VICTORIAN WOMEN WRITERS AND THE OTHER GERMANY

Shedding new light on the alternative, emancipatory Germany discovered and written about by progressive women writers during the long nineteenth century, this illuminating study uncovers a country that offered a degree of freedom and intellectual agency unheard of in England. Opening with the striking account of Anna Jameson and her friendship with Ottilie von Goethe, Linda K. Hughes shows how cultural differences spurred ten writers' advocacy of progressive ideas and provided fresh materials for publishing careers. Alongside well-known writers – Elizabeth Gaskell, George Eliot, Michael Field, Elizabeth von Arnim, and Vernon Lee – this study sheds light on the lesser-known writers Mary and Anna Mary Howitt, Jessie Fothergill, and the important Anglo-Jewish lesbian writer Amy Levy. Armed with their knowledge of the German language, each of these women championed an extraordinarily productive openness to cultural exchange and, by approaching Germany through a female lens, imported an alternative, 'other' Germany into English letters.

LINDA K. HUGHES is Addie Levy Professor of Literature at Texas Christian University. She edited *The Cambridge Companion to Victorian Women's Poetry* (Cambridge University Press, 2019) and has published extensively on long nineteenth-century literature, culture, and women's and gender studies. Her earlier books include *The Cambridge Introduction to Victorian Poetry* (Cambridge University Press, 2010) and *Graham R.: Rosamund Marriott Watson, Woman of Letters* (2005), which received the Colby Prize.

CAMBRIDGE STUDIES IN NINETEENTH-CENTURY LITERATURE
AND CULTURE

FOUNDING EDITORS
Gillian Beer, *University of Cambridge*
Catherine Gallagher, *University of California, Berkeley*

GENERAL EDITORS
Kate Flint, *University of Southern California*
Clare Pettitt, *King's College London*

EDITORIAL BOARD
Isobel Armstrong, *Birkbeck, University of London*
Ali Behdad *University of California, Los Angeles*
Alison Chapman, *University of Victoria*
Hilary Fraser, *Birkbeck, University of London*
Josephine McDonagh, *University of Chicago*
Elizabeth Miller, *University of California, Davis*
Hillis Miller, *University of California, Irvine*
Cannon Schmitt, *University of Toronto*
Sujit Sivasundaram *University of Cambridge*
Herbert Tucker, *University of Virginia*
Mark Turner, *King's College London*

Nineteenth-century literature and culture have proved a rich field for interdisciplinary studies. Since 1994, books in this series have tracked the intersections and tensions between Victorian literature and the visual arts, politics, gender and sexuality, race, social organisation, economic life, technical innovations, scientific thought – in short, culture in its broadest sense. Many of our books are now classics in a field that since the series' inception has seen powerful engagements with Marxism, feminism, visual studies, post-colonialism, critical race studies, new historicism, new formalism, transnationalism, queer studies, human rights and liberalism, disability studies and global studies. Theoretical challenges and historiographical shifts continue to unsettle scholarship on the nineteenth century in productive ways. New work on the body and the senses, the environment and climate, race and the decolonisation of literary studies, biopolitics and materiality, the animal and the human, the local and the global, politics and form, queerness and gender identities, and intersectional theory is re-animating the field. This series aims to accommodate and promote the most interesting work being undertaken on the frontiers of nineteenth-century literary studies, connecting the field with the urgent critical questions that are being asked today. We seek to publish work from a diverse range of authors, and stand for anti-racism, anti-colonialism and against discrimination in all forms.

A complete list of titles published will be found at the end of the book.

VICTORIAN WOMEN WRITERS AND THE OTHER GERMANY

Cross-Cultural Freedoms and Female Opportunity

LINDA K. HUGHES
Texas Christian University

Shaftesbury Road, Cambridge CB2 8EA, United Kingdom

One Liberty Plaza, 20th Floor, New York, NY 10006, USA

477 Williamstown Road, Port Melbourne, VIC 3207, Australia

314–321, 3rd Floor, Plot 3, Splendor Forum, Jasola District Centre, New Delhi – 110025, India

103 Penang Road, #05–06/07, Visioncrest Commercial, Singapore 238467

Cambridge University Press is part of Cambridge University Press & Assessment, a department of the University of Cambridge.

We share the University's mission to contribute to society through the pursuit of education, learning and research at the highest international levels of excellence.

www.cambridge.org
Information on this title: www.cambridge.org/9781009069328

DOI: 10.1017/9781009072243

© Linda K. Hughes 2022

This publication is in copyright. Subject to statutory exception and to the provisions of relevant collective licensing agreements, no reproduction of any part may take place without the written permission of Cambridge University Press & Assessment.

First published 2022
First paperback edition 2025

A catalogue record for this publication is available from the British Library

Library of Congress Cataloging-in-Publication data
NAMES: Hughes, Linda K., author.
TITLE: Victorian women writers and the other Germany : cross-cultural freedoms and female opportunity / Linda Hughes.
OTHER TITLES: Cambridge studies in nineteenth-century literature and culture.
DESCRIPTION: Cambridge, United Kingdom : Cambridge University Press, 2022. | Series: Cambridge studies in nineteenth-century literature and culture | Includes bibliographical references and index.
IDENTIFIERS: LCCN 2022008810 (print) | LCCN 2022008811 (ebook) | ISBN 9781316512845 (hardback) | ISBN 9781009069328 (paperback) | ISBN 9781009072243 (epub)
SUBJECTS: LCSH: Women authors, English–19th century. | Women authors, English–Travel–Germany. | Women authors, English–Attitudes. | English literature–Women authors–History and criticism. | English literature–19th century–History and criticism. | English literature–19th century–German influences. | Germany–Foreign public opinion. | BISAC: LITERARY CRITICISM / European / English, Irish, Scottish, Welsh
CLASSIFICATION: LCC PR115 .H84 2022 (print) | LCC PR115 (ebook) | DDC 820.9/9287–dc23/eng/20220406
LC record available at https://lccn.loc.gov/2022008810
LC ebook record available at https://lccn.loc.gov/2022008811

ISBN   978-1-316-51284-5   Hardback
ISBN   978-1-009-06932-8   Paperback

Cambridge University Press & Assessment has no responsibility for the persistence or accuracy of URLs for external or third-party internet websites referred to in this publication and does not guarantee that any content on such websites is, or will remain, accurate or appropriate.

For Carroll,
life partner and fellow traveller

The Germany I am speaking of is not the one which colonises or makes cheap goods, or frightens the rest of the world in various ways . . .

Vernon Lee, *Genius Loci* (1899)

Contents

List of Figures	*page* viii
Acknowledgements	ix
Preface/Vorwort	xiii

Introduction		1
1	Entrée to the 'Other' Germany: Anna Jameson, Ottilie von Goethe, and Their Women's Network	13
2	Germany through a Female Lens: Anna Jameson's Writings, 1834–1860	32
3	Networked Families in Germany: Mary Howitt, Anna Mary Howitt, and Elizabeth Gaskell	55
4	An Unbeliever in Germany: Marian Evans (George Eliot), 1854–1855	87
5	The Anglo–German Fiction of George Eliot and Jessie Fothergill: *Daniel Deronda* (1876) and *The First Violin* (1878)	107
6	New Woman Travellers and Translators: Michael Field and Amy Levy	129
7	An Anglo–German Expatriate–Citizen: Elizabeth von Arnim	162
8	Queer Borders: Vernon Lee's Haunted Expatriate Writings	187
Nachwort/Afterword		209

Notes	212
Bibliography	259
Index	276

Figures

2.1	Dedication page, *Social Life in Germany* (1840), illustration and text by Anna Jameson. Courtesy Harry Ransom Center, The University of Texas at Austin	*page* 48
3.1	Wilhelm Kaulbach design for inaugural issue of *Howitt's Journal*, 2 January 1847, 9. Courtesy Woman's Collections, Special Collections, Texas Woman's University	59
5.1	From Joachim Raff, *'Lenore' Symphony* March, Book III, Chapter IV, *The First Violin* (2:24–5). Courtesy Rare Book & Manuscript Library, University of Illinois	113
7.1	Fold-out map of Rügen affixed to the boards of *The Adventures of Elizabeth in Rügen*. Courtesy Mary Couts Burnett Library, Special Collections, TCU	168
7.2	Concluding pages, *Fräulein Schmidt and Mr Anstruther* (378–9). Courtesy Mary Couts Burnett Library, Special Collections, TCU	182

Acknowledgements

I am grateful to the Goethe- und Schiller-Archiv, Klassik Stiftung, Weimar, Germany, for permission to quote from unpublished letters between Anna Jameson and Ottilie von Goethe (Signatur 40); to Dr Silke Henke, Department Head, Media Processing and Usage; and to the librarians and staff who assisted me during my four visits to this archive. I thank University of Nottingham Manuscripts and Special Collections for permission to quote from Mary Howitt's letters to her sister Anna Harrison (Ht/1/1/54, Ht/1/1/125); Camellia PLC for permission to transcribe Amy Levy's autograph copy of 'Neue Liebe, Neues Leben'; and Leonie Sturge-Moore and Charmian O'Neil, as well as the British Library, for permission to quote from the Michael Field Diaries (British Library Additional MSS 46778, 46779, 46785, 46786). Additionally, I thank Lindsay Stainton for her assistance with the Amy Levy archive in 2010; Ana Parejo Vadillo for help with Michael Field materials; Kimberly L. Johnson, Director, Special Collections and University Archivist, Woman's Collections, Texas Woman's University, for providing a scan of Wilhelm Kaulbach's initial month design for *Howitt's Journal*; and the Harry Ransom Center, The University of Texas at Austin, for providing a scan of the illustrated dedication to Anna Jameson's *Social Life in Germany*.

At Texas Christian University (TCU) I am indebted to the generous support of the TCU library and librarians, including Julie Christenson and Kerri Menchaca in Special Collections; Ammie Harrison, Humanities librarian; and Kay Edmondson, Jill Kendle, and Kristen Barnes in the Interlibrary Loan office. A 2010 TCU-Research and Creative Activity Fund grant enabled my visits to the Howitt and Amy Levy archives in the United Kingdom; to the British Library, where I consulted the Michael Field Diaries; and to the Goethe- und Schiller-Archiv in Weimar, Germany, for my initial examination of Anna Jameson's holograph letters to Ottilie von Goethe. The Addie Levy Research Fund supported subsequent trips to Weimar and to the Colby College Library in Waterville, Maine, to examine its Vernon Lee collection. Successive English department chairs, including Brad Lucas, Karen Steele, and Theresa Gaul, happily signed off on my reimbursement forms from travel and conferences related to this project and supported my year-long sabbatical in 2016. Office Manager Merry Roberts has helped in more ways than I can name, aided by Executive Assistants Lynn Irving and Regina Lewis. English department work-study students over the years also provided assistance with scans and retrieval of library materials.

I am the grateful beneficiary of a series of superb Addie Levy Research Associates, who each worked with me one academic year. Heidi Hakimi-Hood, Claire Landes, Sofia Prado Huggins, Kaylee Henderson, Dana Shaaban, and Abigayle Farrier, all gifted Ph.D. students, provided research assistance directly related to this book project or on collateral projects that enabled me to sustain ongoing work on this study. My warmest thanks to each of them – and, as this project comes to a close, to another gifted Ph.D. student, Sanjana Chowdhury, creator of this work's index.

I am also indebted to my German teachers, beginning with my first in high school, Helmut Schmeller, who in addition to introducing me to German language study opened a new intellectual world previously unknown to me in my small Kansas town. When I completed an undergraduate German minor, Frau Ellen Mayer did most to advance my speaking and comprehension skills. Decades later, I realised that if I wanted to research Victorian women writers' cultural exchanges with Germany I needed more than my by-now rusty German minor. I was fortunate to be welcomed 'back to school' by my TCU colleagues when I enrolled in undergraduate German classes for two years while continuing to teach in the English Department. Naively, I hoped at the outset of my renewed student life to become fluent in German. That did not happen: I could not make time for immersion experiences amidst my other research, teaching, and family obligations. However, thanks to outstanding teaching by my colleagues Drs Cynthia Chapa (now retired but thankfully still 'meine Freundin'), Scott Williams, and Jeffrey Todd, I sufficiently strengthened my language skills to enable me to read literary and scholarly German-language texts and to speak with German librarians and personnel when I travelled to Weimar. Besides language instruction itself I am grateful to my teacher-colleagues for letting me revive the joys of being a student again (eagerly awaiting marks on my quizzes and assignments like the other students) and learn more about contemporary German politics and culture. I am also grateful to the German undergraduate students, including Rebecca

Stewart, now a Teaching Fellow in Harvard's Department of Germanic Languages and Literatures, and Evan Voorn, most recently a German and Social Studies teacher in Texas and Colorado, with whom I worked in class and on occasional projects; they did me the kindness of forgetting that I was a professor and accepting me as a fellow student.

I owe very special thanks to my Germanist colleague Scott Williams, who went above and beyond mere collegiality. An expert in translation studies, he checked all my German translations in this book, offering advice and, when needed (more than once, I own), corrections. Any remaining errors are of course my own. Scott read not only carefully and attentively but also supportively, and I thank him too for believing in the value of what I was doing.

Bethany Thomas, Literature Commissioning Editor at Cambridge University Press, encouraged this project from the time I first talked to her about it at the North American Victorian Studies Association (NAVSA) conference in 2019. I thank her for her support and for making the submission and review process so congenial. My thanks go also to the Series Editors of Cambridge Studies in Nineteenth-Century Literature and Culture, Kate Flint and Claire Pettitt, for their own warm support and enthusiasm for the project; to my two anonymous readers for their encouragement, insights, and suggestions; to George Paul Laver, Editorial Assistant at Cambridge University Press; to Humanities Content Manager Nicola Maclean; to Straive Production Manager Siddharthan Indra Priyadarshini; and, with special thanks for her discerning eye and attentive care, to copy editor Suzanne Arnold.

Two scholars offered help at the early stages of this project but are no longer living as I finish it; I hope I sufficiently thanked them when I still could. Dr William Boos, philosopher and gifted linguist, provided the earliest help with German translation when I worked on a precursor project that drew upon German classical scholarship ('Discoursing of Xantippe: Amy Levy, Classical Scholarship, and Print Culture', *Philological Quarterly*, 2009). As she expertly drove us from the 2009 NAVSA conference in Cambridge, England, to the Tennyson Bicentenary conference in Lincoln, Dr Linda H. Peterson, so important a scholar in studies of Victorian women writers, autobiography, and poetry, briefed me on the Howitt archives in Nottingham and counselled me on how best to access them – a fond memory that mingles with sadness at her too-early death.

From start to finish during my long process of research and writing this book, I have benefited from three scholars and friends who listened, responded, and offered unfailing encouragement. For years I have learned from Victorianist Dr Florence S. Boos, whose ethically committed scholarship and wealth of knowledge continually inspire me. Our friendship predates my arrival at TCU and has enriched my professional and personal life; thank you for this gift, Florence. My TCU colleague, art historian Dr Babette Bohn, whose groundbreaking book *Women Artists, Their Patrons, and Their Publics in Early Modern Bologna* appeared in 2021, has exemplified excellence in humanities research since she joined TCU's faculty – lucky for me, arriving the same year I did. I thank her for our many talks over lunch as we discussed our research, our teaching, and our ongoing lives; I also thank her for an excellent suggestion about my title. As department chair Dr Fred Erisman hired me at TCU, but we have become friends who meet over lunch at intervals to talk about our research and our reading. Fred 'retired' two decades ago but has since published three scholarly monographs, his latest (*In Their Own Words*, 2021) on pioneering women aviator-journalists.

I close by thanking the person who has been with me and offered support the longest, Dr Carroll W. Hughes, a board-certified clinical psychologist and prolific researcher in dual diagnosis and childhood depression before he retired from the University of Texas Southwestern Medical School. I knew him by another first name when we were both teenagers in high school, when I admired him for his independence, obvious intelligence, willingness to question authority, and irreverent sense of humour. Since we were more or less children ourselves when we became a pair, I rightly claim him as 'life partner', my 'fellow traveller' through our shared lives. He also became my literal fellow traveller as I worked on this book, visiting Weimar with me twice, on one occasion driving us through dangerous fog as we made our way to Weimar from Vienna one November day. He has also travelled with me through this book's manuscript, reading every word – twice – and shoring up my confidence as he did so. I dedicate this book to him as both my life partner and my driver, my patient listener, my reader, whose support all my adult life, as well as during a pandemic, has meant so much.

Preface/Vorwort

Why did so many British women travel to Germany and live there for months or years? This is the question I asked myself when I realised that three writers I had recently written about, Elizabeth Gaskell, George Eliot, and Amy Levy, had done so. Wondering how common such experiences were for women writers, I ventured on a tag search of Germany and 1800–1900 in the *Orlando* database of British women writers edited by Susan Brown, Patricia Clements, and Isobel Grundy, having no idea what to expect. I was startled when some 625 hits suddenly appeared on the computer screen. Why had I never heard of women writers' interest in things German when it was so widespread? I was familiar with the attractions of France and Italy for Victorian women, but their attraction to Germany was a blank.[1] And thus was this project born.

The many reasons for Victorian women's travels and temporary residence in Germany cannot be reduced to a single purpose or goal, which ranged from tourism to boarding school or family arrangements and professional pursuits.[2] What stood out repeatedly for me among these women, however, were the progressive women writers drawn to Germany, to the German language, and to German social and cultural practices. In turn, their interchanges with Germany generated compelling works as a legacy for their Anglophone readers (and, sometimes through German translations, Germans as well). The ten women on whom I focus in this study – Anna Jameson, Mary Howitt, Anna Mary Howitt, Elizabeth Gaskell, George Eliot, Jessie Fothergill, Michael Field (Katharine Bradley and Edith Cooper), Amy Levy, Elizabeth von Arnim, and Vernon Lee – disclosed a new nineteenth-century Germany to me, not the one imported to England by Thomas Carlyle, musicians in British concert halls, biblical scholars affected by German Higher Criticism, or late-century intellectuals immersed in aesthetic theory. The other Germany that drew progressive women to it was a land where middle-class British women could enjoy greater personal and intellectual freedoms in the 1830s and 1840s than they could back home; where throughout the years 1833–1908 German stimuli excited women's imaginations and opened new opportunities for women as professional writers. By the late 1870s, college-educated women like Levy and Michael Field were travelling as femes sole, discovering new German authors or cultural resources and extending the translation work of earlier women writers. From the late nineteenth century into the pre-war years of the twentieth, von Arnim and Lee, living as British expatriates, began to develop the complex identities of twentieth-century and contemporary global citizens characterised by financially independent mobility and daily awareness of more than one culture and language.

Unquestionably cosmopolitanism is part of this story, and Anna Jameson's 1834 theorisation of female cosmopolitanism outlined in the Introduction would hold good for most if not all of her successor women writers my narrative examines. But rather than primarily a study of female cosmopolitanism, this book is a history of nineteenth-century progressive British women and how their experiences in Germany expanded their outlooks, mental tableaux, freedoms, and mobility. One of my overriding interests is seeking to understand how deep-seated cultural exchange occurs when it is impelled by German language facility (however great or minimal), openness to difference (hence the inevitable focus on progressive women), and onsite presence in German lands from northern Germany to Austria and the Swiss Bernese Alps – a concatenation of conditions that intensified these writers' awareness of being a woman, often alone, in a foreign land.[3] Expatriates (like their unprivileged compatriots driven to become immigrants or refugees) have no choice but to enter into a foreign culture if they would not remain socially isolated. This entry, however, can also be a chosen path into greater learning – so that elements of this study anticipate women's participation in academic study abroad as well as global mobility. And in modelling open, deliberate cultural exchange with a culture different from their own, these women are potential teachers of readers and scholars today faced with the imperative of negotiating the inseparable elements of citizenship, multiple differences within nations, and global networks and awareness.

Introduction

> The Germany I am speaking of is not the one which colonises or makes cheap goods, or frightens the rest of the world in various ways ...
>
> Vernon Lee, *Genius Loci* (1899)

Interest in transnationalism has intensified in recent decades among literary scholars and historians, in part due to postcolonial studies, which overturn earlier concepts of centre and periphery, but also in response to world events, mass tourism, and media technologies that bring global dimensions into daily life. Transnational studies proceed under a number of critical terms, from cosmopolitanism, internationalism, mobility studies, and cultural transfer to travel writing. A transnational focus brings with it a question of where to place borders in knowledge as well as spaces when, as ecological studies tell us in a time of increasing crisis, everything is connected to everything else. In this study I draw on scholarship from a number of these scholarly approaches, always aiming to keep in focus how engaging with cultural difference and specifically a foreign culture is at once a challenge, often daunting, and a key to inventing ways to connect and engage in innovative sociability and experiential learning. The writings I examine vary widely, from fiction and poetry to memoirs, travelogues, translations, and children's literature. But all turn upon the processes and results of cultural exchange. US-educated Brazilian anthropologist Mercio Pereira Gomes most aptly theorises my object of study. Gomes denies that deep participation in another culture is exclusive to anthropologists. Rather, he contends that all cultures, while inherently ethnocentric, also contain within them the possibilities for what he calls ethnoexocentrism: 'ethnoexocentrism is a necessary cultural drive that favours a genuine acceptance of other cultures where individuals can relate and intermingle with one another'. Usually dormant, 'it comes to light when called for, particularly when inescapable intercultural relations require it. Ethnoexocentrism is a more complex feeling than ethnocentrism, for it necessitates a self-conscious appraisal of one's own sentiment and the sentiment of the other culture.'[1]

The specific cultural exchange in this study involves Victorian women writers' encounters with what I term, with the help of Vernon Lee, 'the other Germany'. All the women whose writings I examine were privileged in access to income and to learning that enabled their transnational mobility; and with one exception they were also privileged in race. They were also systematically disadvantaged by their gender and sexualities and often rendered vulnerable corporeally, socially, and culturally when they spent periods ranging from months to years in Germany. Focusing on a small group from a given time and nation who experienced both privilege and disadvantage generates a fine-grained representation of cultural engagement with difference that can be approached through the writings these women left behind, whether in letters and diaries or published texts, that, more than describing German scenes and individuals, convey what it was like for British women to interact with those who did not share some or most British middle-class assumptions. Even the fiction I discuss obliquely illuminates these encounters, suggesting how personal transnational experience enabled authors to imagine their way into culturally different German personae.

Today the Victorian woman writer most often linked to Germany is George Eliot.[2] Eliot's influence on other women was profound, whether as a translator, intellectual writer, agnostic, or sexual dissident. Both her books and her scandal in daring to elope to Germany in 1854 with the married George Henry Lewes acted upon other women writers' sense of the possible. But Eliot was not the initial groundbreaking figure who opened the door to Germany for progressive Victorian women writers. That was Anna Jameson two decades earlier – even though on her 1833 trip to Germany, her second, she had little to no German language at her command and relied on Germans' shared knowledge of French or English to interact socially, as well as a letter of introduction from Robert Noel, cousin to Lady Byron and an acquaintance of Ottilie von Goethe.[3]

As progressive women, the writers in this study were all intellectually curious, articulate individuals who welcomed exploration as participant observers of human experiences in a tongue and land not their own. All were also ambitious for writing careers, finding their German experiences a spur to thought, creativity, and profit as they simultaneously enlarged the breadth of the kind of life a nineteenth-century Englishwoman could live. They came to Germany across the long nineteenth century, each finding new modes of entering and encountering German culture as they built upon precursors' experiences.[4] The first group consisted of Anna Jameson (1794–1860), Mary Howitt (1799–1888), Elizabeth Gaskell (1810–65), and Anna Mary Howitt (1824–84). Eliot (1819–80) began as a member of this first set, then pivoted away with her elopement. There followed Jessie Fothergill (1851–91), Michael Field (Katharine Bradley, 1846–1914 and Edith Cooper, 1862–1913), and Amy Levy (1861–89), all of whom benefited from Eliot's own breaks with tradition. The final pair, the expatriates Elizabeth von Arnim (1866–1941) and Vernon Lee (Violet Paget, 1856–1935), registered in their family connections and fluid movements across borders the transnational mobility that increasingly defined modernity from the late nineteenth century into the present.

Their cumulative story thus unfolds the emerging phases of a new modernity for women, from greater mobility and independence (in travel, in finances, in logistics) to analogues of modern study abroad and the expatriate lives so familiar to intellectuals, artists, and global professionals in the following two centuries. What remains specific to them is the interest of their particular stories, their particular framing of what it meant, as middle-class women who were intent (Eliot excepted) on retaining their social standing to travel to a foreign land – not to gawk or to find employment but to live and be interactively with Germans, whether through social and personal connections, ability to read German, or viewing German visual arts in cities and museums. Their enabling disposition was a love precisely of cultural difference, of seeing what was native to themselves (their British middle-class society and its conventions and their individual experiences) through the lens of another society and language.

Once on the Continent, the first generation of women experienced and – especially in the case of Jameson – helped build a social network that functioned as a circle of intellectual and social interchange. In addition to Ottilie von Goethe, the woman at the foundation of Jameson's twenty-seven-year relationship with Germany, Jameson became friends with Goethe's German circle of women and in turn introduced English friends such as Adelaide Kemble Sartoris to the German circle.[5] Hence this particular network spanned both sides of the North Sea and at times also migrated southward to Vienna and Rome. Several women followed Jameson's lead, including Mary Howitt, to whom Jameson furnished letters of introduction for Germany; Gaskell, Howitt's longtime friend; and Howitt's daughter Anna Mary.

Eliot attended one of Jameson's 'literary gatherings' in 1852, and Eliot, along with Jameson, was invited to a dinner at Robert Noel's residence in

February 1854.[6] But after Eliot eloped with George Henry Lewes to Germany that July, the two never saw each other again. That stark dividing line in Eliot's own life also marks a chronological division from the older set, for the younger women followed Eliot's rather than Jameson's lead to Germany. Jessie Fothergill, Michael Field, and Amy Levy all travelled as single women, in contrast to the married Jameson, Howitt, and Gaskell; all were, like Eliot, also freethinkers. Writers in this second group may often have travelled with another woman – Fothergill with her sister, Levy with Blanche Smith (both alumnae of Newnham), or the couple Michael Field – but at crucial moments they found themselves alone, a rather more radical experience than Eliot's in the mid-1850s (as I discuss in more detail in Chapter 4). German texts, which these younger women read in the original language, also acted to draw them to Germany and remained important spurs to their experiences of cultural exchange. Fothergill identified Johann von Goethe as her favourite poet after Robert Browning and William Morris, and Paul Heyse was even more important to her. *The First Violin* (1878), Fothergill's best-selling novel set in Germany, explicitly references Heyse's *Kinder der Welt* (*Children of the World*, 1873), which helped inspire Fothergill's male protagonist. Today Heyse, a 1910 Nobel Prize winner for literature, has been eclipsed, much like Fothergill herself, but his 1873 novel also inspired Levy, who identified her favourite fictional hero in her 'Confessions' book as Heyse's atheist hero Edwin. Heine and Johann von Goethe were two of Levy's favourite poets, and her poetry collections additionally include translations from Emanuel von Geibel and Nikolaus Lenau. Katharine Bradley's first volume of poetry, *The New Minnesinger and Other Poems* (1875), likewise included translations of Johann von Goethe and Heine as well as Schiller. For these younger writers, German texts mingled promiscuously with English works as a given part of their cosmopolitan literary tableaux. In all, this generation's freedom from marriage, spurning of religious belief, university education (excepting Fothergill), mobility, unconventional living arrangements, and assumption of intellectual agency meant that they functioned as New Women, anticipating later developments such as university women's study abroad in Europe.

Neither of the last two writers this study takes up was born in England: Elizabeth von Arnim was born in Australia, Vernon Lee in France. Both writers, known today only through their noms de plume, differed markedly in sexuality, the twice-married serial adulterer von Arnim contrasting the presumed-chaste and woman-loving Lee. If both were defined by their transnational mobility, they also bring my account of Victorian women writers and Germany full circle. For like Mary Howitt, Anna Mary Howitt, and Gaskell, von Arnim and Lee initially experienced Anglo–German cultural exchange through their families – in the later women's case, families that were themselves cosmopolitan. The heavily autobiographical *Elizabeth and Her German Garden* (1898), von Arnim's first book, can be read as a family memoir even though it turns the conventions of domesticity and motherhood inside out. It appeared seven years after the author's marriage to the German Count Henning von Arnim-Schlagenthin. This marriage linked von Arnim to Goethe and hence implicitly to Jameson, since one of the forebears of von Arnim's husband was Bettina von Arnim, whose 1835 epistolary novel *Goethe's Correspondence with a Child* (*Goethes Briefwechsel mit einem Kinde*), published three years after Johann von Goethe's death, established her as a major literary figure. Ottilie von Goethe, moreover, knew Bettina personally. In June 1836, shortly after another of Jameson's visits to Weimar, Goethe wrote a brief essay on contemporary German women who had emancipated and validated German women intellectually.[7] A copy survives in Goethe's papers addressed to Jameson, headed 'Für Anna – Über Rahel, Bettine und Charlotte'.[8]

Vernon Lee is identified with Italy, where she moved permanently in 1873 and for which she had a passion. Prior to that, her itinerant family shuffled back and forth across Germany, Italy, France, and Switzerland. Still, as a 1904 essay by Lee indicates, her German-speaking Bernese governess Marie Schülpach exerted a notable impact on Lee's personal and imaginative development (as I discuss in Chapter 8). German language and culture also surface in others of Lee's works, including a biography of the German wife of Bonnie Prince Charles, known as the Countess of Albany; and some of her best-known stories, including the *Yellow Book* tale 'Prince Alberic and the Snake Lady', are indebted to the legacy of German romanticism channelled through Lee's governess and the precursor tales of E. T. A. Hoffmann. This study finds its fitting conclusion in the earliest novel Lee wrote for adults, *Ottilie, An Eighteenth Century Idyl* (1883), set in Germany. If that title resonates, it should, for while this novel has been linked to Lee's own family history, it also draws upon elements of Johann von Goethe's character Ottilie in *Elective Affinities* (*Die Wahlverwandtschaften*, 1809) and, I further suggest, can be fruitfully read as a reimagining of the life of Ottilie von Goethe, the woman who opened a female-centred Germany to Jameson that had the impact of a revelation.

Over and above the specific reasons that brought middle-class women to Germany, Protestant Germany and Prussia in particular offered Victorian women writers the 'cross-cultural freedoms' my subtitle emphasises.⁹ There they could enjoy local mobilities almost unimaginable back in Britain, where appearing in public required an escort, preferably male, for women to be judged respectable. The earliest eye-witness account of German women's superior freedoms and social standing arrived in Britain through Madame de Staël (1766–1817). Though de Staël is best known today for her novel *Corinne* (1807), her travel book *De L'Allemagne* (*Germany*) appeared in 1813 and was translated and published in London the same year. De Staël's third chapter, 'Of the Women', underscored the limitations imposed on German men by oppressive political rule in contrast to German women:

> The German women have a charm, exclusively their own ... they are modest but less timid than Englishwomen; one sees that they have been less accustomed to meet with their superiors among men, and that they have besides less to apprehend from the severe censures of the public. They endeavour to please by their sensibility, to interest by their imagination; the language of poetry and the fine arts are familiar to them; they coquet with enthusiasm, as they do in France with wit and pleasantry. That perfect loyalty which distinguishes the German character, renders love less dangerous to the happiness of women; and perhaps they admit the advances of this sentiment with the more confidence, as it is invested with romantic colours.¹⁰

If fidelity was the norm, de Staël also noted the ease with which Protestant German women obtained divorces and changed husbands. And rather than French women's *esprit*, German women cultivated idealism:

> [t]heir careful education, and the purity of soul which is natural to them, render the dominion which they exercise soft and equal; they inspire you from day to day with a stronger interest for all that is great and generous, with more of confidence in all noble hopes, and they know how to repel that bitter irony which breathes a death-chill over all the enjoyments of the heart.¹¹

Jameson would recirculate several of these themes in *Visits and Sketches at Home and Abroad* (1834) and *Social Life in Germany* (1840), discussed in my opening chapters. A decade later Florence Nightingale was still startled by the stark difference between German and English female freedoms, as her 1850 letter home from Berlin (just prior to her first visit to Kaiserswerth, the famous centre of nursing training) indicates:

> And it is more particularly of the Prussian women that I was struck with how much freer and fuller their life is than that of Englishwomen ... England ... is inferior to America in political freedom and practical life,

to France in mental organization, to Germany in popular education, and oh! two centuries behind northern Germany in social freedom. In Berlin a girl of any rank walks about quite alone (i.e., by daylight, and not out of the city); a lady wears any dress, goes into any society, or into the market with her basket on the arm, and nobody laughs at her or talks about her. There is absolute freedom to move yourself socially as you please.[12]

For British women writers to interact with educated German women, then, especially in northern Germany in the middle decades of the century, was to experience a more expansive life as a woman that allowed greater physical movement, social interaction, and intellectual equality free from the social policing that in England often labelled such women 'unfeminine'.

Professional opportunities also drew progressive women writers to Germany. Jameson had made an inconsequential trip to Germany with her father in 1829, after which she wrote the early parts of *Visits and Sketches*.[13] Needing to gather further materials for her book, Jameson undertook the trip of 1833 that changed her life and generated part or all of her books for the next seven years.[14]

Mary and William Howitt's determination to live in Germany from June 1840 to April 1843 was both a family and a career decision propelled by reports of inexpensive education and living costs, their earlier exposure in 1830 to the Felicia Hemans–H. F. Chorley circle that pursued study of contemporary German literature, and Queen Victoria's marriage to the German Prince Albert, which the Howitts thought would create interest in publications about German culture.[15] Jameson's letter of introduction for the Howitts to Professor Friedrich Christoph Schlosser (a historian at Heidelberg University) and his wife, whom Jameson had come to know through Goethe, gave the Howitts immediate access to the Schlossers' intellectual circle in that city. Their teenaged daughter Anna Mary became fluent in German as a result of the family's German residence and met many of her parents' literary and artistic acquaintances, including artist Wilhelm Kaulbach, whose illustrations the Howitts featured in *Howitt's Journal* in the late 1840s. Thus when Anna Mary wished to pursue formal art education to prepare for a career in art, she headed to Munich; denied entrance to the Munich academy on the grounds of sex, she received lessons from Kaulbach in his studio for almost two years. This in turn led to her two-volume publication *An Art-Student in Munich* (1853), a fusion of travel writing and professional memoir.

Elizabeth Gaskell first visited Heidelberg in 1841 with her husband William, where they visited the Howitts. In 1858 and 1860, however, Gaskell's visits to Germany involved only herself and her daughters. The

1858 trip was a form of therapy for Gaskell's daughter Meta after a traumatic broken engagement, while the next was a holiday for Gaskell and two other daughters. These residences helped inspire two late stories by Gaskell, her powerful sensation tale 'The Grey Woman' (1861) and the lesser-known but poignant 'Six Weeks at Heppenheim' (1862).

Eliot's reasons for travelling to Germany need no rehearsal here. They had little to do with her own professional opportunities and everything to do with those of George Henry Lewes, who needed to gather materials for his biography of Johann von Goethe (1855) including the personal recollections of the famous writer's connections. Among the younger writers Jessie Fothergill, Michael Field, and Amy Levy, only the Fields travelled to Germany for explicitly professional reasons. In the mid-1870s, Jessie Fothergill lived in Düsseldorf with her sisters for fifteen months, possibly for educational or economic reasons (like the Howitts before them in the 1840s). In the 1880s Amy Levy completed tutorials in classical languages with a German classics instructor in Dresden, and she also did some teaching. But her visits to Germany, Switzerland, and the German-speaking areas of the Vosges Mountains in present-day Alsace-Lorraine suggested no definite end-goal. In contrast, from 1890 to 1891 the Fields were preparing for their 1892 volume *Sight and Song*, consisting of lyrics written in response to paintings, and so visited museums across Europe, gazing at length upon paintings and recording their responses in their collaborative journal. When Edith Cooper fell ill with scarlet fever, their stay in Dresden was necessarily extended, and both inside and outside the hospital where Cooper recovered the women had particularly intense interchanges with German people and culture. The most important results of all these writers' German residences were the works their extended stays inspired, from Fothergill's best-selling novel or Levy's numerous poems and cluster of short stories in the 1880s to Michael Field's *Sight and Sound*, in which lyrics inspired by Dresden paintings – such as 'The Sleeping Venus' – were among the most notable.

Von Arnim's career is quite literally unimaginable without her eighteen-year residence as a citizen of Germany, and while Lee's earliest books were propelled by her fascination with Italian art and music, she never forgot the importance of Germany. As she declared in *The Sentimental Traveller* (1908), 'of all the countries, the first to be good to me was Germany, coming, in the shape of my nurses and of my dear Bernese governess, fairy-like to my christening or thereabouts'.[16]

If this study principally frames these ten writers in relation to ethnoexocentrism and cultural exchange, a gendered cosmopolitanism was unquestionably another feature of their interchanges with Germany; for their German language skills, social networks, and/or professional pursuits enabled them to enter into German culture in ways that casual travellers or tourists could not.[17] Cosmopolitanism is today theorised in various terms, but for my purposes the most useful articulations are by Kwame Anthony Appiah and Steven Vertovec and Robin Cohen, since their conceptualisations share elements with the 'ethnoexocentrism' of Mercio Gomes.[18] Appiah argues that cosmopolitanism demands simultaneously validating cultures not our own (a form of universalism) and attending to the specificities of individuals and the places they inhabit. His identification of 'conversation', 'living together', and 'association' as key facets of cosmopolitanism is particularly relevant to the writers I discuss. Appiah is especially known for endorsing rooted cosmopolitanism, the premise that partiality to our own 'families, our friends, our nations' is not only to be expected but is to be honoured, even as cosmopolitans must also maintain openness to places and persons who are very different.[19] None of the women featured here ever forgot that they were British or sought to exchange German culture for their own. But opening themselves to German culture and friends enriched their emotional and social as well as intellectual and authorial experiences, sometimes in ways they could never have anticipated.

These writers also, in Vertovec and Cohen's words, necessarily evinced 'socio-cultural processes or individual behaviours, values or dispositions manifesting a capacity to engage cultural multiplicity', which demanded that they set aside impulses to judge or exploit a foreign culture and instead engage with it.[20] To transform these cross-cultural personal experiences into writing, additionally, they had to sustain the mobile intellectual and personal orientations that transcended national and family ties and that could generate the imaginative space in which to create highly individual aesthetic expression.

Such orientations were doubly important for women. Denied voting or property rights (the former won partially in 1918 and fully in 1930, the latter in 1882), they were not full-fledged citizens of their own country, much less the citizens of the world that Immanuel Kant envisioned in 'Perpetual Peace' in 1795.[21] Recent scholars have increasingly revised Kantian cosmopolitanism to include women, who often entered alien realms obliquely or unconventionally.[22] These theoretical interventions are far less new than might be supposed, however, for they were anticipated by Anna Jameson and Vernon Lee in 1834 and 1904 respectively. The earliest book that Jameson completed after meeting Goethe opened, as had Jameson's *Characteristics of Women* (1832), with an introductory dialogue between the male interlocutor Medon and Alda, a stand-in for the female author.²³ As Medon observes,

> If nations begin at last to understand each other's true interests – morally and politically, it will be through the agency of gifted men; but if ever they learn to love and sympathise with each other, it will be through the medium of you women ... our [male] prejudices are stronger and bitterer than yours, because they are those which perverted reason builds up on a foundation of pride; but yours, which are generally those of fancy and association, soon melt away before your own kindly affections. More mobile, more impressible, more easily yielding to external circumstances, more easily lending yourselves to different manners and habits, more quick to perceive, more gentle to judge; – yes, it is to you we must look, to break down the outworks of prejudice – you, the advanced guard of humanity and civilization!
> 'The gentle race and dear,
> By whom alone the world is glorified!'²⁴
> Every feeling, well educated, generous, and truly refined woman, who travels, is as a dove sent out on a mission of peace ... It is her part to soften the intercourse between rougher and stronger natures; to aid in the interfusion of the gentler sympathies; to speed the interchange of art and literature from pole to pole ...²⁵

Jameson may strategically reserve politics, government, and moral philosophy to men and invoke women's stereotypical bent towards emotion and 'fancy', but Jameson more forcefully emphasises (like Appiah) 'conversation', 'living together', 'association', and openness to difference as she claims women's capacity for cultural leadership on a world stage. As Alda replies to Medon, 'Thank you! I need not say how entirely I agree with you.'²⁶ Elsewhere Jameson would make clear that women's disposition to 'yield' 'more easily ... to external circumstances' and take the impress of their surroundings resulted from male social and political dominance. In the dialogue above, she immediately repositions such 'yielding' as a form of diplomatic empowerment that enables women to effect intercultural understanding and dismantle long-standing prejudices.

Nor is Jameson really ceding intellectual qualities to men: the educated middle-class woman acquainted with 'art and literature' can directly engage in cultural 'interchange' so that ostensible domestic sequestration 'melts away' like the international prejudices women glide past. She thus clearly signals through the convenient masculine pronouncement of Medon (her fabricated spokesman) that women are in the end the superior diplomats, peace-makers, travellers, and intellectuals of the world. Her gendered cosmopolitanism is rooted in the local, since women's 'pliability' emerges from their British social position at home, which may constrain women there but also more readily enables them to embrace the 'cultural multiplicity' cited by Vertovec and Cohen.

Though Vernon Lee is best known today as an aesthetic theorist, she included in the essay 'In Praise of Governesses' a definition of cosmopolitanism and cultural exchange that is more personal than theoretical and, as in Jameson's 1834 text, inseparable from Germany and women.[27] Lee begins 'In Praise of Governesses' by saluting the German and Swiss governesses who inspired her abiding affection for Germany and its culture, then asserts the importance of engaging closely with cultures not our own:

> I maintain that we are all of us the better, of whatever nationality (and most, perhaps, we rather too-too solid Anglo-Saxons) for such transfusion of a foreign element, correcting our deficiencies and faults, and ripening (as the literature of Italy ripened our Elizabethans) our own intrinsic qualities. It means, apart from negative service against conceit and canting self-aggrandisement, an additional power of taking life intelligently and serenely; a power of adaptation to various climates and diets of the spirit, let alone the added wealth of such varied climates and diets themselves. Italy, somehow, attains this by her mere visible aspect and her history: a pure, high sky, a mountain city, or a row of cypresses can teach as much as Dante, and, indeed, teach us to understand Dante himself. While as to France, that most lucid of articulately-speaking lands, explains herself in her mere books; and we become in a manner French with every clear, delightful page we read, and almost every thought of our own we ever think with definiteness and grace. But the genius of Germany is, like her landscape, homely and sentimental, with the funny goodness and dearness of a good child; and we must learn to know it while we ourselves are children. And therefore it is from our governesses that we learn (with dimmer knowledge of mysterious persons or things 'Ulfilas' – 'Tacitus's Germania,' supposed by me to have been a lady, his daughter perhaps, and the 'seven stars' of German literature) a certain natural affinity with the Germany of humbler and greater days, when no one talked of Teuton superiority or of purity of Teuton idiom; the Germany which gave Kant, and Beethoven, and Goethe and Schiller, and was not ashamed to say 'scharmant'.[28]

Here, like Jameson in *Visits and Sketches*, Lee asserts the necessity of breaking down the outworks of cultural prejudice, mixing sympathetic emotion and intellect in the reception of another culture, and bringing pliable adaptation to our psychological and physical encounters with difference.[29] Though Lee does not assert women's superior cosmopolitanism, she articulates a version consistent with Appiah and Vertovec and Cohen, and does so in the context of women and their role of governessing. These and similar orientations towards the foreign and foreigners opened the writers I examine to the rich process of cultural exchange this study details.

Their exercise of ethnoexocentrism was highly individual, as were their resulting works, which included moments when they or their fictional characters functioned as lone women directly negotiating cultural difference and unfamiliar customs – a highly unusual circumstance at the time.[30] The social freedoms and mobility of German women that Florence Nightingale observed in 1850 form a leitmotif in this study, particularly because, as progressive women, the ten writers were all inclined to push against the normative boundaries of female roles in their time. Their 'other Germany' was thus far more woman-centred than in much of the Victorian masculine writing about that land, not only because they were far more likely to focus on women and women's experiences, but also, finally, because they themselves were at the centre of their own accounts.

Chapter 1 first sets the scene of Jameson's 1833 arrival in Germany and the woman-centred Germany that immediately arose for her on meeting Ottilie von Goethe, whose own circle of German women friends would have an important impact on Jameson personally, intellectually, and culturally. Without this 'other Germany' and Jameson's venturesomeness once she encountered it, we might know far less about how progressive Victorian women writers could embrace cultural exchange or their particular ethnoexocentrism that made exchange and their written accounts of it possible. From Jameson this book moves forward in roughly chronological order across the three generational waves of writers noted earlier who engaged with German-speaking lands and their people, from those in Jameson's circle, to the more unconventional freethinkers and New Women of the century's middle decades into the *fin de siècle*, and ending with the turn-of-the-century expatriate writers von Arnim and Lee.

CHAPTER 1

Entrée to the 'Other' Germany
Anna Jameson, Ottilie von Goethe, and Their Women's Network

If Anna Jameson played a key role in progressive Victorian women writers' engagement with Germany from 1833 onwards, so did Ottilie von Goethe. Without Goethe's mastery of English, her charismatic conversation, and her keen interests in British as well as European literature and the arts, Jameson might have remained another intelligent travel writer who authored sprightly accounts of her experiences rather than a participant in German culture. Both women were disposed to ethnoexocentrism, and their first encounter immediately sparked a profound connection. As Jameson's niece Gerardine Macpherson observes in her biography,

> The attachment that sprang up rapidly between Goethe's fascinating daughter-in-law and the 'liebe Anna' never thenceforth, though put to severest proof, suffered coldness or change. They were dear friends for nearly thirty years, maintaining, through long periods of separation, a faithful correspondence and renewing personal intercourse whenever and wherever possible – in Weimar itself, or in Vienna, Dresden, Venice, Rome, wherever Anna could give or accept a rendezvous with Ottilie.[1]

This chapter reveals how they came to form an intense cross-cultural friendship that drew others into their circle and how they modelled more expansive social and cultural roles for women.

Today Anna Jameson remains surprisingly little known beyond specialists despite being a widely known, well-respected professional writer and, in the 1850s, an influential feminist, as Judith Johnston has shown.[2] Jameson was also an important art critic and precursor art historian whose contributions figure in recent studies by Kimberly VanEsveld Adams, John Paul Kanwit, Hilary Fraser, and Caroline Palmer.[3] I approach her as a crucial cultural mediator between England and Germany whose writings as well as English friendships drew other progressive writers to Germanic lands. She was met more than halfway by Goethe, today a figure even less well known to Anglophone scholars (and only recently of interest to

Germanists beyond her role as Johann von Goethe's daughter-in-law). Goethe was in fact a transnational cultural mediator in her own right.

Anna Jameson's disposition to reach across cultural boundaries was inseparable from her origins. Red-haired and Dublin-born, she was the daughter of an English mother and Irish father, the miniaturist painter Denis Brownell Murphy, and moved with her family at age four to England.[4] From the beginning she was assimilated into the world of art (and would herself illustrate many of her books). Upon her father's appointment as 'Painter in Enamel' to Princess Charlotte in 1810, which took him to Windsor, the young Jameson additionally learned to move easily between privileged aristocratic circles and intellectual members of the middle class.[5] More important, Jameson was endlessly curious and embraced the opportunity to learn about new cultures, languages, and people. When she travelled to Italy as a governess in 1821, she devoted her discretionary time to visiting art galleries and exploring each new city and, for as long as she could afford it, she hired an Italian master to study Italian.[6] Jameson's record of her foreign experiences readily furnished material for books, so that her travel journals were transformed into the *Diary of an Ennuyée* (1826), advertised to the public as a novel, and furnished the parts of *Visits and Sketches* (1834) written before Jameson arrived in Germany in 1833.[7]

Jameson married in 1825 but unhappily, a factor that promoted her independence as a traveller abroad and her opportunities to meet foreign residents of other countries (further supported by her highly effectual letters of introduction). If her de jure marital status conferred instant feminine respectability upon her, her de facto marital separation after being wed four years to Robert Sympson Jameson (1796–1854) increased her determination to earn money from writing to help support her career as well as her sisters, parents, and niece. Her unhappy marriage would also have created rapport with the widowed Goethe, whose marriage to August von Goethe had been deeply unhappy. And Jameson's moment of arrival in Germany was propitious for her warm reception from German writers, artists, and intellectuals. She arrived as the author of a work of Shakespearean criticism, *Characteristics of Women* (1832), copies of which had been sold at a nearby Leipzig bookseller and, due to German interest in Shakespeare, was being translated into German in 1833.[8]

The impact of meeting Goethe was all the stronger because Goethe was Jameson's first real encounter with a German. In 1829 Jameson had toured Germany with her father, her father's patron Sir Gerard Noel, and the patron's daughter, but they travelled in an English barouche '*à la milor*

Anglais ... surrounded with all that could render us entirely independent of the amusements we had come to seek, and of the people among whom we had come to visit'.[9] Jameson's second trip, undertaken to gather additional materials on German culture and art at a time when neither was well known back in England, again began conventionally for Jameson and her sister Charlotte, who accompanied her. As Charlotte's letter home made clear, up to their arrival in Weimar 'We have, as yet, travelled mostly with English people, some of whom came over in the packet from London with us.'[10] In Weimar the cloak of Englishness fell away, and Jameson came face to face with a German woman whose independence, intellect, curiosity, and sociability equalled her own but was filtered through a screen of cultural difference. Goethe, then, was in every sense Jameson's gateway to Germany.[11] Jameson immediately recognised the professional importance of Goethe's acquaintance. To her sisters back home Jameson explained that 'to be introduced, under [Goethe's] auspices, to the best society at Frankfurt and Bonn, ... is of great consequence to me ... She knows every distinguished person in Germany, France and England.'[12]

This impressive social network was a natural result of being Johann von Goethe's daughter-in-law, since international visitors regularly visited Weimar to converse with the renowned author and she was his frequent companion, especially in his late years. But much more was involved in the first meeting of Jameson and Goethe, who welcomed Jameson 'with open arms'.[13] Goethe's own disposition to reach across cultural boundaries – especially when the British isles were involved – likewise had connections to her family, especially her mother Henriette von Pogwisch (1766–1851), a 'Hofdame' (lady of the court) at the Grand Ducal Court of Weimar. Born Henriette Henckel von Donnersmarck, she had been a talented pianist and singer from an early age and was sufficiently educated to serve as governess in a royal household before becoming a lady of a court.[14] She left her position when she fell in love with and married Wilhelm Julius Baron von Pogwisch (1760–1836), then in the military, in 1796 and enjoyed an initially happy marriage. But once Pogwisch left the military, his income from his inherited property was insufficient to support his wife and their two daughters, Ottilie and Ulrike (1798–1875). Henriette thus separated from him in 1802 and moved to Weimar in 1806, securing appointment to the position of Hofdame five years later.[15]

The same year that von Pogwisch moved to Weimar, so did another woman intellectual, the travel writer and novelist Johanna Schopenhauer (1766–1838), and her daughter Adele (1797–1849), who would become Goethe's closest childhood friend.[16] Both von Pogwisch and Pogwisch's mother, Gräfin (Countess) Henckel von Donnersmarck, created a literary family tradition of continuous reading and exploration. The countess, in fact, owned a fine library, and after von Pogwisch's death Goethe inherited her mother's books, many of them in English.[17]

Von Pogwisch formed two reading groups among her Weimar contemporaries, one for German and one for French literature. Her daughter followed suit, and at age twenty, in September 1816, instigated with her sister and Schopenhauer a 'Musenverein' or society of Muses that continued to meet until 1822, within which Goethe was 'Tille-Muse'. The group's purpose was not to inspire other great men to literary achievement but to recite and discuss current works and perform the poems they themselves had written; fittingly, given the nine muses of classical tradition, they ultimately expanded their membership to nine.[18] But though Goethe wrote poems, critical essays, and imaginative tales after the manner of E. T. A. Hoffmann throughout her life, she steadfastly refused to make her writings public. Still, Goethe was both a producer and eager student of literature who readily affirmed women's critical and creative abilities. This background readily inclined her to welcome an Anglo-Irish woman credited with a published novel and a critical book on Shakespeare.

English literature, specifically, was also an early and abiding interest for Goethe. In a letter to her father-in-law in spring 1817 she mentioned her continuing English lessons ('englischen Mysterien'), but she was reading English literature well before that.[19] At the most basic level her English studies fashioned her into a cosmopolitan reader conversant with contemporary letters in England as well as France and Germany. Her English studies and unusually early acquaintance with Romantic writers also led to what became a literary passion: the poetry of George Gordon, Lord Byron.[20] So intense was her response to his work that she responded to his 1816 poem reflecting his scandalous separation from his wife, 'Fare Thee Well', with a prose fantasy of her own.[21] In 'Byron. Ein Traum. Den 27ten October 1822' (Byron: A Dream), the dreamer sees a beautiful maiden seated on a rocky eminence holding a golden harp whose music fills the scene, clearly a muse figure. When a 'kingly' ('königliche') black bird hovers over the maiden and kisses her lips, she then raises a laurel branch to the bird. And, as the dark bird carries it away into the heavens, the maiden sounds the final note of her melody that resembles a 'Fare well' [sic], and the maiden sighs out 'Lebewohl, mein dunkler Liebling' (farewell, my dark beloved) with tears in her eyes.[22]

In 1823, her adoration of Byron coalesced with the entrance into Weimar of the handsome young Irishman Charles Sterling, son of the

British consul in Genoa, who brought with him a letter of introduction from Byron himself. According to Thomas Moore, Byron's earliest biographer, 'a young gentleman, Mr. Sterling, of pleasing person and excellent character, in the spring of 1823, on a journey from Genoa to Weimar, delivered a few lines under the hand of the great man as an introduction'.[23] The effect of the nineteen-year-old Sterling on Goethe, then almost twenty-seven, was electric. Perhaps the biggest mistake of August von Goethe's life, biographer Ruth Rahmeyer speculates, was not seeing that what quickly emerged between his wife and Sterling was more than casual flirtation.[24] Not only was there intense physical attraction between the two young people, but they also shared enthusiasm for Byron, and Sterling could talk with Goethe at length about Byron's work.

By the time Anna Jameson arrived in Weimar in 1833, the affair was over and Sterling had decided to enter the Anglican ministry. But Goethe never got over him. That Jameson was not only an English literary figure in her own right but also a red-haired Irishwoman would have intensified Goethe's deep interest and receptiveness towards her visitor. Something sparked between the two as they met. According to Angele Steidele, Jameson fell in love with Goethe on the spot, an assessment supported by Goethe's own comment to her close friend Adele: 'Anna *liebt mich mehr als sie sollte*' (Anna loves me more than she should).[25] Such was Goethe's personal force that only five days after Jameson and her sister arrived in Weimar, Goethe persuaded them to change plans abruptly and accompany her to Frankfurt and Bonn for a tour on the Rhine. Jameson's erotic response to her new acquaintance is even clearer in her 23 July 1833 letter to Goethe after Jameson and her sister Charlotte had left and travelled on to Mainz:

> I thought of you when we walking [sic] about at Mainz ... – next morning at 8 – I looked at my watch & said 'now she is going to her bath' at 11 I thought – 'Now perhaps Captain Storey is awaiting her' & that thought was not quite pleasant – for whenever it occurs, it is mingled with some surprise how such a woman can allow such a man to amuse her (– forgive me this!) – Then at 12 – I thought 'now she is conjugating her Italian verbs aime, aimi, ama,['] &c. & at one oclock when we passed St Goar, could I otherwise than think of you! – & when four oclock strikes I wonder who is near you at the Table d'Hote, who amuses or perplexes [?] you on the left and who is so happy as to replace me on your right ...[26]

As might be expected over the course of a decades-long friendship between Jameson and Goethe from their initial meeting in 1833 until Jameson's death in 1860, their relationship and conditions in their own lives changed. Goethe never reciprocated Jameson's romantic feelings, but theirs was one of the great women's friendships of the nineteenth century.

The impact of Jameson's and Goethe's meeting each other did not stop with them. Jameson's entrée into Goethe's friendship circle illuminates the fluid gender and sexuality identities possible for intellectual German women as well as their social freedoms. Jameson first met Schopenhauer and, shortly thereafter, Sibylle Mertens-Schaaffhausen (1797–1857), who resided along the Rhine near Bonn and Cologne rather than in Weimar, a friend whom Goethe herself had met in summer 1832 through Schopenhauer.[27] When Jameson met Mertens-Schaaffhausen, they too formed an intimate friendship that was erotically tinged, if not so markedly or sustainedly as Jameson and Goethe's; and Jameson and Mertens-Schaaffhausen remained warm friends until Mertens-Schaaffhausen's death in 1857. Jameson would also sustain her friendship with Schopenhauer. These four women, two in unhappy marriages (Jameson and Mertens-Schaaffhausen), one a widow after an unhappy marriage (Goethe), and one never married, constituted a network of intellectually gifted, widely read women who moved freely about and shared passionate discussions of art, literature, and antiquity through conversations and letters. Their written and spoken exchanges were multilingual: Goethe and Schopenhauer knew English very well, and Goethe's letters to Jameson were principally Anglophone; after intensive study of German beginning in July 1833 Jameson mastered the language sufficiently to read it and converse to a degree.[28] But since Mertens-Schaaffhausen knew scant English and Jameson's German was not developed enough for complex intellectual exchanges in 1833, Mertens-Schaaffhausen and Jameson spoke and initially wrote to each other in French. If Schopenhauer and Mertens-Schaaffhausen, like Goethe, were central to Jameson's experience of cultural exchange, they are little known in English studies, and so I offer details below on their backgrounds and experiences before concluding with the principal forces within Jameson's and Goethe's friendship after 1833.

Adele Schopenhauer and Sibylle Mertens-Schaaffhausen

All who observed Schopenhauer in her lifetime attest to her powerful intellect, creative imagination, and attraction to other women.[29] Men found her ugly, which was no loss to her erotic life but did represent a social barrier: only marriage would have enabled her to leave her mother's house and form her own household. And because her mother, if talented and successful, was also demanding and egocentric, the gifted daughter never had a chance to develop independent professional writing, instead subordinating her gifts to her mother's writing career. In fact, according to Steidele, she often provided the ideas that her mother developed in her novels, but her collaborations were never credited in the authorial signatures or prefaces of her mother's published books.[30] The first woman whom Schopenhauer fell in love with was Goethe. Her October 1816 letter (written when Schopenhauer was nineteen) declared her love and even envisioned a form of same-sex marriage:

> I love you with every fiber of my being, with every feeling that is in me . . . and believe that I cannot live if you aren't happy, for you alone know all my thoughts and feel just as I do . . . you are my everything . . . you were my last thought yesterday and my first thought today . . . of this I am certain: we must always remain united since we are so firmly bound to each other . . . It was the will of God that brought us to each other so that we can go united through a wonderfully intertwined life.[31]

As Steidele sums up the matter, Goethe was Schopenhauer's 'Alpha' and 'Omega'. Only gradually and reluctantly, when Goethe had been married several years, did Schopenhauer finally accept the futility of her passion.[32] She left Weimar in 1827, and in January 1828 she met Mertens-Schaaffhausen in Cologne.

The two women had very different prior histories. The mother of Sibylle Schaaffhausen died a week after giving birth to her daughter; nor did the young daughter experience a close, much less motherly, relationship with her stepmother: they disliked each other. But in contrast to Schopenhauer's missing father (who had committed suicide years before), Schaaffhausen's beloved father played a vital role in his daughter's life, influencing and encouraging her study of antique coins and other Roman artefacts that abounded in Cologne from its days as a Roman colony. And from repeated evenings sitting in the great 'Dom' or cathedral, she grew to love the larger cultural heritage of the city. Her father often took her with him on visits to his close friend Ferdinand Franz Wallraf, co-founder of the city's museum (still called the Wallraf-Richartz-Museum); and seeing the collections at Wallraf's house further inspired her to become a collector and connoisseur as she grew up.[33]

Her father's tutelage, however, and her marked intellectual and artistic talents (she was a superb pianist and composed original music) spared her nothing of the predetermined female roles her German Catholic upbringing enforced. Entirely without love, she was shepherded into marriage at age nineteen to Louis Mertens, a prosperous merchant almost sixteen years her elder. Her obligatory duty to him was fulfilled in the six children she gave birth to before she turned thirty-one. She had scant vocation for motherhood and, while carrying out the tasks of tending and educating her children, otherwise showed little interest in them – perhaps not altogether surprising for one who had never experienced maternal love as a child. Nor was her marriage a success, since husband and wife had tempers as well as entirely different interests.[34] Instead she continued to channel her passions into collecting antiquities and the arts, which led her to open a salon while still in her twenties. This was attended by Romantic philosopher, poet, and critic August von Schlegel (1767–1845) as well as archaeologists, professors, scientists, musicians, and artists, a network that underlay her close involvement in promoting the music and art of Cologne, including the annual Carnival founded in 1823.[35]

If Mertens-Schaaffhausen expediently performed heteronormativity in her domestic life, she fell in love only with women, and the first was Schopenhauer, who entered Mertens-Schaaffhausen's salon during a visit to Cologne in January 1828 and was dazzled by her hostess's range and depth of knowledge, musicianship, and critical acumen. In turn Schopenhauer's obvious intelligence and standing as the daughter of a famous German woman author captivated her hostess. Immediately they began to spend whole days together and, when Schopenhauer fell ill, Mertens-Schaaffhausen waited tirelessly and tenderly upon her, until Schopenhauer wrote to Goethe that she had never in her life 'been so loved'; as Schopenhauer added, 'I love her … [and] I will never again love anyone as I love her.'[36] Clearly Schopenhauer had transferred her former passion for Goethe to a new beloved, and writing thus to Goethe bespoke a touch of recrimination for Goethe's love withheld. In 1829 Schopenhauer and her mother again travelled to Cologne, and from then until 1832 they lived in Mertens-Schaaffhausen's country home along the Rhine in summers and in Bonn during winters.[37]

Turbulence intervened in Mertens-Schaaffhausen and Schopenhauer's relationship, however, due to Louis Mertens's dislike of Schopenhauer and Schopenhauer's outbursts of jealousy, such as when Mertens Schaaffhausen was nursed through an illness by her friend Annette von Droste-Hülshoff (1797–1848), 'the greatest woman poet of nineteenth-century German literature' according to Monika Schafi.[38] The two women reconciled, but Schopenhauer exploded in jealousy again in late 1833 and 1834 over a new rival for Merten-Schaaffhausen's affections – none other than Anna Jameson (discussed below). In the face of Schopenhauer's continued outbursts, Louis Mertens banned Schopenhauer from his house, and there was nothing for it but to suspend the relationship.[39] If Schopenhauer and Mertens-Schaaffhausen defied Mertens's edict for three months in 1840, that too ended in a further ban of Schopenhauer from the Mertens property. With the exception of this interlude, the two women endured a seven-year separation from 1835 to 1842.

During that separation Mertens-Schaaffhausen found new love with Italian noblewoman Laurina Spinola (1806–38), whom Mertens-Schaaffhausen considered her soulmate.[40] Yet the soulmate died in 1838, and so did Johanna Schopenhauer, freeing her daughter at last. When Louis Mertens likewise died in August 1842, Mertens-Schaaffhausen's first letter to Schopenhauer implored her to come, and Schopenhauer arrived the following October.[41] Their reunion, Joey Horsley suggests, began the happiest years of both their lives.[42] Schopenhauer had to travel repeatedly to spas for treatment after the onset of uterine cancer in 1840, but the couple eventually moved to Rome in November 1844, returning to Bonn during summers.[43] In Rome Mertens-Schaaffhausen rose to prominence in archaeological circles through her detailed, exact knowledge, involvements in excavation, and marvellous collections. In Rome, in fact, Emil Braun, secretary of the German Archaeological Institute in Rome, invited Mertens-Schaaffhausen to present a public lecture on the frieze she helped identify – the first woman ever invited to lecture.[44] Schopenhauer, meanwhile, embarked anew on a literary career, publishing fiction and contributing newspaper articles on art from Florence, where she went to study it systematically, always with the energetic support of her partner, who helped edit her articles.[45] By 1849, however, Schopenhauer's illness forced her back to Germany, accompanied by Mertens-Schaaffhausen, who nursed her until her death on 25 August.

Afterward, Mertens-Schaaffhausen tried valiantly to collect her partner's writings and find a publisher, without success – a failure that contributed to Schopenhauer's invisibility as a writer and intellectual in later historical accounts. Nor was Mertens-Schaaffhausen's fate any better. In 1845 her daughter had come to Rome and pronounced her mother's 'eccentric' friendships with women 'wrong, absurd, mad'.[46] Long resentful of their mother's decided preference for spending more time with Schopenhauer or other women than with her husband and children, her heirs took their revenge when Mertens-Schaaffhausen died in Rome on 22 October 1857, no one at her side: they broke up their mother's magnificent collections, which could have won her a place in archaeological history, and sold them off in three massive auctions.[47]

Falling in(to) Love and Friendship: Jameson, Goethe, and Their Shared German Circle

The German circle of friends into which Jameson entered in 1833 was, then, sexually diverse and formed a liminal affective and social space that allowed for same-sex desire alongside Goethe's ever-flourishing attractions to men. From Goethe, whom Jameson and her sister left in Frankfurt in July, the English pair moved on to Bonn, meeting Schopenhauer, her mother Johanna, and Mertens-Schaaffhausen, at one of whose parties Jameson was introduced to Schlegel.[48] When Charlotte returned to England, Jameson extended her stay in Bonn where, according to Schopenhauer (who wrote to Goethe), Jameson was lost without someone to guide her through a country that was still quite foreign to her in manners and language, a reminder of the challenges to cultural exchange when one's grasp of a different language is incomplete.[49] Being shepherded about brought Jameson closer to these new friends, however, and Steidele contends that Jameson closely observed the relationship between Schopenhauer and Mertens-Schaaffhausen just as Schopenhauer surveilled Jameson's emotions. As the former wrote to Goethe on 12 September 1833, 'Anna loves you very much, more since meeting me, and through me, without my being aware of it, received some clarifications about you.'[50] Schopenhauer would have interpreted Jameson's feelings through her own experience of same-sex love, but her letter is additional evidence that Jameson harboured romantic feelings for Goethe that never surfaced in her marriage. And she was all the freer to indulge this queer attraction in the presence of Schopenhauer and Mertens-Schaaffhausen's mutual love.

From Bonn Jameson travelled to Munich but abruptly changed her itinerary again after Goethe wrote that she was ill with severe facial pain (a chronic malady) and asked Jameson to come back to Frankfurt. First Jameson nursed Goethe and, when Jameson then fell ill, Goethe nursed Jameson in turn, further deepening their emotional ties.[51] Goethe herself confessed at this time that 'since [Anna] has been here, I have often felt very soothed to see myself so loved.'[52] Once Goethe returned to Weimar in September, Jameson was off at last to Munich.[53] Jameson's letter to Goethe after their parting veered between romantic and maternal expression as she declared her lasting love for Goethe and warned against a serious flirtation Goethe had begun:

> I think of you, I fear for you, I love you, and there is nothing I can think or fear, which would make me love you less, – nay, I would try to love whatever you thought worthy of being loved … Whether loving or

> beloved, at least, dearest Ottilie, do not perform your threat, which dwells on my mind, and do a foolish thing ... At least before you make any irrevocable engagement in word or deed, be sure you secure that equivalent of happiness and love which alone *can* justify you to yourself, your children – and the world – which, despicable as it is, will always have the power to wound and degrade *them*, through *you*.[54]

Once in Munich Jameson continued to share endearments with Goethe and offered this perceptive assessment of the two women's contrasting characters, hinting at how each fulfilled a need in the other, Jameson's caution benefitting from Goethe's spontaneous freedom and vice versa:

> I love you, dear Ottilie, for that *abandon* and I could almost add that *inconsequence* where yourself are concerned. I respect and esteem in you that delicacy toward your friends which I do not often meet in others. My own nature is so reserved that discretion is in me scarce a virtue, for my mind and heart, tho' always full – too full – seldom overflow. This I think you have seen. But were I inclined to place confidence in anyone I would trust in you, from what I have seen of your character ...[55]

Jameson's estimate of her new friend accords with Goethe's own, as she described herself in a letter to Sarah Austin (1793–1867), the distinguished English translator of *Characteristics of Goethe* (1833), in an undated letter:[56]

> I am horribly lazy and indolent concerning myself, but I have an iron will for whatever touches my friends and pursue it for years through all the turns and twists of life; for it would seem unnatural to me to consider giving up and I can never become resigned. I have inexhaustible enthusiasm for certain ideas and for many am an emotional Don Quixote ready to break a lance defending them. For I see that the prevailing fear of ridicule ... undermines every higher aspiration in society regarding the power of words and example and results in timidity and faint-heartedness. With an inborn wild impulse toward freedom and rebellion, I have always been an utter slave in matters of love, and this duality rules me and is made manifest in the world. So little it would seem in many respects, so fervently as I demand women's emancipation, perhaps there is nobody who could be so happy as I in a harem using all my talents and gifts on behalf of one man – so long as he belonged only to me and I was not burdened with sharing his heart.[57]

Goethe outlines a character strong, fierce, and independent in some respects, as loyal to ideas as friends, yet withal unsteady in purpose where her own interests were concerned and liable to slavish self-subordination with men. All would be borne out in her relationship with Jameson.

From the beginning, Jameson's intimate emotional experiences with Goethe were also intertwined with hard work and professionalism. In Munich Jameson presented yet another letter of introduction to Dr Martius, famous from his travels in Brazil and now Keeper of the Botanic Garden and Professor of Botany. This she obtained because of her freer, unchaperoned travel in Germany, for when she casually chatted with a kindly old gentleman on board a river steamer, he turned out to be an English MP pursuing official business. As Jameson crowed to her father, 'I assure you, dear Papa, that it is much more amusing to travel as I do, than as we did with Sir Gerard Noel.'[58]

Once arrived, she set to work gathering materials on art and literature, which formed the bulk of *Visits and Sketches*. In Stuttgart she called again on sculptor Johann von Danneker, whom she had met in 1829, and in Munich met artist Moritz Retzsch, who inspired Jameson's 1834 edition of his etchings.[59] She also keenly observed the ambitious building projects sponsored by King Ludwig II of Bavaria. When driven away by cold weather, she rejoined Goethe in Weimar for two weeks, then journeyed to Dresden, where she met Romantic poet Ludwig Tieck and toured the famous Zwinger Museum, which Jameson would help make even more famous through her writings about art, especially Raphael's *Sistine Madonna*.[60]

After learning that her father had suffered a stroke and quickly arranging her return to London, she made one more German stop, not in Weimar but in Bonn to see Mertens-Schaaffhausen, who had complained of neglect.[61] Evidently Jameson hoped to make peace with her new friend, but her visit had the opposite effect. Schopenhauer and Mertens-Schaaffhausen both found themselves attracted to Jameson, who responded especially warmly to her wealthy host, Mertens-Schaaffhausen – who after all had the country home, the salon in town, and parallel interests in art and culture.[62] In *Visits and Sketches* Jameson would term Schopenhauer 'one of the most generally accomplished women I ever met with' but exclaim that Mertens-Schaaffhausen was 'a rare creature!', her warmth of feeling registered in the superlative and exclamation point.[63] Mertens-Schaaffhausen's and Jameson's moonlit carriage rides along the Rhine found their way not only into *Visits and Sketches* but also into Jameson's beautiful drawing 'Der romantische Rhein bei Nacht' that she gave to Mertens-Schaaffhausen, which has been preserved in the Anna Amalia Library in Weimar.[64]

After three weeks in a pension, Jameson moved into Mertens-Schaaffhausen's home, now becoming the member of a German household in which no English was spoken, only German or French, and attuned herself to the rhythms of German domestic life. All this time Schopenhauer was excluded from the Mertens-Schaaffhausen home by Louis Mertens and so from many private moments shared by Jameson and Mertens-Schaaffhausen. Inadvertently, Jameson's stop in Bonn caused a rift between the two Germans fuelled by Schopenhauer's jealousy, which helped lead to the German pair's seven-year separation. In a 1 December 1833 letter to Goethe, Schopenhauer expressed her emotional devastation at Jameson's departure and her intense resentment that Mertens-Schaaffhausen seemed to assume an even greater claim to the woman both Germans desired:

> As dear as she is to me, as endlessly as I bewail her, it really astonishes me how she behaves towards me and Mertens, because everyone knew her to be more intimate with me ... Sibylle got tremendously upset and treated me so unkindly due to her ardent love for Jameson, which Sibylle treats as if she were dying from some fatal illness.[65]

Where she meant to bolster loving friendship, Jameson had brought greater strife.

From Weimar, Goethe made it clear that she wanted no part in a Sapphic circle, telling Schopenhauer outright that her problem was having no man to love. Another line in her letter ruled out any response in kind to Jameson's romantic passion: 'this form [of love] between women is not natural'.[66] But Goethe shared this only with Schopenhauer, not Jameson, who wrote to Goethe after leaving Germany of her

> grief, ... deep and bitter grief ... on parting from you. Leaving Germany was leaving *you*, you, round whom some of the deepest feelings of which my nature is capable, had imperceptibly twined themselves – quietly indeed, because my nature is quiet, and not now, as once, confiding and demonstrative but not therefore the less real.[67]

Although Jameson cared very much for all three of her new German friends, Goethe always came first and alone induced Jameson to drop her plans and rush to Goethe's side, even at risk to herself and her career. This occurred in 1834–6, when Goethe's unruly erotic desires and belief that each new prospective lover would realise her ideal nearly brought catastrophe upon her and her family. So long as Johann von Goethe was living, she had been devoted to her father-in-law and his closest companion.[68] But when he died in March 1832, she had sped to Mainz, where Charles Sterling had arrived, for a passionate reunion – though they may not yet have physically consummated their long attraction to one another. Goethe now considered herself linked to him for life and was horrified that, only days after leaving her, he visited prostitutes in Amsterdam – and told her so in a letter.[69] The next month she met Captain Story, and in 1833, after Jameson left Frankfurt in July, spent extended time in his company. In 1834 Goethe returned to Frankfurt in May and saw Story daily the next three months.[70] By July 1834, when Jameson arrived in Germany following the appearance of *Visits and Sketches* to arrange for publication of Retzsch's engravings, Goethe was pregnant.[71]

Jameson, ignorant of the fact, soon reached Weimar and, at the express invitation of Weimar's Grand Duchess, appeared in court accompanied by Goethe's mother and grandmother.[72] Jameson next journeyed to Berlin to see an exhibition but abruptly returned to Weimar when called back by Goethe, who by then realised her condition and the crisis it represented. That Goethe, the unmarried widow and mother of Johann von Goethe's descendants, as well as the former intimate companion of the writer himself, should be pregnant out of wedlock by an Englishman who had no intention of marrying her was well-nigh unthinkable and threatened to tarnish the very name 'Goethe'. The obvious solution was to spirit Goethe out of town accompanied only by Jameson, her most trusted friend. Goethe had stayed in bed the day Jameson appeared in court and, to explain their departure, she pleaded indisposition that required treatment at a spa. The pair then headed to Vienna.[73]

Goethe's secret pregnancy also posed real danger to Jameson, who in 1834 had presented Goethe as the ideal woman in *Visits and Sketches* (see Chapter 2). Were it known in England that Jameson had knowingly shielded the great Johann von Goethe's unmarried daughter-in-law and was present at the birth in mid-February 1835 of an illegitimate daughter whom Goethe named after her, Jameson's spotless name and career as a mobile, respected woman of letters could well have ended.[74] In that case, moreover, Jameson could no longer have helped support her family back home. For Goethe's sake Jameson endured the risk and stood as godmother to little Anna at the infant's baptism. To further salvage Goethe's reputation (although reports of Goethe visibly pregnant in Vienna had reached Johanna Schopenhauer, who gleefully fed Weimar gossip), Goethe then returned to Weimar in June 1835 and resumed her social and family life there.[75]

Jameson stayed on in Vienna to oversee care of the baby, of whom she became very fond. It was a very stressful time due to her lack of experience in infant care and the need to oversee finances and daily transactions with only limited skills in spoken German (she could fall back on French or English only when mingling with the Viennese elite).[76] The sheer busyness of her life there, and its burden, are suggested in Jameson's 20 July 1835 letter to Goethe omitted by Needler from his edition of their correspondence, perhaps because he found maternal and childcare minutiae of little interest:

> I must begin by telling you two things which I forgot in my last letter – first that I am very sorry you are going to send little gowns – it is quite unnecessary – I have made already two – I have the materials for others which I will make – & the weichlichstes[77] [?] being of no use will make the prettiest little jackets you can imagine – & I can contrive it all very well – so if not sent, do not send them – the second thing I had to say was that I sent off a box by Mr Schwarz containing many books & different things belonging to you & to me ... the little one's teeth begin to make her uneasy – if the English necklace is a comfort to you by all means send it – with regard to its efficacy – I have no belief in it & think it an absurdity – so do all the English physicians – but they do not object to it as it quiets mothers & nurses – so Dr Herbert told me – you tell me dearest Ottilie, to send you no details about the arrangements I have made but I must do so – & you must know all exactly that you may continue or alter such arrangements you will find all at the end of this letter –
>
> You ask 'what security or what confidence you can have – [?illegible] after the last bad experiment' you have as much security as any mother has or can have who is obliged by any circumstances to leave her child, as many thousand mothers are – I saw a very tender mother last year part with her infant of 8 months old – not for a year but for 5 or 6 years at least, she was going to India – she placed it necessarily with strangers – having no security but the intelligence & integrity of those she trusted – the rest remained with heaven & nature ... in your first experiment – you paid as you say 4 [?] people to take care of your child & it was dying of neglect – that is you paid 4 [?] vulgar, ignorant, self interested people who were all fighting together. – you will now have to pay two people, one of whom (Seligmann[78]) will be responsible for the health of your child as far as human means can secure it, & the other, an amiable woman & a mother will be responsible for its tender treatment – if any thing happens, I am sure you may trust that it was unavoidable but the dear little thing is so well, & has such an excellent constitution, that there is every hope for you – Seligmann thinks she will prove "un miracle de beauté et d'esprit"[79] as he told me yesterday – he is always in admiration – & once said, she was 'comme une incarnation au quelque chose de divine'[80] – her eyes are wonderfully beautiful & she is full of life & spirit – still delicate & thin, however & requiring care – I must not forget that she shows already a very decided love of music you say that you will not & cannot be separated from your child after September, that is longer than two months – my dear Ottilie, I know your truth, & that you never were guilty of willful exaggeration or affectation – you endured to be parted from your other children for a year nearly, because necessity required

it & you will also try to bear this if necessary (not unless – God forbid) – but surely you who are a really tender & conscientious mother, will not attempt to tell me that here there is an equal necessity? – it is more necessary that you should maintain & preserve your influence in the minds of your other children & hold fast their affection & respect as your best shield against the world, & their best defence against bad friends & bad example than that you should sacrifice all for the mere physical wants of this little Baby, who never will remember the first year or two of its existence, hereafter you may be all to it without sacrificing the others – if too soon you rashly attempt to unite both – for want of generosity & courage to chuse an alternative you will lose both – remember I tell you this from a deep conviction of what [I] say –[81]

The length of this letter attests to Jameson's indefatigable efforts in Vienna, her genuine affection for little Anna, her somewhat maternal advice to her beloved friend, and perhaps her own terror lest Goethe insist on publicly owning the child and so undoing the secrecy Jameson had worked so hard to shore up. By 4 August Jameson was utterly exhausted: 'I am so completely alone that I can with difficulty rouse myself to make any decision – Something I must do for my health & immediately – for I become weaker & weaker – I know dearest Ottilie that a short time would recover me if I had change & perfect rest – but where I am to go?'[82]

She shortly left Vienna and headed 'to the [Austrian] mountains for a few weeks to do nothing but keep quiet, and take cold baths'. After recuperating in Traunkirchen near the Traunsee in the lake district, she returned to Weimar in mid-September, revisited art galleries in Dresden and other northern German sites of professional utility, and finally rejoined Goethe for Christmas in Weimar, staying into the new year.[83] In stepping so far outside her comfort zone during this entire episode, Jameson had expanded her sensibility beyond the limits of her own culture's ideology and gender norms, an enlarged perspective she carried forward into the rest of her life.

She hoped to remain in Germany through the winter. This time her plans changed abruptly due not to Goethe but to her husband, who wrote in August 1835 to insist that she join him temporarily in Canada where he had been appointed Attorney General of Upper Canada, presumably to confer domestic respectability upon him. The bargain they eventually struck was that in return he would agree to a permanent separation and provision of an annual allowance.[84] Jameson left Germany some time in the spring and prepared for the Atlantic voyage onwards to Canada. But she took the fruits of her two-year residence in Germany (including some book chapters) with her. Arriving in Vienna with Goethe in 1834 had given Jameson immediate entrée to the best Viennese social, intellectual, and artistic circles. Her new acquaintances included poet Karoline Pichler; dramatist Franz Grillparzer; Henriette Pereira-Arnstein, a pianist and salonnière who hosted musical evenings attended by Grillparzer and Mendelssohn among others; Countess Zichy, who would invite Jameson to the Austrian spa Ischl after she left Traunkirchen; and the Princess Hohenzollern.[85] Many of these would figure in her next book, *Winter Studies and Summer Rambles* (1838), which also recounted her delightful experiences of Canadian travel and cultural difference when she could leave Robert Jameson behind in Toronto.

In 1839 Jameson was once again in Germany, intent on seeing Goethe to check, if need be, her romance with the decade-younger Gustav Kühne (1806–88), editor of the literary newspaper *Zeitung für die elegante Welt* and member of the 'Young Germany' movement. Goethe was not only assisting his editorial efforts but also acting as a tacit collaborator on his novel about the 1798 Irish rebellion, *Die Rebellen von Irland* (1840).[86] Characteristically Jameson's trip also had a professional end in view, for she had decided during her Canadian sojourn to translate the plays of the royal princess Amalia of Saxony and write accompanying notes that touched on women's status. Goethe was deeply involved in assisting Jameson too, who even before arriving had asked Goethe for explanations about what plays she should consider and the social contexts of their incidents.[87]

Five years later Jameson made an urgent trip back to Goethe's side to help her weather a very different crisis, the sudden death of Goethe's only surviving daughter, Alma von Goethe (1827–44).[88] Alma had been flourishing in Weimar with her grandmother after Goethe moved to Vienna; but to expand Alma's social and intellectual horizons and improve her marital prospects, Goethe insisted that Alma join her in Vienna. It had ended in tragedy when Alma contracted typhoid at a ball and quickly died. Jameson and Goethe reunited in Nuremberg and then travelled to Dresden, Prague, Vienna, and Venice.[89] A six-month German sojourn recurred in 1850, with Jameson first visiting Mertens-Schaaffhausen in Bonn on arriving and again just before she returned to London. Goethe joined her friends in Bonn; Jameson and Goethe then moved on to Düsseldorf and Berlin, where Jameson could combine gallery research for her books on sacred art with as much companionship with Goethe as possible. Later Jameson joined Goethe in Vienna through Christmas and into the new year.[90] The friends were together again in Vienna and Venice in 1855, then a last time in Dresden from August to mid-September 1859 before Jameson died in 1860, a consequence of bodily illness but even more of her persistent drive, determination, and work ethic, for she had walked home in a snowstorm after consulting materials in the British Library.[91]

Both Jameson and Goethe benefited from their long friendship. Jameson's first encounter with Goethe in 1833 led to a trilogy of books, *Visits and Sketches* (1834), the 'Studies' portions of *Winter Studies and Summer Rambles* (1838), and *Social Life in Germany* (1840). Though Jameson then turned to other topics, especially sacred art and women's access to work, her cultural exchange with Germany formed an intellectual foundation that continued to inform her work. And always, for Jameson, Germany wore the face of Goethe. As Jameson wrote to her on 5 May 1836, 'what was once my home is no longer my home – my home is with you'.[92] On her way to Goethe in 1839, Jameson repeated, 'I have arrived thus far on my road to you, my dearest Ottilie – & my joy to see you again will be greater than I can express – I long to be <u>at home</u> again –.'[93] Even in England Jameson's German friends were with her in a very real sense. On 16 July 1843 she told Goethe,

> I am writing in a little room in my mothers cottage which I wish you could see. It is smaller than my little bedroom at Weimar – over the Chimney is a fine drawing after one of Rafael's Madonnas – life size – on one side is your picture, under it, Alma's. On the right Sybille – Countess Zichy & Noel, Fanny Butler and Tieck – over the bookcase the bust of Goethe –.[94]

Goethe's virtual presence led Jameson to claim that even from a distance she could feel her friend's sympathies:

> I will not allow a day to pass without beginning an answer to your letter my dear dear Ottilie – I really believe there is no one in the world who loves me as you love me or who thinks of me so constantly – O du meine Heilige! [Oh you, my saint!] – I was enchanted to have your letter – the news from Vienna & Hungary made me feel anxious about you and I was afraid to write not knowing precisely where you might be – were I but a <u>free</u> woman there is nothing on earth should prevent my going to you – but <u>I</u> am bound at present by family cares & duties & I am not very well or happy – the one being a consequence of the other ... I am glad you like my book, dearest – I can truly say that in many parts of it – I thought of you while I wrote it – & thought of pleasing you – & I felt some of your sympathy ...[95]

Jameson's role in Goethe's life was equally sustaining. So great was the impact of Jameson's death on 17 March 1860 – St Patrick's Day – that Goethe's daily diary went blank for nine months.[96] Materially, too, Goethe attested to the profound meaning Jameson's friendship held for her. Goethe retained every scrap that Jameson wrote to her. The Jameson materials in the Goethe- und Schiller-Archiv, for example, include a series of undated hasty notes written during Jameson's visits to her beloved friend, some clearly written in Italy and at least one in Vienna. The entirety of one reads, 'Why have you not sent me a word dearest to say you are better? – I am afraid it is not so – I shall be with you a little after 12 – I have much to write to make notes &c.' and signed 'Your affect Anna'.[97] On one hand the notes indicate Jameson's practice of combining a fulfilling emotional relationship with her ongoing professional career. The notes additionally confirm that even when reuniting the women maintained separate quarters, most likely because Jameson needed a private place to write. On the other hand, these notes testify to how much Jameson meant to Goethe, who saved even these trivial scribbles from her treasured friend.

In their own time Goethe and Jameson manifestly affected each other's lives profoundly. Today their friendship has a larger significance as well: their every gesture of friendship, their every moment together or in correspondence, enacted cross-cultural exchange. Their decades-long exchange and Jameson's representation of Germany in her writings additionally acted to influence Victorian women readers and writers who came after her. By precedent and precepts alike, Jameson established Germany as a welcoming place to middle-class women writers in search of greater personal freedoms and wider professional opportunities.

CHAPTER 2

Germany through a Female Lens
Anna Jameson's Writings, 1834–1860

The publication of *Visits and Sketches at Home and Abroad* in 1834 launched Jameson as an expert on foreign as well as British art, literature, and culture. German culture would also play major roles in her next two books, so that when she helped Robert and Elizabeth Barrett Browning elope to Italy in 1846 she was known 'as the author of *Winter Studies and Summer Rambles in Canada* (1838) and *Social Life in Germany* (1840)'.[1] After 1840 her career turned more decidedly to art, first in a series of guides to galleries and then the art books for which she is best known today, *Sacred and Legendary Art* (1848–52). Jameson's experiences of Germany and her friendship with Goethe nonetheless informed all her writing from 1834 until her life ended in early 1860, including a brief *Athenaeum* article in 1859. This chapter surveys Jameson's German-inspired work as examples of sustained cultural exchange and explores their literary and social impact in nineteenth-century England and continuing relevance; even today Jameson serves as a useful model of how to engage another culture ethically and productively.

Visits and Sketches at Home and Abroad (1834)

John R. Davis terms *Visits and Sketches* the 'most influential travelogue' of Germany in the 1830s, especially in opening the richness of German art museums and the ferment of new schools of painting and architecture to British audiences.[2] The *Athenaeum* devoted three successive notices to *Visits and Sketches* in June–July 1834, asserting that the volumes

> afford a vivid instance of the strength and reach of the female talent of the present day – they are full of woman's keenness of observation, of her enthusiastic warmth of feelings, of the rich elegance of her imagination; but they betray little or no deficiency of the strength upon the presumed exclusive possession of which, man has been so long used to crest himself.[3]

The *Edinburgh Review* additionally noted her 'eloquent and philosophic female criticism'.[4] Part I, especially the section on Frankfurt, and all of Part II follow the conventions of travel literature, alternating among celebrity accounts, picturesque sights, and guides to art galleries, as would later mass-produced European travel guides and Jameson's own London gallery guides.[5]

But larger aims also surface. As in *Characteristics of Women* (1832), Jameson comments on women's education, but rather than tying this education to women's roles as 'mothers and nurses of legislators and statesmen', as in the earlier book, *Visits and Sketches* celebrates sociable women for whom exercising intellectual powers is an important end in itself.[6] In her opening pages Jameson theorises female cosmopolitanism immediately after contrasting the insular, snobbish young Englishwomen on board a steamer, whom she observed travelling under the wing of their equally haughty 'mamma', with two young German women.[7] Superior to the English females in looks and rank, they interact with other passengers, smile at the young Englishmen eager to loan them their telescopes, and freely walk along the deck rather than huddling apart.[8] The German women, like those on Berlin streets whom Florence Nightingale would observe in 1850, are freer than their English counterparts; more important, they engage in Anglo–German cultural exchange.[9]

Jameson also demonstrates the contrast between openness to difference in cultures and narrow Englishness in herself before and after engaging in Anglo–German sociability. Thus she and her English travelling companion first turned up their noses at what seemed the 'exceedingly disagreeable' old city of Cologne with its 'endless narrow dirty streets, and dull dingy-looking edifices'; but after she met an unnamed friend (Sibylle Mertens-Schaaffhausen), she saw the same city anew, specifically as a sphere of more capaciously conceived female ability and development:

> Cologne has since become most interesting to me from a friendship I formed with a Colonese, a descendant of one of the oldest patrician families of the place. How she loved her old city! – how she worshipped every relic with the most poetical, if not the most pious veneration ... The cathedral she used to call '*mon Berceau* [cradle],' and the three kings '*mes trois pères* [my three fathers].' Her profound knowledge of general history, her minute acquaintance with the local antiquities, the peculiar customs, the wild legends, the solemn superstitions of her birth-place, added to the most lively imagination and admirable descriptive powers, were to me an inexhaustible source of delight and information.[10]

As she later observes of Mertens-Schaaffhausen and Adele Schopenhauer, they are 'very essentially *German*: English society and English education would never have produced two such women'.[11]

Visits withholds from view until the middle of Book I the woman who lay at the heart of Jameson's experience of Germany. 'Goethe and his daughter-in-law' opens with a deeply contemplative Alda in England whose thoughts are 'far – very far' away after reading a passage in Sarah Austin's *Characteristics of Goethe* that

> sent back my thoughts to Weimar. I was again in his house; the faces, the voices of his grandchildren were around me; the room in which he studied, the bed in which he slept, the old chair in which he died, – and, above all, *her* in whose arms he died – from whose lips I heard the detail of his last moments.[12]

On one hand this is celebrity reporting by a privileged insider. But proximity to the daughter-in-law's arms and lips linked to the passage's rhythm of rising emotion marks this as highly personal writing too.[13] Though the passage begins with the greatness of Johann von Goethe, Jameson adroitly adapts his cultural authority as warrants for the highest pinnacle of womanhood Jameson has ever encountered:

> 'That's a piece of nature,' (literally, *das ist eine Natur*, that is a nature) ... from Goethe's lips was considerable praise.
>
> This last phrase threw me back upon my remembrances. I thought of the daughter-in-law of the poet, – the trusted friend, the constant companion, the devoted and careful nurse of his last years. It accounted for the unrivalled influence which apparently she possessed – I will not say *over* his mind – but *in* his mind, in his affections; for in her he found truly *eine Natur* – a piece of nature, which could bear even *his* microscopic examination. All other beings who approached Goethe either were, or had been, or might be, more or less modified by the action of that universal and master spirit ... but HER's was, in comparison, like a transparent medium, through which the rays of that luminary passed, – pervading and enlightening, but leaving no other trace. Conceive a woman, a young, accomplished, enthusiastic woman, who had qualities to attach, talents to amuse, and capacity to appreciate, GOETHE; who, for fourteen or fifteen years, could exist in daily, hourly communication with that gigantic spirit, yet retain, from first to last, the most perfect simplicity of character, and this less from the strength than from the purity and delicacy of the original texture ... Her conversation was the most untiring I ever enjoyed, because the stores which fed that flowing eloquence were all native and unborrowed ...[14]

Jameson goes on to praise the daughter-in-law's gift of 'consummate refinement of thought, and feeling, and expression' and caps this extended eulogium by enunciating the standard Goethe sets for all educated women:

'Quick in perception, yet femininely confiding, uniting a sort of restless vivacity with an indolent gracefulness, she appeared to me by far the most poetical and genuine being, of my own sex I ever knew in highly-cultivated life.'¹⁵ Never passive or mute in the presence of genius, the female Goethe clearly possesses a remarkable mind and broad knowledge inseparable from feminine sympathy, affection, and delightful sociability.

Goethe is also, Jameson makes clear, herself a writer – but one whom the public will never be able to read: 'Of those effusions of her creative and poetical talents, which charm her friends, I say nothing, because in all probability neither you nor the public will ever benefit by them.'¹⁶ When Alda names other talented German women writers who spurn publication, Medon immediately cites the similar report by Abraham Hayward in a recent translation of *Faust* and quotes Hayward's hopes that steps might be taken 'to unlock the stores of fancy and feeling which the Ottilies and the Adèles have hived up'.¹⁷ Jameson is here engaging in intricate intertextuality. On one hand, without herself mentioning the first names of two of her closest German friends, Jameson allows Hayward to do so and also delegates to him regrets about their refusal to publish. On the other hand, in alluding so specifically to Hayward's second edition, which appeared mere months before *Visits* was issued, Jameson publicises Goethe's intellectual status, gives added point to the survey of German women writers that follows her own tribute to Goethe, and engages in self-advertising.¹⁸ For apropos of a commentary on Gretchen in *Faust*, Hayward devotes a paragraph to Jameson herself:

> I wish Mrs. Jameson would devote a chapter in her next work to [Johann von] Goethe's women; she would form, I am sure, a higher and a truer estimate of a Mignon or a Clara, than Madame [de Staël] ... Much as this lady [Jameson] has been admired, she has never yet been adequately spoken of ... [or] her earnest truth of feeling, her passionate intensity of thought, her fine discrimination of character, and daring felicity of illustration.¹⁹

In alluding to Hayward, Jameson reciprocates Hayward's advertisement of her yet offers a tacit riposte. Rather than devoting her writing to Johann von Goethe's fictional women, Jameson surveys living German women authors, making it clear that a number of German women publish, whether Helmina von Chezy, Karoline Pichler, Johanna Schopenhauer, or Fanny Tarnow.²⁰

Hayward concluded his commentary by regretting that 'little or nothing is known in England of the present state of painting, sculpture and engraving in Germany', and he again singled out Jameson as peculiarly gifted with the 'power of making paintings and statues speak to the imagination and understanding through books', another propitiously timed mention preceding the publication of *Visits*.[21] In *Visits*, Jameson presented a guide to the Glyptothek Museum of ancient sculpture in Munich and to Germany's most important contemporary artists, amply fulfilling Hayward's desire. In addition, whenever possible she also mentioned Renaissance and contemporary German women painters, including Madame de Freyburg (an artist and mother), Julie von Egloffstein (an early member of Goethe's Musenverein), Louise Seidlar (Luise Sidlar in *Visits* and like Egloffstein a member of Johann von Goethe's circle, becoming eventual custodian of paintings at the grand ducal court); Mademoiselle de Winkel of Dresden, and Emilie Lachaud de Loqueyssie (whose portraits included miniatures).[22]

In these ways Jameson is truly offering an account of Germany and German culture through a female lens. Perhaps most important, she enacts the liberating possibilities of a German milieu for British women by writing a text in which, working out of surroundings afforded by Germany, she appropriates authority as a woman cultural critic. She additionally aligns the qualities needed in an effective cultural critic with those she identifies with affective female cosmopolitanism in her introduction:

> Certainly [in Britain] we have in these days mean ideas about painting – mean and false ideas! It has become a mere object of luxury and connoisseurship, or *virtù*: unless it be addressed to our personal vanity, or to the puerile taste for ornament, show, furniture, – it is nothing ... The public – the national spirit, is wanting; individual patronage is confined, is misdirected, is arbitrary, demanding of the artist any thing rather than the highest and purest intellectual application of his art ...[23]

True appreciation of painting instead requires '[s]ensibility, imagination, and quick perception of form and colour', 'power of association', a 'mind trained to habitual sympathy with the beautiful and the good', and 'knowledge of the meaning, and the comprehension of the object of the artist'.[24] Like most nineteenth-century art critics, including Ruskin, she adopts a moral approach ('the beautiful and the good'), but her additional terms echo those in her introduction: 'habitual sympathy', 'quick perception', a 'trained' mind, and comprehensive 'knowledge'.[25]

On the basis of these precepts and her assumption of authority, she does not hesitate to assert cases in which German practices are superior to British. When she examines German art inside the new palace being built for King Ludwig in Munich, for example, and watches painter Julius Schnorr and his assistants working on frescoes based on the *Niebelungenlied*, she asks,

> 'What would some of our English painters – Etty, or Hilton, or Briggs, or Martin – O what would they give to have two or three hundred feet of space before them, to cover at will with grand and glorious creations, – scenes from Chaucer, or Spenser, or Shakspeare, or Milton, proud[l]y conscious that they were painting for their country and posterity, spurred on by the spirit of their art and national enthusiasm, and generously emulating each other! Alas! How different! – with us such men as Hilton and Etty illustrate annuals, and the genius of Turner shrinks into a vignette!['].[26]

More than two decades later a plan along these lines would be adopted for the new Houses of Parliament due to a German intervention, Prince Albert's leadership in directing frescoes that celebrated British cultural heritage including Chaucer and Arthurian legend.[27] But if she was receptive to German triumphs, neither did Jameson avoid censuring German faults, as when she criticised the plan to build the monument named Valhalla in the style of a Greek temple.[28] She moreover elevated British portraiture over Germany's:

> If I should whisper that since I came to Germany I have not seen one really fine modern portrait, the Germans would never forgive me ... But before they are angry, and absolutely condemn me, I wish they would place one of their own most admired portraits beside those of Titian or Vandyke, or come to England, and look upon our school of portraiture here! I think they would allow, that with all their merits, they are in the wrong road ... They think too much of the accessories ...[29]

The high point of Jameson's representation of female freedoms and opportunities afforded by Germany comes in a passage on the Glyptothek, which she visits on a day set aside for 'strangers', or non-residents, and finds herself alone as she walks from gallery to gallery of sculpture. In this passage she first theorises the distinctive quality of the ancient sculptures she observes, namely, their combined *'presence of thought, and the absence of volition'*.[30] In an original poem evidently composed in the gallery, she then contrasts and appropriates to herself the union of thought and mobility that characterises literature:

> Alone.
> In the Gallery of Sculpture at Munich.
>
> Ye pale and glorious forms, to whom was given
> All that we mortals covet under heaven –
> Beauty, renown, and immortality,
> And worship! – in your passive grandeur, ye
> Are what we most adore, and least would wish to be!

There's nothing new in life, and nothing old;
The tale that we might tell hath oft been told.
Many have look'd to the bright sun with sadness
Many have look'd to the dark grave with gladness;
Many have griev'd to death – have lov'd to madness!

What has been, is; – what is, will be; – I know
Even while the heart drops blood, it *must* be so.
I live and smile – for O the griefs that kill,
Kill slowly – and I bear within me still
My conscious self, and my unconquer'd will!

And knowing what I have been – what has made
My misery, I will be no more betray'd
By hollow mockeries of the world around,
Or hopes and impulses, which I have found
Like ill-aim'd shafts, that kill by their rebound.

Complaint is for the feeble, and despair
For evil hearts. Mine still can hope – still bear –
Still hope for others what it never knew
Of truth and peace; and silently pursue
A path beset with briers, 'and wet with tears like dew!'[31]

Jameson's iambic pentameter rhymed couplets and triplets creatively respond to her solitary reflection on sculpture's relation to humanity, acknowledging the lack of the ideal embodied by sculptures in herself but claiming both thought and volition that statuary lacks. Hers is the utterance of an Englishwoman whose self-reliance rather than relative existence is extended by cultural mobility and culminates in 'unconquer'd will', a phrase usually reserved for men. Publicly representing this intensely personal moment also demonstrates to her closest German friends the potential benefits if they would likewise share with women readers and a broader public their poems and contemplative prose. Jameson's poem is thus the climax of *Visits* and what it represents. Combined with Jameson's assertion that in Germany and especially Prussia 'no where could an unprotected female journey with more complete comfort and security', Jameson telegraphed to other women the mobility and intellectual promise that Germany offered them too.[32]

Winter Studies and Summer Rambles in Canada (1838)

When Jameson reluctantly left Germany in 1836 and travelled to England to prepare for a transatlantic journey that took her to her husband in

Canada, she could not know that she would also be sailing into Canadian literary history. Jameson is today a minor figure relative to George Eliot or Elizabeth Gaskell, but *Winter Studies and Summer Rambles in Canada* (1838) has remained in print since its first appearance and is a canonical Canadian text.[33] The 'summer rambles' of Jameson's third volume featuring her 'adoption' by the Ojibwa ('Chippewas' to Jameson) are best known. But according to Alessa Johns and Judith Johnston, *Winter Studies and Summer Rambles* (hereafter *WSSR*) also has an intimate connection to her experiences in Germany. As Johnston says of *WSSR* epigraphs taken from German women,

> by these judicious quotations, Jameson writes herself into a circle of German women (I am including von Goethe), all of whom have literary and artistic connections, a writing-in which perhaps eases the pain of displacement and exile. However . . . , she also appeals to women readers beyond the work's first and most intimate putative reader, Ottilie von Goethe, readers who are both English and German, as *Winter Studies and Summer Rambles in Canada* was translated and published in Braunschwieg (near Hanover), by F. Biewig in 1839).[34]

Throughout, *WSSR* drew upon her German experiences as a woman, intimate friend, thinker, and professional writer.[35] Even her openness to 'Chippewa' women and cultural difference was shaped in part by Jameson's prior experience of ethnoexocentrism in Germany. But *WSSR* extends Jameson's ethnoexocentrism in its quadrilateral cultural exchange among Britain, Germany, Canada, and the US and invites readers to become equally open to cultural difference.

As Jameson's preface explains, she wrote *WSSR* in the form of 'fragments' of a journal written to 'a friend'.[36] That friend is clearly Goethe, as a number of passages in Jameson's three volumes confirm. Early in volume I Jameson, chafing against confinement in Toronto, remarks that 'Resignation comes in a form which reminds me of Ottilie's definition – "Resignation, my dear, is only a despair, which does not beat people."' Later Jameson asks, 'Why do you not finish your translation of [Johann von Goethe's] Egmont? who will ever do it as you *can*?', a pointed reference to Goethe's earlier collaboration with Englishman Charles des Voeux on a translation of *Tasso*, although the reference was veiled to any readers unfamiliar with Goethe's role.[37] This dear friend likewise hovers in the background of Jameson's extended discussion of Eckermann's *Gespräche mit Goethe* (conversations with Goethe), since she had been physically present at many conversations that Eckermann recorded.[38]

Even when Jameson narrates her adventure in the Canadian west among its First Nations peoples, she suddenly addresses Goethe as 'you' and covertly refers to their shared secret of Jameson's exhaustion in 1835 from tending to Goethe's infant daughter Anna in Vienna:

> Two summers ago I was lingering . . . alone, and convalescent, on the banks of the Traun-See in Upper Austria. O that I could convey to you in intelligible words all the difference between *there* and *here*! – between *then* and *now*! – between *that* solitude and *this* solitude! There I was alone with nature and my own heart, bathed in mountain torrents, and floated for hours together on the bosom of that delicious lake, not thinking, not observing, only enjoying and dreaming! . . . What a contrast between that still, sublime loneliness, that vague, tender, tranquil, blessed mood, and the noisy excitement of this restless yet idle existence, where attention is continually fatigued and never satisfied! . . . What a contrast between my pretty Tyrolean *batelière* singing as she slowly pulled her oar, and my wild Indian boy flourishing his paddle! – between the cloud-capped Traunstein and gleaming glaciers, and these flat marshy shores . . .
>
> But it is well to have known and seen both. Nothing so soon passes away from the mind as the recollection of physical inconvenience and pain – nothing is so permanent as the picture once impressed on the fancy; and *this* picture will be to me a pleasure and an inalienable property, like that of the Traun-See, when this irksome languor of the sinking spirit will be quite forgotten and effaced.[39]

In these interwoven references Goethe buckles the German and Canadian parts of *WSSR* together and gives it such unity as it has.[40]

At one point Jameson compares Eckermann's book to S. T. Coleridge's *Table Talk*, an aside that illuminates the form of Jameson's own *Winter Studies*. Insofar as all three works represent mobile intelligences discoursing on varied topics in a sociable context, Jameson's *Winter Studies* is an Anglo-German female counterpart to Johann von Goethe's *Conversations* and Coleridge's *Table Talk* with appeal to German and English readers alike.[41] This generic format clarifies not just her wide-ranging comments on German and Anglophone literature but also the emotional and psychological function of Jameson's critical commentaries in providing the virtual companionship of the beloved German friend she had so recently left behind. Jameson was 'accompanied' by Goethe in her solitary Toronto room in material ways too, since while writing Jameson drew upon the 'MS notes you were so good as to write me. For the latter I cannot sufficiently thank you, my dear kind friend!'[42]

Approaching *Winter Studies* as female-centred conversation gains further credence from the epigraph gracing Jameson's title page in all three volumes below Jameson's authorial name: '*Leid, und Kunst, und Scherz* [Sorrow, and Art, and Jest]. / Rahel''. Jameson's epigraph derives from the famous German woman conversationalist Rahel Varnhagen von Ense (née Rahel Levin), the Berlin Jewish salonnière who 'was perceived as a pioneer of women's intellectual emancipation by her contemporaries, including [Johann von] Goethe [and] Heinrich Heine'. Rahel is by now a key figure in histories of German Jewish life, women writers, and Romanticism.[43] But when *Winter Studies* appeared in November 1838, Rahel was unknown to the British public. As Jameson observes in a footnote, 'The book of "Rahel" is famous from one end of Germany to the other, but remains, I believe, a sealed fountain still for English readers.'[44] A month later, Carlyle published the lengthy essay-review 'Varnhagen Von Ense's Memoirs' in the *Westminster Review*, contending that Rahel was a 'true genius' but 'did not write'.[45] Carlyle, who would designate the specifically gendered *man* of letters a modern hero in *On Heroes, Hero-Worship, and the Heroic* (1841), refused to recognise the over 10,000 private letters from a woman's pen as writing, despite German opinion to the contrary. As noted earlier, Goethe knew Rahel and in her privately written 'Für Anna' declared, 'The Germans only really gained an appreciation of female genius through Rahel and Bettina [von Armin]. These two women actually brought about the intellectual emancipation of women.'[46] 'Rahel' on the title page of *WSSR*'s three volumes, then, is a signifier of the female intellectual conversationalist and pays oblique homage both to Rahel and to Goethe, for whom Rahel functioned as a 'role model'.[47] The personal significance of the Rahel epigraph – which points to Jameson's themes of sorrow, art, and lively wit in her three volumes – is even clearer in Jameson's private letter to Goethe as she prepared to leave for Canada: 'all things connected with *you* must go with me. I cannot part with them. And in my cabin I take the *Rahel* you marked for me, and all the M.S.S. notes which you made for me.'[48]

Though volumes II and III of *WSSR* are both titled *Summer Rambles*, volume II is structured to bring German and Canadian cultures together in an Anglo-German textual space. For Jameson takes her German studies with her on the road, associating German studies with physical as well as cultural mobility, modelling for transatlantic Anglophone women the enrichment afforded by international reading and cultural exchange. Rather than a binary between serious winter studies to ward off depression (volume I) and lifted spirits and sociability rekindled with warm weather (volume II), Jameson positions study as a pleasure easily blending with others. Her preliminary expeditions westwards are thus punctuated by comments on Baron Sternberg's fiction, Schiller's dramas, and the poet Joseph von Eichendorff.

Only in volume III do German studies largely disappear as she recounts her travels among Canadian and US Indigenes, when she could take no more than her notebooks and sketchbooks – and, I would add, the cultural practices she had acquired in part from her German travels.[49] Just as personal letters of introduction had facilitated her entry into German circles, so in Canada she likewise relied on a personal network, having met in Toronto Charlotte MacMurray, 'otherwise O-ge-ne-bu-go-quay, (i.e. *the wild rose*)', the biracial wife of Ojibwa descent married to the Christian missionary William MacMurray.[50] Tellingly, Jameson links the voice of Mrs MacMurray to Goethe's, thereby connecting both to Jameson's affective life and to her mobile practice of cultural exchange:

> The first glance, the first sound of her voice, struck me with a pleased surprise ... She speaks English well, with a slightly foreign intonation, not the less pleasing to my ear that it reminded me of the voice and accent of some of my German friends. In two minutes I was seated by her – my hand kindly folded in hers – and we were talking over the possibility of my plans.[51]

In this trilateral cultural exchange among German, British, and Canadian First Nations women, Jameson exemplifies women's talent for affective cosmopolitanism due to their 'kindly affections' that render them more 'mobile' and able to 'lend' themselves 'to different manners and habits'.[52]

Volume III foregrounds travel writing, enlivened by Jameson's breathless excitement and delight in her new-found physical mobility, adventurousness, and unprecedented experiences.[53] She first visits the American agent and ethnologist Henry Schoolcraft and June Johnston Schoolcraft, the pioneering Native American writer and Charlotte MacMurray's American sister, on Mackinac Island.[54] With June Schoolcraft, Jameson shares encounters that are more overtly grounded in affect and ready sympathy across difference, as she had in Germany:

> Mrs. Schoolcraft's features are more decidedly Indian than those of her sister Mrs. MacMurray. Her accent is slightly foreign – her choice of language pure and remarkably elegant. In the course of an hour's talk, all my sympathies were enlisted in her behalf, and I thought that I perceived that she, on her part, was inclined to return these benignant feelings ... I am here a lonely stranger, thrown upon her sufferance; but she is good, gentle, and in most delicate health, and there are a thousand quiet ways in which woman may be kind and useful to her sister woman.[55]

As with Goethe, Schoolcraft's fluent English forms a bridge to her British visitor (as did their shared Christianity), though Jameson has more blind spots than in Europe and reverts to the 'doomed Indian' trope identified by Kate Flint when she mentions the melancholy tone of Schoolcraft's conversation.[56]

Accompanied by Schoolcraft, Jameson next travels to Sault Ste Marie, Canada, to visit Schoolcraft's mother, a full-blooded 'Chippewa' Indian who speaks no English, has never lived among Anglo-Europeans, and has the 'habits and manners' of 'a genuine Indian squaw'.[57] As Jameson becomes closely acquainted with the mother, however, she presents a less conventional travel account, one that represents receptiveness, adaptability, and ready affection on both sides. On arriving in Sault Ste Marie, for example, Jameson was ill and 'fevered', and the mother 'took me in her arms, laid me down on a couch, and began to rub my feet, soothing and caressing me. She called me Nindannis, daughter, and I called her Neengai, mother, (though how different from my own fair mother, I thought, as I looked up gratefully in her dark Indian face!).'[58] Jameson responds to the opportunity to enter another culture by immediately studying her host culture's language, though with perhaps more limited success than in Germany: 'My attempts to speak Indian caused, of course, considerable amusement; if I do not make progress, it will not be for want of teaching and teachers.'[59]

As numerous scholars observe, Jameson also begins to adopt subject positions unusual for a European woman.[60] To give one example of many, she revises prevailing notions of cultural superiority in warfare after comparing the history of rape among Indian, Teutonic, and Latin nations (to the detriment of the last):

> A war-party of Indians, perhaps two or three hundred, (and that is a very large number,) dance their war-dance, go out and burn a village, and bring back twenty or thirty scalps. *They* are savages and heathens. We Europeans fight a battle, leave fifty thousand dead or dying by inches on the field, and a hundred thousand to mourn them, desolate; but *we* are civilised *and* Christians ... Really I do not see that an Indian warrior, flourishing his tomahawk, and smeared with his enemy's blood, is so very much a greater savage than the pipe-clayed, padded, embroidered personage, who, without cause or motive, has sold himself to slay or be slain: one scalps his enemy, the other rips him open with a sabre ... and to me, femininely speaking, there is not a needle's point difference between the one and the other.[61]

Becoming 'the first European female who had ever' shot the rapids in a canoe, she is then adopted by her hosts, a more formal marker of entrance

into another culture than she had experienced in Germany: 'I was
... adopted into the family by the name of Wah,sàh,ge,wah,nó,quà. ...
the bright foam, or more properly, with the feminine adjunct *qua*, *the
woman of the bright foam*; and by this name I am henceforth to be known
among the Chippewas.'[62]

As in almost all her works, Jameson integrates discussion of women's
social position into her subject matter, here within a hybrid cultural
framework.[63] For in concluding her account of the Ojibwa, Jameson
attempts to view the condition of women from both a First Nations and
a European perspective:

> Then, when we speak of the drudgery of the women, we must note the equal
> division of labour; there is no class of women privileged to sit still while others
> work... Compare [such a woman's] life with the refined leisure of an elegant
> woman in the higher classes of our society, and it is wretched and abject; but
> compare her life with that of a servant-maid of all work, or a factory girl, –
> I do say that the condition of the squaw is gracious in comparison, dignified
> by domestic feelings, and by equality with all around her.[64]

Reading volume III of *WSSR* in tandem with *Visits and Sketches* and
awareness of Jameson's personal letters clarifies how pervasively
Jameson's earlier German experiences prepared for and inform *WSSR*,
even as her Canadian rambles extended her receptivity to a culture much
different from any she had previously known. Together, these first two
German books offer important representations of nineteenth-century
women's transnational practice of ethnoexocentrism that contributed to
women's social and intellectual empowerment in Jameson's time and that
enhance understanding of transnational possibilities past and present.

Social Life in Germany (1840)

In February 1837, while still in North America, Jameson told Goethe that
she had read 'all your notes on the [plays of] the P[rincess] Amelia' and
asked, 'can you give me an analysis of those I have *not* seen'.[65] By late
November 1838, now back in London, Jameson had decided 'to translate
the Princess Amelia's dramas into English' and asked Goethe, 'Pray ... get
for me any information about them you can. I want the dates of their first
appearance, ... and in short any particulars about them and the sensation
they have caused and the manner in which they have been played in
Germany.'[66] Having spent almost two years in North America, Jameson
still turned towards her second home in Germany. Her letter clarifies to
what degree *Social Life in Germany*, like *Winter Studies and Summer*

Rambles, was a collaboration with Goethe, whose book it was as well: 'I shall give a selection, not for their excellence, but those which you recommend as true to German social life.'[67]

The result was a decidedly Anglo-German book, one titled to take advantage of the current publishing market. Jameson did not title hers a translation but (in full) *Social Life in Germany, Illustrated in the Acted Dramas of Her Royal Highness the Princess Amelia of Saxony*. Her title implicitly echoed that of Harriet Martineau's *Society in America*, an enormous transatlantic publishing success of 1837.[68] Jameson knew Martineau; as she commented to Goethe in August 1836, shortly before leaving for Canada, 'Miss Martineau has returned from America, and when I can find time I shall run and see her.'[69] Taking advantage of audience interest in social analysis created by Martineau, Jameson proceeded similarly but less systematically in *Social Life* to provide a picture of middle-class life in northern Germany seen from the inside. Judith Johnston in fact asserts that *Social Life* is more 'sociological' than literary.[70]

Jameson also enhanced the commercial appeal of *Social Life* by calibrating its release date. On 9 February 1840, an advert in the *Examiner* announced, 'Mrs. Jameson's New Work. / Now ready', giving its full title and appending this quote from Jameson's preface: 'A Royal lady on [sic] this our Nineteenth Century has stepped from her Palace into the arena of literature, and has written very beautifully for her own sex and for her own people.'[71] The next day, 10 February 1840, Queen Victoria married Prince Albert of Saxe-Coburg in the Chapel Royal, St James. Here, then, was a German-generated publishing opportunity that extended both Jameson's readership and British interest in Germany. One of the plays Jameson translated not only came from the pen of a distant relative of the prince (both he and Princess Amalia were descendants of the House of Wettin) but also illuminated his background. For *The Princely Bride* (*Die Fürstenbraut*) was based on a royal author's immediate experience of the 'court of a petty prince,' the social milieu of Albert's rearing, and gave a royal insider's view:

> Never, perhaps, was a courtly group sketched off with such finished delicacy – such life-like truth – such perfect knowledge of and command over the materials employed. We have no other instance, I think, of the portrait of a princess delineated by the hand of a princess, and informed with sentiments and feelings drawn possibly from her own nature, or at least suggested by her own position. It is easy to conceive that one cause of this drama not being oftener performed, is the very truth of the picture it represents.[72]

In the play the royal title character arrives for the royal wedding. Perhaps Jameson hoped that readers would see in the sterling character of her protagonist the qualities of England's new Anglo-German prince. The Princess is self-effacing, loving, wise, and steadfast in duty to the point of assuming blame for breaking off the royal wedding when she realises the deception practiced on the bridegroom (and herself) when her lady in waiting was passed off as the Princess when the affianced prince had earlier visited in disguise. Having fallen in love with him through his letters, the Princess plainly sees her intended bridegroom's shock and recoil on her arrival. Eventually the prince sees his affianced princess's virtues and determines to marry her after all. She assents, disillusioned but determined to do her duty to her father and abide by the dictates of her royal role.

Jameson's introduction to the play dourly paints the life that awaits her, one that she will pass on to her children in turn:

> The daughters of the Princess-Bride are brought up as their mother was before them: sighing, she sees them one after another depart from her to fulfil a destiny similar to her own; but without a suspicion that all this is not in the essential nature of things: and the once hopeful and feeling heart, and the once bright and aspiring mind, subdued at last to the element in which she moves, she goes through her state and court duties, holds her *grand et petit cercle* with habitual grace and suppressed *ennui*, plays piquet every night with the prince, sees every day the same faces, and does and says every day the same things; – and so she dies, leaving behind her, perhaps, one favourite *Hofdame* [court lady] to grieve for her, and the pensioners on her bounty to weep for her – or for their pensions, – and there an end![73]

Jameson's *Athenaeum* reviewer saw the immediate relevance of this play in giving a 'glimpse into one nook of the world in Germany, which the events of the hour make a more than usually interesting object of contemplation to all British subjects', adding, 'Let us hope that something more of reciprocal obligation, of hearty affection, than is displayed in this melancholy sketch of the destiny of a German princess, may enter into the story of the married life of a German prince!'[74]

The *Athenaeum* saw more in *Social Life* than an opportune commercial publication, however, revealing how well Jameson had solidified her position as a writer of distinction by 1840:

> Like all Mrs. Jameson's works, the one under notice bears that stamp of individual thought and earnest purpose, which distinguishes authorship from book-manufacture. Her increasing desire is to improve the social position of her own sex; to emancipate woman ... This purpose is advanced by every new display of original intellect and moral strength in female literature, – and the present offering to the public is happily marked by both characteristics.[75]

The glum forecast of the royal princess's future also tacitly warned young Englishwomen brought up never to question the roles they inherited of possible disappointments in marriage. Unsurprisingly, Judith Johnston and others have focused principally on feminist commentary in *Social Life*. As always Jameson carefully hedged her assertiveness, underscoring that she was not rejecting women's traditional roles as wife and mother or disputing men's claims to the public sphere of politics and governance. Still, it is in this book that she first publicly states a feminist credo through her mouthpiece Alda in another dialogue with Medon:

> My profession of faith, since you call for it, may be summed up in few words. I believe that men and women were created *one* in species; equally rational beings with improvable faculties; equally responsible to God for the use or abuse of the faculties entrusted to them; eqully free to choose the good and refuse the evil; equally destined to an equal immortality.[76]

Social Life shares elements of a conduct book with *Characteristics of Women*, but Jameson draws on female life in Germany rather than Shakespeare to model proto-feminist conduct. As in *Characteristics*, notably, Jameson again placed her dedication in a visual frame of her own devising (see Figure 2.1), not to single out a beloved friend this time, but to address a community of young Englishwomen whose lives and sense of female possibility she hoped to improve by showing important cultural alternatives to life as her middle-class readers knew it.

The dedication necessarily stressed moral probity as well as the German author's refined taste, since in the notes (often silently contributed by Goethe) Jameson presented female models that were highly unconventional in England at the time. Fifteen years after *Social Life*, Marian Evans would inform *Fraser's* readers that women thought nothing of attending theatre by themselves in Weimar – a startling behaviour even then.[77] Jameson conveyed the point in 1840 in a note to the first play, *Falsehood and Truth* (*Lüge und Wahrheit*): 'in the small towns, where every one is known, young ladies may be seen alone at the theatre without any impropriety. The beautiful little theatre at Weimar is in this respect like a family drawing-room.' In the introduction to *The Uncle* (*Der Oheim*), she reiterated, 'in the north of Germany, as Weimar, Cobourg, Stettin, Dessau, &c., ... a young lady, rich, noble, and beautiful, might put on her bonnet and walk through the streets unattended, with perfect propriety'.[78]

Besides modelling physical and social mobility for women, she was also suggesting revised courtship practices. Her explanation of the *Verlobung* or formal engagement ceremony in her introduction to *The Young Ward* (*Der Zögling*) underscored the importance of an engaged couple's getting to

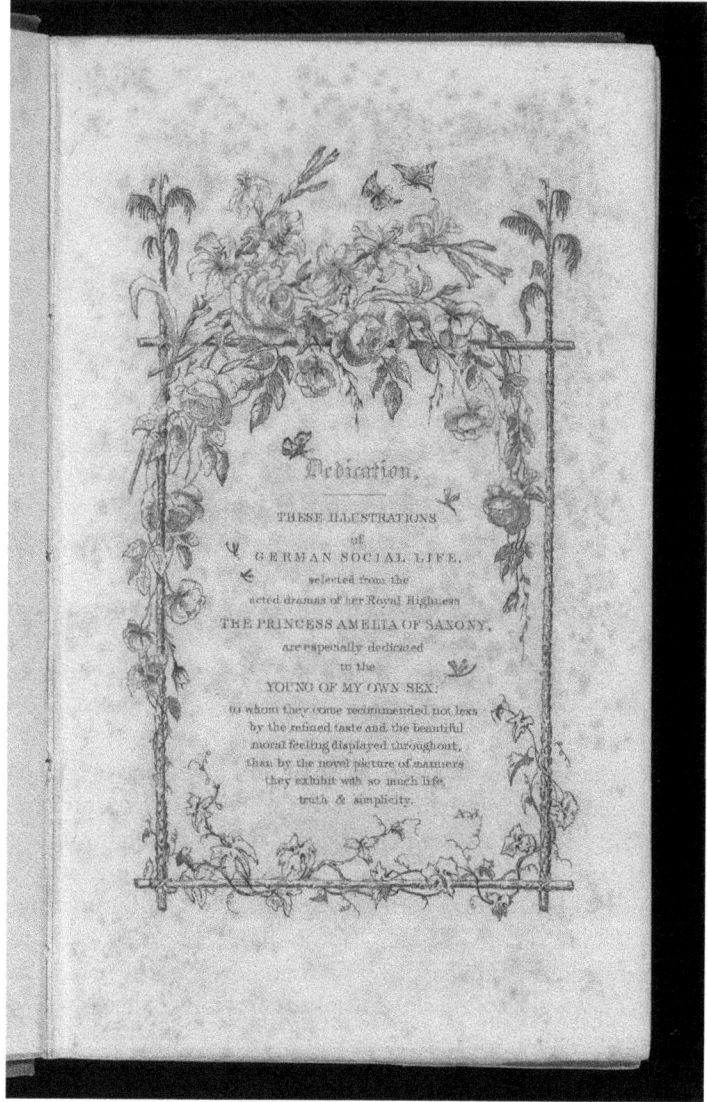

Figure 2.1. Dedication page, *Social Life in Germany* (1840), illustration and text by Anna Jameson. Courtesy Harry Ransom Center, The University of Texas at Austin

know each other before they married, a practice that in Germany sometimes led to a broken engagement with no blame assigned to either party.[79] More daringly, Jameson explained in reference to the play's mention of divorce that in Protestant Germany, divorce could be both ethical and justifiable, since in Saxony divorce did not imply the wife's impropriety, the sole ground on which an Englishman could then sue for divorce: 'the legal pleas for divorce are several; viz. 1. The proved infidelity of *either* party ... 2. Bigamy on either side. 3. Desertion of home ... by either party'.[80] The repetition of 'either' highlighted the equality of German men and women before the law, an indirect endorsement of English equality of the sexes at home. She then added (in addition to outright crimes against a spouse) '4. Quasi-desertion; that is ... when the husband and wife have agreed to be separated for life without other cause than mutual aversion, disparity of temper or character &c.; and coercive measures have been tried, or apparently tried, without result'.[81] If Henriette von Pogwisch had divorced her husband on precisely these grounds after their lengthy separation (see Chapter 1), Jameson, now legally and permanently separated from the man with whom she could not live amicably, may have been telegraphing a message to him in Canada through the public medium of print. In Germany Jameson could have divorced him (especially after he began an affair in Canada in subsequent years); as an Englishwoman she was forced to remain tethered to him and depend only on his good will to fulfil the promise of leaving her his money at the time of death (which he did not do). Without ever saying so directly, she demonstrated by looking at German models that divorce on the grounds of incompatibility was a morally upright position – a common enough assumption in the twentieth century but rarely articulated in English writing by men or women until then.

In one other important respect *Social Life* addressed female community on a larger scale, for it was the earliest of Jameson's extended discussions of secular sisterhoods at a time when these were unfamiliar; indeed, it would be five years before the first Anglican sisterhood was founded in London.[82] The discussion surfaced because the 'princely bride' speaks of taking shelter temporarily in a convent, and Jameson wanted to indicate that the princess refers not to a nunnery but to a *Damenstift*, one of numerous lay-convents endowed for unmarried noblewomen. Jameson already knew a little of *Damenstifte* through Goethe's younger sister Ulrike, whose name had been entered as a candidate for a *Damenstift* in the St Johannis-Kloster in Schleswig in 1807.[83] That the topic meant more than mere information to Jameson, however, is evidenced by her returning to these institutions again in her books of 1855 and 1856 and in one of her last periodical articles. Their interest for Jameson once again lay in their feminist implications:

> *Damenstifter*, or *lay-convents*, exist both in the Protestant and Catholic countries of Germany ... in almost all, a descent of unstained nobility is

a first requisite; in *all*, want of fortune and celibacy are necessary qualifications; but no vows are necessary, and no restraint is exercised, only when a lady marries she vacates her place and privileges to another; neither is constant residence within the walls of the institution required, but merely for some months or weeks every year, and at the chapters held for the arrangement of the domestic affairs of the community ... In some of the *Stifter* the Superior possesses considerable power and responsibility, in others scarce any; she has generally the title of *Höchst-würdige Frau*, (most honourable lady). There is also generally a prioress and a deaconess, (*Prieurin* and *Dechantin*). The other ladies are styled *Stiftsdame*, (in French, *Chanoinesse*;) ... They frequently wear, when residing in their *Stift*, a particular costume, with a long white or black veil, and in full dress, on all occasions, a decoration or badge (*orden*) attached to a broad watered ribbon, blue, white, or crimson, suspended from the shoulder across the bosom or otherwise. It is very pretty, at a court ball in Germany, to see a number of noble girls thus decorated; one has at least the pleasant conviction that they will not be *obliged* to marry to secure a station in society – a refuge, a home; their order confers a certain dignity, besides an elegant maintenance ...[84]

She concluded by singling out an Anglo-German *Stift* founded in 1829 by the British Hanoverian king George IV designed to assist daughters of men who had served the Hanoverian state; these did not require noble birth.[85] The idea of secular residences for women associated with civil service contributions would become a keynote of her discussions of *Stifte* in 1855.

Jameson gleefully wrote to Goethe on 3 March 1840, 'My translation of the Princess's drama is published and has great success, more than I hoped. I have seen *ten* reviews of it, and all most favourable.'[86] Jameson hoped that she and Goethe could collaborate again, and suggested a series of biographies of women artists and 'their social position philosophically and morally considered'.[87] But when Goethe failed to respond to this or other suggested collaborations, Jameson instead concentrated her energies on art criticism for the next twelve years, beginning with gallery guides for London and culminating in her best-known work today, *Sacred and Legendary Art* (1848–52). Jameson and Goethe continued to correspond regularly and visit at intervals, but Jameson would publish no more books specifically focused on Germany. Yet Germany would never entirely disappear as a reference point for her.

Female Communities at Home and Abroad

Jameson's writings about female communities in the 1850s are her most overtly feminist. She had always urged the vital importance of women's education and educational access. Turning sixty in 1854 seemed to free her to speak more openly, even though she continued to calibrate her feminism for public consumption, maintaining distance on 'women's rights' and repeatedly affirming respect for men.[88] Nonetheless, she increased her advocacy for access to paid employment for middle-class women and better wages for working-class women so that all could achieve independence and maintain themselves decently. She also stressed men's and women's *inter*dependence in a 'communion of labour', which entailed public recognition of women's integral role in the larger society as well.

Two factors supported her activism: her increasing interactions with a network of younger women in the Langham Place Group, and the National Association for the Promotion of Social Science, founded in 1857, which featured rational, evidence-based discourse at mixed-sex meetings in which women as well as men were welcome to speak publicly – one of the first British organisations to follow this policy.[89] Such public validation of women in their intellectual *and* sociable capacities provided female experiences in England akin to those Jameson had so eagerly sought in Germany two decades earlier.

Several of the younger women whom Jameson called her 'nieces' also had ties to Germany.[90] As Chapter 3 details, Anna Mary Howitt developed fluent German from living in Heidelberg with her parents William and Mary as a teenager; she returned to Munich as an aspiring artist in 1850 to study art and published *An Art Student in Munich* in 1853. In Germany she was visited by her friend, painter Barbara Leigh Smith, later Bodichon, an integral member of the Langham Place Group. And Bodichon introduced Anna Mary to Bessie Rayner Parkes, another Langham Place Group leader to whom, according to Clara Thomas, Jameson suggested the founding of the *English Woman's Journal*.[91]

Thomas draws a direct line from Jameson's assertion of the fundamental equality of women and men in *Social Life* to her last two books published in her lifetime: *Sisters of Charity Catholic and Protestant, Abroad and at Home* (1855) and *The Communion of Labour* (1856), both of which began as private lectures given in the home of Elizabeth Jesser Reid in Regent's Park.[92] Johnston gives an important analysis of these two works' roots in English feminism and feminist networks. But the first of these, *Sisters of Charity*, is also a late 'Germany' book given Jameson's attention to German women's employment in hospitals, prisons, and charitable institutions. As always, Jameson shrewdly timed the release of her book: Florence Nightingale and her female nurses, several drawn from Catholic and Anglican sisterhoods, were in the Crimea and becoming famous at the very moment Jameson was lecturing and publishing. Nightingale was herself intimately tied to Germany through her training in Kaiserswerth near Düsseldorf. In her preface to *Sisters of Charity* Jameson acknowledged her indebtedness to the pamphlet '"Kaiserswerth on the Rhine" (published by Hookham)'; in the text proper she devoted some eight pages to the Kaiserswerth hospital founded by Protestant pastor Theodor Fliedner and his wife, then drew out its immediate relevance: 'Let me add, for it is a matter of interest at the present, that Miss Florence Nightingale went through a regular course of training at Kaiserswerth, before she took charge of the Female Sanitarium in London.'[93] The anonymous 'Kaiserswerth' pamphlet Jameson cites in her preface was in fact written by Nightingale, as Jameson likely knew.[94]

Jameson also referenced the German Ursulines, secular schools, reformed prisons, and Kaiserswerth when noting attempts to found similar facilities in England.[95] And she describes in detail a Viennese hospital run by Elizabethan Sisters:

> On the ground-floor was an extensive 'Pharmacie,' a sort of Apothecaries' Hall; part of this was divided off by a long table or counter, and surrounded by shelves filled with drugs, much like an apothecary's shop; behind the counter two Sisters, with their sleeves tucked up, were busy weighing and compounding medicines, with such a delicacy, neatness, and exactitude as women use in these matters. On the outside of this counter, seated on benches or standing, were a number of sick and infirm, pale, dirty, ragged patients; and among them moved two other Sisters, speaking to each individually in a low gentle voice, and with a quiet authority of manner, that in itself had something tranquilising. A physician and surgeon, appointed by the Government, visited this hospital, and were resorted to in cases of difficulty or where operations were necessary. Here was another instance in which men and women worked harmoniously and efficiently.[96]

In 1855, however, Jameson's reportage was transnational, and sisterhoods in France and Italy were equally crucial in helping Jameson make the case that providing public, socially productive work for women (salaried or accompanied by residential support) was both feasible and desirable.

Jameson's next lecture and book, *The Communion of Labour*, was more strictly English in focus. But as she revised both her published lectures for an 'Enlarged and Improved edition with a Prefatory Letter to The Right Hon. Lord John Russell, President of the National Association for the Promotion of Social Science on the Present Condition and Requirement of the Women of England', she hoped to include the subject of *Damenstifte*, the German female communities she first described in the *Social Life* notes to *The Princely Bride*. She asked Goethe for more details about these on 8 March 1856: 'my letter, containing a long list of questions relative to the government of the Stifter – remains without any reply & as I promised to give some information, I have felt uncomfortable not to do so – I wish I could be present at the ceremony of your Sister entering the Stift – but wishes and plans seem to be equally in vain'.[97] Two months later she wrote to thank Goethe for details received, and in November 1857 made explicit that her queries related to her plans for the new edition of her lectures: 'I am going to publish a new edition of the *Sisters of Charity* and the *Communion of Labour*. The question has made such great progress in England that I must make alterations. I wish I could give some good account of the German Stifter.'[98]

Jameson's feminist activism and long connection with Germany coalesced in her final German writing, a letter signed 'A. J.' and titled 'The Damen-Stifter in Germany' published in the *Athenaeum* on 1 January 1859, fifteen months prior to her death. It was also her final collaboration with Goethe, or at least a Goethe family member. Goethe was in Venice at the time and could not lay her hands on all the answers to questions that Jameson posed – everything from the precise numbers of *Damenstifte* in various German states to sources of funding required or numbers of residents in the largest and smallest. So she delegated her elder son Walther to compile a list and send it directly to Jameson.[99]

In her *Athenaeum* letter, as in so much of her writing, Jameson carefully inserted the timely relevance of her publication and a prominent man's endorsement of her position:

> It is a pleasant – and not less a significant – sign of the times that a mere passing allusion made by Lord Brougham to the German 'Damen-Stifter' (chapters or endowments for unmarried ladies) should have excited in this country so much interest and inquiry. It is announced that a future number of the *English Woman's Journal* will contain some account of the origin, details of management, and statistics of these admirable institutions.[100]

Anticipating potential religious anxiety among *Athenaeum* readers, she also underscored the Protestantism of most German *Stifte*: 'Many of these institutions date from the Reformation, and, so far as I can understand, they are more numerous in the Protestant than in the Catholic states.' She further enhanced her letter's timeliness by reporting a new *Stift* founded in Weimar by the Dowager Grand Duchess, adapting its details to her feminist ends. For she followed with a succession of important roles played by Weimar's Grand Duchesses, who endowed philanthropies and initiated building projects, and the Duchess Louisa, who saved Weimar after

Napoleon's victory at Jena. The tacit argument here was that women could govern and improve the well-being of their societies through their efforts. Jameson shrewdly drew the German women into even closer relation with Englishwomen by noting the marriage of Victoria, Princess Royal, to the Grand Duchess's grandson – clearly implying that England should follow Germany in endowing similar women's philanthropic communities in England.[101]

Though only a minor publication, this public letter was in some ways a fitting climax to Jameson's explorations of Germany through a female lens: it involved female networks, reflected her longstanding tie to Weimar, reinforced her deep commitment to reforming women's social and intellectual positions, and above all registered her intimate friendship with Goethe that spilled over into collaborative publications as well as letters. Jameson was presumably planning to contribute to the upcoming special number of *English Woman's Journal* devoted to *Stifte*, but this never materialised. Instead, a week after Jameson's *Athenaeum* letter appeared, a riposte appeared in the form of another *Athenaeum* letter from S. A. – possibly Sarah Austin, long an English authority on German culture and the early friend of both Jameson and Goethe. S. A. publicly impugned Jameson's assertions about *Stifte*, bringing Jameson's authority into question.[102] Jameson left no record of her response to this embarrassing repudiation and exposure even of her errors in forming German plurals. Jameson's silence on *Stifte* afterwards tacitly conceded the victory to her opponent.

This reversal resulting from implicit trust in all that Goethe sent, however, was also the consequence of one of the best things she had enjoyed in her busy life and career, her loving friendship with Goethe. Months after 'Damen-Stifter' appeared in the *Athenaeum*, Jameson again paid an extended visit to Goethe (noted in Chapter 1). Considering that Jameson died so quickly after contracting pneumonia in March 1860, her last hurrah of writing about German female communities and visit with Goethe in 1859 comprise a meaningful coda to Jameson's pioneering female cosmopolitanism and ethnoexocentrism, her embodied practice of Anglo-German cultural exchange in public and private writings, and, not least for a professional woman writer, an opportunity to earn a living by sharing her observations of Germany through a female lens.

CHAPTER 3

Networked Families in Germany
Mary Howitt, Anna Mary Howitt, and Elizabeth Gaskell

Anna Jameson could experience rich Anglo–German exchange in part because neither husband nor children tethered her to a home, and she was free to travel and work relentlessly. But ethnoexocentrism in no way relies on cutting domestic ties. The German residences of three mid-Victorian women, Mary Howitt (1799–1888), Ann Mary Howitt (1824–84), and Elizabeth Gaskell (1810–65), unfolded in the context of family; and the German-related fiction of Mary Howitt and Gaskell was partly inspired by these mothers' preoccupations and concerns for their daughters.[1] These two friends also formed a literary network.[2] In 1840 Howitt, William Howitt (1792–1879), and their children including Anna Mary, whom Howitt had early on trained in journalism, settled in Heidelberg for a three-year residence.[3] William Howitt had lifted Gaskell's account of Clopton Hall, which she had visited as a schoolgirl and described in a letter to the Howitts in 1838, and incorporated it into *Visits to Remarkable Places* (1840) – Gaskell's first solo work in print. In summer 1841 Gaskell then arrived in Heidelberg with her husband, Unitarian clergyman William Gaskell (1805–84), with whom Gaskell had earlier co-authored the poem 'Sketches among the Poor, No. 1' in *Blackwood's Edinburgh Magazine* (January 1837). This was Gaskell's first face-to-face meeting with Howitt and Anna Mary.[4] Later, William Howitt secured the crucial placement of Gaskell's first novel *Mary Barton* (1848) with Chapman and Hall after the manuscript had been rejected by most London publishers.[5]

When Anna Mary returned to Germany in May 1850 to study art with Wilhelm Kaulbach, whom she and her parents had met during their 1840s German sojourn, some of Anna Mary's letters home became articles on Germany and German art after her mother transcribed and forwarded them to the *Ladies' Companion*, *Athenaeum*, and *Household Words*. These Gaskell encouraged Anna Mary to expand into the book-length work that became *An Art-Student in Munich* (1853) following the younger woman's two-year course of art study.[6]

By 1858, when the Howitts' fortunes had declined while Gaskell was increasingly famous, Gaskell returned to Heidelberg with Meta and Florence, two of her four daughters, and stayed for almost three months, a trip designed to help Meta overcome the trauma of a broken engagement to Captain Charles Hill of the Madras Engineers. In July 1860, Gaskell again settled in Heidelberg, this time with daughters Florence and Julia, for two months.[7] Her repeated immersion in Heidelberg and German culture inspired two of Gaskell's most intriguing short stories, 'The Grey Woman' (1861) and 'Six Weeks at Heppenheim' (1862). Both deal with fraught engagements of young women to unworthy or unstable men and the aftermath, an indication of the intersection among Gaskell's roles as mother, fictionist, and participant in Anglo–German exchange.

Together, the Howitt women and Gaskell reflected – and extended – the legacy of Jameson. Just as Robert Noel's 1833 letter of introduction opened up Germany for Jameson and her life-changing friendship with Goethe, so in 1840 Jameson provided the Howitts with a letter of introduction to Friedrich Schlosser (1776–1861), Professor of History at the University of Heidelberg, and his wife, whom Jameson mentions in *Visits and Sketches*.[8] The Schlossers formed the nucleus of the Howitts's intellectual circle in Heidelberg, and they in turn introduced Gaskell to the Schlossers, and to Heidelberg, in the summer of 1841. Because Howitt's, Anna Mary's, and Gaskell's experiences in Germany extended over two decades (1840–60) and generated very distinctive works, I examine each writer separately below.

Mary Howitt: Creating the Cosmopolitan Child

Howitt has long been known for her children's writing. 'The Spider and the Fly' ('"Will you come into my parlour," said the Spider to the Fly') remains an enduring favourite.[9] Yet Howitt worked in many modalities throughout her long career. While living in Germany from 1840 to 1843, she was active as a poet, translator, and editor as well as children's writer, producing an inventive translation of German children's verse and a young adult novel that addresses the central issue of this study: cross-cultural exchanges and freedoms. She later wrote an 1853 novella about the German opportunities open to an English woman artist. In all this work she had travelled far from her beginnings as a Midlands Quaker child in Uttoxeter, Staffordshire, and it is helpful to understand how she got there.

She married William Howitt in 1821 at age twenty-two and they soon settled in Nottingham, where she bore several children even while pursuing a literary partnership with her husband. They became interested in learning German through their acquaintance with Romantic poet Felicia Hemans (1793–1835), journalist Henry Fothergill Chorley (1808–72), and Chorley's two brothers, all of whom were enthusiastic about German Romanticism.[10] As Howitt wrote to her sister Anna on 30 September 1829, 'We are "pushing on" as William says with German – we read with tolerable ease our first books – how we shall find German poetry I don't know as yet we have not tried. What we want most however is instruction in pronunciation...'[11] They did not want merely to read German; they wanted to speak and hear it, the key skills that enable entrance into another culture.

They and their five children arrived in Germany in June 1840, drawn by cheaper living conditions and educational opportunities for the children. In Heidelberg Howitt had a nanny for her youngest but still had to manage a household of five children while continuing her literary labours, some of it contracted in advance in England.[12] She was named editor of *Fisher's Drawing-Room Scrapbook*, for which Howitt was paid £100 a year, after the marriage and death of Letitia Landon (1802–38). Though Howitt considered the poems she wrote to fill the 1840 and 1841 volumes of *Fisher's* mediocre, the 1842 *Fisher's* marks a change, for it registers the happiest phase of the Howitt family's life in Germany.[13] Howitt's prefatory poem to the 1842 annual, with a Heidelberg byline and date, idealised her German surroundings:

Preface

TO THE PUBLIC.
In this fair land where I am writing now,
    Whom they would honour, they salute with flowers;
Flowers wreath the cup, and garlands bind the brow;
    They grace the saddest and the brightest hours.
This is the wreath that I for you have twined,
    A wreath of song – may it be evergreen!
A wreath of love round loving brows to bind,
    Roses fresh blown with myrtle sprays between...
                    M. H.
HEIDELBERG, August, 1841.[14]

She further associates her present life with freedom in 'Heidelberg, on the Neckar': 'My blessing on thee, pleasant little town! / ... Crowned with free woods, which freest nature fills.'[15] To this lyric she appended a long note for English tourists extolling the rich treasures of Heidelberg Castle as well as the beauty, fecundity, and literary heritage of this delightful spot, thoughts in keeping with the sentiments of most literary annuals as well as travel literature and the nascent Victorian tourist industry. Far more subtly, Howitt infused progressive politics into her lyric 'Boaz and Ruth. / A Harvest Scene', which opens, 'This land, it is not England', at first a seeming reference to a biblical past. If the peasants toil 'Like beasts of burden', they are simultaneously empowered since this 'bounteous land' is 'possessed / By the glad many, not the few'. Against the backdrop of Chartist agitation in England in 1842 and the byline 'HEIDELBERG, SEPT. 1840' attached to 'Boaz and Ruth', 'This land … not England' also suggested a better alternative in Germany.[16]

Howitt likewise adopted a progressive role in translating contemporary German poets for *Fisher's*, including Clemens Brentano (1778–1842), Heinrich Heine (1797–1856), and Ferdinand Freiligrath (1810–76). Like Jameson, Howitt effected a cultural transfer of German work into the English literary scene that differed strongly from Carlyle's focus on Goethe and other revered figures of German Romanticism. Jameson and Howitt showcased writers who repudiated German hierarchies and authoritarianism, whether Freiligrath or Heine, whom Howitt was making better known more than a decade before Marian Evans's or Matthew Arnold's essays on Heine.[17]

After William Howitt returned from publishing negotiations in London in summer 1841 equipped with new letters of introduction from Jameson to literary and artistic eminences in Germany, the family travelled about Germany, less to imitate the German custom of a *Herbstreise* or 'autumn tour' than to gather copy for writing and extend their Anglo–German social and publishing networks.[18] The bloom came off the rose suddenly when on returning to Heidelberg the Howitts discovered that their servants had long been thieving from them. William vented his spleen at length in *German Experiences: Addressed to the English; Both Stayers at Home, and Goers Abroad*.[19] Mary's response was more tempered, though she too expressed dismay over the revelation of their servants' dishonesty in a letter to her sister. Still, when it was time for them to return to England she was sad to go.[20]

If disillusioned about university towns in Germany, the Howitts were newly prosperous from William Howitt's well-received books on Germany and the couple's other literary works. To enhance their income while also working to support reformist politics, they founded *Howitt's Journal* (1847–8).[21] The periodical is best known today for its progressive features

Mary Howitt: Creating the Cosmopolitan Child 59

Figure 3.1. Wilhelm Kaulbach design for inaugural issue of *Howitt's Journal*, 2 January 1847, 9. Courtesy Woman's Collections, Special Collections, Texas Woman's University

on workers, including worker-poets, and Gaskell's early stories published under the pseudonym Cotton Mather Mills. I want briefly to note its importance in extending the Howitts' Anglo–German exchange and their cultural transfer of contemporary German arts and letters into England. Almost every issue of volume I reported news from Germany or featured German content in essays and translations of literary works. The journal's visuality itself signalled Anglo–German exchange, for the designs heading every 'The Month in Prospect' feature were by Wilhelm Kaulbach (see Figure 3.1).[22]

Mary's translation of 'The Lover' by Heinrich Voss, a Heidelberg professor, was highlighted in the cover illustration of the 20 February 1847 issue.[23] And volumes II and III included her translations of Ferdinand Freiligraths's poems and a short tale by Berthold Auerbach. In sum, this later venture registered their continuing interest in German art, culture, and politics and the fruits of their Anglo–German professional and social networks.

Beyond her work as poet, translator, and editor, however, her children's writing is some of Howitt's most intriguing Anglo–German work. In 1838, Nottingham publisher Thomas Tegg had invited her to produce thirteen children's tales that illustrated 'household virtues' for the round sum of £1,000; and she continued this series in Germany.[24] The fifth tale, written in Heidelberg where the story is set, is a Victorian young adult novel: *Which Is the Wiser: or, People Abroad. A Tale for Youth* (1842). It seamlessly merges the standard courtship plot of a heroine's choice between two suitors with a cross-cultural plot that turns on whether the would-be lovers can embrace cultural difference. If the novel's moral instruction hinges on choosing the better or worse life partner, its other lesson is teaching young adult readers how to welcome and respectfully explore cultural difference rather than ignoring or sneering at it.

In the story the widow Mrs Palmer and her daughter Caroline ('Lina'), an intelligent, talented, beautiful young Englishwoman, have lived in Germany for fourteen months, where Mrs Palmer enjoys privileged social standing while avoiding English high prices. In contrast to her mother, who disdains interest in Germany or Germans, Lina has acquired fluent German and seeks sociable interchange with German neighbours.[25] The two Englishwomen thus pose at the outset the title's question of whether Lina or her mother takes the wiser course.

Even before Howitt introduces the Palmers, she introduces young readers to German customs, such as the Verlobung or formal engagement that even widows observe annually as an anniversary (9), and a few German words, such as 'Haupt Strasse, or High Street' (5) and '"Herein," or walk in' (9), thereby nudging young readers into textual cultural exchange. Above the Palmers lives the widow Hoffmann, who married wisely. She is visited by her handsome son Karl, a medical student, who is first attracted by Lina's voice when he hears her singing German songs, then by her beauty, and ultimately by her intelligence and open interchange emerging from her interest in him and the larger German community.

If Lina is an exponent of ethnoexocentrism, Mrs Hoffmann is as prejudiced against the English as Mrs Palmer and her circle are against the Germans. When she hears that Mrs Palmer's rich English friends are coming to Heidelberg for a few months, Mrs Hoffmann objects in disgust,

> 'I wish such English people would not come here ... they do us great mischief. We might as well have an army of French, laying waste ... as these troops of frivolous, money-loving, money-wasting English. Germany, dear, home-loving Germany, has more deep and grave cause of fear from these smiling, flattering, yet deriding visitors, than from a whole nation of Frenchmen ... [T]hey love dissipation more than enjoyment; they value money not for the good it will do, but for the show it will make, they think to pass here for princes, and they only make themselves the laughing-stock of our people...' (21)

She dislikes Lina simply because Lina, too, is English.

Howitt injects these two prejudiced mothers into her courtship plot, triangulating not only Lina's choice between an English and a German suitor but also Lina's and Karl's choice between their mothers and their attraction to each other. Mrs Palmer's greatest wish is to see her daughter financially secure because of her own uncertain health. Though Lina falls in love with Karl through their conversations and shared love of music, she is also attracted to the wealthy heir Arthur Burnett among the privileged English visitors: 'there was something in the dashing, off-hand, uncounting-of-cost, and decided manner and style of the new English associates, which was captivating' (90). Both as a dutiful daughter and as a means to secure her financial future, she feels impelled to accept Arthur's attentions, especially after Bell Ponsonby, a haughty, imperious, calculating young woman, joins the Wilkinson party who are visiting Mrs Palmer and overtly competes to win Arthur for herself.[26]

Howitt makes clear that Karl appeals to Lina's best self. But her mother values the moneyed English suitor far more, so that, were Lina to choose Karl, she would forfeit the approval of her English mother and far more:

> She preferred his mind and his manners infinitely to Burnett's; she thought him much handsomer also; but with him she could only expect the ridicule of all these her English friends, with no chance of forgiveness from her mother; and she herself must sink down into the manager of a frugal German family, dressing plainly, and counting the cost of everything. The prospect was not inviting ... (128).

Which is the wiser course indeed? But consistent with her generic innovation of a cross-cultural courtship plot, Howitt embeds the clearest revelation of Arthur's undesirability in his refusal of ethnoexocentrism, his refusal to see the German setting as anything but a backdrop for his English pursuit of pleasures. These include horseback riding through town, when the English visitors fill the main streets and sideline German pedestrians, which the Heidelberg townspeople find insulting and insensitive.

When one day Bell touches Lina's horse as the party rides out, the horse bounds ahead and, while Lina keeps her seat, Arthur gallops to the rescue and in the process rides over a disabled boy being pulled in a 'child's chaise' who cannot get out of the way. Rather than stopping to investigate, Arthur merely dispatches a groom with money to pay off the boy's family (133–5). The horrified Lina, who befriended this boy earlier, rushes to call on him at his grandfather's, where she learns that, through Karl's agency, the boy had been admitted to art school and was due to matriculate the next week (146). The Wilkinsons, too, are horrified, but only by a call at their residence by a gendarme who expects justice more than cash. Arthur is merely annoyed by it all.

Yet Lina still accepts Arthur's offer of marriage, an unexpected plot twist precipitated by the revelation that Mr Wilkinson, a financier, has lost all Mrs Palmer's money in a failed speculation he represented as certain. Lina sees the wiser choice of suitors but feels forced to accept the inferior but wealthy man:

> 'I am like someone before whom two roads lay – the one right, the other wrong; difficulties, great, untold difficulties, lay at the entrance of the right road; I have shrunk from encountering them; I have taken the other, though I know it to be wrong ... and please God that I may only not know the misery my choice has occasioned another!' (157–8)

In following the 'wiser' English financial course, she destroys Karl's hopes and her own. All for naught, it turns out. Mr Wilkinson, Arthur's trustee, flatly forbids his marriage to a penniless girl, and the youth capitulates, later taking a rich wife of whom he is not proud. The injured boy recovers enough to attend art school, and Karl, who has left the same night he learns of Lina's decision, falls ill for some time before he can commence the medical studies which his brilliant exam results have made possible. Mrs Palmer, too, falls seriously ill and the Wilkinsons depart. Lina is saved only because of her earlier Anglo–German friendship with Madame von Vöhning, who counsels her to return to Stuttgart, where they met, and teach French, English, and harp lessons to support herself and her mother. From there, Lina secures a position as governess for the family of a new German ambassador to England, whom the Palmers accompany back to their native land (175).

The final chapter is set three years later, when Lina is now governess in an immensely wealthy English family that hosts a grand musical soiree at which the newest musical sensation, Von Rosenberg, will perform. In Heidelberg Von Rosenberg was Karl's dear friend, with whom he set off on a walking tour the night of Arthur's proposal.[27] When her employer asks her to take her young charge into the drawing room, Lina, now dressed in black for her mother's death a month earlier, is presented to Von Rosenberg, who instantly recognises his former Heidelberg friend and reports that Karl now resides in Berlin at the young Prussian king's express invitation, gathering the brightest medical minds of his generation around him. The chapter breaks off, then returns full circle to Heidelberg and another lesson for young readers on German culture: the tradition of the Christmas tree, then little known in England. Karl is coming to the celebration at his mother's home with his young wife, along with Von Rosenberg. Howitt momentarily teases readers with the suggestion that the courtship plot foundered by withholding the wife's name. But it is Lina, whom Karl travelled to see in England as soon as Von Rosenberg wrote, and who has preceded her arrival with a letter to Mrs Hoffmann in perfect German; 'the calligraphy too was German, and the sentiments those of the most cordial affection – worthy, said the kind mother-in-law, of the warmest German heart' (181). Even though Lina is known as Karl's 'English wife' (183), Mrs Hoffmann has moved beyond her earlier prejudice and fully accepts Lina as a daughter. If Lina has at last made the wiser choice, so has Mrs Hoffmann.

Lina could make this right moral and emotional choice because she met cultural difference with warmth, interest, and a desire to learn. Without an ability to speak German or her sociable openness to Germans and their customs, she could never have found happiness with Karl, to whom her own foreignness was never an obstacle. Both Howitt's innovative plotting and her desire to write a story illustrating how one might engage in cultural exchange with lasting benefit on both sides deserve greater visibility in English studies today.

This young adult novel was partly inspired by William and Mary Howitt's experience of Anglo–German romance in their own household. William's first German book, *Student Life in Germany* (1841), was actually his translation of the narrative he asked German student Cornelius to write out in German. Since Cornelius also knew English, he came to the house nightly to assist as William's work proceeded. In the course of these visits he fell in love with Anna Mary and, when William's work was two-thirds complete, proposed to her. Whether or not the decision was entirely her own, Anna Mary refused Cornelius's proposal. Yet, as his work was not yet finished, he kept coming nightly, promising unbidden that he would never again mention his feelings for her. As Howitt wrote to her sister, 'all through he has behaved so nobly and beautifully, that we are all of us apparently as warm and dear friends as ever . . . I only hope that neither A.M. nor I may ever again have to pass through such deep suffering as we have endured principally because we know this young man to be so good.'[28] Having seen up close how easily Anglo–German romance might develop and the difficulties it might cause, Howitt transferred some of these to her fictional Anglo–German romance. But in *Which Is the Wiser* events conspire in the young lovers' favour as Howitt rewrites broken romance and anguish into a joyous ending even as she teaches her young readers what new worlds cultural exchange and foreign language study could open for them.[29]

Another distinctive contribution to children's literature, and one of Howitt's most financially successful, appeared the year after her return to England, the *Child's Picture and Verse Book: Commonly Called Otto Speckter's Fables* (1844), a work beloved throughout Germany and first translated into English by Howitt.[30] Her prefatory poem constructs a bridge from Germany

To English Children

This little Book comes from the hand,
    Dear Children, of a friend –
Throughout the kindred German land,
    'T is loved from end to end.
'T is when sternest winter chills;
    When summer gilds the vine;
From Russia to the Tyrol hills;
    From the Black Sea to the Rhine.
'T is loved within the peasant's shed,
    By children brown and wild;
Within the noblest hall 'tis read,
    By many a high-born child.
With many a flower-enwoven wreath,
    On birth-days is it given;
It lies the Christmas-tree beneath,
    As'twere a gift from Heaven.
O then, ye Children dear, receive
    This little Book I pray,
'Twill waken love, much joy will give,
    For many and many a day.[31]

In short, Howitt promised, this book could appeal across classes, regions, and complexions. The poem was signed M. H. and dated 18 December 1843, hinting that this book would make a fine Christmas gift for children.

According to David Blamires, Howitt actually combined two works, *Funfzig Fabeln für Kinder* (Fifty Fables for Children) and *Noch Funfzig Fabeln für Kinder* (Another Fifty Fables for Children). Only the illustrations were by Speckter, who received full credit in England though the German verses were written by William Hey, a Protestant pastor and teacher. As Blamires adds, the original's two-sestet selections were 'skillfully crafted to the understanding of small children and expressing pleasure at the small things in daily life', and Howitt's translations (which used a range of rhyme schemes) were 'very close' to Hey's original.[32] The result was a popular English children's book that went into an additional four editions.³³ Some poems are humorous (e.g. 'Little Pug and Little Cur', in which a well-groomed but greedy pug gets its comeuppance from a scrappy and clever mongrel); others are religious or teach a gentle moral lesson.³⁴

Howitt's truly brilliant stroke was to create a trilingual version of each poem, the first in French (a more familiar language to British families than German), then the original German, and finally Howitt's English translation.³⁵ She may have been influenced by William Howitt's 1843 translation of Adelbert von Chamisso's *Peter Schlemihl* in a dual-language version published in Nuremberg and London.³⁶ But Howitt's trilingual book created not merely a translation but also a well-thought-out international educational text that reminded children with every turn of the page that there were multiple languages in the world besides English and that helped children begin learning the rudiments of two languages as they puzzled out the relation of the German or French to the English words. Howitt's reviewers took note. *Tait's Edinburgh Magazine* observed 'the advantage of offering to the juvenile reader a useful exercise in the French and German languages', while the *Eclectic Review* confirmed the popularity of the 'Fabel-buch' in Germany, identified the book's appropriate age range of two to seven, and underscored the difficulty of translating German into English verse that had the requisite 'simple' English and 'vivacity' suited to children.³⁷

Howitt's most lasting creation of a cosmopolitan child, of course, was her own daughter Anna Mary. Even before the Howitts arrived in Heidelberg Anna Mary was studying German.³⁸ With three years' residence in Heidelberg, she fully mastered the language and in addition met Wilhelm Kaulbach, her Munich art instructor. Her ambition to become a professional painter was longstanding, but it may have been needful for Anna Mary to have means to support herself after disaster befell her parents and abruptly ended *Howitt's Journal* in 1848. Due to William Howitt's initial investment in a prior English journal partnership, he was held liable for its debts and forced into bankruptcy. The family regrouped as best they could, but the Howitts's heyday as authors was at an end.

They had to rely on writing careers to live nonetheless, and it is unsurprising that Howitt quickly repurposed Anna Mary's letters home from Munich into paying magazine articles (discussed below). Howitt also drew on her daughter's 1850s German art study in another way. Anna Mary returned from her Munich studies to England in 1852 due to another dramatic change in the family's circumstances: that June William Howitt set off for Australia to try recouping the family's fortunes in the gold rush (another unsuccessful venture) and was absent two years.

It was imperative that Anna Mary return before his departure to help see him off on a journey about which the only thing certain was that it would mean physical rigours and rough living conditions oceans away.

In 1853 Howitt's novella *Margaret von Ehrenberg, The Artist-Wife* (hereafter *The Artist-Wife*) appeared in *Stories of English and Foreign Life* by William and Mary Howitt. Some of the collection's ten tales were by William Howitt, but *The Artist-Wife* was reissued in the US solely under Howitt's signature in *Popular Tales for Household Reading* (1857), confirming her authorship. Yet this tale was still collaborative – with Anna Mary, whose actual art-study in Munich formed the basis for Howitt's imagined life of an Anglo-German wife and professional artist.

Anna Mary was living with Howitt while both were completing books about woman artists in Germany. *The Artist-Wife* appeared in mid-March 1853, Anna Mary's *An Art-Student in Munich* in early May 1853.[39] The considerable overlap between the mother's and daughter's descriptions of the Munich Artist's Ball points to synchronous composition if not actual collaborative writing. The Artist's Ball is the climax of Margaret von Ehrenberg's Munich life with her husband in Howitt's sixth chapter:

> they stood within the theatre itself, the pit converted into a vast ball-room, from the centre of which arose a fairy pavilion of golden gothic tracery, festooned with living wreaths of the most lovely exotic creepers, with golden dolphins spouting forth streams of ruddy wine into a golden fountain beneath the golden pavilion; with the richly emblazoned banners of the different artist-corps, floating in gorgeous folds and streamers from above it, with the spaces between the boxes draped with the same corps colours, and with ivy and moss garlands, binding together artistic trophies of palettes and brushes, alternating with groups of musical instruments: and the whole vast space was one moving mass of brilliant colour, whilst the walls were peopled with quaint and gorgeous crowds gazing down upon the quaint and gorgeous crowds below, and over all, and through all, sounded gay laughter, and shrill cries, and a maddening hum of frantic merriment.[40]

And here is Anna Mary's description:

> what a magic vision bursts upon us when we enter the ball-room itself! In the centre rises a pavilion, stolen certainly out of Fairyland! Graceful and slender Byzantine arches of white and gold, and with delicate vermilion tracery upon them, cluster together … Ivy and vine cluster around, and festoon the graceful arches; tall, golden tripods rise, heaped up with flowers; wreaths of fresh greenery, and golden tambourines and pipes and flutes, hang around the base of the pavilion in joyous symmetry; beneath the pavilion, nestling amid a grove of odorous shrubs and flowers, four magical swans, with white and golden plumage, arch their necks and pour from

their open bills ruddy streams of wine! The fairy vision towers to the very ceiling of the lofty Odeon hall, where, from a wreath of roses red and white, spring forth long silken streamers.[41]

The mother's and daughter's chapters even share a mysterious hooded figure who watches over all. In Howitt 'a stranger, an Indian, whose swarthy countenance and gleaming eyes she now recollected had been fixed upon her ever and anon for hours, and her steps dogged by him, – who was he? – not her husband, she was certain' (*The Artist-Wife*, 58). In *Art-Student* there 'sits crouching' a 'half hidden' figure, 'a Bedouin in his long, spectral bernouse; he props his dark face upon a dark arm, and looks up' . . .[42] In the daughter's autobiographical writing, the ball signifies joy and confirms her chosen vocation; in the mother's novella, it marks the onset of disaster and suffering for the English-born married artist until she wins through to reaffirm her artistic vocation in the end.

Howitt's *Artist-Wife* extends her earlier work in *Which Is the Wiser?* insofar as it, too, explores the opportunities and dangers of life abroad. Only the 1853 tale, however, offers in an Anglo–German context the adult themes of troubled marriage and the challenges faced by women who pursue professional careers. The young English artist Margaret Harwood, denied professional training at home, seizes an opportunity to travel with her mother to Dresden to copy gallery paintings on commission. In Dresden her sickly mother dies; and rather than return home and resign herself to blighted aspirations, Margaret remains, soon moving on to Munich, a vibrant art centre under the Bavarian King Ludwig, as the English public knew from Jameson's *Visits and Sketches*. There she first meets the 'Frau Doctorin' Ludmilla, the widow of a doctor, the daughter of a Hofrath or king's privy councillor, and a progressive woman intellectual. Ludmilla immediately perceives Margaret's talent, befriends her, and networks her into Munich's art world and society. In this Ludmilla differs from other German women, who are shocked by Margaret's anatomical studies and by any 'Englishwomen' who are '*emancipated*' (29).

At a Munich artists' gathering Margaret also meets the dashing Baron von Ehrenberg, who marries her after a whirlwind romance. Deeply in love, Margaret cannot see what readers can, that he is extravagant and likely unfaithful, or that he wilfully exploits Margaret (along with his friends) to obtain money for his luxurious tastes and habits. He thus encourages her professionalism, basking in attention she earns, and readily agrees that they will lead independent daytime schedules so that she can paint and he pursue his own affairs before they rejoin each other every evening.

But the baron encourages Margaret to pursue lower forms of her art, especially profitable society portraiture, rather than the landscape and history painting that interest her.[43] He ignores two sketches that Margaret exhibits anonymously, to which King Ludwig and other connoisseurs gravitate, and even lies when the king asks if he knows who painted them. Both sketches foreshadow later events in Margaret's life. One shows an idyllic mountain landscape at sunset and 'a human group bathed in the sunlight of love and nature – a father, mother, and child.' The companion sketch shows the same scene at sunrise, now a site of devastation and agony since the family's hut has been crushed by a tree and their garden destroyed, the father now a corpse while his wife grieves in agony and the child stares in bewilderment. To the paired sketches Margaret gives the title 'Life also hath her hurricanes' (4–5).[44]

Margaret's 'hurricane' comes when the baron signs a bill to two ruthless moneylenders, making Margaret responsible for his debts so that he can outfit himself gorgeously for the annual Artist's Ball. He then empties her bank account and decamps. The arrival of gendarmes who enter her studio to arrest her for debt shatters all her former illusions. Her earnings and loans from an art dealer are insufficient to cover the debt, and Margaret narrowly evades debtors' prison only because she insists that as an Englishwoman she will keep her word to pay off the sum (81).[45] She sells many of her paintings and most household furnishings to cover her immediate debts and then, for months after, works doggedly to churn out portrait after portrait and pay off the rest.[46]

Determined to return to England afterwards, Margaret hears the voice of her husband on the quay at Calais, for he is headed to England in search of a new victim he can exploit. If the baron represents the potential dangers of marriage, he also exemplifies the dangers of a cosmopolitanism that harbours no loyalties anywhere. Finding his way to Margaret's wealthy aunt, he so charms her that when she dies she leaves him the bulk of her fortune. Only her estate of Flimbsted goes to her nephew Henry Lushington, a young widower and father, and a small settlement to Margaret. The baron, in effect, robs his wife of her money twice. Ultimately the baron is quickly dispatched when he goes to Paris, is caught up in the 1848 revolution, and is shot on the barricades. Ironically hailed by the French at his funeral as a martyr to *Liberté*, *Egalité*, and *Fraternité*, he has at last aided his wife's fortunes, and Margaret inherits her aunt's money after all.

In the final chapter, set three years later, Margaret is in her own studio-cottage on the Flimbsted estate where she continues her breakthroughs in landscape painting. Henry Lushington, a positive model of ethnoexocentrism who responds to cultural difference with interest and respect, had earlier visited Margaret in Munich, fallen in love with Ludmilla, and married her, after which the couple made their home at Flimbsted. Margaret now happily mentors Henry's elder daughter Signild, who aspires to a painting career herself, and goes with her when she studies art in Munich for a year. Henry and Ludmilla's successful Anglo–German marriage counters Margaret's disastrous one, and the novel culminates in the Flimbsted christening of a newly born Lushington daughter, Margaret Ludmilla.

The Artist-Wife is a story of in-depth Anglo–German exchange: the principal English and German characters (Margaret, the baron, Henry, Ludmilla, and Signild) travel in both directions between England and Germany and form Anglo–German families. Even Margaret's cottage is Anglo–German. She lives in her own English home on English property, but the architecture derives from designs that Margaret had admired in Munich. *The Artist-Wife* is also, notably, a proto-feminist narrative, a view shared by Antonia Losano.[47] The novel tacitly argues the need to re-conceive ideas about careers for married women; at one point Margaret explicitly recognises 'how blessed her lot was in one respect above the ordinary lot of women – she first perceived how terrible a curse her gifts of imagination would have been to her, as to many another of her sisters, but for a channel discovered for its free career under ordinary circumstances in her profession' (116).

The novella also aligns emancipation with female networks, a practice earlier glimpsed in Jameson's formative German experiences. The baron chafes at Margaret's friendship with Ludmilla: 'There's a glance of emancipation in her sharp dark eyes, and an extravagant idealism that is only fuel to the fire of my wife's absurdities about independence and perfectibility' (8). On inheriting the baron's money, Margaret's first thought is how her riches might relieve the suffering of other women and artists (135). Howitt even inserts her own female network into the story in noting that Margaret possesses a miniature of her mother 'painted from a girlish sketch of hers by Margaret Gillies, one of our best miniature painters' (145). Margaret Gillies (whose first name perhaps suggested that of Howitt's protagonist) was a practising artist in England whose 'life and art', according to Wettlaufer, 'directly inspired Anna Mary Howitt'.[48] Howitt further drew upon her own experiences as a married professional woman and, I surmise, the future she had earlier imagined for Anna Mary, who arrived in Munich engaged to Edward La Trobe Bateman (1816–97), an artist and illustrator on the fringes of the Pre-Raphaelite circle.[49] As Anna Mary's letters to her friend Barbara Leigh Smith (later Bodichon) attest, Anna Mary was as dreamily and hopelessly in love with 'Edward' as Margaret is with the baron early in Howitt's novella.[50] Anna Mary thus came very close to being an artist-wife in Munich herself, and in one letter to Leigh Smith she fantasised about lecturing to a Female Art Academy as 'Mrs. Bateman'. Anna Mary, however, broke the engagement in spring 1852, a denouement that perhaps likewise influenced Howitt's representation of unhappy marriage.[51] If Howitt as mother helped create a cosmopolitan child who became a professional artist, her daughter in turn helped create the mother's narrative of an Anglo–German professional artist-wife.

Anna Mary Howitt: From Daughter to Feminist Forerunner

As well as being mother-daughter authors, Howitt and Anna Mary were active in the early 1850s in a London feminist circle that included Anna Jameson, Barbara Leigh Smith, and Bessie Parkes.[52] While mother and daughter were preparing their 1853 books for publication, Anna Mary was simultaneously serialising her feminist novella *Sisters in Art* (July–December 1852) in the *Illustrated Exhibitor*, a story of three young women determined to be fully trained professionals who band together to found a women's art school. Set principally in England, *Sisters in Art* has attracted more attention in recent scholarship than *An Art-Student in Munich*. In the nineteenth century their relative weighting was reversed. *Sisters* appeared only in the ephemeral *Illustrated Exhibitor and Magazine of Art* and was never reprinted. *Art-Student*, in contrast, was published four times during Anna Mary's life: first in instalments appearing variously in *Ladies' Companion*, *Household Words*, and the *Athenaeum* (1850–1); in the British first edition (1853); in an American first edition (1854); and in a second British edition (1880). Not only was the reach of *Art-Student* wider and longer, but as historian Richard Scully attests, it also had a larger cultural impact in its time, in part due to its account of the decadal Miracle Play at Oberammergau, which Anna Mary attended in 1850. Noting the rarity of an Englishwoman's travelling to Oberammergau and Anna Mary's 'astonishment that such an archaic form of Catholic worship could still exist in the nineteenth century', Scully asserts that her 'hugely popular book' inspired the vogue for Oberammergau that developed among 'British travelers who were perversely eager to share in her disapproval of the "child-like faith" of the majority-Catholic Bavarians'. The 1880 restaging of the Miracle Play, Scully adds, inspired Anna Mary's London publisher to reissue a second edition that year. The decade-long wait for the play had intensified interest, and in the words of an advertising blurb, 'The "Passion-Spiel" at Ober-Ammergau ... has attained the perilous distinction of fashion.'[53]

The idea of writing about Oberammergau first came from the Howitts's long-time friend Henry Chorley. Shortly after Anna Mary and fellow English art student Jane Benham left for Munich, according to Howitt,

> Henry Chorley ... came to tell me he had accepted from Messrs. Bradbury & Evans the editorship of *The Ladies' Companion*; and he wanted Annie, as we all now called my daughter, to go to a great miracle-play of the Passion, performed that year by the devout peasants of Ober-Ammergau ... [A]nd he begged her to write for him a description of the whole thing, from the setting-out in the morning to the end of the play. She willingly complied, and thus first made known this remarkably striking, pathetic, but now trite subject to the English public.[54]

Anna Mary's *Ladies' Companion* letters, reprinted verbatim as Chapter IV of *Art-Student*, were her earliest writings from Munich to be published.[55] Anna Mary's periodical essays might, like the chapters of *Sisters in Art*, have remained ephemera but for the intervention of Gaskell. In a late December letter of 1850, Howitt told her daughter that Gaskell as well as Anna Mary's fiancé had spent Christmas Eve with them. At this point Anna Mary's *Ladies' Companion* letters, three letters on German art in the *Athenaeum*'s 'Foreign Correspondence' section, and 'Bits of Life in Munich' in the 2 November *Household Words* had all appeared. As her mother happily reported, 'Mrs. Gaskell is much pleased with your writings. She says you do not make the reader see the things with your eyes, but you present the scene itself to him. She hopes, on your return, you will collect and publish your letters in a volume – a sort of "Art Life in Munich".'[56]

Recovering the full publishing history of *Art-Student* clarifies other matters. Scully is right to underscore Anna Mary's 'disapproval of the "child-like faith" of the majority-Catholic Bavarians'. The first *Ladies' Companion* instalment also pointed out the occasional 'frightfully deformed or diseased wretch' begging alms, 'disgusting fungi of Catholicism [that] were a strange comment on the scene'.[57] This outburst of Protestant repulsion emerged from a complex context, however. Jameson had gravitated to Weimar, Howitt and Gaskell to Heidelberg, both part of Protestant Germany. Anna Mary was the first woman writer in this study to settle in Catholic Bavaria, and this religious alterity posed a more challenging encounter with cultural difference.

Anna Mary was also travelling to a Catholic destination at a fraught time. On receiving her account of the consecration of the new Munich basilica, her mother warned how parts of it might be received:

> I shall copy your account of the consecration of the Basilica for the *Athenæum*, but I am afraid it is too gloriously papistical for the present time in England. You can have no idea what a tide of popular feeling has set in against everything Catholic. 'No Popery' is written over all the walls of London. Public meetings are held everywhere, and petitions and protests are got up by all parties against Papacy. There never was so anti-Catholic a nation as this. However your account is very beautiful and picturesque, and they may give it as news.[58]

The cause of such hostile fervour was the Catholic See newly established by the Roman Catholic Church in England in 1850. A subsequent Howitt letter indicated the risks that a woman writer ran if she seemed overly sympathetic to Catholics. Eliza Meteyard ('Silverpen' in the former *Howitt's Journal* and elsewhere), who also spent Christmas Eve with the Howitts in 1850, was under duress 'because people are beginning to discover *popery* in her little book'. In fact Meteyard's publishers refused to publish Meteyard's next book on this account.[59]

If Protestant national identity mandated Anna Mary's self-regulating barrier against Catholicism in parts of her Oberammergau narrative, the passage singled out by Scully does not represent the whole. She also admitted to tears at the sight of so many peasants walking up the steep road, 'earnest, grave, yet cheerful', for whom the play was not mere entertainment but 'a deep religious object'. Tobias Flunger, who acted the role of Christ, struck her as a 'gentleman' as well as a man who strangely resembled Christ in the work of 'early Italian painters', and she found herself unexpectedly moved by the play as well.[60] If her letter remained a Protestant outsider's response, placing it early in her published book enabled a larger design: the 1853 narrative enactment of increasing openness to difference and cross-cultural exchange that reaches its climax when the English art student is also one of the community of Munich artists in the joyous artist's ball.

Before turning to this narrative arc it is helpful to clarify a question of authorship. Though the published essays certainly depended on Howitt's transmission of copy to editors, the evidence indicates that Howitt (busy with her own writing commitments) acted as amanuensis rather than her daughter's collaborator and managing editor in 1850–1.[61] An 1851 letter makes this clear. After Barbara Leigh Smith offered some criticisms of her friend's *Household Words* 'Bits', Anna Mary replied on 10 February, 'There are ... faults I myself do find in those Household Words articles which deserve, it seems to me, criticism – and they would not have been there had I at all expected these descriptions would have been made public – or if I had chanced to be at dearest Mamma's elbow when she copied them – things that for public reading seem to be rather in bad taste.'[62] She would later remove some of those personal references as she revised extant essays and added thirty new chapters to complete a book in two volumes.[63]

A feminist framework is integral to *Art-Student*. Anna Mary was forced to become a private student of Wilhelm Kaulbach, court painter to King Ludwig and director of Munich's Kunstakademie (Art Academy), because the academy admitted only men, like Britain's Royal Academy at that time.[64] But the patriarchal constraint was inseparable from great female freedom and agency for this art student. In Chapter VII, 'Justina's Visit. – A Group of Art Sisters' (a non-fiction version of *Sisters in Art*), 'Justina', Anna Mary's pseudonym for Leigh Smith, is astonished by the Englishwomen's bohemian freedoms to walk about on streets, dine informally, and carry their own latch keys – those insignias of New Women in the 1890s: 'She declared again and again that there never was such a delicious, free, poetical life as ours.'[65]

Art-Student enfolds multiple genres beyond elements of New Woman fiction; it is a travel book, an ekphrastic guide to the art of Munich akin to Jameson's *Visits and Sketches*, a family memoir, and an artist's life writing.[66] In a specifically Anglo–German context, however, the principal importance of *Art-Student* is as a narrative of transformation from nationalism to ethnoexocentrism – that is, from more strictly English Protestant identity to genuine openness to difference and to participation in another culture. The opening chapters of *Art-Student* replay some old prejudices; even the standard British tourist's complaint about 'German stenches' surfaces.[67] By mid-narrative, Anna Mary accommodates Catholicism on Easter Sunday. And near the book's end her chapter on Christmas in Munich makes room for starker differences on a global as well as Anglo–German scale before the book culminates in the artist's ball.

Anna Mary's account of 'The Holy Week' and 'Easter Eve' in *Household Words* on 7 June 1851 marks how far she had shifted her orientation towards Catholicism after living for a year in Bavaria. True, she begins by frankly conceding that on Good Friday 'I had come to [St Peter's] church with a feeling of utter disgust towards the ceremony which I was about to witness – a representation of Christ borne to the sepulcher'; and she associates an 'emaciated' priest she sees in St Peter's Church with 'the most fearful vice of priestcraft'.[68] But her tone softens when she gives in to the experience of sitting that afternoon in St Michael's Church:

> Above the human mass, high up, suspended in the air, beneath the boldly swelling arches of the richly ornamented roof, and casting a warm, golden light upon the nearest stone-wreaths, and angels, and glimmering in a warm, dark haze at the farthest end of the church, burned and blazed a mighty cross of fire. The effect was thrillingly beautiful ...

Music then suddenly 'burst like a whirlwind through the church moaning, lamenting, pleading', and she was 'strangely affected by the whole scene; moved to the inmost soul with a vast pity and grief by that sad lament – and, no wonder, for was it not *the Miserere*?' Though a Protestant, she experiences a deeply religious moment among an enormous German Catholic crowd as one of the congregation.[69]

Anna Mary then fashions an Anglo–German liminal space that allows for her English Protestantism to touch without merging into Catholicism when she goes into the country on Easter Sunday. As 'people streamed into' her 'favourite old [Catholic] church', she remains outside on the 'fresh grass', a metaphorical and cultural positioning that leaves her free to meditate as a Protestant on the meaning of the Resurrection and offer prayers directly to God while maintaining proximity to German worship. Then comes a passage added only in 1853:

> sitting where I did, the voice of the priest praying came to me, sweetly and distinctly. It was much more beautiful listening to the service than being within the church among the people! I heard the little organ peal forth, and the singing of the quire. There was one fresh young voice that sang like a very angel. This voice celebrated the Resurrection. My eyes overflowed with warm tears, and my soul responded, though I sat, a heretic and an alien, outside the walls of the little church.[70]

She here slips into more profound cultural exchange. As an Englishwoman she stays at a distance but responds deeply, moved to her very 'soul'. When she calls herself a 'heretic and an alien', however, she is seeing herself as the Germans do. In this liminal space she is both inside and outside the church and national alignments in her sympathies, emotions, and mental tableau. William A. Cohen contends that Victorian writers were interested in the senses because 'sense perception' demonstrated 'how the world of objects – including other bodies – enters the body of the subject and remakes its interior entities'.[71] The Easter sections represent a cross-cultural sensory transformation of Anna Mary's subjectivity, marking how far she had come since her early visit to

Oberammergau as the intimacy of sound, touch, and visual beauty enter freely and leave her in a state of reverence.

Another new chapter added to volume 2, 'Christmas-Day – A Christmas Tree in a Beautiful Home', dated 'Christmas-Day 1851', takes readers to an even more unconventional celebration of a religious holiday. Its title suggests a sentimental scene capitalising on the German Christmas tree that her parents had helped to make well known in the 1840s. But not so. It begins with Anna Mary in a state of religious doubt consequent upon 'reading lately' through 'old Catholic legends': 'What had Christmas availed in the world? what real earnest hold had Christ's blessed words upon the world? The masses were brutal and superstitious; the few were faithless ... But of Christ's own pure, blessed words there were *no* questionings.'[72] This time she finds solace and comfort within, not outside, a Catholic church, rather like Lucy Snowe in *Villette* at a time of psychic and cultural fragmentation. Though the 'ornaments' she sees 'are vile, judged by one's standard of purity, beauty, and simplicity; still, this morning the effect was poetical ... as [i]ncense filled the whole chapel, meeting one on entrance as if with a bodily presence; and music from a concealed choir flooded the chapel'. The music, from angelic praise or 'wild hallelujahs' to 'mournful murmurs', leads her to a firmer affirmation of faith:

> I felt my spirit bow in worship with that ignorant crowd of poor people who filled the chapel. Ah! how beautiful, how holy, was faith! though I was as ignorant, as superstitious, as the most ignorant peasant there, what mattered it? Better love a phantom than nothing; to be without love was to be without faith or joy.
>
> The spirit of God had spoken in that music as it spoke of old to Saul when David touched the golden strings of his harp; all the demons of doubt had fled, and I *could* alone believe in the strength of goodness![73]

She is one *of* and *with* the congregants here, even as she exercises English freedom of thought and shares a rare Victorian literary representation of female religious doubt in a middle-class woman. Perhaps Anna Mary knew Robert Browning's *Christmas-Eve and Easter-Day* (1850), since her mother mentions the Brownings in a 3 September 1852 letter to her husband in Australia while Anna Mary was living with her.[74] Anna Mary's brief Christmas Eve passage is in some respects a prose counterpart to his poem, which opens as his narrator seeks refuge from the rain in a dissenting chapel filled with unattractive working-class worshippers before it moves to a German university classroom associated with Göttingen, a hotbed of Higher Criticism (which applied methods of textual and mythological studies to the Bible). Unlike Browning's narrator, however, Anna Mary finds faith in a Catholic Church and identifies with the peasants among whom she sits. When she passes outside and sees two priests carrying the host to a 'sick person' and witnesses a 'lady in her silks and satins, and a little ragged urchin' kneel and cross themselves in the snow as the host passes by, she remarks, 'I paused also, longing almost for the faith which taught them to believe that the body of Christ had really passed before them, making sacred the very air through which it moved.'[75] Religious difference is here no barrier to sympathy and cross-cultural response.

The narrative continues to the home of a Court Councillor's wife on St Stephen's Day to see the lighting of the Christmas tree, another note of Anglo–German ecumenicism since she calls it St Stephen's, though it falls on the same date as England's Boxing Day. The unfolding scene inside is neither German nor merely Anglo–German. As the host's five blonde daughters show Anna Mary and 'Isabel' the Christmas presents they have received,

> the door flew open, and the eldest son of the house entered, followed by nine youths with swarthy faces, black eyes, and scarlet *fezes*. They were the nine noble Egyptian youths sent over by the Pacha of Egypt to study at Munich. There was Salem Salem Awad, son of a great philosopher and poet; Prince Murad Ibrahim, son of Pascha Amurad; Prince Hassan Hassan, son of an Admiral and Pascha; Prince Jussuph Katschador, son of a Bey; and five other equally noble Egyptians ... and smiling, they pressed their right hands upon their hearts, their lips, and brows, – saluting the ladies with the oriental *salaam*.[76]

This global encounter of Christians and Muslims, dark- and light-skinned youths, depends on the Egyptian students' elite social and economic status, and some of Anna Mary's descriptors are conventionally Orientalist, as when she imagines the 'swarthy oriental countenances, contrasting with these delicate complexions and golden hair of the north' appealing to painter William Etty. Still, when the group sits down, with the Egyptians (wearing their *fezes* at table) 'seated alternately with the blond-haired, blue-eyed sisters', dark-skinned Muslims are neither feminised nor positioned as threats to virginal blond femininity.[77] Instead the text identifies the two Englishwomen as the cultural outsiders: 'We two foreigners were introduced to the Egyptians', another instance in which Anna Mary sees herself as the Germans do.[78]

Exchange across difference pervades this multicultural celebration of a Western religious holiday. Like Anna Mary, the German Councillor's daughter Emilia has studied abroad, in her case music in Milan. The

Egyptian youths are studying abroad in Germany, and they know other international students in London, as Anna discovers when she converses with them: "'I have heard in England much about the Egyptians studying in London,' said I to one of the youths; 'are they friends of yours?'" She promises to inquire back home about the Egyptians studying in Manchester, about whom the Munich group are worried because 'there is no blue sky, and no sun as in Egypt'.[79] The whole is an intriguing fore-glimpse of global studies in the twentieth and twenty-first centuries. More important for *Art-Studies* itself, the scene marks the dramatic cultural distance the narrator has traversed from her earliest reactions in Oberammergau.

As Julie Codell rightly remarks of Anna Mary's culminating description of the artists' ball, it celebrates freedom, carnivalesque merriment, and artistic creativity.[80] The artists' spontaneous play and creativity are cross-cultural both imaginatively and actually, given the Englishwomen's presence: the artists design costumes for themselves as 'Americans, Armenians, Turks, Portuguese, Italian peasants, Venetian senators, knights and ladies of the German legions' and also as Arabs and indigenous and Spanish-American Mexicans. Anna Mary and 'Isabel' freely participate in the scene rather than keeping their distance, donning the variegated, brightly coloured fools' caps all men and women received with their tickets of admission.[81] The ludic festivities culminate in an untranslated toast that seals the narrator's identity as one among a society of artists who all pledge allegiance to German art:

> And thus the night wore on in full embodiment of the painters' motto emblazoned on their decorations and upon their cards:
>
> > 'Tages Arbeit; Abends Gäste!
> > Saure Wochen! Frohe Feste!'
>
> Never, surely, was there a more joyous festival, or one more graceful, and fantastic, and poetic, than this *Künstler Bal* of 1852. Long lives and merry ones to the joyous artists! let us cry: and long, long life and a glorious immortality to the joyous, genial German art! A right hearty – *Lebe Hoch für die Stadt München, für Münchener Kunst und Künstler!*[82]

Anna Mary's entry into Munich culture builds upon her parents' Anglo–German networks but is also enabled because she has a designated profession and, as a feminist forerunner, enjoys urban mobility within the city and friendships that criss-cross international borders. *Art-Student* is also a striking representation of early forms of study abroad and global cultural exchange.

Wives and Daughters in Germany

A tacit globalism haunts Gaskell's two stories set wholly or partly in Germany: the Indian Rebellion of 1857 forms a partial backdrop to both 'The Grey Woman' and 'Six Weeks at Heppenheim'. Earlier that year Gaskell and her daughters were on a ship to Rome for Gaskell's well-deserved holiday after completing *The Life of Charlotte Brontë* (1857). On board they were joined by Captain Charles Hill, an engineer with the Madras Engineers in India, who continued to accompany the Gaskells during their Italian holiday. Soon after the Gaskells returned to Manchester, Hill and Gaskell's daughter Meta became engaged. Hill was visiting the Gaskell household in Plymouth Grove when news of the Indian Rebellion broke and he was ordered back to India. Plans remained for Meta to travel with her father to Egypt the succeeding winter, where the couple would marry, then live in India for four years.[83] Hill himself was never in any personal danger, but now Gaskell had to entertain thoughts of a daughter far away in a land that was not always peaceful, a frightening prospect for a mother who cared deeply for her children.

In the end the wedding did not come off, for Hill had not been entirely forthcoming about his finances, and Meta later learned that he had unpaid gambling debts.[84] An engagement that first brought worries about her daughter's survival in India now gave way to worries about Meta's mental and emotional suffering from having all her hopes for the future destroyed. It was largely to help Meta through her pain that Gaskell took her and another daughter to Heidelberg for some three months in 1858. This context is the back story to Gaskell's two German stories in which a daughter travels far from home to a site of murderous violence after marriage ('The Grey Woman', 1861) or suffers heartbreak from a man whose drinking, womanising, and gambling debts destroy earlier hopes of marriage ('Six Weeks at Heppenheim', 1862). 'The Grey Woman', set in Carlsruhe and the Vosges mountains, is notable for elements of sensation fiction, queer sexuality, and feminist themes.[85] 'Heppenheim', in contrast, is a quiet tale set in a village north of Heidelberg. Yet both portray the effects of crossing cultural borders.

If William Gaskell was fluent in German, Gaskell was not, and William mediated between English and German speakers during Gaskell's first trip to Heidelberg in 1841.[86] By 1858 Gaskell had her own Anglo–German contacts. Around 1850 she met Chevalier Christian Bunsen, Prussian ambassador to England from 1841 to 1854, who gave her a book of his devotions inscribed to 'my well beloved friend'; he was now a Heidelberg resident.[87] After her 1858 visit Gaskell boasted to her friend Charles Eliot Norton, the American man of letters, on 9 March 1858 that 'we knew nearly every body in Heidelberg', a mostly English-speaking circle.[88] Still, Germanist Peter Skrine and Gaskell scholar J. A. V. Chapple note Gaskell's deft, informed use of German words and phrases in her German stories, and Skrine ultimately credits her with at least basic knowledge of traveller's German.[89]

'The Grey Woman', published in three parts in Dickens's *All the Year Round*, begins as a tourist story at a mill just outside Heidelberg in the 1840s, when a sudden rain shower drives the English narrator and her German-speaking friend indoors. The story's careful attention to languages is immediately apparent when the narrator must ask her friend, 'What did she say?' after the miller's daughter makes a joke about the rain that inspires laughter. Indoors, while the friend pursues an animated exchange with the miller's wife, Frau Scherer, the narrator has leisure to look about while they converse in 'a language which I but half understood'. The opening also registers cross-cultural contexts when the friend mentions Herr Scherer's hatred of the French after Napoleon's invasion of Prussia in 1806, which prepares for the story's 'invasion' of M de Tourelle, whose estate lies in the Vosges Mountains, into the previously sheltered life of Gaskell's protagonist, Anna Scherer.[90]

When the present-day English visitor sees a portrait of a beautiful young woman in a corner and asks about it, she learns that it is the miller's aunt, whose 'sad history' included such fright from 'one of those hellish Frenchman' that she 'lost her colour' and became known as 'the Grey Woman'. The miller has his aunt's manuscript of her personal history and offers to let his guests take it home and read through its 'crabbed German writing'. This the friends do, and over the 'ensuing winter' they collaborate on translating and abridging Anna Scherer's narrative, which unfolds uninterrupted after the tourist-prologue. The tale of the 'Grey Woman' is positioned in consequence as an Anglo–German literary production that moves between Anna Scherer's German and the friends' English rendition. It is also the narrative of a mother determined to 'end ... her daughter's engagement' and prevent a disastrous marriage.[91] 'The Grey Woman', then, enacts at once a mother's intervention in her daughter's life and a sympathetic cultural, literary, and linguistic Anglo–German exchange.

The story's geographic criss-crossing from Germany to France, France to Germany against the backdrop of the French Revolution is a reminder that Anna's is also a cross-cultural marriage. Though her aristocratic husband, like Margaret von Ehrenberg's in Howitt's *Artist-Wife*, turns out to be a villain, there is a signal difference between Margaret's and Anna Scherer's marital experiences. Margaret has a profession, speaks German fluently, and has formed a social and professional network before she marries. Anna's range of experience prior to marriage is painfully narrow. Though she is literate and speaks French, her education has done nothing to curb her naivety about the world beyond the mill. Her limited curiosity and powers of reflection obstruct agency and leave her vulnerable to the depredations of M de Tourelle, who uses his cosmopolitan mastery of French and German as well as aristocratic mobility to mask his thefts and murders. For he is leader of a band of chauffeurs, notorious for torturing and murdering their victims. Ruthless domestically too, Tourelle dazzles Anna and the Carlsruhe friends she visits with his rank and sartorial glamour, knowing as he courts her that the moment she becomes inconvenient or dull after marriage he can dispose of her with no qualms of conscience. Anna passively understands Tourelle's French on first meeting him but lacks the confidence to reply, a foreshadowing of her passivity in marriage, which takes place quickly after they meet. Her beauty and pliability nonetheless sufficiently charm him that he directs a Paris milliner to hire a middle-aged lady's maid for Anna to keep her company during his long absences. His sole generous act as a husband will be the means of saving Anna's life.

The new maid is from Normandy, not Paris, a site intrinsic to English history and language dating to the Norman Conquest, perhaps Gaskell's means of encouraging ready acceptance of this figure by English readers. Amante's arrival introduces diversity into the isolated castle hidden in the Vosges Mountains as well as into Anna's daily existence. It is Amante's difference, as well as her maturity, intelligence, and knowledge of a tailor's life (her father having turned tailor after ceasing to farm), that enable her to fend for Anna and herself immediately after they discover the dead body of a noble neighbour murdered by Tourelle and his chauffeurs. First Amante contrives their escape from the castle and next disguises herself as a tailor, assuming the role of husband to Anna, who is disguised as a peasant wife with brown rather than blonde hair. But when as 'husband' and wife they settle in Frankfurt, Amante faces new challenges because she does not know German: 'Amante was a stranger in the place, speaking only French, moreover, and the good Germans were hating the French people right heartily.'[92] It is not her monolingualism that precipitates Amante's murder by the vengeful chauffeurs but a cruel irony: Amante previously sold a distinctive ring (Tourelle's gift to Anna) to a French pedlar to support herself and Anna before they crossed the Rhine. The pedlar resurfaces in

Frankfurt, immediately recognises the 'tailor', and informs Tourelle. The chauffeurs' murderous code of silencing witnesses is relentless, and Amante dies accordingly.

Ultimately Anna bigamously marries the kindly Dr Voss, who attends her pregnancy and birth of a daughter. As a Protestant Lutheran rather than Roman Catholic, Anna could have legally divorced Tourelle in Germany. But she is so terrified that she will be seen by Tourelle and murdered that she never leaves her room – as confined in Frankfurt by him as if she were still at his castle Les Rochers.[93] Finally apprehended, Tourelle is executed, and after Dr Voss's death Anna and her daughter Ursula return to Heidelberg and Anna's childhood home. There Anna writes the letter that the English narrator helps 'translate'. For Anna the story is transactional, written to intervene in Ursula's engagement. In it she reveals the truth of Ursula's biological father and ensures that her daughter will never marry her French fiancé, who has (like his prospective mother-in-law and fiancée) been living under an assumed name. The fiancé is the son of Tourelle's murder victim Maurice de Poissy, whose dead body dumped beside Anna hiding in her husband's room precipitates the rest of the tale. 'The Grey Woman' thus narrativises the potential dangers of cross-cultural marriages for a wife, especially when she has incomplete knowledge of the culture and social context she seeks to enter.

The very different 'Six Weeks at Heppenheim', published in May 1862 in *Cornhill Magazine* (which allocated less space to sensation fiction than *All the Year Round*), unfolds as the grape harvest approaches in rural Hesse. Its narrator is a recent Oxford graduate taking a walking holiday in Europe prior to buckling down to law study in London. To economise he frequents the same hotels as Germans rather than the luxury hotels favoured by British tourists – the 'wiser' course recommended in Howitt's young adult novel. He commands enough German to negotiate rooms and engage in brief German-language conversations, but the rapid German of other guests in the hotel is more challenging. He has neared the end of his walking tour when he arrives in Heppenheim. Having overtaxed his bodily strength on his journey, he falls into serious illness and, as Chapple notes, Gaskell beautifully conveys his fever-induced delirium through vivid, disjointed details that register his disordered subjectivity and distorted sensory perceptions in the presence of fever.[94]

In his illness the Englishman is cared for by Thekla, an innkeeper's daughter from Rhineland-Palatinate northwest of Heppenheim who has travelled more than 135 miles to work as a hotel maid to earn enough for the household linens and kitchen furnishings she will need when she marries her handsome childhood sweetheart. As the English narrator recovers he realises all that Thekla has done for him, quietly performing every service to perfection despite constantly being harried by her employer's acerbic sister. The narrative quickly rules out potential romance between the Englishman and Thekla. Not only is she engaged already, but they are very different in education, class, and culture. The challenge of cross-cultural communication rather than marriage takes centre stage here, in mostly desultory conversation between the two given the narrator's persisting weakness and limited German, and Thekla's constant duties. He and Thekla, however, are largely friendless in Heppenheim, both having come from afar. The Oxonian becomes interested in Thekla when he repeatedly sees her weeping and pulling out a letter when she thinks him asleep in night-watches. His interest results not so much from voyeurism to relieve the tedium of recovery but from increasing empathy. Ultimately he learns the source of her sorrows and assists her in arriving at a happy resolution against a backdrop of pastoral plenitude during the vine harvest.

Yet there are convergences between the quiet 'Heppenheim' and sensational 'Grey Woman'. 'Heppenheim', too, is intrinsically Anglo–German and cross-class. Moreover, German terms or turns of phrase are scattered throughout, and to counterbalance an allusion near the tale's end to 'Mrs. Inchbald's pretty description of Dorriforth's anxiety in feeding Miss Milner', Gaskell inserts into the mainstream English *Cornhill* a note with an untranslated German harvest hymn ('Heppenheim', 586, 584).[95] As well, the story demonstrates the kind of Anglo–German exchange that Jameson, as far back as *Visits and Sketches*, extolled as a benefit to civilisation. As might be expected of an Oxonian proud of English freedom from government intrusion into Englishmen's lives, the narrator disdains the German ducal regulation that forbids grape harvest to begin so much as one day before the legal date fixed annually even if some vineyards have grown past optimal ripeness. As he mutters on hearing this detail, 'What a strange kind of paternal law' (572). He repeats the point in a later conversation with the inn owner Fritz Müller: 'What a paternal government! How does it know when the grapes will be ripe? Why cannot every man fix his own time for gathering his own grapes?' Instead of conceding his English guest's privilege to pass judgment on German custom, the innkeeper counters with a contextualised explanation and reminder of the limits of English practice:

> 'There are people employed by the government to examine the vines, and report when the grapes are ripe. It is necessary to make laws about it; for, as

you must have seen, there is nothing but the fear of the law to protect our vineyards and fruit-trees; there are no enclosures along the Berg-Strasse [mountain roadway], as you tell me you have in England; but, as people are only allowed to go into the vineyards on stated days, no one under pretence of gathering his own produce can stray into his neighbour's grounds and help himself without some of the Duke's foresters seeing him'. (580)

The narrator maintains his views and local allegiances, but this open exchange mediates – and moderates – his entrenched English assumptions: '"Well," said I, "to each country its own laws"' (580).

The mystery of Thekla's sorrow is ultimately revealed quietly rather than sensationally, yet in terms that resonate with 'The Grey Woman' and Gaskell's own family experiences. The fiancé, Franz Weber, was the son of the other town innkeeper who shared a close friendship with Thekla's father. The fathers promoted marriage between their children and Franz duly presented Thekla with a ring. But Franz, who grows ever more handsome as he nears adulthood, enjoys the notice he wins from other young women (569). When his father asks him to visit other hotels in Germany and Switzerland to learn more about the hotel business he will inherit, Franz takes up gambling, writing to Thekla for money when he needs help. Ultimately he writes the letter from Switzerland that causes Thekla's grief. He thanks her for the money she has already loaned him, then seeks her advice on 'the desirability of his marrying' a pretty young girl whose father is a prosperous shopkeeper, 'adding with coarse coxcombry his belief that he was not indifferent to the maiden herself' (568). The crisis comes when Franz turns up at Thekla's Heppenheim inn, bringing down upon her the severe judgement of Fritz Müller's sister against a young woman who without being engaged (Thekla hides the ring she still keeps) has attracted the notice of such a disreputable man. On her side, Thekla is shocked by startling changes in Franz, who is now seedy and shabby, and by news that Franz has not married after all and instead wants to marry Thekla and return to their home town. Facing unemployment on one hand and disillusion with a gambling, unfaithful, heavy-drinking man on the other, she is torn between the virtue of fidelity to love and her new repugnance for him. She vows never to marry and to leave Heppenheim immediately, going she knows not where.

The story's Anglo–German alliance resolves all. Because the narrator so readily welcomes conversation with Fritz Müller, he learns that the widowed innkeeper and father to the young Max, who is happiest in Thekla's arms, has fallen in love with Thekla not as a substitute mother or housekeeper but for herself. Indeed, he loves her sufficiently that he was willing – until the vagabond Franz showed up – to conspire with the narrator to help Thekla marry her first love. Conspiring with Müller anew, the Englishman sympathetically reasons Thekla out of her reluctance to be 'off with the old love and on with the new' until she realises that the higher virtue would be to bring happiness to herself, Müller, and Max. Unlike 'The Grey Woman', then, a cross-cultural alliance augments rather than destroys potential happiness in marriage in 'Heppenheim'.

A final convergence between 'Heppenheim' and 'Grey Woman' is less expected: both turn on gender reversals. If Amante was masculinised in 'Grey Woman', Gaskell's sympathetic male narrator is feminised.[96] Illness, in essence (like Rochester's disability in *Jane Eyre*), takes English masculinity down a notch so that the man learns the empathy and listening skills conventionally ascribed to women, shifting from an athletic, independent Oxonian to the confidante who provides emotional support to a young woman. He had at first brushed off Thekla's concerned inquiry whether he is ill, not wanting to be the object of a foreign female gaze when he was beginning to feel weak (561). He concedes later how dramatically his status has shifted: he is now 'weak as a new-born babe' (562) and is nursed along with Max by Thekla. When after his fever has broken the doctor and inn-owner ask if they should let family members in England know why his return is delayed, he is suddenly reminded of his father, mother, and sister, all dead, and begins to cry (563). He even asks Thekla to think of him as a mother after she resists help from him as a brother: 'tell me all about it, as you would to your mother if she were alive' (568). He gains influence over Thekla only through continued empathy and emotional support, not through masculine initiative and assertion.

Thekla for her part resembles the masculinised Amante, who is 'tall and handsome, though upwards of forty, and somewhat gaunt'.[97] The narrator first describes Thekla as

> a tall young woman, with a fine strong figure, a pleasant face, expressive of goodness and sense, and with a good deal of comeliness about it, too, although the fair complexion was bronzed and reddened by weather ... She had white teeth, however, and well-opened blue eyes – grave-looking eyes which had shed tears for past sorrow – plenty of light-brown hair, rather elaborately plaited, and fastened up by two great silver pins. (561)

Markedly gentle in manners and her care for Max and her English invalid, Thekla gains the Oxonian's notice with her strength more than her 'comeliness': 'She passed her arm under the pillow on which my head rested, and raised me a very little; her support was as firm as a man's could have been' (563–4). She is in fact the story's hero. She suffers and endures, seeking with unwavering honour to live by her commitments and take the consequences if she fails, working hard to help support her unworthy fiancé, nursing the narrator back to health, and then saving Max (who falls seriously ill near the story's end) with her unceasing care. Far more than Müller's abrasive sister, she ensures the smooth operation of the inn's daily services.

Skrine suggests that Schiller's Thekla in the *Death of Wallenstein* may be a source for Gaskell's character. He characterises Schiller's heroine as one who 'wins all hearts' and points to the paired names of Thekla and Max in 'Heppenheim' as further evidence of Schiller's precedent, since Schiller's Thekla loves the hero Max, who with her provides the moral centre of *Wallenstein*.[98] There is no evidence that Gaskell read Schiller's play, though Samuel Taylor Coleridge's 1800 translation was sufficiently well known for Jameson to posit Thekla as an illuminating counterpart to Shakespeare's Juliet in *Characteristics of Women*. As Jameson remarks,

> Thekla and Max in the Wallenstein [are] two angels of light amid the darkest and harshest, the most debased and revolting aspects of humanity ... I remember no dramatic character, conveying the same impression of singleness of purpose, and devotion of heart and soul [as Juliet], except the Thekla of Schiller's Wallenstein; she is the German Juliet ... the love of Thekla is more calm, and reposes more on itself ... The love of Thekla stands unalterable, and enduring as the rock.[99]

Of course Schiller's Thekla is a princess, Gaskell's an innkeeper's daughter working as a servant; Schiller's heroine dies tragically on her beloved's grave while Gaskell's finds happiness (and motherhood) in a marriage in a last-minute plot twist. If Gaskell was alluding to Schiller (or Jameson), she would thereby be associating elevated heroism with her lowly German maid – perhaps not a far-fetched notion for the author of *Cousin Phillis*. But this happy resolution occurs only because an Englishman is exploring Germany and German cultural practices with an open mind and learns to welcome friendships from those he meets. In teaching him the humanity of cultural others, the Germans act on him even as he acts to influence Thekla and assist the innkeeper's happiness in turn.

In her innovative representations of masculinity and femininity Gaskell, I suggest, was aided by her German settings and her own experiences abroad, which generated a kind of free space for imaginative play within the stories and distanced Gaskell from England and English assumptions.

Altogether Howitt, Anna Mary, and Gaskell represent fresh approaches to ethnoexocentrism and Anglo–German exchange within an array of genres. The range of their work, from children's literature to tales of cross-cultural marriage, representations of religious difference, and historical fiction, helps to indicate the rich literary creativity that could result from Anglo–German exchange and that residence abroad helped to foster.

CHAPTER 4

An Unbeliever in Germany
Marian Evans (George Eliot), 1854–1855

More ink has been expended on George Eliot (1819–80) than any other writer in this study. Even among those who have only casual interests in British literature, two things are widely known about this canonical author: she left England in 1854 with the married George Henry Lewes (1817–78) and lived openly with him until his death, and she was an agnostic who left organised religion to endorse an ethic of compassion and sympathy that she called the religion of humanity.[1] Rather than the canonical Eliot, I focus in this chapter, like Fionnuala Dillane, on the writer 'before George Eliot' – especially her first direct encounter with German culture in 1854–5. In her earliest German travels with Lewes she was 'Miss Evans' since 'George Eliot' did not yet exist and Lewes's German circle of writers and intellectuals knew that he was married to the former Agnes Jervis.[2] As late as September 1857 Lewes still referred to 'Miss Evans' in letters to German correspondents, and his partner signed herself 'Marian Evans' in the notes she enclosed in Lewes's.[3] Her first visit to Germany has received extensive attention from Eliot scholars, especially Gerlinde Röder-Bolton, who traces Evans's travels and the multiple cultural contexts in which these unfolded.[4] Generally scholars have emphasised the impact of Evans's first encounter with German culture on George Eliot's later thought and writing.

A rather different picture emerges when Jameson's, the Howitts', and Gaskell's sojourns in Germany are juxtaposed to Evans's. Like Jameson, Evans began her most important encounter with Germany in Weimar, where she resided with Lewes from 2 August to 3 November 1854. They arrived in Weimar after following a tourist itinerary through Belgium and the Rhine valley (where she and Lewes breakfasted in Cologne with David Friedrich Strauss, whose *Das Leben Jesu* Evans had translated in 1846), making a two-day stop in Frankfurt so that Lewes could visit Johann von Goethe's birthplace in preparation for a biography.[5] After leaving Weimar the couple settled in Berlin from 3 November 1854 to 11 March 1855.[6]

In 1858 Evans and Lewes would return to Germany, staying in Munich from 7 April to 7 July. The day after arrival, Evans was reading Anna Mary Howitt's *An Art-Student in Munich* and soon also visited the Glyptothek.[7] From Munich, the couple travelled on to Prague and then Dresden, where Evans sat before Raphael's *Sistine Madonna* with Lewes at her side and responded as reverently to the painting as Jameson had in 1834: 'all other art seems only a preparation for feeling the superiority of the Madonna di San Sisto the more', she wrote to Sara Hennell.[8]

But despite such overlapping moments, the divergences between Evans's earliest German experiences and those of the Victorian women writers discussed in Chapters 2 and 3 are striking. First and perhaps most telling, she did not travel to Germany or reside there alone, as Jameson did often. Mary and Anna Mary Howitt arrived with William Howitt in Germany, but when he left to arrange publication details in England, mother and daughter along with the younger Howitt children fended for themselves in Heidelberg, as Anna Mary did in Munich after Jane Benham returned to England in 1850. And Gaskell's 1858 residence in Heidelberg (soon after Evans's departure from Munich) was spouseless as well.

In contrast, even as 'George Eliot' this writer never travelled alone in Germany. From 1854 to 1878, the year of his death, she travelled with Lewes. On her last trip to Germany – to Munich via Innsbruck, Augsburg, Stuttgart, Wildbad, and Baden before heading to France and then home – she travelled as Mrs Cross, escorted by her new husband. When John W. Cross, formerly the financial adviser and manager for both Eliot and Lewes, had to be fished out of a canal in Venice and fell ill, Cross's older brother Willie joined the pair and stayed almost a month until they were comfortably settled at a spa in Wildbad and 'Johnnie' had largely recovered.[9]

The sixty-year-old bride, an international celebrity author who knew Continental literature and art so much better than her businessman-husband twenty years younger, had far more agency on this last visit. Lewes and Eliot had never visited the spa town of Wildbad, so Eliot might have suggested this stop for her honeymoon.[10] But the more likely source was Willie Cross, since Eliot referred to Willie's knowledge of German spas worth visiting in a mid-July 1880 letter to Lewes's son Charles.[11] The point remains: unlike Jameson or Anna Mary Howitt, this canonical woman writer never experienced the kind of immersion in German culture that forced her to negotiate cultural exchange directly. Nor did she articulate a vision of female cosmopolitanism as Jameson did or explore cross-cultural exchange in her fiction in the same depth as the Howitts and

Gaskell – though she placed Gwendolen Harleth in a German gambling casino at the outset of *Daniel Deronda*.[12] Paradoxically, on her first German visit in 1854–5, the woman willing to waive belief in legal marriage until 1880 most closely resembled conventional traveller-wives, including 'Mrs Gaskell' on her initial trip to Germany with husband William in 1841.

This matters a great deal. Lewes was adept at living in Germany on German terms. He had resided in Germany and Vienna from August 1838 to July 1839, when he met Varnhagen von Ense and others in Berlin through the offices of Carlyle, who had nurtured his developing interests in German philosophy and culture.[13] As Lewes commented in 1841, Carlyle's letter of introduction was a 'patent for cordial reception' throughout Germany, which enabled him to form a German social network (as Jameson had with her female friends in Weimar and Cologne).[14] He also later claimed to have met Liszt in Vienna.[15] Perhaps most crucially, by living alone in Germany, surrounded by Germans, Lewes acquired fluency in German, a crucial linguistic skill that he deepened when he visited Berlin again in 1845 and reconnected with Varnhagen von Ense; he then also met writer Adolf Stahr (1805–76) and German novelist Fanny Lewald (1811–89).[16] In 1854 Lewes was therefore making his third trip to Germany, in contrast to Evans's first. Knowledgeable in travel routes and German customs, able to speak readily with railway or hotel clerks and porters as well as former acquaintances, Lewes naturally became the first point of contact between the travelling couple and anyone they encountered. Evans did not bring so much as a guidebook to consult, instead relying entirely on Lewes.[17] Lewes's earlier network and the new letters of introduction he brought (written specifically for *him*) also meant that everyone the couple met or socialised with were his contacts. In sum, virtually all that Evans saw or experienced in 1854–5 was filtered through Lewes.

There was good reason for this. Though Evans had already translated two very demanding texts by Strauss and Feuerbach before setting foot on German soil, she knew German as an expert reader, not a speaker. Lacking the ability to speak and comprehend others' spoken German rapidly enough to engage in conversation, she was often rendered mute in larger gatherings, a further inducement to silence and retreat rather than active exchange with German speakers. Of course being the gifted intellectual that she was, Evans deliberately set to work on her listening and speaking skills, going to the theatre with Lewes to practise listening to the language and, under the kind encouragement of acquaintance Adolf Schöll

(1805–82), Director of the Art Institute in Weimar (to whom Lewes had an introduction from Strauss), practised German conversation with him.[18]

Still, she was largely insulated from the culture in which she resided, and the painful knowledge that she and Lewes had become the objects of scandalous gossip back in England intensified this tendency. The nature of the gossip is clear in the 15 October letter Evans wrote to John Chapman, her *Westminster Review* editor: 'We have been told of a silly story about a "message" sent by me "in a letter to Miss Martineau" which letter has been shown at the Reform Club. It is hardly necessary to tell you that I have had no communication with Miss Martineau, and that if I had, she is one of the last persons to whom I should speak as to a confidante.'[19] The speed of spreading rumours is indicated by a 15 November letter to Charles Bray (1811–84), Evans's longtime Coventry friend, from phrenologist George Combe (1788–1858). In 1852 Combe and Evans were friendly enough that she stayed with him and his wife in Edinburgh before travelling on to Ambleside for a briefer visit with Martineau.[20] Now Combe wrote to Bray,

> The conclusion, then, is irresistible that the reports are too true. – They are spread everywhere, and we now meet them in society. We are deeply mortified and distressed; and I should like to know whether there is insanity in Miss Evans's family ... an educated woman who, in the face of the world, volunteers to live as a wife, with a man who already has a living wife and children, appears to me to pursue a course and to set an example calculated only to degrade herself and her sex, if she be sane.[21]

The still-living wife was the sticking point that also led Jameson to repudiate Eliot in a 15 March 1856 letter to Goethe. After confirming the story about Evans and Lewes (which Goethe appears not to have known in 1854), Jameson explained that she had interacted with Evans before her elopement; after praising Evans's intellect and ability she concluded, 'I do not well understand how a good and conscientious woman can run away with another woman's husband.'[22]

It was due to Jameson's and Evans's shared contacts that news of the Lewes–Evans relationship reached London so soon after the couple left England – through Robert Noel, cousin to Lady Byron, who, it will be recalled, gave Jameson a letter of introduction to Goethe in 1833. Evans had met Noel at the home of Barbara Leigh Smith on 6 December 1852; and on 23 June 1853 Jameson and Noel twice called on Evans but found her away from home.[23] By chance, Noel was on the same boat to Antwerp as Evans and Lewes, and he did not hesitate to let others know that he had seen the unmarried pair together.[24] This gave Evans further reasons to be cautious about reaching out to Germans, for she never knew who had been told her story and what they thought.[25]

The Germans in Lewes's network were far less troubled by two unmarried persons cohabiting than George Combe and his associates. Unsurprisingly, Evans and Lewes enjoyed a warm relationship in Weimar with Liszt and his unmarried companion Princess Wittgenstein, and in Berlin with Adolf Stahr, still married to another woman, and Fanny Lewald.[26] Both Adolf Schöll and his wife, moreover, welcomed Evans as well as Lewes in Weimar.[27] Still, if James Marshall, private secretary of the Grand Duchess Sophie, was quite friendly with Evans and called repeatedly on the couple in Weimar, he never invited Evans to meet his wife or to visit their home.[28] That Lewes went out so often alone to dine at the home of Marquis Ferrière de Vayal, the French ambassador in Weimar who was married to the former Mlle Roederer, also suggests that Evans was not invited; like Marshall, the Marquis called on Lewes and Evans several times, but always alone.[29] Evans was also absent when Lewes was invited to present himself at Court by Grand Duke Karl Alexander in September, which went unmentioned in Evans's journal. Lewes, in contrast, crowed after the fact in a 27 September 1854 letter to his sons:

> The other day the Grand Duke sent word that he should be glad to see me at his summer palace. As I had never paid a visit to a crowned head before I felt very uncomfortable lest I should not behave myself according to strict *etiquette*. How should you have felt, Charley? – However the Grand Duke at once made me feel at home, and except that I called him 'Royal Highness,' I did not behave otherwise than I should to any gentleman whom I might visit for the first time. He was very kind to me, and begged me not to hesitate to ask him any service I might desire. He has a just regard for the English. When the Grand Duchess comes to Weimar he is to present me to her.[30]

In 1836 Jameson had also been presented at court and was given a private audience with the former Grand Duchess Maria Pavlovna, yet another outgrowth of her close friendship with Goethe and, in consequence, Goethe's mother Henriette von Pogwisch, a Weimar lady of the court.[31] But without such contacts, Evans spent the day alone.

In 1854 Goethe herself was residing principally in Vienna, but she returned to Weimar while Lewes and Evans were there, shuttling between Weimar and Berlin while negotiating the rights of descendants in the publication of Johann von Goethe's complete works.[32] Lewes had no letter of introduction to her so had to take the initiative and wrote the following on 10 August:

> It is a great and unexpected pleasure to me to hear of your return to Weimar as I may now hope for the fulfillment of a desire formed fifteen years ago

when my friends Madam Betty Beer and Varnhagen von Ense so often spoke to me of you – the desire of making your personal acquaintance. You will understand that desire when I add that not only have German and English friends frequently spoken of you but that I have been many years occupied writing a *Life of Goethe*, and must necessarily therefore be interested in one so near and dear to him as yourself. When en route for Weimar our friend Mr Robert Noel told me you were in Italy; but yesterday I learned of your arrival and hastened to write to ask if it would be disagreeable to you to allow me to pay my respects?

Pray excuse the want of formality of this note, but indeed I cannot write like a mere stranger to one towards whom I do not feel like a stranger. In spite of your acquaintance with English literature I dare not hope that my name has reached you and am forced therefore to back myself by friends.[33]

The letter skilfully drops the name of Varnhagen von Ense, with whom Goethe remained in touch – visiting him in Berlin the following month, in fact.[34] Lewes then speaks of Goethe's dear friend Noel in the casual way only someone who was well-acquainted with him would. But above all, Lewes gives Goethe a compelling personal reason to meet because he was writing the first English-language biography of Johann von Goethe, which would bring further attention to and enhance demand for his works, which Goethe and her sons were negotiating to publish.

The letter says nothing of his household companion Marian Evans, however. And so it was that Lewes went alone to meet Goethe and to receive permission to view Johann von Goethe's study and the bedroom in which he died, a space off limits to most visitors. Evans in consequence never met Goethe herself.[35] Whether Goethe explicitly gave permission to Lewes to bring an unnamed companion is unknown. Certainly Evans's June 1855 travel essay on Weimar for *Fraser's Magazine* implies that she was present:

> it is a sad pity that Goethe's study, bedroom, and library, so fitted to call up ... sympathy, because they are preserved just as he left them, should be shut out from all but the specially privileged. We were happy enough to be amongst these, – to look through the mist of rising tears at the dull study with its two small windows, and without a single object chosen for the sake of luxury or beauty; at the dark little bedroom with the bed on which he died, and the arm-chair where he took his morning coffee as he read; at the library with its common deal shelves, and books containing his own paper marks.[36]

No mention is made of 'her in whose arms he died', so central a presence in Jameson's description of the same scene twenty years earlier.[37] Evans's only reference to the female Goethe, in fact, is not a complimentary one:

'It is to be regretted that a large sum offered for this house by the German Diet, was refused by the Goethe family in the hope, it is said, of obtaining a still larger sum from that mythical English Crœsus always ready to turn fabulous sums into dead capital, who haunts the imagination of continental people.'[38]

Nor did the daughter-in-law figure as more than a twice-mentioned sidelight in Lewes's 1855 biography. In noting the marriage of the great man's son, Lewes termed her 'the gayest and most brilliant of the Weimar circle' who 'became a privileged favourite' with her father-in-law, so that in his final days 'The name of Ottilie was frequently on his lips' and she was by his side at his death.[39] Goethe recorded no response to her appearance in Lewes's book but, as the first to have heard Johann von Goethe read aloud Part II of *Faust*, she resented his judgement that the continuation 'in both conception and execution [was] an elaborate mistake'.[40] After that August 1854 encounter Goethe and Lewes never saw each again. And Lewes made so little impression on her that she did not mention him in her letter ten days later to Jameson, only her hope of seeing Noel in Dresden to get his advice on her family affairs.[41]

Evans's sceptical gaze at the Goethe family also extended to Germans generally in her journal: 'during the whole seven months of our stay in Germany we never heard one witticism or even one felicitous idea or expression from a German!'[42] It bespeaks one consequence of her limited ability to form friendships or exchange views with Germans that might otherwise have been a first step toward ethnoexocentrism. Both Röder-Bolton and the editors of Eliot's journals comment on the narrow, naïve, and at times highly negative impressions of Germany that Evans registered on this first trip.[43] Like so many more conventional English travellers, Evans was offended by lurking German stenches, and she disliked German beds (a matter of genuine concern on what amounted to a honeymoon trip). Röder-Bolton is particularly acute on Evans's susceptibility to racial stereotyping, as when Eliot noted that in Adolf Schöll 'there is no German heaviness either in his appearance or his mind'. Noting that in fact Schöll was Austrian, Röder-Bolton suggests that Evans's quick impulse to type him and others racially points to her participation in Victorian 'preoccupation with cultural identity and racial difference'. Nor was Evans always sensitive to class difference. Evans and Lewes once jumped to the conclusion that their coach companion was a grocer when he turned out to be a government official.[44] In later years of course Eliot's perceptions would expand, but her reactions in that first visit were predicated on her relative insulation from German culture at large in all its diversity.

She also perceived gender in surprisingly narrow terms: for Evans, Germany was a male-centred country, the home of the great man Johann von Goethe and the living men in her immediate circles in Weimar and Berlin. To be sure, she responded warmly in private to Princess Wittgenstein and appears to have had a cordial relationship with Madame Schöll, but as Cheri Hoeckley observes, Evans's July 1855 *Fraser's* essay on 'Liszt, Wagner and Weimar' 'remains completely silent about the princess'.[45] This essay did, however, note with appreciation the freedom of Weimar women to attend the theatre or concerts by themselves, the cultural difference that had struck Jameson, Barbara Leigh Smith, and Florence Nightingale before her.[46] Evans's anonymous book reviews suggest as well how much more readily she sought out German men's thoughts and conversations than women's, though this may partly have resulted from her editors' preferences. She reviewed Adolf Stahr's multivolume *Torso* three times in addition to Edward Vehse's memoir of the Austrian court and Otto Gruppe's book on German philosophy – not to mention Lewes's own Goethe biography, which she reviewed for the *Leader*, Lewes's former periodical.[47]

Her other journalism mentioned German women writers briefly or not at all. Novelist Henriette von Paalzow, whose *Citizen of Prague* was translated by Mary Howitt in 1846 and whose translated novel *Jacob van der Néess* (originally *Jakob van der Rees*) was serialised in *Ainsworth's Magazine* 1849–50, came in for a single sentence in Evans's notice of 'a small volume entitled "Ein Schriftsteller-Leben [a writer's life]"'. In her first of two reviews of Edward Vehse's work Evans also mentioned in passing Caroline Pichler.[48] And though Evans proposed an essay on German women to John Chapman, which he turned down, this was to have focused only on German women's historical development, 'not simply the modern German woman, who is not a very fertile subject'.[49]

More unexpected still are her comments and silences about women in two of her three reviews of Heinrich Heine's work. Heine's European cosmopolitanism, religious scepticism, and frank references to sexuality were contentious in Britain, which raised the stakes of discussing his work. But progressive women writers tended to welcome him: Mary Howitt translated some of his lyrics in the 1840s, and Heine was a key Jewish precursor for Amy Levy in the 1880s. Evans's own representations of women in discussing him were uneven. In 'German Wit' (1856) Evans noted Heine's 'profound admiration and regard' for Rahel, to whom he dedicated the 'Heimkehr' or homecoming section of *Buch der Lieder* (book of songs) (1827). She added that Heine's early Berlin network also included 'the poetess Elise von Hohenhausen, the translator of Byron', who swiftly recognised Heine's talent.[50] Yet she ended her essay-review by quoting without comment Heine's belittlement of women authors and Countess Hahn-Hahn in particular: 'O the women! ... When they write, they have always one eye on the paper and the other on a man; and this is true of all authoresses, except the Countess Hahn-Hahn, who has only one eye.'[51] Similarly, in Evans's review of reminiscences of Heine by Alfred Meissner in the 23 August 1856 *Leader*, Evans quotes Meissner's contention (in a passage she translated) that 'Heine had a true horror of a learned and strong-minded woman, a blue-stocking, and a feminine reasoner'; but she did not point out Meissner's own inconsistency in remarking that 'in the very last months Heine was soothed by the visits of a new friend, a young lady of "unusual intellectual powers"'.[52] In this review Evans did, however, dare to talk about extra-legal marital unions sympathetically, presenting the words as Meissner's rather than her own:

> 'He had lived several years with his wife – Crescence Mathilde Mirat was her full name – without being married to her. It was one of those unions which are so frequent in Paris that they are almost legitimized in the eyes of the world, and are called *mènages Parisiens*. Innumerable are the marriages of this kind, especially among artists; the woman enjoys all the rights of a legitimate wife ...'[53]

This was in the spirit of Heine as well as her own example.

Since Evans's public silences about or dismissals of German women could be explained by a periodical's 'house style' or audience expectations, it is especially useful to compare her reviews to responses to women in her private journal and letters.[54] There is in truth little difference between them: her private journal also generally focused on the men she met or talked to rather than the women. Even when she noted having seen or talked with a woman, she rarely provided details. Of 29 September in Weimar, she merely recorded, 'the Princess Wittgenstein called and chatted pleasantly'.[55] She mentioned meeting women more frequently in Berlin, where she and Lewes often attended the salon of Henriette Solmar (1794–1888), a distant relative of Rahel's who had known the more famous salonnière and like her was a Christian convert.[56] Evans clearly liked Solmar, finding her 'extremely agreeable' in one entry and noting a 'pleasant evening' at her salon in another. And in Evans's unpublished 'Recollections of Berlin' she elaborated,

> Fräulein Solmar is a remarkably accomplished woman, probably between fifty and sixty, but of that agreeable *Wesen* [nature] which is so free from

anything startling in person or manner and so at home in everything one can talk of, that you think of her simply as a delightful presence, and not as a woman of any particular age. She converses perfectly in French, well in English and well also, as we were told, in Italian. There is not the slightest warmth of manner or expression in her, but always the same even cheerfulness and intelligence – in fact she is the true type of the mistress of the salon.[57]

It would have been illuminating to know what Evans and Solmar discussed, but that remains unmentioned.

Through Varnhagen, who had recognised Lewes when he and Evans walked out into the city two days after arrival in Berlin, they also met his niece Ludmilla Assing (1821–80), a writer and translator who in 1857 published a biography of her friend Countess Elise von Ahlefeldt (1788–1855), another salonnière who had been divorced by her military husband due to her long affair with a writer.[58] Assing loaned her own copy of Heine's poems to Evans as she and Lewes left Varnhagen's 'coffee' on 9 November, thus inspiring Evans's steady reading of Heine's works during the rest of her Berlin residence. Evans and Assing had much in common and were roughly of an age, but Evans merely mentions Assing's name before passing on in her journal, either because she had not asked Assing about her writing career and the people she knew or did not consider her comments worthy of note. Here, by way of contrast, is a journal excerpt from 24 November, when sculptor Christian Rauch called on her and Lewes: 'In the evening Rauch, the sculptor came – the finest old man I ever saw and the most charming. His head is noble, his features harmonious and his expression extremely winning. He told us many interesting things about Goethe whom he knew well, and thoroughly agreed with G's quotation from Jung Stilling.'[59]

Of other women Evans had even less to say. One night when she and Lewes called at Solmar's salon, they 'found only a small knot of insignificant women', while her 10 May 1858 letter to Sara Hennell expressed impatience at being stuck with Bavarian women on social occasions:

> It is quite an exception to meet with a woman who seems to expect any sort of companionship from the men, and I shudder at the sight of a woman in society, for I know I shall have to sit on the sofa with her all the evening listening to her stupidities, while the men on the other side of the table are discussing all the subjects I care to hear about.[60]

Even Evans's extended exchanges with the novelist and travel writer Fanny Lewald (1811–89), likewise living with a married man, are largely effaced in the journal though she and Evans would seem to have had so much in common. Lewald had been part of the Goethe–Schopenhauer–Mertens-Schaaffhausen circle since the mid-1840s and might have helped link Evans to a vibrant female intellectual network akin to what Evans had enjoyed in London prior to eloping with Lewes. This same Goethe–Schopenhauer–Mertens-Schaaffhausen network had brought Lewald and her married lover Stahr together in Rome when they were 'formally introduced' at 'one of Mertens-Schaaffhausen's gatherings' late in November 1845. Through this salon attended by a cross-section of the Roman intelligentsia – scholars, diplomats, papal administrators, European visitors, artists, and writers – Lewald also met Goethe and Adele Schopenhauer. Lewald at first found the Goethe name intimidating, but Ottilie von Goethe soon revealed herself as the same 'high-spirited and warm-hearted friend' that had captivated Jameson.[61]

Lewald, then, might have introduced Evans to female-centred intellectual circles, but this remained an untapped possibility. Lewald had travelled to England and Scotland in 1850 and developed a lasting friendship with Geraldine Jewsbury, Jane Carlyle's closest friend.[62] Perhaps Lewald's English connections, including Anna Jameson (whom Lewald met in 1850), made Evans nervous given the rumours back home.[63] And Lewald's recent writing success with her novel *Wandlungen* (Changes) (1853), which follows several characters against the backdrop of European revolutions from 1830 to 1848, might have intimidated the younger, as yet unfledged novelist.[64] Evans read *Wandlungen* by 1 December 1854 before attending the 'coffee' of Varnhagen on 4 December, where Stahr and Lewald were present. Of this evening Evans's journal tersely recorded, 'I talked principally with Prof. Stahr, about German style, Lessing, Spinoza, History of Jesus etc.'[65]

In 'Recollections of Berlin', written later, Evans did go into greater depth in describing her relationship with Lewald:

> Professor Stahr [was] pale, nervous, sickly looking, with scarcely any moral radiation, so to speak. Fanny Lewald, whom he married whilst we were at Berlin, after nine years of waiting, is a Jewish looking woman, of soft voice and friendly manners. She seems to have caught or to have naturally something of the literary egoism which is almost ludicrously prominent in Professor Stahr, but, this apart, she is an agreeable person.[66]

Possibly 'literary egoism' was in the eye of the beholder.

Evans's comment on the Jewish appearance of Lewald, who had converted to Christianity as a young adult, is also noteworthy, since she did not similarly comment about this when it came to her other ethnically Jewish German friends, including Solmar. In light of her later reputed philosemitism in *Daniel Deronda*, Evans's orientation towards the Jews whom she knew, read, or wrote about during and after her first visit to Germany is additionally important for assessing her encounters with cultural difference.[67] Several of her private comments register receptivity to Jews, an orientation that expanded as she developed her career.[68] Several scholars reference Evans's amused disapproval of overt anti-Semitism when Otto Gruppe's wife and sister-in-law spouted virulent attacks after Lewes acted Shakespeare's Shylock one evening: 'I was amused to see that the young women's feeling towards the Jews was not much above that of Gratiano and so on. Frau Gruppe when running through the wonderful speech "Hath not a Jew eyes" etc turned round to us and said "They don't feel – they don't care how they are used."'[69] Lewes and Evans continued to see the Gruppe couple, however. Later Evans's responses to racial difference were more overtly positive. When she and Lewes visited Prague's Jewish cemetery and synagogue in 1858, she recorded a distinctly sympathetic response, noting the curious shapes of tombs and singling out compelling Jews: 'We saw a lovely dark eyed Jewish child here, which we were glad to kiss in all its dirt. Then came the somber old synagogue with its smoked groins, and lamp for ever burning. An intelligent Jew was our cicerone and read us some Hebrew out of the precious old book of the Law.'[70]

Her published reviews and essays were less affirming. In these she tended to erase Jewishness from any acquaintaince or author she admired and at times her remarks verged on anti-Semitism. To be sure, she had to conform to a periodical's house style, and anti-Semitism was pervasive in British culture. Still, her silences and occasional belittlements seem gratuitous. For example, her first review of Heine in the *Leader* opened with unprompted racial slurs that implied a Jew could not truly be German, nor for that matter a German witty (this last a private opinion also recorded in her 'Recollections of Berlin'):

> Nature one day resolved to make a witty German. But as this supreme paradox was not to be achieved all at once, it happened that in the ardour of a great purpose she mistook Hebrew blood for German, and while she was busy adding the wit, allowed the best moral qualities of the German to slip out of her hands. So, instead of the witty Teuton she intended, she would have produced merely a Voltairian Jew speaking the German language, if she had not, perceiving her mistake before it was too late, superadded, as some compensation for the want of *morale*, a passionate heart blending its emotions with the most delicate and imaginative sensibility to the beauties of earth and sky, and a supreme lyrical genius, which could weave the wit, and the passion, and the imagination into songs light and lovely as the rainbows on the spray of the summer torrent.[71]

When, in the remainder of the review, Evans called Heine's lyric (if not his moral) power equal to that of Johann von Goethe's, the word 'Jew' disappeared, enabling a discussion of Heine separate from his ethnic origins.

Assessing the treatment of Jewishness in Evans's more significant essay, 'German Wit: Heinrich Heine' in the January 1856 *Westminster Review*, requires some understanding of Heine's reputation and reception in Britain at the time. John Rignall's claim that Eliot 'was instrumental in making Heine known in Britain' is dubious: Heine was already well known to English readers from translations dating to the late 1820s and 1830s and critical notices beginning in the 1830s.[72] Moreover, Evans published anonymously, and digitised databases of Victorian periodicals give no indication that Evans's essay was cited by others following publication. 'German Wit' became known as a significant critical essay only when it was identified as by 'George Eliot' in her posthumously published *Essays and Leaves from a Note-book* (1884). The essay's impact after 1884 is clear, but not before.

Still, Evans's four reviews of Heine in 1855 and 1856 helped clear a space for Heine's emergence as a major literary figure in the 1860s. She did so by intervening in two problems Heine's work posed for English readers in the 1850s. The first was Heine's brazen defiance of decorum.[73] Even Abraham Hayward's 1835 review of Heine commented in closing that the reviewer had been forced to '*mutilate* some of the passages which seemed to us deserving of quotation'.[74] It was a charge repeated in a two-part survey of Heine's life and works in *Tait's Edinburgh Magazine* five years before 'German Wit' appeared. If reporting that Heine's 'very detractors are at length resigned to admiration', the *Tait's* reviewer still was forced to concede that his prose works sparkling with wit and evincing brilliant diction 'are full of trifling and gross frivolity – so much so, that they can never come before the English public in the shape of a translation of Henry Heine's works'.[75] Conceding Heine's 'want of *morale*' in her own review of his poems, Evans coupled this want with the virtues of 'a passionate heart blending its emotions with the most delicate and imaginative sensibility' and 'lyrical genius'.[76] Her 1855 review thus augmented other attempts to mediate Heine's standing in the English press.

Evans's 'German Wit' continued to reframe Heine's reputation for English audiences in additional ways. First, she elevated Heine's cultural status while also showcasing her own intellect and commanding prose style. She began by theorising wit and humour, arguing that humour is deeply affirming and human, thus strongly linked to poetry, whereas wit is razor sharp and quicksilver, even sometimes pitiless and cruel in its unexpected reversals of thought, and is thus aligned with intellect. Linking this distinction to a stadial Enlightenment theory of civilisation's progress, she regarded humour as universal, found even among rude or barbaric peoples, whereas wit could be found only in later stages of development, relying as it did on intellect, tact, and taste. Anticipating Matthew Arnold's characterisation of the function of criticism in his 1864 essay, Evans then argued that wit, even if sometimes expressed in attacks, was crucial to intellectual progress because it deflated naïve sentimentality and refreshed thought and writing by calling into question cultural assumptions that threatened to become dogmas or encouraged self-satisfied emotion.[77] In so arguing, she was granting to Heine, hitherto an outlaw figure, a major role in world letters that would allow her to place him alongside, rather than in opposition to, the great man of letters Johann von Goethe.

To create sympathy for Heine, as she would for her flawed protagonists in her later fiction, Evans also adopted Lewes's method in his biography of Johann von Goethe, weaving together the life and literary works to construct the complex whole of a multifaceted human subject who was also an 'artist in prose literature'. She noted Heine's anguish and lingering guilt at having caused the death of a childhood playmate when the youth followed Heine's suggestion that he rescue a drowning kitten, pointed out Heine's later resistance to cultural stereotypes when he visited England even though he was appalled by so much in English culture, indicated his escape from threatened imprisonment in Germany because of his progressive political beliefs, and, as did almost all other accounts of Heine, narrated his imprisonment on his 'Matratzengruft' (mattress grave) in his last years of life, unable to rise or even open both eyes unaided.[78] If he was sometimes licentious or irreverent to the point of blasphemy or offence, Heine's composite life and works suggested on the whole a deeply sympathetic man and artist of great depth and tenderness whose scepticism and fellow-feelings combined to create great art.

But if the fully rounded character she fashioned generated receptivity to Heine among *Westminster Review*'s progressive readers, Evans's portrait did not eliminate a second challenge that Heine posed to English audiences: his Jewish identity. Fully to embrace Heine's Jewishness while ranking Heine as the near-equal of the great Johann von Goethe was to threaten or at least radically qualify white British assumptions that Christian Anglo-Saxon culture was superior to 'Oriental' Jewish culture. Making the case for Heine's universal appeal, moreover, sat ill with specifying his ethnic and religious divergence from mainstream English culture. Evans responded to this second challenge by systematically erasing Heine's Jewish origins in her essay and treating him as part of a larger Christian communal tradition (if one that also generated humane, Christian-influenced scepticism). In contrast to her opening paragraph in the *Leader* carefully distinguishing Hebrew from German blood, her *Westminster* essay-review termed Heine German, backtracked to concede partial Jewish heritage, then erased his Jewishness altogether:

> HEINRICH HEINE [is] a German born with the present century, who, to Teutonic imagination, sensibility, and humour, adds an amount of *esprit* that would make him brilliant among the most brilliant of Frenchmen. True, this unique German wit is half a Hebrew; but he and his ancestors spent their youth in German air, and were reared on *Wurst* and *Sauerkraut*, so that he is as much a German as a pheasant is an English bird, or a potato an Irish vegetable. But whatever else he may be, Heine is one of the most remarkable men of this age: no echo, but a real voice, and therefore, like all genuine things in this world, worth studying.[79]

Laudation was Evans's end point in this introduction of Heine's name, but reducing Jewish Germans (or their half-Jewish offspring) to essentialist animal and vegetable types entered dangerous ground. Her analogy to the Irish potato easily summoned kindred racial stereotypes, since 'Celtic' Irish people were seen as 'other' and less than Anglo-Saxons; and because the potato reference summoned up the recent Irish famine, it also implied the shared suffering of Irish and Jewish peoples.

Her separation of Heine from Jewishness relied on the very different claim that Heine's mother 'was not of Hebrew, but of Teutonic blood', an especially sensitive point since Jewish identity is traced through the mother rather than father.[80] To be fair, Eliot was not the first English writer to assert this. The 1851 *Tait's Edinburgh Magazine* asserted,

> Young Henry Heine ... lived in a dense atmosphere of tradition, scandal, and – garlic. For his father was a Jew, while his mother belonged to a poor Christian family ... Bred up in the Protestant faith as he was, but painfully sensitive of his descent from the hated Hebrew race, he seemed anxious to assert his Christianity and to conceal a parentage which exposed him to contempt and scorn.[81]

Nothing of the kind was true. Heine's mother, as Jeffrey Sammons explains, was 'Peira van Geldern (1771–1859), known to everyone as Betty, [who] came from a family of considerable standing in the German Jewish community'. Her father and brother were physicians, and her grandfather had been 'a wealthy court Jew' who served as 'a financial advisor to the ducal court of Jülich-Berg, of which Düsseldorf [where Heine grew up] was the chief city'. Sammons also explains how such dramatic misunderstanding of Heine's identity could emerge, tracing it to none other than Heine himself, who occasionally 'hint[ed]' that the family name was not 'van Geldern' but 'von Geldern', which would imply descent from German aristocrats.[82] And German nobles were exclusively Christian. Heine did not actively mislead others about his descent, but he was evasive, as a check of his German passage describing his early years in Düsseldorf in his *Reisebilder* indicates. For rather than writing out van Geldern, he wrote 'v. Geldern', leaving it to others to presume what 'v.' stood for. And Evans presumed it stood for 'von'.[83]

At least Evans, unlike the *Tait's* reviewer, did not link Heine's ostensibly divided heritage to garlic and self-hatred. But her apparent dislike of Heine's birth name ('Harry, for that was his baptismal name, which he afterwards had the good taste to change') seems tinged with cultural revulsion. She followed this expression with her translation of the humorous passage in *Reisebilder* that mocked German Jews and applied the word 'crucify' to Heine's treatment by other Jews, as if Heine were radically distanced from them: 'With Hebrew it went somewhat better, for I had always a great liking for the Jews, though to this very hour they crucify my good name; but I could never get on so far in Hebrew as my watch, which had much familiar intercourse with pawnbrokers, and in this way contracted many Jewish habits – for example, it wouldn't go on Saturdays.'[84]

Because Evans presumes that Heine received Christian baptism at birth, she must work around his conversion to Christianity as a young man, a crux in almost all interpretations of Heine's life and career. Instead, she turns 'conversion' into an act of pragmatism and community-building (note the word 'united'): 'It was apparently during this residence in Berlin that Heine united himself with the Lutheran Church. He would willingly, like many of his friends, he tells us, have remained free from all ecclesiastical ties if the authorities there had not forbidden residence in Prussia, and especially in Berlin, to every one who did not belong to one of the positive religions recognised by the State.' Evans left 'positive' undefined, but it clearly excluded the Jewish faith.[85] In the remainder of her essay, 'conversion' arose only in Christian contexts, first when she discussed Heine's rumoured conversion to Catholicism when he married: 'in deference to the sentiments of his wife, [he] married according to the rites of the Catholic Church. On this fact busy rumour afterwards founded the story of his conversion to Catholicism.' Later, she noted his reorientation towards theism when confined to his mattress-grave, when 'Catholics and

Protestants by turns claim[ed] him as a convert', another 'charge' against which Heine's agnostic reviewer defended him.[86] The only other time the word 'Jew' appeared after the essay's early pages, in contrast, was in another translated Heine excerpt in which 'Jew' referred not to Heine's family or personal identity but to Jesus as the successor to Homeric gods:

> Then suddenly approached, panting, a pale Jew, with drops of blood on his brow, with a crown of thorns on his head, and a great cross laid on his shoulders; and he threw the cross on the high table of the gods, so that the golden cups tottered, and the gods became dumb and pale, and grew ever paler, till they at last melted away into vapour.

Rather than a deracinated Jew, Evans's Heine is a Gallicised German and, according to another Heine passage she translated, 'a Hellene – sensuous, realistic, exquisitely alive to the beautiful'.[87]

Having erased Heine's Jewish identity, Evans could wholly commend him to the journal's readers as a free-thinking, transnational great artist in prose whose captious wit dislodged reified ideas and simultaneously sounded an extraordinary range of tones and emotions in exquisite diction. Recommending a Jew to English audiences as Johann von Goethe's literary successor in 1856 would have been a very hard go, especially coupled with his reputation for scurrilous obscenity.

Yet the degree of Evans's misreporting of Heine's Jewish roots on which her commendation depended remains surprising. On the very night Ludmilla Assing loaned her a copy of Heine's poems in Berlin, she read aloud Heine's ballad 'Donna Clara'.[88] The title refers to the anti-Semitic princess who, when her unknown knight asks for her love, swears her love by the Saviour whom the Jews murdered (*'Bei dem Heiland sei's geschworen, / Den die gottverfluchten Juden / Boshaft tückish einst ermordet'*). All her succeeding declarations are also laced with attacks on Jews, while her lover's refrain is to let the Jews alone (e.g. *'Laß den Heiland und die Juden'*) and think only of love. In the end, though a very king's daughter, she makes love with her mysterious knight outdoors on the grass. When they part the next morning she demands to know his name, and the ballad ends when the knight, laughing and kissing her once more, announces that he is the son of the learned Rabbi Israel von Saragossa (*'Bin der Sohn des vielbelobten / Großen, schriftgelehrten Rabbi / Israel von Saragossa'*).[89] The keen satire on Jew-haters is unmistakable, and the Jewish deflowering of a Christian Spanish princess is humorous if by Victorian standards obscene. The ballad appeared in *Die Heimkehr* (homecoming), dated 1823–4, which was dedicated to Rahel, the Jewish salonnière who after Christian conversion and marriage to Varnhagen von Ense opened a new salon attended by Heine. That Evans would have remained oblivious of the Jewish context here strains credibility, especially since Evans knew of Rahel's prominence quite well. As she wrote to Sara Hennell on 23 June 1855, 'Varnhagen has written "Denkwurdigkeiten" [memoirs] and all sorts of literature and is or rather *was* the husband of *Rahel*, the greatest of German women'.[90] She did note the dedication of *Heimkehr* to Rahel in 'German Wit' and observed that Heine 'frequently refers to her or quotes her in a way that indicates how he valued her influence', but she skated past Rahel's Jewish origin after introducing her as 'Rahel (Varnhagen's wife)' as well as the basis for Heine's close friendship with her.[91]

Evans finished her essay on Alfred Meissner's *Recollections of Heine* on 4 August 1856, so perhaps she had not read Meissner's book before she completed 'German Wit' in late November 1855.[92] Certainly a long passage she translated in her Meissner review would have amended her earlier mistake about Heine's heritage:

> At the end of a long conversation on the Jews, recorded by Meissner, Heine sums up his feeling towards them this way: –
> 'You hear, by [sic] dear Meissner, how I almost in one breath ridicule and compassionate the Jews; in fact, they appear to me at once ludicrous and venerable. I could not devote myself to them entirely . . .; I unite myself with no party, whether republicans or patriots, Christians or Jews. I have this in common with all artists who write not for enthusiastic moments, but for centuries – not for one land, but for the world – not for one race, but for mankind. It would be absurd and petty in me if, as people pretend, I had ever been ashamed of being a Jew; but it would be just as ridiculous if I declared myself to be a Jew . . . . [sic]. As I was born to deliver over the bad and the rotten, the false and the foolish, to eternal ridicule, so it is equally in my nature to feel what is sublime, to admire what is great, and to venerate whatever has true life.' Heine had spoken the last words with deep earnestness, and had become thoughtful. But, as if laughter must always resume its wonted seat on his lips, he added playfully, 'If our little friend Weill comes to see us soon, you shall have another proof of my piety towards primitive Mosaism. Weill was formerly a singer in the synagogue . . . and chants the old songs of Judah in all their traditional purity, from their earliest monotonous simplicity to their latest point of Old Testament finish. My good wife, who has no notion that I am a Jew, was not a little amazed when she heard this strange musical lament, this shaking and quivering. When Weill began his first song, Minko the dog crept under the sofa, and Cocotte the parrot tried to hang himself between the bars of his cage. "Monsieur Weill! Monsieur Weill!" Matilda cried out, in alarm, "don't carry the joke too far!" Weill went on. Matilda turned to me and said, "Henry, tell me what songs are these?" "They are our German national songs," I answered; and I have obstinately persisted in this assertion.'[93]

This was the longest excerpt from Meissner's German in Evans's *Leader* review, and the time Evans devoted to translating it may indicate the importance she attached to the passage. In representing Heine's secularism, witty writing, complex sensibility, and frank assertion of Jewish identity, this review served as a corrective to her *Westminster* essay published nine months earlier. Because both her *Leader* review of Meissner and 'German Wit' were anonymous, however, there was no reason for anyone beyond close friends to connect one with the other, or for her to revise her *Westminster* essay.

She returned to the essay in her final years, however, when, according to Lewes's son Charles Lee (1842–91), Eliot 'made some time before her death a collection of such of her fugitive writing as she considered deserving of a permanent form; carefully revised them for the press; and left them, in the order in which they here appear', giving the essays 'the advantage of such corrections and alterations as a revision long subsequent to the period of writing may have suggested to her'.[94] The mystery is why Eliot did not correct her mistake about Heine's parentage then. She did make one change, dropping the misogynist comment of Heine about women writers and the Countess Hahn-Hahn with which her 1856 essay had ended.[95] My supposition is that a Christianised Heine was so integrally embedded in the artful unity of her essay that Eliot could not correct her error without rewriting the whole substantially.

It was, then, not Eliot's 'German Wit' but Matthew Arnold's 1863 essay on Heine in *Cornhill Magazine* that elevated Heine's status in Britain; and in this essay Heine's Jewish identity was unequivocal, as central to Arnold's argument as the Christianised Heine was to Evans's. Arnold laid the groundwork for *Culture and Anarchy* (1868–9) by emphasising Heine's cosmopolitanism and his role as a 'soldier in the war of liberation of humanity' precisely because he had detached himself from his roots in favour of a wider culture: 'Heine, far more than Tieck or Jean Paul Richter, is the continuator of that which, in Goethe's varied activity, is the most powerful and vital', for he, 'a young man of genius, born at Hamburg, and with all the culture of Germany, but by race a Jew; [had] warm sympathies for France, whose revolution had given to his race the rights of citizenship'.[96]

In 1864 George Eliot (now known privately as 'Mrs Lewes') wrote to Hedwig Sauppe, daughter of the director of a Weimar grammar school whom she had met in 1854:

> I remember well the happy day we spent at Tiefurt, my own want of appreciation for the Sauer-milch, my bungling attempt to speak German, the thunderstorm, the tiny rooms, and the entertainment Prof. Sauppe gave

> us by reading aloud ... from the MS. of Goethe's 'Jahrmarkt' ... Indeed the memory of the Weimar days is very dear to me, and I often think with wondering gratitude how kind people were to me there – half dumb foreigner as I was.[97]

In the nine years since her first visit, Eliot's perspectives had dramatically widened, and she could see in retrospect how little she had been able to enter into German culture on that initial journey. Eliot's Germanism was always an important part of her career and is recognised as such today. But relative to Jameson and the Howitts especially, Marian Evans was far less able than they to engage in the deep-seated cultural exchange of ethnoexocentrism. Her example is a reminder that even a woman of extraordinary intellect and command of written German could remain a sheltered, dependent Englishwoman rather than empowered woman directly encountering cultural differences if she did not also negotiate some of her own arrangements or interact sufficiently with Germans.

During her 1858 German residence she was writing *Adam Bede*, the novel that would carry her to the forefront of contemporary novelists. By the time she returned to Germany in 1870, she was no bystander but a fluent speaker and the central attraction when she and Lewes attended the salon hosted by Fanny Lewald.[98] Equally important, by her example of outstanding fiction and ability to work outside marriage and doctrinal Christianity, Eliot set the stage for writers who followed her, including Jessie Fothergill, the aunt and niece who wrote as Michael Field, and Amy Levy, each of whose experiences in Germany I detail in the following chapters.

CHAPTER 5

The Anglo–German Fiction of George Eliot and Jessie Fothergill
Daniel Deronda *(1876)* and The First Violin *(1878)*

This chapter takes up a giant of literature and, so to speak, a gadfly of fame, well known and then gone. With the success of *Middlemarch* (1871–2), George Eliot was compared to Shakespeare and her next novel eagerly awaited. The culminating Jewish plot of *Daniel Deronda*, serialised from February to September 1876, surprised Victorians and continues an object of debate today even as it remains a reference point in studies of realism, national identities, and cosmopolitanism. *The First Violin* by Jessie Fothergill (1851–91), serialised in *Temple Bar* from January to December 1878, won notice for its original plot involving professional musicians and had reached a tenth edition by 1895; in 1898 it was adapted for the New York stage.[1] But its lasting power into the twentieth century was nugatory.[2] Still, there is good reason to pair these two works since they mutually illuminate each other's approach to Anglo–German exchange in the 1870s, including their interchanges with German-Jewish writer Paul Heyse (1830–1914), who won the Nobel Prize for literature in 1910.[3]

If *Deronda*'s principal focus is its Jewish plot, a secondary focus on music, which involves Gwendolen Harleth, Mirah Lapidoth, Herr Klesmer, and the Alcharisi, comes to the fore in *The First Violin*, which combines music with the feminist theme of careers for women.[4] Like Eliot, Fothergill was agnostic, as is her principal female character May Wedderburn, the free-thinking daughter of a provincial clergyman whom readers first encounter on English ground before she – and the narrative – remove to Germany. Both Eliot and Fothergill were fluent in German and spent considerable time in Germany, Fothergill in Düsseldorf for fifteen months, where she lived in a boarding house with her sister and two friends.[5] If cultural difference is an essential dimension of *Daniel Deronda*, its Anglo–German exchange is centred in English characters' responses to Herr Klesmer, and a key episode has a likely German source in Heyse. *The First Violin*, in contrast, is Anglo–German throughout in setting, structure, and sources. As the *New York Times* asserted, the novel's 'German flavor ... belongs to the very structure of the plot and the turn of the scenes. Whoever Jessie Fothergill may be, she has lived long in Germany and imbibed much of the German novelistic spirit without losing her special characteristics as an English woman.'[6] At the same time, Fothergill, still in her twenties, partly shaped her novel as an intertextual conversation with Eliot. *Deronda*'s serialisation ended only sixteen months before *First Violin*'s began, so that *Deronda* formed a 'horizon of expectation', to use Hans Robert Jauss's term, that made Fothergill's echoes of Eliot and her deliberate departures from *Deronda* readily visible.[7] Partly homage, these echoes also critiqued Eliot insofar as Fothergill took a road Eliot chose not to, making her principal female character a talented singer with the potential for an operatic career.

Daniel Deronda and Its Anglo–German Conversations

In the opening pages of this novel, Daniel Deronda observes Gwendolen Harleth in Leubrunn gambling; later, in the Frankfurt synagogue, Deronda encounters his grandfather's friend who passes along Deronda's family patrimony to him. Germany is more often a matter of back stories and distant origins, however, rather than a culture that actively exerts a shaping force on the plot or its leading characters' imaginative and emotional lives. Eliot instead brings the two cultures together through a German immigrant who finds an English bride and stays – the reverse story of Karl and Lina in Howitt's young adult novel *Which Is the Wiser?* Herr Klesmer is, more accurately, a cosmopolitan figure in whom the German, Slav, and Jew can meet. Whenever Klesmer enters, and at times when Mirah sings, German words mix with Eliot's English-language text, a lexical hybridity that mirrors the cultural hybridity of drawing rooms where German music is heard (as it so often was in Britain's private homes and performance halls). Hybrid culture and language merge early in the narrative when Klesmer plays his composition inspired by a Johann von Goethe lyric, '*Freudvoll, Leidvoll, Gedankenvoll*' (joyful, sorrowful, thankful).[8] A number of Eliot's chapters also feature German-language epigraphs drawn from Heinrich Heine, Leopold Zunz (1794–1886), and Goethe.[9] Henry James had some reason to send up the novel's German elements in an imaginary conversation about *Daniel Deronda* in *Partial Portraits* (1888), in which Pulcheria, a decided sceptic about the work's merits, proclaims, 'The tone is not English, it is German.'[10]

Klesmer manages his mixed bloodlines and heritages because he absorbs them all into the larger identity of an original artist who wields the powerful aesthetic medium of music, which enters into ears and hearts before auditors can raise cultural barriers to withstand it. Narrow English characters like the politician Mr Bult cannot fathom how to respond to this 'alien' dropped into his midst (205–7). The Arrowpoint family, in contrast, model the development of positive responses to cultural difference. Catherine Arrowpoint, the musically gifted daughter of the house, loves Klesmer and says so when he declares his love for her. German music and words alike become the medium enabling his declaration as he plays 'so as to give with the delicacy of an echo in the far distance a melody which he had set to Heine's "Ich hab' dich geliebet and liebe dich noch"' (I have loved you and love you still) (208). Catherine's parents at first exemplify English prejudice, demanding that she uphold the family name (and wealth) as well as English national identity rather than yoking herself to an itinerant musician with no established income or musical reputation. As her father says, 'He won't do at the head of estates. He has a deuced foreign look – is an unpractical man', to which Catherine astutely retorts, 'England has often passed into the hands of foreigners – Dutch soldiers, sons of foreign women of bad character: – if our land were sold tomorrow it would very likely pass into the hands of some foreign merchant on Change ... How can I stem that tide?' (210–11). Catherine's determination prevails, and in the end the Arrowpoints find after all that they can merge the German-Slav-Semite Klesmer with their English family to the benefit of all. As Sir Hugo reports months later, they spend Christmas harmoniously with their unconventional son-in-law and daughter at Quetcham (349), and Klesmer's meteoric rise in the English musical world gives him the opportunity to create his own wealth and live in Grosvenor Square as 'a patron and prince among musical professors' (518). He in fact becomes a sponsor for his in-laws, granting the provincial Arrowsmiths access to higher reaches of London society in Grosvenor Square than they could ever know otherwise.

Mathilde Blind, the German-Jewish immigrant, poet, and earliest biographer of Eliot, proposes an additional Anglo–German exchange in *Deronda*. The drowning scene of Grandcourt, Blind contends, was suggested by a parallel scene in a short story by Heyse, whom Eliot met in Munich in 1858.[11] Blind makes this assertion in discussing Eliot's *Westminster Review* essays. Noting the very similar views about realism in Eliot's essays on Riehl and Heine (1856) and in George Henry Lewes's 'Realism in Art: Recent German Fiction' in *Westminster Review* (October 1858), Blind speculates that Eliot's views influenced Lewes's.[12] Blind then notes Lewes's attention to the work of Paul Heyse and Heyse's possible relation to *Deronda*:

> Among German novelists, (or rather writers of short stories), Paul Heyse is one of the few who is singled out for special praise in this review. And it is curious that there should be a tale by this eminent author called 'The Lonely Ones' (which also appeared in 1858), in which an incident occurs forcibly recalling the catastrophe of Grandcourt's death in 'Daniel Deronda': the incident – though unskillfully introduced – of a Neapolitan fisherman whose momentary murderous hesitation to rescue his drowning friend ends in lifelong remorse for his death.[13]

Since Lewes's review focuses on Heyse's 'Das Mädchen von Treppi' (The Girl from Treppi) and never mentions the story cited by Blind ('Die Einsamen'), his review offers scant evidence for Blind's claim about *Deronda*, which Eliot did not begin writing until the early 1870s. But Heyse's story recirculated among Anglophone audiences in October 1869 when a new translation of the tale under the title 'The Lonely Ones' – as Blind calls it – was published in *Lippincott's Magazine* and reissued as a pamphlet in 1870.[14] Around this time, in early summer 1871, a Munich friend informed Eliot of the recent death of Heyse's son, to which Eliot replied in June, 'Poor Heyse! How much trouble he has had mingled with his gifts of genius and beauty! I think the boy whom he has lost must be the one I saw when I was first at Munich.'[15]

The textual parallels of 'The Lonely Ones' and *Deronda*'s fatal yachting scene are notable, and these similarities, plus Eliot's 1871 letter reflecting interest in Heyse at the time she began writing *Deronda*, strengthen Blind's suggestion. Both drownings are set off Italian city coasts, Genoa in *Deronda* and Naples in 'The Lonely Ones', and are connected to rich men and a backdrop of adulterous desire. In the Heyse tale a German poet visiting Italy, struck by an Italian woman of great beauty who lives with her brother Tomaso, inveigles an invitation to their home and ultimately learns why Tomaso never leaves his isolated home and has vowed never to look upon the sea again. Tomaso's best friend Nino had been professionally trained as a singer thanks to his rich uncle and was slated for his operatic debut when he and Tomaso rowed out together and only Tomaso returned. As Tomaso's sister explains,

> 'The heavy net drew [Nino] down. The peg to which it was fastened came suddenly out of the joint and shot overboard; and he, bending over the side, with his arms extended to seize the net, was caught in the meshes: the boat turned over, and when Tomaso rose to the surface he saw the empty boat floating calmly in the evening glow'.[16]

Tomaso, the poet alone learns, had fallen in love with the rich uncle's wife, and she with Tomaso. Nino had seen the lovers' adulterous desire and sought his best friend's promise that he would not betray the uncle to whom Nino owed so much. But Nino does not survive:

> '"Tomà," said he, "if you do not promise me by our old friendship to give this up, it will be my ruin ... My brother," said he, "I demand it of you. I could go and warn my uncle, but then he would be undeceived in his beloved wife ... Promise me, then. I surely deserve this one sacrifice at your hands."
> ...
> 'The story I told [when I returned alone] was the true one: the net drew him down, his feet became entangled: I did not overturn the boat. But that is not all: I was seated in safety at the stern while he was struggling in the water! My limbs seemed ice. My eyes were fixed on the eddying pool beside me which had just closed over his head: I saw the bubbles rise as if they called to me: he was still breathing below there. And now, now, one of his hands rose above the water and groped for the firm hand of his friend, only a boat's length off. A silver ring on his finger gleamed in the evening sunlight. I had but to reach out the oar and he was saved! Did I not wish to reach it to him? Must I not have wished it? I held the oar upon my knees: one bend of my arm and the hand with the silver ring would have closed around it. But the demon sat in my breast and chained every nerve and froze every drop of blood. I sat as if in a dream – my head swam, I strove to cry out – ever staring at the hand. And the hand sank – now to the ring, now to the finger tips, now it was gone! Then the demon seemed to set me free. I cried like a madman. I sprang overboard, upsetting the boat, and dived down, and rose, and down again, without finding him, though I have a hundred times brought up a tiny coin from the bottom of the sea'.[17]

Tomaso, like Gwendolen in *Deronda*, withholds rescue only to plunge into the sea when it is too late. Heyse's story ends in bitter irony. The sister thinks she has triumphed when Tomaso spurns marriage to the woman he loved after the rich uncle dies: '"Tomà!" she cried sobbing, but with wild triumph in her voice, ... "you have refused! You are mine! We shall belong only to each other!"' Only the visiting poet knows that Tomaso has steeled himself to permanent isolation and guilt for the rest of his life.[18]

The contexts of Heyse's and Eliot's Italian scenes are quite different: Tomaso is driven by passionate desire and furore at Nino for blocking it, Gwendolen by passionate hatred. But their refused rescues both lead to psychological torture rather than escape from unendurable emotions. The structural frameworks for their revelatory confessions also resemble each other. The Genovese boatmen tell Deronda that 'her husband had gone down irrecoverably, and that his boat was left floating empty. He and his comrade had heard a cry, had come up in time to see the lady jump in after her husband, and had got her out fast enough to save her from much damage' (588). At the hotel next morning, Gwendolen unfolds a very different first-hand account after explaining that 'I felt a hatred in me that was always working like an evil spirit' (591):

> 'I saw him sink, and my heart gave a leap as if it were going out of me. I think I did not move. I kept my hands tight. It was long enough for me to be glad, and yet to think it was no use – he would come up again. And he *was* come – farther off – the boat had moved. It was all like lightning. "The rope!" he called out in a voice – not his own – I hear it now – and I stooped for the rope – I felt I must – I felt sure he could swim, and he would come back whether or not, and I dreaded him. That was in my mind – he would come back. But he was gone down again – and I had the rope in my hand – no, there he was again – his face above the water – and he cried again – and I held my hand, and my heart said, "Die!" – and he sank; and I felt "It is done – I am wicked, I am lost!" – and I had the rope in my hand – I don't know what I thought – I was leaping away from myself – I would have saved him then. I was leaping from my crime . . .' (596–7).

In both scenes, initially exculpatory narratives of a witnessed drowning give way to confessions of withheld rescue and panicked leaps into the sea when rescue is impossible, leaving haunting guilt and psychological agony in their wakes.

Nowhere do Eliot's journals state that she read the English or German versions of Heyse's tale. But she would have had access to the 1858 collection of tales that Lewes reviewed (which included 'Die Einsamen') and notices or issues of *Lippincott's Magazine*. Heyse's Jewish antecedents as well as his recent loss of a beloved child might plausibly have given Eliot reason to think of him as she began to develop ideas for a new novel that turns on Jewish life. Even if in the end Blind's observation cannot be confirmed, it suggests an Anglo–German literary exchange that merits renewed consideration.

The First Violin: A Hybrid Anglo–German Novel

Like *Deronda*, *First Violin* features a proud beautiful woman subjected to psychological oppression and torture after she marries a controlling English aristocrat. *First Violin* also features a woman of great talent who follows the yoked trajectories of Eliot's Alcharisi and Mirah: she trains as a diva, only reluctantly sings in public, and ends up marrying a Continental nobleman. As with the Alcharisi, furthermore, her religious upbringing means little to

The First Violin: A Hybrid Anglo–German Novel 113

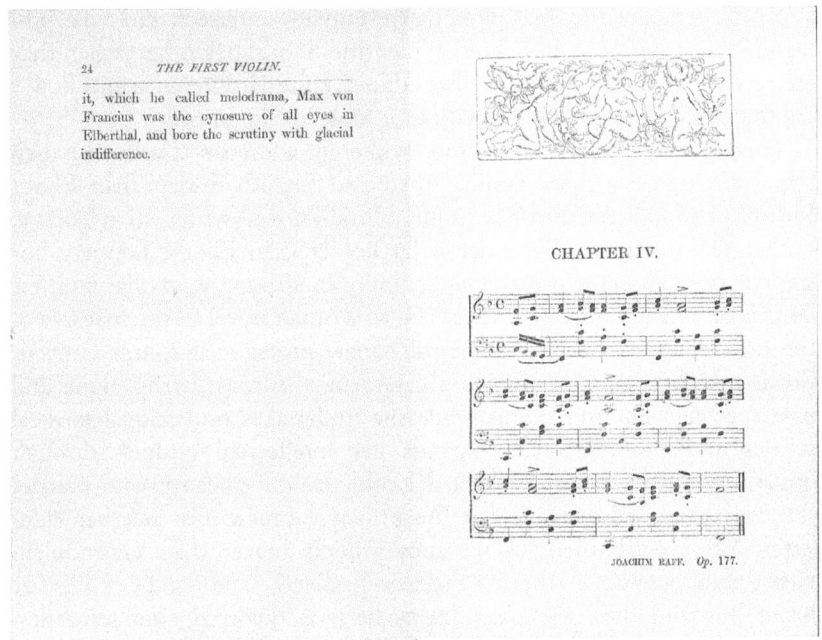

Figure 5.1. From Joachim Raff, 'Lenore' Symphony March, Book III, Chapter IV, *The First Violin* (2:24–5). Courtesy Rare Book & Manuscript Library, University of Illinois

her and she easily abandons it without regret. Music is as intrinsic to Fothergill's plot and characterisation as it is to Eliot's. But rather than building up a series of operatic textual allusions that foreshadow future developments or underscore character traits, as when Mirah sings '*O patria mia*' to Klesmer and reinforces the cause of nationhood to which Deronda pledges himself at the end, Fothergill weaves into the fabric of her novel a musical leitmotif that recurs when the male protagonist, the concertmaster violinist, enters the scene. Fothergill reproduces the printed staves of this leitmotif from the score (see Figure 5.1) as well as staves from other instrumental works, so that the sounds of words and of music (for those who can read music) coalesce. Fothergill also includes among her secondary characters one who resembles Klesmer: a tall, striking 'rather Jewish-looking' German conductor who is committed to Wagner's new music, teaches music on the side, and is both a composer and a commanding pianist. The settings of both Eliot's and Fothergill's novels shift between provincial England, the Continent, and back again. More substantively, homosocial and romantic male friendships play pivotal roles in both novels and help generate the dual plots that eventually intersect; the male protagonists, furthermore, have hidden identities that shock others when they are revealed. Finally, both novelists address cultural difference and how a culture can best negotiate diversity as it looks to the future.

There are salient differences too. Fothergill addresses class rather than ethnic prejudice, a more familiar theme to English readers than Eliot's Jewish plot and easier for a young, little-known writer to negotiate. Fothergill's treatment of gender is far bolder than Eliot's, however, for she not only revises normative masculinity in striking ways that had few British precedents but also writes a New Woman novel in the first five of the novel's six books. Her principal female protagonist spurns conventional marriage, opts to pursue a career in music, and lives alone and unchaperoned far from home while she undertakes professional musical studies and simultaneously expands her intellectual outlook through literature and philosophy. The pale, cold, haughty beauty who marries the controlling aristocrat is not the principal protagonist but her elder sister. Yet even Fothergill's unhappy wife is braver than Gwendolen: rather than staying in the marriage or passively standing by while her hated husband dies, the sister leaves hers, is divorced, and remarries, finding more acceptance in Germany than she could at home because of the long German Protestant tradition of divorce and remarriage.[19] Her defiance of English norms ultimately brings happiness, if not unalloyed, after initial shame and humiliation, and she is highly respected in her adopted country.

To focus only on Fothergill's intertextual relation to Eliot, however, is to distort its fundamental innovation. Of all the prose works examined in this study, *First Violin* goes furthest in its saturated Anglo–Germanism that looks towards both countries, both languages, both literatures at once. From Book II forward, *Violin* is in continuous conversation with Paul Heyse's three-volume novel *Kinder der Welt* (Children of the World) (1873), which appeared while or just before Fothergill lived in Germany.[20] Eliot's dual narrative of Deronda's and Gwendolen's stories, which are isomorphic with Eliot's dual Jewish–Protestant English plot, is mirrored in Fothergill's double narrative of a German man and the English female protagonist. Heyse, however, played the largest role in suggesting Fothergill's representations of gender and her plot's structure. First serialised in Berlin's newspaper *Spener Zeitung*, *Kinder der Welt* was divided into six books, as is Fothergill's *First Violin*.[21] Heyse's text is an explicitly agnostic novel that distinguishes 'children of the world', who are committed to a secular philosophical quest for truth, from the 'children of

God' content to rest in inherited religion and observances. Edwin, the hero, is a philosopher who refuses to avow dogma to attain an academic post and works independently on his philosophical treatise, which argues for the compatibility of morality with unbelief.

Heyse's novel challenges traditional gender roles throughout. An orphan, Edwin cares for his invalid younger brother Balder, acting at once as parent, wife, and brother to him. Above them lives Christiane, a brilliant but harsh-featured pianist unable to attract Edwin, whom she loves. She can outlive this disappointment, but when Lorinser, a hypocritical Christian fanatic rapes her after she refuses his attempts at conversion and his sexual advances, she attempts suicide. In this work, notably, rape disqualifies her neither for marriage nor sociability. One of Edwin's bohemian friends, Herr Mohr, an aspiring amateur musician, has long been drawn to Christiane and eventually persuades her to marry him; and when they have a child he becomes the principal caretaker for their son so that Christiane can devote herself to her music career. She becomes a renowned pianist and the de facto music director of the town where they settle. Edwin for his part loves the beautiful Toinette, whom he meets in the Berlin Tiergarten (zoo) one day. But she declares herself unable to love and is already the mistress of a Count who furnishes her fine home, so that Edwin must content himself with being merely her intellectual and social companion.

Fothergill overtly signals that Heyse is a German intertext of *The First Violin*: one of her German characters cites *Kinder der Welt* and its 'hero' Edwin in Book II of the English novel, and Fothergill's Book IV is entitled 'Children of the World'. In so overtly announcing the importance of Heyse's novel for her own, Fothergill signals the degree of her Anglo–German exchange, which she deepens by so intermixing German with English words on the page that she creates a hybrid linguistic text that is neither wholly English nor German: the two languages cannot be pulled apart.[22]

The novel does not begin that way, however. It opens as a provincial novel and first-person narrative of a young daughter whose father is barely able to support his family on his vicar's salary. At seventeen, May Wedderburn considers herself the least intelligent, beautiful, and talented of the vicar's three daughters, yet she must fend off the wealthy, middle-aged Sir Peter le Marchant, who has returned to his estate after a long absence and directs his predatory gaze on her: 'I hated him from the moment in which I saw him looking at me with expression of approval.'[23] The novel's opening pages mention Jane Austen, whose works Stella,

May's sister, loves to read, but Fothergill swiftly displaces a novel focused on three unmarried sisters in search of husbands. May is as intelligent as Elizabeth Bennet and also possesses feminist insight, so that in the marriage proposal Sir Peter offers she sees that he merely 'offered to buy my youth, and such poor beauty as I might have, with his money' (1:23). Her beautiful sister Adelaide is furious at May's refusal, since wedding Sir Peter would ensure the financial security of all three sisters whose minimal education unfits them to earn a living should their father die. Triangulated between Sir Peter's aggressions and Adelaide's anger, May escapes to Germany with her neighbour Miss Hallam, a deep-voiced older woman who never attends church, and who now seeks a young companion who can travel with her to Germany while she consults a prominent ophthalmologist, her last hope to ward off blindness. May notes in her interview that she has modest singing ability, which she demonstrates with Robert Schumann's *Lied* set to Heine's 'Die Lotosblume'; Miss Hallam then offers to exchange May's assistance for expert music lessons in Germany that can prepare May to earn her living as a music teacher on her return. May leaps at the chance.

Book I is entitled *Res Angusta Domi* (financial straits at home) to signify May's starting point. Book II, which shifts to Germany, is aptly entitled 'Life', since for May Germany will offer the kind of revelation reminiscent of Anna Jameson's own four decades earlier. Fothergill offers no counterpart to Jameson's affective female cosmopolitanism, however. Rather than suggesting that feminine sympathy and receptivity are key to cross-cultural encounters, Fothergill approaches ethnoexocentrism within a feminist framework: repeatedly *First Violin* correlates May's discovery of new cultural and intellectual perspectives with resisting norms for young middle-class Englishwomen's behaviour.

Book II opens in the Cologne rail station and vividly represents what it is like for a young woman arriving in a foreign country with no knowledge of the language or customs to face a crisis while unable to ask for help. At Cologne en route to Elberthal, Fothergill's fictional town based on Düsseldorf, Miss Hallam and May must change trains, and May suddenly realises she cannot find Miss Hallam's shawl left in her care.[24] May fights a crowd back to the waiting room, finds the door locked, races towards the arrival hall, gets the wrong door again, hurries through a deserted station wing and past the sign '*Gepäck-Expedition*' (baggage delivery office), and finally spots the door labelled '*Ausgang*' (exit): 'There was the magic word, and I, not knowing it, stared at it and was none the wiser for its friendly sign.' She finally gets back to the station entrance and spots a uniformed

The First Violin: A Hybrid Anglo–German Novel

porter, not considering that in her flustered state she will inconvenience him, albeit as a pretty, naïve foreign girl:

> 'Elberthal?' said he in a guttural bass; '*Wollt ihr nach Elberthal, Fräuleinchen!* [Do you want to go to Elberthal, miss?]
> There was an impudent twinkle in his eye, as [if] it were impertinence trying to get the better of beer, and I reiterated 'Elberthal,' going very red, and cursing all foreign speeches by my gods . . .'
> '*Schon fort, Fräulein* [already gone],' he continued, with a grin. (1:47–50)

Suddenly the porter assumes 'a more respectful demeanour' as a 'gentleman sauntering along' approaches. May now must decide whether to violate the prohibition taught to all middle-class women against speaking to a strange man. This man (in contrast to Sir Peter and the porter) has noticed neither May nor her looks, for as he walks along 'his fingers drummed a tune upon his chest' and he is 'humming something', which we later learn is 'the air of the march from Raff's Fifth Symphonie, the "Lenore"' (1:50–1), the novel's leitmotif.[25] It is Elberthal's concertmaster known as Eugen Courvoisier.[26] Placing faith in his bearing as a gentleman, May defies English if not class rules and plants herself in front of him; he looks up, startled, with a 'keen' and 'commanding' glance that modulates to detached amusement as he takes in the situation. May's provincial upbringing has provided no comparable acquaintance, and she thinks – oblivious to her own foreign status – 'Not an Englishman. I should have known him for an outlander anywhere' (1:51–2). The 'handsome' man offers an Anglo–German response: he bows German-style and asks in 'excellent' English how he can help her. When May realises that she has no money (having left her purse with Miss Hallam's maid), she sees no alternative but to accept his help and assents when he suggests that they get something to eat while waiting for the Elberthal train, which he too has missed.[27] She is startled to reflect how far and how quickly she has come from English norms: 'It was unheard of, horrible, this possibility of falling into the power of a total, utter stranger – a foreigner – a – heaven only knew what! . . . I was parading about the streets of Köln with a man of whose very existence I had half an hour ago been ignorant.'[28] She can justify herself only by repeating 'he was a gentleman' (1:59–60).

The vicar's daughter transgresses again when she enters a public hotel dining room with a strange man to share a meal; she does not immediately recognise herself when she passes a mirror on being shown to their table, possibly Fothergill's symbolic touch to register May's first step towards a new self. She surprises herself again when, as he takes up the newspaper on the table, she thinks, 'I was not happy, and yet I could not feel all the unhappiness which I considered appropriate to the circumstances' (1:61–2). As he peruses the paper, it is May who directs an erotic gaze upon the man, noticing his 'indescribable grace, ease, and negligent beauty' as he leans his head on his hand, letting his thick fine long hair sweep across his brow, and perceives too that 'All his lines were lines of beauty' fused with an intellectual face, 'masculine strength', and a recurring mournful expression (1:63–4). He is aware of her gaze the whole time but, rather than confronting or flirting, asks when he looks up, '*Nun* [now], have you decided?' (1:66) – i.e. have you decided to trust me? His cosmopolitan detachment dispels her fears of sexual predation, and she relaxes into amicable conversation despite knowing that what she is doing is 'Bohemian, irregular, and not respectable' (1:68).

This recognition in a foreign land that 'wrong' feminine behaviour can be very pleasant is quickly followed by a momentous cultural revelation when he asks if she would like to visit the cathedral (*Kölner Dom*) before their train leaves. May longs passionately to learn more than her provincial home afforded, and she leaps at this opportunity to broaden her experience too. She has never been in a cathedral, much less a Catholic one, and is astonished by its sublime grandeur. As she had earlier with Miss Hallam, she readily confides more than she needs to Courvoisier and makes sufficiently clear that she is happy to have left home after an unwelcome marriage proposal and hopes to support herself as a music teacher after her return to England. Rather than presume upon her innocent candour, he instead cautions her against so readily revealing herself and suggests that she learn to 'mask' her 'face, which is too expressive' (1:77) – a good piece of advice for young international travellers even today. But he is interrupted by a soprano and organist's rehearsal for an approaching service.

May is transfixed as she hears German music for the very first time:

> There suddenly filled the air a sound of deep, heavenly melody, which swept solemnly adown the aisles, and filled with its melodious thunder every corner of the great building. I listened with my face upraised, my lips parted. It was the organ, and presently, after a wonderful melody, which set my heart beating – a melody full of the most witchingly sweet high notes, and a breadth and grandeur of low ones such as only two composers have ever attainted to, a voice – a single woman's voice – was upraised. She was invisible, and she sung till the very sunshine seemed turned to melody, and all the world was music – the greatest, most glorious of earthly things. (1:78–9)

Fothergill prints a stanza from the German libretto of J. S. Bach's *St. Matthew's Passion* ('Matthäus Passion') to indicate which soprano solo

May hears ('Blute nur, liebes Herz!' [bleed on, dear heart]) (1:79). It is a revelation not only of great German music but also of the narrowness of her previous monocultural life in England: 'And such music was in the world, had been sung for years, and I had not heard it' (1:80). She hears it now because she is alone rather than chaperoned at the rail station and has violated English etiquette in visiting the cathedral with this man.

That night he puts her into a coach headed to Miss Hallam's door and disappears, having swept the impressionable May into a new world of music as well as enchantment with him. Miss Hallam, of course, is horrified when she hears of May's unchaperoned interlude with a man who could have brought her back on an earlier train: '"no gentleman would have done anything of the kind"' (1:88). Miss Hallam astutely points to the first task at hand: 'It is evident ... that you must at once begin to learn German, and then if you do get lost at a railway station again, you will be able to ask your way' (1:89). But it is the organ, the soprano's voice, and Courvoisier's words that keep May from sleep for hours.

When in contrast to her first day in Germany May conforms to English principles, her experiences and cultural outlook narrow. Miss Hallam and May are the only Englishwomen at the boarding house, and May must pass a gauntlet of young male European students who giggle when she enters for the midday meal. Already on her guard, she firmly resists the overtures of art student Anna Sartorius, put off by her cropped hair, direct conversation, and 'masculine' assertiveness (1:96) – all signifiers of a New Woman – though she had admired Miss Hallam's brusquerie when on home ground. In retrospect she takes herself to task for English prejudice:

> Anna took me on a tour round the town ... She did her best to entertain me, and I, with a childish prejudice against her abrupt manner, and the free, somewhat challenging look of her black eyes, was reserved, unresponsive, stupid. I took a prejudice against her – I own it – and for that and other sins committed against a woman who would have been my friend if I would have let her, I say humbly, *Mea culpa*! ... I have since, with wider knowledge of her country and its men and women, got to see that what made her so inharmonious was, that she had a woman's form, and a man's disposition and love of freedom. (1:102, 104)

A worse closing down of cross-cultural receptivity from English class prejudice occurs the night May attends her first opera, Wagner's *Lohengrin*.[29] Still thinking of Courvoisier and wondering whether he might be an artist, military captain, or perhaps amateur singer in the chorus performing for his amusement, she looks anxiously about the audience and is shocked when he suddenly appears,

> a man, carrying a violin, ... with a nod here, a half smile there, a tap on the shoulder in another direction ... I certainly realised as nearly as possible that *im*possible sensation, the turning upside down of the world ... I waited, spell-bound ... He *was* Eugen Courvoisier, and he looked braver, handsomer, gallanter, and more apart from the crowd. (1:141–2)

When he recognises her in the audience, 'I did the most cowardly and treacherous thing ... I saw a look of recognition flash into his eyes – upon his face. I saw that he was *going* to bow to me. With ... my head swimming, my heart beating, I dropped my eyes to the play-bill upon my lap' (1:143). At the very moment of erotic possibility, her middle-class English prejudice drives her to cut him, and when she dares to look up again he looks back at her with no recognition as he would to a complete stranger:

> I did not know whether to be most distressed at my own disloyalty to a kind friend, or most appalled to find that the man with whom I had spent a whole afternoon in the firm conviction that he was outwardly, as well as inwardly, my equal and a gentleman – ... the man of whom I had assuredly thought and dreamed many and many a time and oft was – a professional musician, a man in a band, a German band, playing in the public orchestra of a provincial town. Well! well! (1:144–5)

Having overturned readers' expectations of romance, Fothergill diverts the novel into a New Woman plot that intensifies her representation of profound cultural exchange in the story of a young woman's life in Germany. Before *Lohengrin*, May attended a 'Probe' or rehearsal of Anton Rubinstein's 'Paradise Lost' (*Das verlorene Paradies*) and met the music director, Max von Francius, who placed her among amateurs in the chorus. On detecting her voice, he asks her to try some solo work.[30] She chooses the soprano solo in Bach's 'Blute noch, liebes Herz' after finding a libretto in English amidst the sheet music to which von Francius directs her, and all that she heard and felt in the Köln Dom is now channelled into her complete immersion in the music. When von Francius informs Miss Hallam and May the day after that with training May could become a prima donna on the stage, Miss Hallam is dismayed and May agrees without reflection, 'shrink[ing] away from the ideas conjured up by that word, the "stage"' (1:131). Even to receive sufficient training to teach, he rejoins, mere months would not be sufficient for her to realise her gift.

Thus begins the professional training that dominates Books II–V, a contrast between May's story and Gwendolen's in *Deronda*.[31] It is von Francius who first quotes Heyse's *Kinder der Welt* in explaining that he must work alone with his new student; more directly he adds, 'You must understand that it is not pleasure or child's play which you are undertaking. It is a work in order to accomplish which you must strain every nerve, and give up everything which in any way interferes with it' (1:132). When May balks at singing onstage in a local concert, von Francius reminds her of the 'responsibility' she owes her 'gifts' (1:166) and, unlike Mirah Lapidoth, May changes her mind the more readily when she learns she will be paid 50 thalers for her onstage solo work, since her ultimate purpose is to acquire sufficient expertise to earn a living and escape mercenary marriage. She now begins life in earnest as a student abroad training for a profession – a fictional counterpart to Anna Mary Howitt's private art study in Munich in 1850–1.

More radical departures from May's old village life soon follow. When Miss Hallam realises that her German ophthalmologist can give her no hope and decides to return to England after only six weeks, von Francius bluntly states the options now facing May: 'Will you go home and stagnate there, or will you remain here, fight down your difficulties, and become a worthy artiste?' (1:212). He persuades Miss Hallam to continue supporting May's study even though it means Miss Hallam will lose the young companion who brings her comfort and the respectable English clergyman's daughter she brought to Germany will live as a *feme sole*, a scenario that George Egerton, Sarah Grand, and George Gissing would make familiar only in the 1890s. Setting her novel outside England, in Germany, thus helped Fothergill represent a New Woman even before Olive Schreiner's Lyndall appeared in *Story of an African Farm* (1883).

Beyond her regular practice of scales and 'shakes' (trills), von Francius persuades her that a leading role in the public performance of the *Messiah* or *St Matthew's Passion* is part of her artistic training. He also begins to develop her intellectual powers while mentoring her on practical matters:

> He would converse with me about Schiller and Göthe, true; he would also caution me against such and such shopkeepers as extortioners, and tell me the place where they gave the largest discount on music paid for on the spot: would discuss [Beethoven's] *Waldstein* or *Appassionata* with me, or the beauties of Rubinstein or the deep meanings of Schumann, also the relative cost of living *en pension* or providing for oneself. (2:61)

Shocking by English standards, he visits her alone in her room to teach and converse with her, but he remains her mentor and friend, never a potential love interest. The romance plot begun at the Köln rail station remains, but it too is inseparable from feminism. When May moves into her new apartment fitted out with the one piece of furniture necessary to a diva in training – a piano – she discovers that her room is across the street from the building where Courvoisier rooms with the assistant concertmaster, whom she can see from her front window. This reignites May's erotic gazing, but she enjoys its pleasures only because she is pursuing professional studies abroad to prepare for a career.

May's athleticism, another New Woman marker, leads to her next direct encounter with Courvoisier, when May, an expert skater from childhood, skates on the local pond to offset the lonely tedium of her December practice. Arriving as the moon rises and many skaters leave, she skates towards the furthest reaches of the pond when she perceives that a solitary skater is Courvoisier, and to experience the joy of swift movement without feeling inhibited by his presence, she skates near the reeds marking the pond's bounds, not realising that she has reached a very shallow spot. Suddenly the ice cracks and she falls through, facing drowning or freezing had he not been nearby, humming Raff's march as he approaches. Rescuing her from distress a second time, he lifts her out, removes her skates, and, because she is too cold and weak to skate or walk on her own, puts his arm about her waist while she holds on to his shoulder and he skates them to the pond's entrance (2:76–81). After losing consciousness she wakes in a strange room on a sofa at the end of which Courvoisier sits smiling and an unknown woman offers her hot spirits. She breaks another English social command when, after first resisting, she drinks the hot schnapps when Courvoisier insists that it will help revive her. Oblivious of her looks, she changes into the bulky but warm woollen uniform of an orphan asylum matron offered to her by the matron to whom Courvoisier has brought her, and they walk home together. But when they are near their rooms and May tries to converse with him about their shared music profession, he snubs her, declaring that he is a humble musician while she is training to be a prima donna, and when she demurs at her talent he cynically comments that 'handsome' looks will win a woman fame nonetheless (2:91–2). May is angry, claiming that her voice and ability to love those who are kind to her are her only talents, and he promptly declares that he will then strive to be disagreeable so that she has the good sense to hate him. Thwarted in romance once more, May redoubles her focus on professional training and embarks on serious piano studies.

In the last of the romance scenes in Book V, in a chapter headed by two staves of Schumann's *Träumerei* (reverie) (2:232), May awakens from a dream of Courvoisier the night after she attends the Artist's Ball dressed as Wagner's Elsa.[32] Too jaded and lonely after her dream to find satisfaction in her books and music, she leaves her austere apartment on impulse, walks to the concert hall, and enters a chamber that she assumes will be empty.

But she hears a piano playing and on opening the door sees that it is Courvoisier, who has glimpsed her before she can leave undiscovered. She pretends to search for a piece of music out of prideful determination not to let him think that she is again vulnerable to slights or a snub. But he speaks to her as one professional colleague to another and asks her to help him practise by playing the piano accompaniment to a duet for piano and violin. Her piano studies enable this, and though they are joined by two other members of the orchestra, those others leave to fetch music for a quartet adaptation of Beethoven's Fourth Symphony, leaving Courvoisier and May briefly alone. Unexpectedly he reverts to the *Lohengrin* concert and asks her forgiveness for his putting his pride above her earlier attempts to apologise. If a clear romantic moment, it too is enabled by May's independent life and her growing professionalism as a musician. Just as non-verbal music staves front the chapter, so now the instrumental quartet rather than words enacts a union beyond the physical as the four musicians co-create musical beauty, moving on to Schumann's *Träumerei* and other selections from the *Kinderszenen* (childhood scenes), never needing to speak because performing music generates intimate companionship and shared joy.

Fothergill's romance fiction grounded in feminist aims nonetheless still conforms to Victorian novels' obligatory love story. But to this English convention Fothergill welds a German novel plot that radically departs from Victorian fiction and masculinities. For Courvoisier occupies a space equally consistent with magnetic heterosexuality and queer masculinity through a romantic male friendship and nurturing fatherhood.[33] Mirroring this polarity, the novel has two narrators and an English and a German plot that never quite fuse yet are inseparable. Courvoisier's story cannot be understood apart from Fothergill's second narrator, the assistant concertmaster Friedhelm Helfen, whose name suggests peace, protection, and help.[34] May first notices Friedhelm when she accompanies Miss Hallam to the ophthalmologist's office. She is immediately drawn to him, albeit not romantically:

> he had, I thought, one of the gentlest, most attractive faces I had ever seen; boyishly open and innocent at the first glance; at the second, endued with a certain reticent calm and intellectual radiance which took away the first youthfulness of his appearance. Soft, yet luminous brown eyes, loose brown hair hanging round his face, a certain manner which for me at least had a charm. (1:94)

He is Courvoisier's roommate as well as assistant, whom Courvoisier greets fondly on the night May attends *Lohengrin*: 'Arrived at the empty chair,

[Courvoisier] laid his hand upon Helfen's shoulder, and bending over him, spoke to him as he seated himself. He kept his hand on that shoulder, as if he liked it to be there. Helfen's eyes said as plainly as possible that *he* liked it' (1:142). A momentary hand on the shoulder of a male friend is common in English fiction; a lingering touch is not.

As the novel's other narrator, Friedhelm, whom Courvoisier often addresses by the affectionate diminutive Friedel, fills in the details that May cannot know, and his every word testifies to the men's closeness. In Book III, 'Eugen Courvoisier', one chapter is titled 'Friedhelm's Story' but is headed by three staves from Eugen's leitmotif from Raff's 'Lenore' symphony, as if the two men blended selves (2:25). Friedhelm, not May (married to 'Eugen' by this point), even gets the last word in the novel, which celebrates love between two men:

> Between me and Eugen there has never come a cloud, nor the faintest shadow of one. Builded upon days passed together in storm and sunshine, weal and woe, good report and evil report, our union stands upon a firm foundation of that nether rock of friendship, perfect trust, perfect faith, love stronger than death, which makes a peace in our hearts, a mighty influence in our lives which very truly 'passeth understanding.' (3:271)

Fothergill's mix of feminist romance and queer masculinity begins early in the novel when, trespassing the safeguards for sexually innocent Englishwomen, May follows Courvoisier and Friedhelm home one night and visits them unaccompanied in their room rather than returning immediately to the safe confines of her boarding house. All have just finished a dress rehearsal (*Hauptprobe*) for the oratorio in which she has a solo part.[35] Desperate to apologise for her rudeness at the *Lohengrin* concert, she invents the pretext of paying back what Courvoisier spent on their meals and rail tickets in Köln. Next to the door she sees 'Prinz Eugen, der edle Ritter' (Prince Eugen, the noble knight) chalked in red and enters in response to their '*Herein*'. She walks in on an embrace, though not between the two violinists:

> there, with the light falling upon his earnest young face, was Helfen, the violinist, and near to him sat Courvoisier, with a child upon his knee, a little lad with immense dark eyes, tumbled black hair, and flushed, just awakened face . . . Courvoisier held the two delicate little hands in one of his own, and was looking down with love unutterable upon the beautiful, dazzling child-face. Despite the different complexion and a different style of feature too, there was so great a likeness in the two faces, particularly in the broad, noble brow, as to leave no doubt of the relationship. My musician and the boy were father and son. (1:177–8)

The First Violin: *A Hybrid Anglo–German Novel* 125

Fothergill's romantic hero is thus a single father who deeply loves his young son, and May has walked in on a queer family of two male parents and a child.

Friedhelm narrates their back story in Book III. At twenty-two, 'literally alone in the world', Friedhelm turned 'misanthrope' after losing his passion for music under the influence of pessimistic philosophy (1:228).[36] He was beginning to contemplate suicide as a rational solution to his unhappiness (1:230) when a knock at the door revealed Courvoisier, instantly as attractive to Friedhelm as he was to May, but first revealed as a violinist and father: 'There entered a tall and stately man, with one of those rare faces, beautiful in feature, bright in expression, which one ... never forgets. He carried what I took at first for a bundle done up in a dark-green plaid, but as I stood up and looked at him I perceived that the plaid was wrapped round a child' (1:233–4).

The newly arrived Courvoisier urgently requires a room for his two-year-old son the eve before he is to begin his appointment as first violin. Like May, Friedhelm is struck by the son's beauty and the father's tender love as Courvoisier lays the child 'upon the bed, and arranged the plaid around it as skilfully and as quickly as a woman would have done it' (1:238). Friedhelm rescues Courvoisier from difficulty when he opens his door to him and soon suggests that all three of them move into a larger set of two rooms (with Courvoisier and the child Sigmund in the bedroom). Yet Courvoisier and Sigmund also rescue Friedhelm from despair and suicide, and he quickly assumes the role of co-parent (1:251).

As Friedhelm declares, 'it has fallen to my lot to be blessed with that most precious of *all* earthly possessions, the "friend" that "sticketh closer than a brother." Our union has grown and remained not merely "*fest und treu*" [firm and faithful] but immovable, unshakable' (1:253); Courvoisier was 'the man who had become my other self ... I loved him – because I could not help it; he me, because – upon my word, I can think of no good reason – probably because he did' (2:2). Courvoisier in turn later announces their mutual love to orchestra members: 'from the time when I arrived; when Friedhelm Helfen, here, took me in, gave me every help and assistance in his power, and showed how appropriate his name was; ... so began a friendship which, please heaven, shall last till death divides us, and perhaps go on afterward' (2:180) – the kind of afterlife usually linked only to heterosexual marriage in Victorian novels. Their queer family suffers a terrible loss, one foreseen by Eugen that partly explains his shifting moods and self-imposed restraints, when he loses custody of Sigmund after an agent sent by his family takes the child away. Prior to that point, their Elberthal family is affectionately represented, perhaps most charmingly and queerly when Courvoisier and Friedhelm go shopping for new stockings for Sigmund and are the only men in the shop (2:10–5). The friends differ only in one respect. Friedhelm has never and can never imagine being in love with a woman (1:280). Courvoisier has indeed loved before and been loved in turn, but awakened one day to find his life 'spoiled' (1:282).

Fothergill freely acknowledges the role of Heyse's *Kinder der Welt* in suggesting elements of *The First Violin*. When Courvoisier and Friedhelm have lived together three years, Courvoisier brings home a 'brand-new novel', an extravagant purchase that shocks Friedhelm, and announces, 'here is some mental dissipation for to-night. Drop that Schopenhauer, and study Heyse. Here is *Die Kinder der Welt* – it will suit our case exactly, for it is what we are ourselves' (2:3). Book IV of *First Violin* is itself entitled 'Children of the World', and near the end of Book V May applies the phrase to Adelaide, who has never followed religion as a guide, to von Francius, and to herself: 'were we not all children of the world, and not of light? ... Religion was for both of us an utter abstraction; it touched us not' (3:60, 62).

May further extends reference to *Kinder der Welt* in Book VI, but only after radical shifts in plot indebted both to Heyse and to Eliot. This requires some explanation of Fothergill's German source. In Heyse, four years after Edwin's beloved brother Balder dies, Edwin and Lea, an artist, are in a happy dual-career companionate marriage. Christiane the pianist and Mohr are parents of a three-year-old, and Toinette, the woman Edwin first met and desired, is well off after marrying the count. But rapid revolutions in perspective ensue. A doctor seeks Edwin out when the count fears that his wife Toinette is going mad, and the doctor reasons that Edwin may be able to help her resist despair. Arriving at the count's grand castle, Edwin realises to his horror that his passion for Toinette has only lain dormant, and now Toinette declares her love for him. They exchange a passionate embrace, yet in keeping with his high sense of morality, Edwin leaves for home and Lea; still driven by his rigorous moral standards, he confesses all to Lea, who out of love for Edwin decides she must leave him to allow Toinette and him to be together. Ultimately Edwin realises that his true passion is for Lea, and Toinette commits suicide. At the novel's end two years later, Lea and Edwin have a daughter, Edwin has published his philosophy book, becoming a hero to a younger generation, and Edwin pays tribute in a final gesture to Toinette's own moral integrity.[37]

In its six-book structure and successive revolutions late in the narrative that layer one sensational event upon another, *First Violin* resembles *Kinder der Welt*. Book V, 'Vae Victis' (woe to the vanquished), culminates when an orchestra member publicly repeats the rumour that Courvoisier forged his wealthy brother's signature on a check, and since he does not deny the accusation, Courvoisier's only recourse is to resign and leave town. 'Der edle Ritter' Eugen was in fact Count Eugen von Rothenfels, the younger son of a proud German baron. Impulsive, extravagant, and democratic in sympathies, Eugen married the beautiful Italian governess Vittoria with whom he fell in love. It was she, Sigmund's mother, who forged the check, and, convinced that he drove Vittoria to crime after he improvidently bet on a horse race and lost most of their money, Eugen takes the obloquy and dishonour on himself, leaves his noble family in disgrace, and takes his young son Sigmund with him (Vittoria having expressed little interest in the child), relying on his highly developed musicianship to support them both. In quick succession, Friedhelm leaves the orchestra to follow Eugen, Von Francius takes a new post, Adelaide elopes, and, May, bewildered to think how she could have fallen so deeply in love with an illusion, falls ill and is ordered home to England. Thus ends the New Woman plot of *First Violin*.

But she has promised to sing for one of von Francius's concerts and returns after the Franco-Prussian war ends.[38] First visiting a villa near Elberthal, May decides to walk to Elberthal to escape the tedium of her hosts' mundane conversation even though a gale is rising. The gale develops into a cyclone, with windspeeds so fierce and the river rising so rapidly that the bridge onto which May walks cracks at either end and breaks off.[39] An almost unbelievable coincidence follows, except that it is borrowed from Eliot's *Mill on the Floss* and maintains the novel's Anglo-Germanism in its German denouement. May is not alone on her makeshift raft floating rapidly downriver, as she realises when she hears someone humming the march from Raff's 'Lenore' and knows either that she is hallucinating or that it is Eugen. It is he, back from the Prussian war to see his old colleagues. Eugen and May expect to die at any moment, like Maggie Tulliver and her brother Tom on their raft on the flooded St Ogg's, an extremity that at last frees them to speak honestly. They declare their love and May affirms her belief in him despite all the evidence ranged against him; she also vows (disappointingly) that if they survive she wants a strong man and master as husband. Yet she proposes to resume her singing career as well to earn income, foreseeing a dual-career marriage akin to Edwin and Lea's in *Kinder der Welt*, an allusion intensified when May thinks, 'My happiness, I am and was well aware, was quite set upon things below; if I lost Eugen I lost everything, for I, like him, and like all those who have been and are dearest to both of us, was a Child of the World' (3:155–6).

They survive, and May agrees to visit the nearby castle of Rothenfels, ignorant of Eugen's connection to it. When May is invited to wander through the halls, she hears a violin playing, seeks it out, and discovers Sigmund practising to become like the father he still adores even though he has been told never to mention him again. All is soon revealed, and rather than marrying a poor dishonoured musician, she is engaged to a count who, soon cleared of all wrongdoing, represents an intimidating standard of brave endurance and honour.

Yet he resumes his family role only on the condition that his natal family accept Friedhelm as a respected guest and equal (3:255). In the final chapter set at Christmas a few years later, the widowed Adelaide von Francius, May's younger sister Stella, Friedhelm, and another musician and his bourgeois wife gather at Rothenfels to celebrate. It is not quite a happily-ever-after conclusion. May has retired from public performance to focus on Sigmund's upbringing with Eugen, a far more traditional role.[40] Nor does marriage entirely banish sadness for Eugen:

> he is not a very cheerful man – his face is melancholy. In his eyes is a shadow which never wholly disappears – lines upon his broad and tranquil brow which are indelible. He has honour and titles, and a name clean and high before men, but it was not always so. That terrible bringing to reason – that six years' grinding lesson of suffering, self-suppression – ay, self-effacement – have left their marks, a 'shadow plain to see,' and will never leave him. (3:269)

Fothergill thus subverts a Victorian romance's happy ending, leaving readers with a saddened bridegroom and the enduring German homosocial love between two men that tilts *The First Violin* towards the German pole of Fothergill's hybrid Anglo–German novel. *Daniel Deronda* will remain better known, but reading *Deronda* alongside *First Violin* highlights the authorial choices of each author and the inspiration that Fothergill drew from Eliot's story of Gwendolen and Grandcourt, which she put in conversation with Heyse's 1873 German novel. The result in Fothergill is an intricately woven fabric of Anglo–German cultural exchange and language that anticipates New Woman fiction and, like all works discussed in this study, demonstrates the rich possibilities and opportunities that Victorian women writers and their fictional characters discovered in Germany.

CHAPTER 6

New Woman Travellers and Translators
Michael Field and Amy Levy

The early chapters of this study address women who travelled to Germany for professional reasons (Anna Jameson and Anna Mary Howitt), erotic reasons (Marian Evans), and family reasons (Mary Howitt and Elizabeth Gaskell), whose cross-cultural experiences inspired writing in multiple genres from 1834 to 1862. Chapter 5, turning to the 1870s, explores alongside *Daniel Deronda* the significance of Jessie Fothergill's story of a single woman who travels to Germany for professional reasons and who, once arrived, takes up the life of a New Woman with her own latchkey and freedom to walk alone on city streets or interact unchaperoned with men as she actively pursues her career. Yet none of the women writers considered thus far, or their fictional characters, could attend a university or royal academy. With Michael Field – Katharine Bradley (1846–1914) and her niece and lover Edith Cooper (1862–1913) – and Amy Levy (1861–89), that circumstance changed. Bradley was five years older than Fothergill, but collectively Michael Field and Levy represent a rising generation who could live as New Women materially and physically, not just in books. Bradley completed a term at the Collège de France in 1868 and a vacation term in October 1874 at Newnham College, Cambridge (founded 1871); on the cusp of the 1880s the aunt and niece attended University College, Bristol, which from its founding (1876) had opened its doors equally to women and men. Levy matriculated at Newnham in October 1879 and remained until some time in 1881.[1] College-educated women travelling on the Continent in pairs were far rarer in their day than ours and could face occasional threats. But as university-educated women they were better equipped to travel on their own terms independent of parental or tour guides' interference as they encountered German culture.[2] That these three women were all lesbian further buffered them against conventional domesticity, and, since their desires lay outside social norms, they were presumably more open generally to new avenues of experience and perspectives.

129

This chapter approaches the Fields and Levy as New Woman travellers, translators, and writers of poetry, drama, and fiction. The chapter's aim is less a comparison – no evidence indicates that they ever interacted, though they shared acquaintances in common including Vernon Lee – than an exploration of how ethnoexocentric encounters with and in Germany continued to propel women writers in the 1880s and '90s as they enjoyed expanded freedoms and a nascent sense of global mobility. Germany was by then a unified modern state with a fully developed rail network, which enhanced these women's mobility.[3] Sometimes their experiences could involve sexual danger, as revealed in the candour of the Fields' and Levy's private writings (another indication of 'New' perspectives). As public writers Bradley and Levy, both of whom had studied German growing up, benefited from the opportunities their educations provided for translations of German poetry that helped found their poetic careers at the outset.[4] Mary Howitt had translated German poets decades before, but Bradley and Levy grouped translations alongside feminist verse in their poetry collections, as Howitt did not. I begin by briefly looking at Katharine Bradley's translations in her earliest volume, to which she gave an Anglo–German feminist title, *The New Minnesinger* (1875), before devoting more sustained attention to Michael Field's collaboratively written private journal entries about their German travels, their drama *Stephania*, and selective poems they published from 1892 to 1908. I follow a slightly different order with Amy Levy since her private records of travel in Germanic lands and short fiction demand less space than her early translation work and the deep, lasting impact of Heinrich Heine on the entire arc of her poetic career that ended so tragically with her suicide in 1889.

Michael Field

The New *[Woman]* Minnesinger *(1875)*

If Lesa Scholl argues that translation of foreign works enabled 'foreign' ideas outside Englishness and its feminine norms to circulate freely among Victorian women, Annemarie Drury maintains that translation is vital to understanding Victorian poetry itself since a desire to incorporate the foreign was intrinsic to poetry in an era of imperialism and global exchanges in commerce, exploration, and print. Moreover, translation was a vital conduit of poetic experimentation because translators had to seek poetic strategies that could recreate for English readers of poetry the impression and impact of a source text outside their own language.⁵ Current feminist translation theorists suggest yet another reason why translations could appeal to progressive women seeking careers. Rather than treating translation as subordinate to a dominant 'original' and 'fidelity' to it as the sole criterion of merit, these scholars emphasise the creativity and personal agency involved in translation.⁶

Even before readers opened *The New Minnesinger*, Bradley declared its connection to Germany and her artistic agency as a 'new' troubadour who sings differently from her male precursors about love and chivalry. As her identically named title poem asserts, girlhood subjectivity and girls' transition to womanhood had yet to be told from a woman's perspective:

> Yes, Woman, she whose life doth lie
> In virgin haunts of poesie, –
> How have men woven into creeds
> The unrecorded life she leads!
> . . . . . .
> what she to herself may be
> They see not, or but dream they see.⁷

In 'Youth Time', a cycle of seven songs responding to the death of a young Frenchman with whom Bradley fell in love in Paris, the fifth song is headed by a German epigraph, '*Geistern bin ich noch verbunden*' (I remain joined in soul), from Ludwig Uhland's 'Auf der Überfahrt' (The Crossing). Appropriate in context, the epigraph also looks ahead to the volume's second section of seventeen translations of German lyrics, Bradley's only published verse translations; these, based on lyrics by Johann von Goethe, Schiller, Heine, and others, were praised by the *Academy* as 'graceful translations'.⁸ Bradley translated loosely and creatively indeed with Goethe's 'Das Veilchen' (the violet). Goethe's three witty German stanzas tell how a modest violet, seeing the approach of a young shepherdess ('junge Schäferin'), wishes it could be the most beautiful flower in the meadow so as to be plucked and pressed against her bosom. But the shepherdess never sees the violet and treads on it, though the blossom rejoices that it dies through her. Bradley drops the shepherdess, who becomes merely the 'Beloved' addressed by the violet and ends with sententiousness that is not in Goethe's poem: 'True love hath only life to shed, / And then away!'⁹

Her translation of Gretchen's famous spinning song in Part I of *Faust*, however, 'Mein Ruh ist hin', skilfully replicates Goethe's rhythms and repetitions that suggest a spinning wheel going round and round:

> My peace is gone,
> My heart is sore;
> I shall find it never,
> O nevermore!
>
> Where he may not be
> 'Tis the grave to me;
> The whole earth round
> Is desert ground.
>
> My poor tired head
> Is fever-toss'd,
> My poor sick brain
> Is daz'd and cross'd.
>
> My peace is gone,
> My heart is sore;
> I shall find it never,
> O nevermore!
>
> For him I'm watching
> The live-long day,
> For him I wander
> From home away.
>
> So kingly-fashion'd,
> So hero-wise;
> His wooing laughter,
> His conquering eyes;
>
> His pleading whisper's
> Magic bliss;
> His thrilling touches,
> And oh, his kiss!
>
> My peace is gone,
> My heart is sore;
> I shall find it never,
> O, nevermore...[10]

Her very choice to translate Goethe and Schiller, the two giants of Weimar classicism whose work influenced Coleridge, Byron, and Carlyle, bespeaks her ambition and claim to authority. But she also gains standing as a translator by including less well-known German poets such as Wilhelm Müller, whose 'Vineta' invokes the legendary sunken island off the north German coast that draws a sailor to it who sees its magical reflex at sunset, just as the isle's magic sparkles within the writer's imagination.

This lyric had a tacit English connection too, since the poet's son was the prominent philologist and German-born British citizen Max Müller, who had reissued his father's volumes in Germany in 1868.[11] This lyric seems to have had particular meaning for Michael Field, since a journal entry from 1889 mentions Bradley reading it aloud to Cooper.[12]

Bradley's best translations are of Heine's work, which effectively convey his tone, rhythms, rhymes, and substance. Rather than drawing all these from his best-known *Buch der Lieder* she also translated 'Neuer Frühling XIII' ('Die blauen Frühlingsaugen') (new spring, no. 13 [the blue eyes of spring]) from his *Neue Gedichte* (new poems) of 1844.[13] As a translator, then, Bradley exhibits wide-ranging literary tastes and in-depth knowledge of German. Her Heine translations further attest to Heine's appeal to women poets from Mary Howitt to Levy, and Bradley's were well timed insofar as they appeared before the heyday of Heine translation in the 1880s.[14] Still, her knowledge was principally of written German, like Marian Evans's before her German travels.

Michael Field's Private Travel Writing and Stephania *(1892),* Sight and Song *(1892),* Wagner, *and* Wild Honey from Various Thyme *(1908)*

The Fields's Anglo–German exchange was more limited than Levy's or many writers in prior chapters. Financially independent and answerable to no one but themselves, they needed Germany and its opportunities less than some. And, as just noted, their speaking and listening skills in German were minimal, as they quickly discovered during their 1891 journey. As Cooper wryly records of their arrival in Dresden in their collaborative journal:

> The train unexpectedly stops – Altstadt, Dresden! The spectral, weary travelling is over. Sim's [Bradley's] excellent knowledge of German literature and grammer [sic] has availed nothing after twenty years' neglect. We were as dumb as sheep, carried on through places no map had ever shown to us ... .[sic] angry with ourselves, shamed, helpless, unrepentant, & contemptuous of all things German, as Sim had been when she said we should go through Dresden in blinkers at the Gallery.[15]

Neither did the couple carry letters of introduction, like many earlier writers, or settle like Fothergill in a German boarding house that would have forced them to speak to Germans more often. Nor were their German travels motivated by German culture itself. As Bradley recorded on the eve of their August 1891 departure, 'Our eyes are preparing for <the> a great pilgrimage. What washing from advertisements, vile cuttings, & all the parodies that life presents they need before they can enter into the Muses' joy.'[16] The 'Muses' joy' was tethered not to a geographic locale but to the immaterial realm of beauty and intellect, which had no borders. For them, the journal suggests, Europe was an aesthetic theatre in which to encounter great paintings, opera, and drama as means to enhance their artistic creativity through new aesthetic stimuli. Moreover, the Fields, like Evans with Lewes, travelled *as* an intimate couple and most readily turned to each other; couples-travel effectively insulated them from direct contact with foreign surroundings.

They had nearly finished their verse drama *Stephania: A Trialogue* (1892) before setting off, which motivated a stopover in Aachen to visit the tombs of Charlemagne and Otho III and a material exchange with this German site. Having kissed the steps leading up to Otho's resting place they had a

> Sudden thought: The M.S. of the 1st two Acts of Otho w^{d} lack consecration unless laid on the pale astounding marble he trod aforetime. I leave Sim watching the full light of afternoon making the dim throne hoar – I fly across the market-place almost swept and garnished, with but few chattering, bonneted elders left – down the main street, I turn aside for The Dragon d'Or <to> the precious sheets within it. I am soon back warm with sun, at the Dom, & soon the M.S. <soon> lies a flake of white on the grizzled mass of stone.[17]

Only *this* place, in *that* moment, would allow for their embodied encounter with the German past. But this was not ethnoexocentrism. Their manuscript's brief rest upon the stony tomb of the Holy Roman Emperor, both tribute and consecration, represented Michael Field's private English projection onto a foreign scene. Though deeply felt and meant, their gesture was not so different from other tourists' touching of foreign artifacts or sites that had personal meaning. At least the Fields' private ritual left a light footprint on Germany after their departure.

Their play was set in 1002 shortly before the German-born Holy Roman Emperor Otho III dies of poison from Stephania, the widow of the Roman leader whom Otho III has ousted and slain. The play thus presents German culture in a largely negative light. Otho not only has executed the Roman leader Crescentius and displayed the beheaded body publicly but has also disposed of Crescentius's widow Stephania by turning her over to his German troops who rape her, thereafter forcing her into the life of a courtesan. The play's greater interest lies in its two clashing love triangles, one homosexual, the other heterosexual: the young Otho calls both his former tutor and mentor Gerbert, now Pope, and Stephania, who seduces him with her beauty, 'Beloved' in Act III.[18] James Bryce's history of the Holy Roman Empire, which inspired the plot of *Stephania*, referred in passing to 'the rebel Crescentius, in whom modern enthusiasm has seen a patriotic republican' and an analogue of 'rude' Bavarian troops occupying Rome to Austrians occupying Italy prior to the Risorgimento.[19] *Stephania* would not have predisposed the Fields to see a positive cultural model in Germany – though they remained eager to see Wagner operas in Wagner's own land.[20]

They next travelled on to Dresden, still insulated from their German environs:

> We stop at a nameless Station – the elder of the Norns,[21] out of breath and sisterly, struggle into the carriage – that guard's face is behind them. For a long time they recover; we venture English, French – but the Norns understand only German. They smile sunken misty smiles; then they bind up their heads from the air, and the shortest mounting the seat closes the vampire-eyelids of the gas-lamp fatefully, as a rite –
>
> Something that is not Sleep falls . . .
>
> The Fates sleep – every now and then an anomalous sound, hardly voices, passes between them – they sleep – one has her chin bound up with a handkerchief – of course in Greece she would be Atropo. They stir and weakly drink from a little flask . . .
> [O]ne lies among one's wraps in feverous damp without shame while it is still dawn. The little stations are mere huts, the lines of the horizon come very near to one – there is revolt in one's <eyes> gaze against the magnifying illusions of night. The world looks common, and very black – poor little patch as it is! One is hungry – one feels <as> that one's eyes are purple and swollen as if one had fought with an adversary. I look at the Fates, – they are two ordinary little Old Maids, dreadful to see in the shiny, heated condition of dishabille [sic], with stray hairs on the cheek & wraps falling from their features – nothing terrible about them . . .
> Suddenly there is sweetness in the world as one looks out – the Sun himself introduces light . . . Then shame comes, and one hastens to the sponge, the comb, the mirror – one must not remain peculiar now that familiarity is given back to the universe of wh: one is a part.
> One begins the comedy of Toilet in the space of a sq. yard – one re-seats oneself curiously reconciled to the view and one's fellow-passengers.[22]

As poets, they mythologise the old women, and their journey becomes a quest undertaken against the Fates. Unable to converse in German and connect with the women, the Fields view them from a distance as pathetic and unlovely, even while the journal's micro-travel narrative vividly conveys the mundane realities that face overnight women travellers and the phantasmagoric imagery wrought by the train's speeding journey through a nocturnal landscape.

Their distance from Anglo–German exchange, however, disappeared instantly when Cooper contracted scarlet fever in Dresden and was forced into a German hospital, where a kind young German doctor allowed Bradley against the rules to enter with Cooper on that first terrifying, disorienting night in a strange place in a foreign city.[23] They now had to interact with German hospital doctors, nurses, and attendants one on one, and, importantly, experienced Germany and Germans alone when separated from one another. Cooper entered the hospital on 17 August. By 8 September, German words and phrases begin to appear in the journal, especially after Cooper playfully, even flirtatiously, learned some German phrases to please a young handsome doctor who knew some English.[24] Bradley now began to master German speaking skills during their extended Dresden residence and recorded a series of 'Ausgangs', her term for expeditions outside the hospital. Most mention gifts that she buys for Cooper, but one is a brief account of the freedoms and exhilaration that residence in another culture bolstered by ability to speak with its inhabitants makes possible:

> I go forth finally to Theater Platz – I see again the Bacchus & Ariadne, the close darkness of the Georgen Thur, the pleasant broken spaces by the Elbe, the trim quiet of Hôtel Belle Vue. I tremendously enjoy myself. How densely foreign it all seems, and am I not still 'im Werden' [in process, becoming] – <u>throating</u> German in & out of the shops, & meeting with response from stranger faces. I love the tall, irregular roofs, the peculiar, compressed darkness of Schloss-Strasse, the soft-coloured, woollen goods in the shops everywhere.[25]

But their direct Anglo–German exchange would also expose Cooper to sexual danger from a quarter the Fields did not anticipate. The couple often spoke with the principal nun who nursed Cooper, and the three were sufficiently acquainted that the Fields told Schwester [Sister] Christiane of their drama about Otho III, which puzzled the nurse:

> 'Wofür besingen Sie solch ein Mann?' she asked. [Why do you sing about such a man?] When we told her he had sinned & repented, she was quite willing we should continue to <u>besing</u> him. Yet she could not discover the attraction, & when we gave her the date of our hero found it 'ein Bischen lange her' [a rather long time ago].
>
> Tonight she has been talking of many things – the healthfulness of wearing 4 pr. of stockings, strong boots &c. We begged of her when writing

to Amy to persuade the child to eat flesh. But she said 'Amy ist eine ganz gutes mädchen – Der Menchens Wille ist sein Himmelsreich' [Amy is a very good girl; a man's will is his heaven]. Amy, she is convinced, lives by her principles, & must not be forced. She showed us her portrait – a clear transcript of the rough, serviceable, consecrated face.[26]

Here, truly, is cultural exchange. When the nun cannot fathom why they write about Otho, they explain rather than dismissing her for imperviousness to art and their high mission; Sister Christiane in turn feels able to offer an alternative perspective on the vegetarianism of Cooper's younger sister that the Fields might otherwise resist.

But this same nun also turned stalker and sexual aggressor when Sister Christiane fell in love with the much younger Cooper. T. Sturge Moore and D. C. Sturge Moore include most of the episode in their print edition of *Works and Days*, including Cooper's perceptive analysis after the nun-nurse embraces and kisses her, and lets her hands roam over Cooper's breasts and belly while declaring how hungry she is for love ('Ich bin so hungrig'): 'My experiences with Nurse are painful – she is under the possession of terrible fleshly love, [which] she does not conceive [of] as such, and as such I will not receive it.'[27] Exercising continued sympathetic understanding, Cooper obliged Sister Christiane with a German poem after the older woman suggested they poeticise together about the contrast between a red rose (Cooper) and last rose (Christiane):

> Here is my ignorant, exhausted attempt:
>
> Die erste Rose Sommer bringt,
> Dennoch sie ist des Sommers Werke.
> Von Liebe, Liebe Jugend singt –
> Und Liebe giebt ihm alle Stärke.
>
> Dir Rose hat in Mai ein' Gluth
> Dass fehlt Ihr in der heisseren Sonne,
> Und erste Liebe hat ein' Wuth
> Dass fehlt des Lebens letzen Wonne.[28]

When the Fields left the hospital in mid-September, Cooper gave the nun a parting gift of a writing-case and expressed deep gratitude to the doctors whose own complex humanity had become much clearer to her. Their judgemental stance toward the old 'Norns' in the train had been left behind, replaced by their far greater openness to German culture and people.

As Marion Thain remarks, 'Paradox is the paradigm underlying Michael Field's poetry.'[29] 'Paradox' also characterises Germany's role in *Sight and*

Song, the work that motivated the Fields's visits to art galleries in Britain, France, and Germany in 1890–1. They explicitly identified their aim in this volume as 'to translate into verse what the lines and colours of certain chosen pictures sing in themselves; to express not so much what these pictures are to the poet, but rather what poetry they objectively incarnate'.[30] Their theory of inter-arts translation, as well as the implied sexuality of merging two female bodies and sets of eyes in gallery spaces into the figure of a masculine-named poet, have commanded the greatest scholarly attention.[31] But the spaces in which such gazing occurred were literal European spaces, and except for relevant museum names affixed to each poem's title, Germany went unmentioned.

At the same time, the volume's successive pages constructed a virtual map and route of museum visits that registered New Women's mobility and freedom to travel to see art. The opening pages take readers from the Louvre to London's National Gallery to the Accademia of Venice, back to the Louvre, and on to the Uffizi.[32] A later sequence follows a German route, beginning with two successive Veneto paintings at the Städel'sche Institut at Frankfurt before moving to Dresden, back to the Städel'sche, back to Dresden and then returning to England at the National Gallery.[33] Like a guidebook, the volume tacitly constructed a network of museums and potential routes between them that readers could imaginatively travel, though readers might alter 'routes' by reading poems out of order. Michael Field thus offered a purely textual counterpart to the virtual travel provided by the dioramas and guidebooks that often assumed readers' prior familiarity with the scenes depicted – just as the Fields assumed audiences' familiarity with the paintings that their poems 'translated'.[34]

German museums recur in three later poem titles, including 'The Sleeping Venus / Giorgione / The Dresden Gallery' and 'A Pen-Drawing of Leda / Sodoma / The Grand Duke's Palace at Weimar'.[35] This last site, which Ottilie von Goethe and her mother would have frequented, and mention of the Dresden art gallery are reminders that the Fields were partially following the precedent of Jameson's visits to German galleries.[36] Yet that awareness underscores the palpable absence from *Sight and Sound* of the Dresden painting that Jameson (and later George Eliot) considered its greatest, Raphael's *Sistine Madonna*. Self-avowed pagans, the Fields displaced the *Sistine Madonna* and installed Giorgione's *The Sleeping Venus* as the *ne plus ultra* of paintings of the female form and celebrated the pagan goddess of love identified with bodily beauty and pleasure rather than the 'grace, and purity' of Christ's virgin mother:

> Here is Venus by our homes,
> And resting on the verdant swell
> Of a soft country flanked with mountain domes:
> . . . .
> There is a sympathy between
>   Her and Earth of largest reach,
>   For the sex that forms them each
>   Is a bond, a holiness,
>   That unconsciously must bless
>   And unite them, as they lie
>   Shameless underneath the sky.[37]

Their 'tour' of the Dresden Gallery thus rewrote Jameson as they foregrounded a New Woman's freedom to look at and appreciate a nude female body rather than reverentially standing before Raphael's image of the Virgin and child.

Another poem earlier in the volume, 'The Rescue', inspired by Tintoretto's painting at Dresden, revels likewise in female nudity and power – muscular, ocular, and erotic. This three-sonnet lyric displaces middle-class, mid-Victorian femininity by again revising Jameson, who deemed Tintoretto's 1565 *Crucifixion* his best painting and regretted the 'exuberance' and 'excess' of his Dresden work, and also Tennyson's 'The Lady of Shalott'. The Michael Field poem, like Tennyson's, features a 'Grey tower', 'armour', and shining surfaces that dazzle; but the knight's armour is 'dark' against the large female's 'shining nakedness', and he 'staggers' under the 'weight' of her 'powerful' limbs as, rather than weakly succumbing to rescue, she 'Bows to confer / Herself on her deliverer' and boldly appropriates a female gaze as she looks into his face. Her naked 'sister-captive' ignores the knight altogether as a matter of indifference and 'Strikes her right ankle, eager to discumber it of chain'. Rather than she, it is the 'rose-frocked rower-boy' who, 'in absent fit / Or modesty, surveys his toe', a humourous reversal of conventional gender roles as well as narratives of chivalric 'rescue'.[38] This understudied lyric in *Sight and Song* thus likewise registers New Woman erotic and aesthetic freedom.

On returning to England from their first German visit the Fields were sufficiently interested in the culture to engage German teacher Jaakoff Prelooker. A Russian Jewish exile and advocate of women's rights, Prelooker had taught himself German, met the socialist feminist Lina

Morgenstern in Berlin, and emigrated to Britain in July 1891.[39] Cooper's 10 December 1891 journal entry indicates how well Bradley had mastered German and Cooper's lesser skills – and interest:

> Our German Prof . . . Herr Prelooker makes his first visit. He is a Russian from Odessa. He has been deeply inspired by <u>W</u>oman, & his work in <their> her cause has driven him from his country. His pamphlets have been suppressed. All this would have kindled one in one's youth, but I rest on the oar of my thirty years totally unmoved. I understand much of the conversation – Sim converses as if by nature. Two mortal hours we keep the ball flying – on the subject of lectures, the deeds of women in history, women nihilists, Germany, & Dresden Experiences. I had ejected <u>Weh</u>! [woe] – in the letter to nurse Prelooker overlooked – with regard to the loss of my hair. He smiled frankly and said the interjection was <u>zu stark</u> [too strong]. How dense the two sexes are to each other's stand points! He is very Slavonic in type – ugly, good, simple – using the hand much for courtesy in the foreign way – has a splendid brow, small intelligent eyes, & the fervour to die for ideals – in wh: he alone is wealthy. He is disappointed in the English ladies – their learning is not <u>gründlich</u> [thorough].[40]

Though their first visit to Germany had been traumatic at times, the Fields's unfulfilled desire to hear more music by Wagner led them back five years later to hear the complete *Ring* cycle in August 1896. To reach Bayreuth they travelled through German-speaking locales in Switzerland and Austria and were at first repelled by Swiss mountains and architecture: 'We launch epigrams against Switzerland – its mountain-crushed people – The horror of mountains! They produce valleys & <u>goitres</u> & petty picturesqueness in building.' But as earlier, their refusal of openness melted away, and when they left Pontresina Cooper wrote, 'We leave Pontresina, loving it. We like its situation, air, Alps, attendance – single street of hotels & <u>chic</u> little shops. Fashion combines charmingly with chamois.'[41]

Upon their arrival in Innsbruck, haunting reminders of their stay in Dresden resurfaced when the 'noble velvet-pile' of their hotel room recalled their Dresden lodging. More tellingly, when given the choice to see Wagner's *Tannhäuser* or a production entitled *Heimat* (native land), 'we chose *Heimat*: we do not feel that we dare to hear <u>Tan.</u> under conditions that might remind us of Dresden – in a German town, on the edge of seeking Bayreuth'.[42] But in Munich Cooper was elated to discover another German city rich in art, especially in the Pinakothek, and wrote about paintings in their journal much as she had in 1891–2.

Their stay in Bayreuth began badly and they almost left, repelled by its foreign smells and unattractive vistas. These, too, reminded Cooper of Dresden: 'No-one has ever told me that Bayreuth is vulgar, suburban, defaming with its Tannhauser Cafés & Siegfried-strasse, its smells, its untidy manners. It is as Michael [Bradley] says a German Redhill ... And the smell that rises up is like to the stench that struck me down at Dresden.'[43] Nor was Cooper, an experienced dramatist herself, impressed by Wagner the poet when she read his libretto before seeing *Das Rheingold*: 'At its best his text only suggests psychologically not aesthetically – the splendid dramatic imagination is not transfused into the language.'

Hearing Wagner's music was another thing altogether, and Cooper began to 'translate' the effect of listening to Wagner's music as the Fields had earlier 'translated' paintings, aiming less at recording subjective thoughts or emotions that the music inspired than at what the music seemed to 'speak'. Of the opening strains in *Das Rheingold* she wrote, 'the most wonderful music begins – the melling of all the waters under the firmament. Let there be rivers! This is the sound of their creation.'[44] Her response to *Die Walküre* paralleled her response to Giorgione's *Sleeping Venus* insofar as it too bespoke female eroticism: 'Sieglinda makes love with a beautiful abandon – . How women lead men in the world of Emotion – they are the protagonists ... all women who succeed take this pre-eminence without question & leave to men all other worlds they like to claim.' As her long passage on the opera concluded, 'The music at the end is the very triumph of the world-creating Eros – rapture acknowledged to the height & depth.'[45] Still, Germany figured more on this trip as another aesthetic theatre rather than opportunity unto itself, and when the Fields left Bayreuth, Cooper contrasted their 'hunger of the pilgrim' on arrival with the 'plenitude of the Initiate' at their exit.[46]

They took two more trips to Switzerland a year later but neither by choice nor desire. In June 1897 James Cooper, father and uncle to the pair, fell to his death while walking in the mountains outside Zermatt. Since his body had not been recovered and there were suspicions of murder, the Fields rushed to Zermatt to help ensure that the search went on. This horrendous context rendered moot any thought of the tourist outings of the year before or sociable interactions with Swiss residents. Instead they met principally with Swiss officials who wished to resolve the case quickly, creating distance and distrust in the Fields. Yet two days after arriving Bradley recorded, 'For a few moments I have intense happiness, watching Henry [Cooper] gathering Alpine flowers on a safe, high meadow slope'; and the following day Cooper lyricised on the Alpine scenery and its intimate association with both her mother and father:

> What blueness ... forget-me-not & turquoise, blue of flowers & bluest stone, have been dreamt of together by this sleeping Lake Geneva, loved so dearly by my beloved mother – what help, what benediction! ... The Rhone Valley, the stifling mountains, the great stream – its fury, its elastic

speed, its grimness & the thought of the sweet lovely gray hair it may be swirling along.[47]

Fragments of German language again began to surface as they further opened themselves to the Alps, as in Cooper's confession of momentary joy amidst searching for her father: 'The morning is "herrlich wie am ersten Tag" [glorious as on the first day]. By five we are ascending Riffel & hearing from Franz that father surely fell in the torrent. Even while speaking of death, the exhilaration of living on such a day & climbing toward the highest Alps is irresistible in its triumph.'[48] After three fruitless weeks' searching, they 'retire[d] beyond the Matterhorn Bridge into a cup-like meadow by the torrent & [sat] in the shade'; Bradley read the Burial of the Dead; and they threw 'clods of sweet Earth' into the stream below.[49] Below this entry they pasted in a small photograph (one of several) of the Matterhorn looming over the hotel, which seems less a tourist souvenir than a *memento mori*. For the daughter and niece of the dead, Zermatt was the site where James Cooper's corporeality, like his life, dissolved and dispersed into the landscape.

Around the time they left Zermatt they began an elegiac sonnet sequence in memory of James Cooper: 'Burial', dated 27 November 1897, and a draft of 'Turning Homeward' followed the final Zermatt entry in their journal for 1897. But they were suddenly called back to Switzerland when James Cooper's body was found. For the third time their travel to a Germanic land involved trauma, first to retrace their steps to Zermatt where they had said their goodbyes, then to identify the deceased's belongings, and worst of all for Bradley, to endure having 'Photographs of the rock [from which he fell] & one of the dear body ... brutally ... put into her hand without a word of warning.'[50] They would return to Zermatt a final time in 1898 for an Alpine Bacchic ceremony to rededicate themselves to life and love, a meaningful counterpart to the Alpine burial ceremony prematurely conducted in July 1897.[51] Their cultural interest in Switzerland was thereafter nil. Their memorial sonnet sequence titled 'The Longer Allegiance', twenty-four alternating Petrarchan and Shakespearean sonnets and a concluding lyric titled 'The Halcyon', appeared in *Wild Honey from Various Thyme* (1908). According to Jill Ehnenn, 'The Longer Allegiance' represents a process

> whereby the poets work through their libidinal attachment to the events surrounding James's death ... [and] stages a series of visits to and meditations upon the woodland site of James's fall and death. In so doing, it praises the untamed yet enduring powers of Nature, God, love, death and

memory, asserts the paradoxical presence of the deceased, and ultimately substitutes a celebration of the poets' own love and life together for their grief.[52]

Michael Field's journal and poetry alike testify to the Fields's mobile travels and engagement with others in German-speaking lands. Yet ultimately they preferred their own intimate companionship and creative collaboration to sustained Anglo–German exchange. In this they form a notable contrast to Amy Levy, who never had the good fortune to find an erotic partner and whose writing registered a sustained, profound interchange with German literature and culture.

Amy Levy

Anglo–German Exchange in Levy's New Woman Fiction and Travels

Like Bradley's and Cooper's families, Levy's was affluent, enabling her to receive a good education with a governess followed by boarding school and the progressive Brighton High School for Girls, where some teachers were college-educated women. Levy then matriculated at Newnham College. Her parents had no connection to the publishing world – her father was a stockbroker – but from age thirteen Levy was both writing and publishing her work, starting with her poem 'Ida Grey' in the feminist journal *The Pelican*.[53] Nearly fluent in German, Levy merged her publishing experience, language proficiency, and German travels to produce an 1884 series of short stories about university-educated New Women abroad aimed at a popular audience. Though they are slight compared to Levy's novels, the stories repay attention because of the queer sexuality nested in their plots and their production alongside Levy's private travel writing in letters. Her public and private representations of New Woman travel diverge in ways that illuminate not only Levy's imaginative processes but also the publishing strategies she and other women writers adopted (and what they left out) to represent New Woman mobility abroad. For example, none of Levy's fictional New Woman travellers is Jewish. The tales appeared in the monthly *London Society*, subtitled 'An Illustrated Magazine of Light and Amusing Literature for the Hours of Relaxation', and Levy crafted her content accordingly. Since themes of holiday travel were a magazine feature, Levy's August 1884 story 'In Holiday Humour' was aptly titled.[54]

This is set by Lake Lucerne in Switzerland, where Girton-educated Olivia Longcroft is enjoying a three-week holiday, often accompanied by the attractive Sydney Tressider. The action opens as Olivia and her friends travel across the lake by steamer from the Pension Sonnenthal ('sunny valley'), where they stay, to Lucerne. Their party consists of four young women (Olivia, her sister Marian, and Sydney's two sisters), three young men, and forty-year-old Caroline Meldrum, who plays unwitting chaperone to the group. The story conveys the sheer fun and merriment available to young people abroad, as well as the pleasures of al fresco dining with a glorious view of mountains ringing the lake: 'The young people were in high spirits; they scampered from one end of the boat to the other; they bought fruit of the dull-eyed peasants; they made a great many jokes about nothing at all ... They lunched in a shady garden affording a distant glimpse of the lake; there were coffee and omelettes, honey and ices, and great piles of scarlet mountain-strawberries.'[55]

The story's title and epigraph come from *As You Like It*, when Rosalind directs Orlando, 'Come, woo me, woo me; for I am in holiday humour, and like enough to consent', a forecast of Olivia and Sydney as they enjoy desultory conversation, the lake's languorous air, and the warm sun until Sydney asks whether he should join a men's walking party the next morning or stay. This leads to his declaration of love and Olivia's assent to an engagement. But that is not the story's end. The romance takes a sudden turn when the couple and Miss Meldrum (caught napping) miss the steamer back to their hotel and endure a frightening ride across the lake in a flimsy boat amidst a sudden violent storm. Olivia, rigid with fear during their journey, realises that it would mean nothing to her to die beside Sydney and declares at the end 'I cannot marry you' – a New Woman outcome indeed. When he compels her to give a reason she stutters out, 'In the boat – in the boat, I – I thought of some one else!' The story quickly ends with Sydney ready to join the walking party after all and the two formally thanking each other for a 'pleasant holiday'.[56]

More significant for readers today than the story's Shakespearean title and epigraph is the Shakespearean allusion embedded in Olivia's name, which opens the story to queer readings: in *Twelfth Night*, Olivia is the Countess who falls in love with the cross-dressed Viola when Orsino sends Viola to woo Olivia in his place. While the collapse of a summer heterosexual romance is hardly daring – if consistent with New Woman repudiation of obligatory marriage – the fact that the gender of the person Olivia thinks of during her dangerous boat ride is left unstated extends the story's queer possibilities. A popular summer reading audience could readily absorb a story of college students' Swiss travels abroad, their potential encounters with physical danger, and the free intermingling of the sexes.

But for those who cared to look, readers could also see a New Woman tale of queer relations that a foreign setting made easier to hint at.

Levy's next story in the series was the epistolary 'In Retreat: A Long Vacation Experience', set in the Vosges Mountains – part of France today but Prussian territory from 1871 to 1918.[57] In this light-hearted narration of a university reading vacation taken by two women students, one studying anatomy, the other Greek, the women book rooms at the Convent of St Odile.[58] German words appear throughout: the evening meal is the *Abendessen*, and when the narrator's companion demands water for the 'travelling "tub"' she has brought with her, the Mother Superior retorts, 'Dann gehen Sie in den Hohwald' (Then go to the upper forest [to bathe]) – which the students refuse to do. The Catholic setting brings cultural difference to the fore, as well as lingering English stereotypes from which the 'advanced' women are not exempt; the narrator first describes the Mother Superior as 'a wicked-looking old woman, with a malevolent eye' and hints in a letter that a visiting monk carries on a clandestine flirtation with a nun.[59] Eventually the university women prevail in the battle of the tub water, and by the story's end their experience of Anglo–German exchange results in a more open, less prejudiced view of the Convent: 'though the prices seem rather high at starting, we have decided that the place is cheap. If not generous, the old Mother is just, and our bills are quite clear from the usual list of "extras".'[60] The brief tale thus represents women in the process of learning to practise ethnoexocentrism while abroad; the students are clear about their own values but have learned to acknowledge the legitimacy of other cultures and orientations.

The story's travelling New Women are modelled on Cambridge students; the verses one of them writes about Strasburg will be sent to the '*Camford Review*', a play upon the River Cam and *Cambridge Review*, to which Levy contributed translations and original poems while in college.[61] Levy further frames her characters by drawing on a former Cambridge student-poet, Tennyson, and his 1847 poem *The Princess*, in which Princess Ida founds a separatist women's university rather than submit to arranged marriage with a prince.[62] Levy's narrator Melissa travels with Psyche and writes to Blanche; all bear names of Tennyson characters at Ida's university. 'In Retreat', moreover, is set in the separatist female community of a convent visited by British 'chums', the word Levy used in private writing for her friends. These homosocial relations again support a possible queer reading of the tale and its New Women, which ends looking ahead to travel in the Black Forest.

The next month 'In the Black Forest' duly appeared in *London Society*.⁶³ There is the merest hint of heterosexual romance between Psyche and a village schoolmaster in Lenzkirch. More prominent is Melissa's love for this part of Germany, with its old-fashioned yellow coaches, coachmen in shiny hats, and the Black Forest itself: 'It is such a fair, smiling, home-like country, with its fragrant woods and meadows, its quiet villages nestling among the hills; its babbling streams and running brooks – such a contrast to that grim Vosges country, with its solitary ruins and endless forests, and where there was always a skull carved at the base of the wayside crosses.' More characters named after *The Princess* surface, including Gama, here a younger man sporting a 'Camford boating-suit' who gives the women a consolatory row on the lake the day they arrive to find that the hotel is full and that they must spend the first night in a coaching inn where their bedroom is separated from cows only by a 'thin partition'. Hilarion, whom they meet for coffee one day, lives in a village higher up. But for the most part the women are on their own, exploring the neighbouring villages, planning an expedition at the story's end to the Black Forest's highest mountain where they hope to camp and see the sun rise, and generally leading an idyllic life of rowing, reading, walking, bathing, and sheer lounging about. As Melissa exults to Blanche, 'Don't we sound healthy, wealthy, and wise? No tea, no cram, no midnight oil. I hope everybody at Princess Ida's University will profit by our example.'⁶⁴ Here are the freedoms of New Woman travellers indeed.

Levy more specifically conjoins New Womanhood and Anglo–German exchange at the outset as Melissa and Psyche travel by coach to 'Freyburg'. The only other passengers are a recently married German couple. The wife proudly, even jealously, upholds traditional female roles in contrast to the university women who are educated enough to speak good German and whose very presence in the coach signifies a new female order:

> [T]he woman [was] shrill, sharp-featured, with light hair and eyelashes, very voracious over the ham-sandwiches and hard-boiled eggs with which her husband plied her; very vigilant over the husband, a meek and cheerful little person, evidently much in awe of his wife. I was determined to talk to the man, in spite of the she-dragon, and assailed him with questions in my fluent German – Psyche says it was a positive case of assault.
>
> The woman expressed much shrill surprise at the fact of our travelling alone.
>
> 'And you always go *ganz allein* [entirely alone]? without a gentleman?' And she clutched at her miserable specimen of manhood with complacent triumph.
>
> You can imagine our scorn. I wonder when the German Hausfrau will consider the question of casting off the yoke!⁶⁵

Their 'New' politics emerge again when Psyche asks to visit the Lenzkirch school. As Melissa notes, 'Girls and boys learn together in the school, but only the latter are taught drilling, which is a great pity: don't you think so?' She approves of co-education but censures unequal standards even if it spares the girls tedious repetition; and as she makes the point she glances towards the unconventional mix of 'thick boots and Liberty handkerchiefs' she and Psyche wear to visit the school.[66] In portraying the fun as well as freedoms apportioned to New Woman travellers, 'In the Black Forest' and 'In Retreat' implicitly invite *London Society*'s younger leisure-hour readers to consider how their own lives might improve should they attend university and throw off old limits imposed on unchaperoned women at home and abroad.[67]

Levy's private letters to friends and family during her time in Dresden, Lucerne, and the Black Forest confirm that she too experienced fun and freedoms while travelling, as well as some complications absent from her fiction. Our picture is incomplete since she left so few letters behind, but she would surely have known about racist attitudes towards Jews led by some German Protestant pastors at the time. At seventeen Levy was reading the *Jewish Chronicle*, which regularly covered news from Germany.[68] In 1880 and 1882, the timing of Levy's early visits to German lands, this London weekly paper reported the anti-Semitic campaign led by Adolf Stöcker, Imperial court chaplain, and history Professor Heinrich von Treitschke, whose standing as a German historian, according to the *Chronicle*, paralleled Lord Macaulay's in England.[69] By late February 1880 the populist movement led by those two inspired the headline 'The "Judenhetze" [persecution of Jews] in Germany', though the paper also reported the Kaiser's and Crown Prince's clear repudiation of Stöcker.[70] If later instances of anti-Semitic propaganda were duly reported, so were ripostes from Christian and Jewish leaders that swiftly followed. By 1882 anti-Semitic agitation in Germany had quieted, and from a Jewish perspective German troubles were overshadowed by pogroms in Russia. Thus 'The Jews of Frankfurt' seems representative of the paper's attitude towards Germany as a whole at this time. The city where Johann von Goethe was born, according to the *Chronicle*, 'illustrates better the past and present circumstances of the Jews, and their gradual transition from the despised condition in which they lived in former times to the general esteem and respect they now command, and the active and important part they take in political and social matters, literature, arts, sciences, &c.'[71] As an educated woman of the press, Levy presumably was keenly aware that in some quarters, especially among clergy influenced by Stöcker, an Anglo-Jewish traveller in Germany might encounter hostility, but also that Jews, especially with talent and education, were readily accepted.

The letters preserved from Levy's months in Dresden, where Levy turned twenty on 20 November 1881, omitted any mention of the famous art gallery that so profoundly affected Michael Field and their poems in *Sight and Sound*.[72] Nor on this first trip did she mention any sustained interactions with German speakers, perhaps unsurprisingly since she travelled with her friend Madge. If she joined a literary club, the crowd there seems to have been largely Anglophone. She did, though, teach English to a young German woman and reported, in addition to some Germans staying at the same boarding house as she, a German Herr Minden who invited her and Madge to walk with him (Levy declined).[73] It was not the thought of unchaperoned contact with men that prompted her response. She was entirely unconcerned at the thought of teaching English to German youths just three or four years younger than she or of studying Greek in Dresden with a married man from Cambridge. But her parents back in Britain objected so strongly that she conformed to her father's wishes and gave up teaching 'boys' for the time.[74]

On her next trip to Lucerne, Switzerland, in July 1883 she travelled with Ellen Crofts, a lecturer in English at Newnham and the fiancée of Francis Darwin, son of the famous father.[75] Rather than in a boarding house, the two women stayed at the Hotel Sonnenberg, a fine hotel of over 300 rooms that became the 'Hotel Sonnenthal' of 'In Holiday Humour'. That story's Swiss boatmen who 'stood up strong and sturdy, skillfully wielding the long poles' as they guide their 'light flat boat' across Lake Lucerne also chime with Levy's own athletic experience as a rower. As her 18 July 1883 letter recounts, 'Monday morning I walked down to Lake Lucerne with three of the party & we took a most remarkable boat with very quaint oars; we had to stand up to row, but it was rather fun.' The night before she and men and women in the party 'went down in the dark to the little lake near here & hired the solitary tub & drifted about for an hour'.[76] As a traveller Levy was more athletic than her character Olivia, who is passively conveyed; and while Levy experienced being set adrift on the lake, she was quite safe in contrast to the danger in which she placed Olivia to prompt an emotional crisis.

As for her response to the beautiful Swiss scenery, this and her bohemian freedoms dominate one of her surviving letters home:

> Today the weather has been all that could be wished; a cloudless blue sky, lots of sun and a gentle breeze. This morning we started on an exploring party – to find out a good place for working. We lighted upon a small rocky

pine-grown peninsula jutting over a small secluded blue lake, lying in the midst of the mountains. It is to be our permanent camping out place, indeed I am at present writing this letter stretched out on a rug over a moss grown rock with a wonderful view of blue lake & green hills & blue sky stretching before me ... Would it be a great trouble to send me my bathing gown ... we are going to bathe early in the morning in the small lake ... This afternoon we had a most exciting time making tea in Miss Croft's 'Aetna' ... wh. we drank out of a tooth glass, & 'milked' with Swiss milk out of a tin wh. we had to break open on a stone ... Excuse more as I am beginning to get rather dreamy ... The sheep bells are sounding as I write ... the sky is blue as it can be and there is sun all over the place ...[77]

Full of what would have been middle-class improprieties back home such as stretching out on the ground and drinking tea from a 'tooth glass', the letter also suggests the sensuosity of balmy airs that lulled her into dreams. Of additional interest in her Lucerne letters is her mention of Mr and Miss Cross, the widower and sister-in-law of George Eliot. Levy and Eleanor Cross evidently took to each other since they maintained the friendship back in Britain, and other hotel guests included the Quaker philanthropist John Rowlinson Ford and Helen Ford, an active suffragist who edited a women's suffrage magazine to which Levy planned to contribute.[78] Here again, as with her vigorous boating and plans to swim, Levy's actual travel experiences were more overtly feminist than those she added to 'In Holiday Humour'.

No letters survive from Levy's residence in the Vosges mountains, so far as we know. But her travelling 'chum' Blanche Smith, a former Newnham student who had read in natural sciences (as Levy's 'Psyche' studies anatomy), readily explains why she might have thought of Tennyson and *The Princess* when writing her story based there.[79] From the Vosges, Levy and Smith travelled to the Black Forest and found rooms at the Gasthaus zum Titisee outside Baden, Germany. Levy spent part of her time with an Anglophone crowd, so much so that she worried in a letter to her sister, 'Everyone speaks English here – I don't know where my German has gone.'[80] But the same letter mentions a planned excursion to Lenzkirch, the destination of Melissa and Psyche to visit a local school in Levy's Black Forest tale. And the Lenzkirch excursion led to a far more direct encounter with German culture in the nearby village of Saig. The Ochs (Ox) Hotel was entirely frequented by Germans, with some of whom Levy enjoyed unconstrained conversation:

> There is a little group of simple-hearted Studenten [male students] with whom I rather chum. One, strange to say, is a friend of Walter Gottheil; he

> is a Wagner-schwaermer [enthusiast], & is going to play me bits of the *Walküre* to-night. Yr. hair wd. have stood on end to have seen me last night, after dinner, sitting at the table with no less than three German mashers engaged in animated converse. I think the matrons believe me to be no better than I shd. be, but my men are awfully nice & polite.[81]

No such episode occurs in Levy's 'In the Black Forest'. Levy's letter thus provides a welcome window onto the lively exchanges that a young British woman two years out from university could enjoy with German male students sans chaperone – a clear anticipation of study abroad freedoms that would become the norm decades later.

The first part of her letter from Saig, however, indicates the risks posed by international travel to women. The comic mix-up at the hotel that lands Melissa and Psyche in a room next to the cows' stall in Levy's Black Forest tale was based on a truly frightening experience, though Levy's letter home customarily made light of it. Here is the passage in full:

> Behold me in my village retreat! I am living in a state of naked impropriety, altogether unchaperoned. My first night of exile was a failure. I didn't get rooms at the Ochs, [the Gasthof Ochsen] so had one found at the Pfarrer-house [the priest's house], with the arrangement that I was to board at the inn. The word Pfarrer suggested a homely domestic soul to myself & Miss Corfe who led me up. Not till I was fairly established did I identify it with the grim individual in a cassock who is to be seen curtseying about the churchyard at all hours of the day. When I came back from supper at the Ochs a sort of funk seized me. I bolted my room & put chairs against an inner door. The nasty old woman who brought my bath saw the chairs and scoffed at my fears, & I tried to settle down with my books. Presently a knock came. I opened the door & beheld a tall figure in a cassock, candle in hand, grinning & chuckling in a way which when taken with his normal solemnity, was grim in the extreme. He came to soothe my fears (o irony) assured me that I was 'bei ihm' [at his house] & that the hostess at the inn had been wrong, & that my room was not besetzt [occupied] for the next night. He kept on repeating 'Ich behalte Sie so lange als Sie wolle' [You can stay as long as you like], so often & with such fervour, & coming so close, that had it not been for his profession I might have considered myself entitled to hang up my 'at in the 'all. I kept the door very narrowly open, tho' he was evidently anxious to pay me a pastorly visit, & waxed pale & funky, wh. was silly, for of course he meant well – but he was a hale man in the 30s & I was quite at his mercy. I had a grim night; kept on remembering that all the villains ... in German tales are priests.[82]

Beckman rightly connects this letter to Levy's 'keen' grasp 'of her vulnerability to sexual assault'.[83] Since the priest's use of 'behalten' can also imply to hold onto or retain, the sexual dimension in Levy's scenario is overt.

Which German tales with villainous priests Levy had in mind is unclear.[84] If she could not overlook sexual danger at Saig, neither would she have forgotten that she was Jewish or the contemporary 'Judenhetze'. One reason the *Jewish Chronicle* dispatched a correspondent to Oberammergau in 1880, when (as Chapter 3 notes) the Passion Play was restaged, was to see how this anti-Semitic work in conservative, largely Catholic southern Germany would affect the standing of German Jews during the Judenhetze.[85] The confrontation with a priest at her door in full-length cassock who was 'grinning & chuckling' must have been terrifying indeed. So while New Women travellers had more freedoms than many of their precursors, they still faced some risks, whether sexual or from prejudices against them, and had to monitor the very independence that also expanded their horizons.

Levy's New Woman Verse Translations and Anglo–German Poetic Exchange

In all Levy published sixteen poems either translated from or indebted to German poetry (see the chapter appendix). In Levy's 'Confessions Book', which reflects sophisticated reading and literary tastes, German literature plays a significant role.[86] Her 'favourite prose authors' included not only Gaskell, Brontë, Thackeray, Anne Thackeray Ritchie, and Henry James but also Johann von Goethe and Heyse. Heyse struck a particular chord since she placed Edwin from *Kinder der Welt* at the head of her 'favourite heroes in fiction' (if mistakenly writing 'Edward').[87] Two of her 'favourite poets' were likewise German: Heine and Goethe (in that order, after Swinburne and Robert Browning). Her subsequent translations and poetic Anglo–German exchange would illuminate her complex emotions as a Jew, woman, and poet.

As Annemarie Drury notes, John Dryden's three modes of verse translation remained influential in nineteenth-century Britain: metaphrase (word-for-word literal translation), paraphrase (which allowed for latitude in word choice but always kept the meaning and effect of the original in view), and imitation ('libertine' translation for which the source text served as a model or point of departure but controlled neither the thought nor language of the new English poem).[88] Levy distinguished among these three modes herself, using 'from' in translation titles for paraphrase and 'after' for imitations. Her earliest verse translation appeared during her first year at Newnham in the 9 June 1880 *Cambridge Review*, which began its long run on 15 October 1879. Her translation's placement was astute, since the *Review* had already published several verse translations from foreign literatures and the classics. Her choice of a little-known Goethe lyric as her source-text was also telling. Selecting Goethe (as had Bradley) linked her effort to mainstream literary tradition and Goethe's prestige. But Levy chose a minor, ironic lyric about a feckless shepherd, 'Der Schäfer' (1779), rather than a passage from *Faust* or the better-known 'Schäfers Klagelied' (The Shepherd's Lament). To clarify what Levy did and did not do in her first published verse translation, I reproduce both Goethe's poem and Levy's translation as a backdrop to the skill she quickly acquired:

Der Schäfer

Es war ein fauler Schäfer,
Ein rechter Siebenschläfer,
Ihn kümmerte kein Schaf.

Ein Mädchen konnt' ihn fassen,
Da war der Tropf verlassen,
Fort Appetit und Schlaf!

Es trieb ihn in die Ferne,
Des Nachts zählt' er die Sterne,
Er klagt' und härmt' sich brav.

Nun, da sie ihn genommen,
Ist alles wieder kommen,
Durst, Appetit und Schlaf.

The Shepherd.
(From Goethe.)

There was an idle shepherd, fond of sleep,
Who never troubled him about his sheep.

But by a maiden was he captive led –
He left the bottle, sleep and hunger fled.

His passion drove him to unrest and flight;
He'd moan and groan and count the stars at night!
* * * * *
But when, at length, the maiden he had ta'en,
Sleep, hunger, thirst – they all came back again.[89]

Turning four German tercets into four English couplets required extreme compression and invention to capture the swiftness and ironic ending of Goethe's frothy lyric. But she departed markedly from his prosody and rhyme, perhaps an assertion of Englishness insofar as she discarded Goethe's trimeter lines and replaced them with iambic pentameter.[90] But Levy also dropped Goethe's witty rhyme scheme (aab ccb ddb eeb) and his repeated words in the second and fourth stanzas and wrote in rhymed couplets instead. She successfully conveyed the sense of Goethe's lyric but relinquished his formal strategies that gave zest to his lyric trifle. She must have been dissatisfied with the results since she never reprinted 'The Shepherd'.

Nor did she ever reprint 'From Grillparzer's Sappho' in the 1 February 1882 *Cambridge Review*. By then Levy had travelled in Germany and read deeply in German literature during her Dresden residence.[91] If rarely mentioned in English studies today, Grillparzer, a leading dramatist in Vienna and Germany in the 1830s, figured importantly in Anna Jameson's *Winter Studies and Summer Rambles*, which identified his *Sappho* (1818) and *Medea* (1821) as his two best dramas and his Sappho as a 'type of the woman of genius'.[92] Levy selected Grillparzer's *Sappho* for translation after the *Cambridge Review* praised her *Xantippe, and Other Verse* (1881) in a June 1881 notice.[93] Her choice of a modern drama referencing a classical female figure implicitly advertised by association her own earlier reinterpretation of Socrates's wife Xantippe. Since Levy began writing 'Medea (A Fragment in Drama Form)' while in Dresden, perhaps Grillparzer's precedent of turning from *Sappho* to *Medea* played some role in Levy's own compositional history.[94] More than in her first attempt with Goethe's lyric, Levy's translation closely followed both Grillparzer's iambic pentameter form and content, a successful blending of English and German materials.[95] Her 'metaphrase' (line-by-line translation) began promisingly in a New Woman mode as Sappho appropriates sexual agency and the power of the gaze to say of Phaon, 'A beauteous body is a beauteous gift.' But Levy ended with Grillparzer's lines in which Sappho bewails her abandonment by Phaon, omitting Grillparzer's more heroic ending in which Sappho dismisses Phaon when he sues for love a second time and commits suicide to ascend to the gods' realm. Levy's 'From Grillparzer's Sappho' attained a higher standard of translation, but Levy found no reason to reprint it.

In contrast, 'Translated from Geibel' appeared in *Xantippe, and Other Verse*, which Englished Emanuel Geibel's 'In der Ferne' (In the distance).[96] This, too, adhered closely to the content and formal features of Geibel (six quatrains, each with three pentameter lines and a concluding dimeter, though Levy's abcb stanzas depart from Geibel's abab). Harmony between German and English expression and form was important to Levy as a translator, then, as well as congenial tone and thought: the Geibel lyric was a pessimistic acceptance of disappointment in love and refusal to escape from memories of joy into forgetfulness. Anglo–German translation enabled Levy to demonstrate her skill in verse and express her characteristic pessimism while adopting Geibel's German original as an intermediary.

Heinrich Heine's poetry, however, undergirded Levy's most important Anglo–German exchange. Though she contributed translations of his verse to the *Cambridge Review*, she preferred to take inspiration from Heine by fully entering into his philosophical orientation, forms, and tone while speaking independently in situation and word choice, a means of deep-seated cultural and personal exchange.⁹⁷ A prime example among her early poems is the moving 'Imitation of Heine' in the 7 December 1881 *Cambridge Review*, later titled 'A Farewell. / (After Heine.)' in *A Minor Poet* (1884):

> The sad rain falls from Heaven,
> A sad bird pipes and sings;
> I am sitting here at my window
> And watching the spires of 'King's.'
>
> O fairest of all fair places,
> Sweetest of all sweet towns!
> With the birds, and the greyness and greenness,
> And men in caps and gowns.
>
> All they that dwell within thee,
> To leave are ever loth,
> For one man gets friends, and another
> Gets honour, and one gets both.
>
> The sad rain falls from Heaven;
> My heart is great with woe –
> I have neither a friend nor honour,
> Yet I am sorry to go.⁹⁸

There could be no exact counterpart to this work in Heine, who travelled to England (which he did not much like) but had no connection with Cambridge University.⁹⁹ His lyric 29 in 'Die Heimkehr' section of *Buch der Lieder*, 'Das ist ein schlechtes Wetter'(The weather is bad) might have suggested Levy's poem, however. In Heine's first stanza the poet too sits at the window looking out ('Ich sitze am Fenster und schaue / Hinaus in die Dunkelheit' [I sit at the window and look out into the dark]).¹⁰⁰ Heine's scene beyond the window is very different from Levy's though: an old woman hauls ingredients in the foul weather to prepare a cake for her beautiful daughter, who sits, protected and nurtured, safe from the elements – and from the speaker. But in their larger effects the German and English lyrics were kindred: both represented loving bonds from which the alienated poets were excluded. Levy incorporated, too, Heine's characteristic ambivalence that could not rest in a single emotion: the 'sad' rain and melancholy tone bespeak a lonely, unsuccessful Cambridge residence, yet the speaker is reluctant to depart from the lovely community that excluded her. Levy's poem invites specific interpretation as the alienated university experience of a Jew – the heritage she shared with Heine.¹⁰¹ Heine, then, suggested to Levy's poetic imagination a stance, an orientation, and a characteristic rhythm and tone; entering into these, Levy peopled

Heine's forms with her distinctive experiences, her foreign intermediary distancing her from personal experience while her 'assimilative creativity' drew from Heine to invent a new, distinctive Amy Levy poem.[102]

Levy's creative assimilation of Heine runs like a thread through all her volumes of poems. The epigraph to Levy's 1881 debut volume consisted of untranslated lines from Heine's lyric 36 in the 'Lyrisches Intermezzo' section of *Buch der Lieder*: 'Aus meinen grossen Schmerzen / Mach' ich die kleinen Lieder' (Out of my great pain I make these little songs).[103] Several poems in her last volume, *A London Plane-Tree and Other Verse* (1889), also intersected with Heine, including 'In the Black Forest' (earlier titled 'After Heine') and 'The Birch-Tree at Loschwitz'. Levy erased Heine's name from her English titles or subtitles in 1889, leaving it to those who knew Heine's poetry to appreciate his inspiration for her work and simultaneously demonstrating such thorough assimilation of his poetics into her subjectivity and imagination that the voice in many poems was an Anglo–German hybrid of her own creation. 'The Old House', for example, conducts an interchange with Heine's 'Still ist die Nacht' (The night is still), lyric 20 of 'Die Heimkehr'. Heine's poet-speaker visits the house formerly occupied by his beloved, who has long since left the city and reports seeing a man in front who wrings his hands in pain; but when the moon shows him the man's form, it is his own – 'meine eigne Gestalt. / Du Doppelgänger!'.[104] Levy's 'The Old House' represents the poet-speaker revisiting the house of her girlhood once known so well, where the ghosts of the dead come to meet her. Then the speaker sees a 'flitting shade ... / She turned, – I saw her face, – O God, it wore / The face I used to wear when I was young!'.[105] The speaker grieves for this young, 'eager', dreamy self who cannot know what disillusionment lies ahead and turns away. Alex Goody singles out Levy's arresting doppelgänger, which Goody reads as an image of the poet-speaker's 'fractured ... self.[106] Reading Levy's lyric alongside Heine's underscores both her reversal of Heine's genders and her erasure of his heterosexual framework.

I conclude this chapter with the five poems that Amy Levy, writing from London, enclosed in a letter to Vernon Lee dated 26 November 1886: 'The Birch-Tree at Loeschwitz[sic]', 'To Vernon Lee', 'Lohengrin', 'Sonnet' (reprinted as 'The Two Terrors' in 1889), and 'Neue Liebe, Neues Leben' (retitled 'New Love, New Life' in 1889).[107] Though 'Lohengrin' had already appeared in the 20 March 1886 *Academy*, the rest were first published in *A London Plane-Tree*. Yet in Levy's letter the poems formed a highly personal overture with encoded meanings apparent in neither the periodical nor the 1889 volume.

In 1886, Levy and her close friend Clementina Black (1853–1922), the social activist, had spent the winter and early spring in Florence, Italy, where they met Vernon Lee – with whom Levy fell in love.[108] One of the bonds between Levy and Lee, besides writing careers, was their shared knowledge of German language and culture. Another was agnosticism. The German scaffolding of Wagner's 1850 opera provided a metaphor and pretext for a poetic declaration in absolute terms of God's non-existence, a point driven home in Levy's sonnet by the terminal punctuation of lines 9 and 11:

> Back to the mystic shore beyond the main
> The mystic craft has sped, and left no trace.
>   Ah, nevermore may she behold his face,
> Nor touch his hand, nor hear his voice again!
> With hidden front she crouches; all in vain
> The proffered balm. A vessel nears the place;
> They bring her young, lost brother; see her strain
> The new-found nursling in a close embrace.
>
> God, we have lost Thee with much questioning.
> In vain we seek Thy trace by sea and land,
> And in Thine empty fanes where no men sing.
> What shall we do through all the weary days?
> Thus wail we and lament. Our eyes we raise,
> And, lo, our Brother with an outstretched hand![109]

Turning a widely circulating print text into private manuscript sent to a woman to whom Levy was erotically attracted suggests latent personal meaning in the act – whether it was mere pride in the lyric's craftsmanship or the touch of the poet's hand in transforming impersonal print into a personal gift for Lee's eyes only.

Levy spoke more directly in three of the other German-related lyrics, all love poems. Below, quoted from the Amy Levy Archive, is 'Neue Liebe, Neues Leben':

> I.
>
> She who so long has lain
>   Stone-stiff with folded wings –
> Within my heart again
>   The brown bird wakes & sings.
>
> Brown nightingale, whose strain
>   Is heard by day, by night –
> She sings of love & pain,
>   Of sorrow & delight –

II.

Why did you come to my dreams last night,
And wring my heart with the old, old pain?
Did you come in love, did you come in despite,
   yr. coming was vain.
For the old, old pain is dead,
And there is a new pain in its stead.

III.

Nay my friend,
  I wd. not deny,
What none can know
  So well as I.

'Tis time; in other days
Have I unbarred the door;
He knows the walks & ways,
Love has been here before.

Love blest & Love accurst
Was here in days long past; –
This time is not the first,
But this time is the last.[110]

Why Levy decided to cut lines 9–18 from the manuscript version in *A London Plane-Tree*, by which time she knew that Lee did not return her feelings, is unclear.[111] In 1886, still under the spell of Lee's magnetism during their shared Italian interlude, Levy added urgency and force to the lyric by shattering the regular trimeter lines of her first and last stanzas. The middle stanzas, in contrast, adopt an irregular mix of tetrameter and dimeter lines that swell and sink as if in agitation or pain. Levy's 1886 German title, moreover, could harbour a lesbian love message that was effaced in Levy's 1889 English substitution. In a German-language context, the opening 'She' of the poem becomes aligned with the German feminine noun *Liebe* in the title and potentially puns on the lower-case German female pronoun 'sie' that could refer back to 'Liebe' or the unidentified 'She'. The German-language title, in other words, enabled Levy to imply a female love object and personification of love before the poem shifted to the more conventional masculine referent for Love in the lyric's conclusion.

In the same November letter, Levy wrote out 'The Birch-Tree at Loeschwitz' immediately below her signature, and 'To Vernon Lee' on the other side of the page.[112] This materiality positioned the two lyrics as paired poems, another relationship effaced in *A London Plane-Tree*. 'To Vernon Lee', a poem of the warm south, places the friends in an Italian spring landscape above Florence in the opening lines:

> On Bellosguardo, when the year was young,
>   We wandered, seeking for the daffodil
>   And dark anemone, whose purples fill
>   The peasant's plot, between the corn-shoots sprung.

Amidst this scene of renewed life and fecundity, the speaker reaches for a branch of beautiful blossoms in the sonnet's sestet:

> A snowy blackthorn flowered beyond my reach;
>   You broke a branch and gave it to me there;
>   I found for you a scarlet blossom rare.

If 'a scarlet blossom' implies the intense passion the poet offers to Lee, the flowering blackthorn branch lies out of reach, a metaphor both of the desired woman and the poet's futile yearning. The sonnet's conclusion then spells out the lesson of this flower language: 'Hope unto you, and unto me Despair'.[113]

The northern spring of 'The Birch-Tree', in contrast to the warm, verdant south of 'To Vernon Lee', is notably cool: 'At Loschwitz above the city / The air is sunny and chill'. In this lyric another tree, a 'Lone' 'silver' birch tree, stands in for the woman the speaker desires, and it is in the cold north, paradoxically, that 'passionate' desire erupts into expression. Indeed, the adjective 'passionate' twice appears in the second and final stanzas to describe what is unseen but full of force – the 'wind' – until the speaker is driven to physical response:

>   Lone and tall, with silver stem,
>   A birch-tree stands apart;
>   The passionate wind of spring-time
>   Stirs in its leafy heart.
>
>   I lean against the birch-tree,
>   My arms around it twine;
>   It pulses, and leaps, and quivers,
>   Like a human heart to mine.

Embracing this stand-in for the beloved brings no relief, however, and the desolated speaker cries out her solitude and unsated passion at the poem's close: 'O God! the lonely hillside, / The passionate wind of spring!'[114]

The German context for the birch-tree is obvious since Loschwitz is a hillside village above Dresden. But as paired poems 'The Birch-Tree' and 'To Vernon Lee' enact a subtle, moving German allusion that Lee would presumably have recognised.[115] For the juxtaposed trees on hillsides in the cold north and warm south invoke one of Heinrich Heine's most famous lyrics, 'Ein Fichtenbaum steht einsam' (A fir-tree stands lonely):

> Ein Fichtenbaum steht einsam
> Im Norden auf kahler Höh'.
> Ihn schläfert; mit weißer Decke
> Umhüllen ihn Eis und Schnee.
>
> Er träumt von einer Palme,
> Die, fern im Morgenland,
> Einsam und schweigend trauert
> Auf brennender Felsenwand.[116]

The repeated 'einsam' literally designating two lone, solitary trees but also connoting what is lonely, secret, or desolate, and the cold height versus burning rock provide a resonant medium through which Levy could filter her Anglophone lyrics of desire. Levy simultaneously revised gender as she drew inspiration from Heine. His fir (or pine) tree is masculinised; as Philipp Veit comments, Heine transformed the feminine noun 'Fichte' into the masculine 'Fichtenbaum' that longs for a feminine 'Palme'. In contrast, the birch embraced by Levy's speaker is culturally coded as female, a means of intensifying the lyric's lesbian undertones.[117] Since in *A London Plane-Tree* Levy separated 'To Vernon Lee' from 'The Birch-Tree' by thirty-four pages, it is only by way of Levy's private letter to Lee that Levy's craft and sophisticated intertextuality with one of Heine's most famous poems becomes legible.

As her friend Eleanor Marx said of Levy, 'her affinity was with Heine, the sublimated essence of Jewish genius'.[118] Levy herself provided a gloss on her long Anglo–German exchange with Heine in 'Jewish Humour' published in the *Jewish Chronicle* three months before she wrote her November letter to Lee. In it she identified Heine's ability to 'crack ... jests, as it were, in the face of Fortune' as the essence of Jewish humour, singling out his lines from 'Wer zum ersten Male liebt' (Whoever loves for the first time) in illustration:

> Sonne, Monde und Sterne lachen;
> Und ich lache mit – und sterbe.
> Sun and moon and stars are laughing;
> I am laughing too – and dying.[119]

Heine's title clarifies why at a time she was newly in love with Lee, this poem might have come to mind. In any case, only Fothergill and Lee herself, perhaps, exhibit the depth of Anglo–German literary exchange evident in Levy's poetry and poetics, and it was no coincidence that she turned so often to an alienated, free-thinking Jewish precursor. But to this literary inspiration she added, like Michael Field, the experience of German travels and translation as a New Woman.

Appendix: Germany/German-related publications of Amy Levy (periodical information from Beckman)

Poems

'The Shepherd (From Goethe)' [translation of 'Der Schäfer'], *Cambridge Review*, 9 June 1880, 158.

'Translated from Geibel' [translation of 'In der Ferne'], *Xantippe, and Other Verse* (1881), 23–4.

'Imitation of Heine', *Cambridge Review*, 7 December 1881, 127; rpt as 'A Farewell,' *A Minor Poet*.

'From Grillparzer's Sappho' [translations of excerpts from Acts I, IV], *Cambridge Review*, 1 February 1882, 141.

'The Sick Man in the Garden. (From Lenau)' [translation of 'Der Kranke im Garten'], *Cambridge Review*, 8 February 1882, 157; rpt. as 'The Sick Man and the Nightingale. (From Lenau)', *A Minor Poet*.

'To Death. (From Lenau)' [translation of 'An den Tod'], *Cambridge Review*, 8 February 1882, 157; rpt. *A Minor Poet*.

'From Heine' [translation of 'Mein Herz, mein Herz ist traurig'], *Cambridge Review*, 26 April 1882, 270.

'A Cross-Road Epitaph' (with a German epigraph from Heine), *Cambridge Review*, 9 May 1883, 353; rpt. *A Minor Poet*.

'In Switzerland', *London Society*, July 1884, 120.

'After Heine', *Cambridge Review*, 3 December 1884, 123–4; rpt. as 'In the Black Forest,' *A London Plane-Tree*.

'A Dirge' (German epigraph), *A Minor Poet* (1884).

'Lohengrin', *Academy* 20 March 1886, 201; rpt. *A London Plane-Tree*.

'To E.', *London Society* 49 (May 1886), 447; rpt. *A London Plane-Tree*.

Translation of Heine's '*Sie haben dir viel erzählt*', *Buch der Lieder*, *Jewish Portraits*, ed. Lady Magnus, 1888.

'The Old House' [intertextual relation to Heine's 'Still ist die Nacht'], *Spectator* 20 April 1889, 15.

'The Birch-Tree at Loeschwitz', *Woman's World*, 1889, 429; rpt. *A London Plane-Tree*.

Essays
'Jewish Humour' (on Heine), *Jewish Chronicle*, 20 August 1886, 9–10.

Short Stories
'In Holiday Humour', *London Society*, August 1884, 177–84.
'In Retreat', *London Society*, September 1884, 332–5.
'In the Black Forest', *London Society*, October 1884, 392–4.

CHAPTER 7

An Anglo–German Expatriate–Citizen
Elizabeth von Arnim

The final chapters of this study focus on writers who had no need to seek opportunities in Germany; they were there by rights as family members and even, in the case of Elizabeth von Arnim (née Mary Beauchamp, 1866–1941), as a German citizen.[1] Both von Arnim and Vernon Lee (née Violet Paget, 1856–1935) lived more years away from England than in it and were themselves daughters of expatriates. Both were foot-dragging feminists (versus Fothergill, Michael Field, and Levy) who relished freedoms and career opportunities trailblazed by New Women but hung back from openly advocating them. Both were known in their lifetimes and today by their authorial pseudonyms rather than given names and of course were fluent in German, though English was their mother tongue.

The similarities stop there, and given their divergent careers I consider each separately. Born in Australia, von Arnim grew up in England from age three, when her English-born father (wealthy from his Australian merchant shipping company) moved back to England. Fiercely intelligent and a gifted musician, von Arnim originally planned to attend Cambridge University but missed the entrance examinations due to illness and instead studied organ at the Royal Academy of Music from 1885 to 1888.[2] In 1891, she married Count Henning von Arnim-Schlagenthin, whom she had met two years earlier. Her education had included study of German, but her husband demanded that she become fluent and the German state that she become a citizen to marry. The couple settled in Berlin and von Arnim, remarkably fertile, bore three daughters in as many years, eventually becoming the mother of five, including the son whom her husband looked to as his heir. Exiled from her home country and earlier solitary reading and music practice, she found an aesthetic outlet and occasional time alone in the garden she began once the family removed from Berlin to Nasssenheide, her husband's family property, in 1896.

By a historical coincidence, the earlier part-owners of that estate were Ottilie von Goethe and her sons, who as young men spent some pleasant summers at Nassenheide and the nearby resort isle of Rügen.[3] If German marriage and motherhood deprived von Arnim of solitude, Nassenheide birthed her writing career, and in 1898 *Elizabeth and Her German Garden* became a best-seller. From 1898 to 1909, when she left Germany, the author quite literally embodied Anglo-German hybridity.[4] English in descent and rearing, steeped in English literary tradition, published by London publishers, she was also a German wife, mother, and citizen with in-depth knowledge of works by Johann von Goethe and Bettina von Arnim (her husband's forbear) and created stories about Germany, Germans, and Anglo-Germans. Even her *nom de plume* was Anglo-German: von Arnim was a noble name on the German side; the English personal name 'Elizabeth' was not merely noble but royal, glancing back to the famous queen.[5] But von Arnim was something more as well: a modern expatriate. It is worth pausing to consider expatriate identity and the literary sensibility it can generate.

Recent studies of expatriates focus principally on refugees fleeing wars, oppression, and threatened violence or economic refugees seeking improved livelihoods – though some attention is given by business professionals to finance and information technology employees placed in international offices. Von Arnim was instead what migration scholar Amanda Klekowski von Koppenfels terms an 'accidental immigrant' – one who migrates due to a personal relationship.[6] Von Arnim was privileged in education, skin colour, and rank, leaving behind Miss Mary Beauchamp to become Gräfin von Arnim-Schlagenthin. But she still had to negotiate cultural difference daily and manage a subjectivity anchored in two places at once – England and Germany.

Though von Arnim faced none of his political burdens, Palestinian-American Edward Said memorably articulates the nature of expatriate subjectivity in ways that apply to her:

> as any real exile will confirm, once you leave your home, wherever you end up you cannot simply take up life and become just another citizen of the new place. Or if you do, there is a good deal of awkwardness involved in the effort, which scarcely seems worth it. You can spend a lot of time regretting what you lost ... On the other hand, as Rilke once said, you can become a beginner in your circumstances, and this allows you an unconventional style of life, and above all, a different, often very eccentric career.[7]

Some social scientists even suggest that being 'bicultural' enhances creativity.[8] In von Arnim's case expatriate identity certainly did generate 'eccentric' Anglo-German perspectives that fuelled the delicious humour of her early books and her creative literary invention. As Said adds, the exile possesses 'a double perspective that never sees things in isolation. Every scene or situation in the new country necessarily draws on its counterpart in the old country'; and because the exile is 'never ... fully adjusted' an intellectual expatriate develops a sensibility characterised by 'restlessness, movement, constantly being unsettled, and unsettling others' – a condition necessary to humour as well as mature literary innovation.[9]

In the three Edwardian novels on which this chapter focuses, *The Adventures of Elizabeth in Rügen* (1904), *Princess Priscilla's Fortnight* (1905), and *Fräulein Schmidt and Mr Anstruther* (1907), von Arnim's expatriate identity is manifested in the first two as the narrator's quicksilver movements of consciousness flip unpredictably between German and English perspectives and back again.[10] In the 1907 novel von Arnim's fluid cultural perspectives result in a masterful proto-modernist work for which she invents a subliminal narrative flowing beneath the surface of her half-German, half-English narrator's letters to the Englishman who proposes, jilts her, and proposes again. Because the resurgence of interest in von Arnim's work this past decade often focuses on her first book, however, I briefly explain why this Victorian work is the most English of her German novels and not yet expatriate expression.[11]

Elizabeth and Her German Garden (1898): Proto-Expatriate Fiction

Elizabeth and Her German Garden is narrated by a marital immigrant who flees from German customs and neighbours into her garden and aesthetic delight.[12] Three pages into the narrative, 'Elizabeth' contrasts 'happy days' amidst 'the oasis of bird cherries and greenery' with her 'reluctant nights' indoors, confessing that she foregoes meals at table to eat salad outdoors, as she had when she regaled herself with 'the blessedness of being alone as I was then alone!' before other family members arrived at the house.[13] Only the 'babies' named by their birth months rather than given names display hybrid identities, 'adulterating the purity of their native tongue by putting in English words in the middle of a German sentence. It always reminds me of Justice tempered by Mercy' (29). Her satiric capping remark indicates just how far she is from identifying with the German language she necessarily speaks as she happily writes in English.

Gradually her perspective begins to evolve. She may resist the duties of a German hausfrau (37–40) and regret that 'The people I love are always somewhere else' (57), but when she visits England she finds herself not quite at home either. For the first time when she stands on English (hence very damp) soil, she recognises herself as a German 'foreigner' and uses the Englished German term 'Fatherland' for Germany itself: 'it was raining, and except the beautiful lawns (not to be had in the Fatherland) and the infinite possibilities, there was nothing to interest the intelligent and garden-loving foreigner, for the good reason that you cannot be interested in gardens under an umbrella' (71). She returns to what she now accepts as her German home to find blue skies and 'three beaming babies awaiting me' and 'wonder[s] why I had gone away at all' (72).

Her distance from England and growing identification with German home life also informs her reactions to the English governess she hires for her children. Miss Jones shoots her employer a hostile look when the mother who refuses to act like an English *or* German mother remarks after an unexpectedly erudite remark from her daughter, '"If you are not careful, April, . . . you'll be a genius when you grow up and disgrace your parents."' Seeing the hostile look, 'Elizabeth' comments, 'I am afraid she despises us because she thinks we are foreigners – an attitude of mind quite British and wholly to her credit; but we, on the other hand, regard *her* as a foreigner, which, of course, makes things very complicated' (88). Here an expatriate perspective comes into view: she understands perfectly the British sensibility of Miss Jones because she formerly shared it but quickly shifts to an alternate 'we' in the same breath.

Her developing expatriate sensibility is most visible when the Englishwoman Minora arrives for an extended visit along with the narrator's German friend Irais. Neither visitor's name is pegged to her culture of origin: Minora is a Latin term today most commonly used in naming female genitalia; here it suggests the possessor's very 'minor' talents. Irais is French-sounding ('j'irais' designates 'I would go') but also summons up a garden's beautiful iris blooms and, contrarily, the Greek goddess of discord. An English art student at Dresden, Minora is gathering 'copy' for a book on Germany and arrives full of self-importance on a bicycle, that symbol of New Womanhood. She thinks she speaks fluent German, yet no Germans can understand her. She thinks she is a keen observer but misses all the telling clues to the family members' relationships with each other. More offensively still, she spouts surface feminism, then treats 'the Man of Wrath' – the domineering sexist husband of 'Elizabeth' – as a font of wisdom whose every word is venerable truth. Juliane Römhild approaches the ironic parallels between 'Elizabeth' and Minora (like Minora 'Elizabeth' is English in origin, is creating copy for a book, pursues aesthetic beauty, and rejects conventional femininity) in terms of von

Arnim's ambivalence towards feminism and her own writing career.[14] But for my purposes the interactions of 'Elizabeth' and her ungainly visitor are a practice piece for the more artful, self-aware performance of expatriate identity in *The Adventures of Elizabeth in Rügen*. Allowing Minora to declare to 'Elizabeth' without comment that 'You speak English very well' telegraphs at once Minora's ignorance and the narrator's command of German so complete that Minora mistakes her hostess's national origin. 'Elizabeth' further distances herself from her Englishness and flips to her German side when she observes that Minora 'spoke very loud, as English people always do to foreigners' and colludes with 'Irais' to invent silly names ('*Drivel from Dresden*', '*Bosh from Berlin*') for the book Minora plans to write (92–5). They also suppress their true opinions of the Man of Wrath when Minora, hearing Irais's ironic application of 'Sage' to him, asks, '"Oh, do you call him Sage? . . . and always in English?"': 'Irais and I looked at each other. We knew what we did call him, and were afraid Minora would in time ferret it out and enter it in her note-book' (95). Yet in a twinkling German customs are foreign when 'Elizabeth' frowns at her daughter's 'Teutonic' Christmas apparel and expresses dislike of traditional German *Glühwein*, which she finds 'nasty' (99, 111). Less than any single comment, it is the movement of mind passing in and out of English and German standpoints during Minora's visit that is significant. Tellingly, this episode occurs near the novel's end, by which point the narrator's perspective can no longer rest in a non-German identity any more than it can be defined by Englishness.

Expatriate Performance in *The Adventures of Elizabeth in Rügen* (1904)

Like her first 'Elizabeth' book, *The Adventures of Elizabeth in Rügen* (hereafter *Rügen*) is a novel rather than thinly disguised diary and continues the theme of desired escape into solitude. At the outset 'Elizabeth' longs to go on a walking tour of Rügen, Germany's largest island in the Baltic Sea, but can find no one to go with her. Lighting upon a copy of Marianne North's *Recollections of a Happy Life* (1894) in the family library and its description of Rügen, 'Elizabeth' immediately decides to go round the island accompanied only by her taciturn maid Gertrud and carriage driver August. Von Arnim herself travelled round Rügen several times, first with her English friend 'Mouse' and then on multiple trips with her children before going once more with her English friend Oona, their two maids, a driver, and a cart of baggage in 1901. It was this last visit on which she based her fictional travelogue. As Römhild asserts, *Rügen*, the 'most complex ... of the Elizabeth diaries', takes a newly experimental form by fusing the genres of 'travel guide and a comedy of manners'.[15] *Rügen* is also, I suggest, an expatriate novel.

Jane Stabler poses the question of 'how we read the literary result of [bicultural] awareness – as a new hybrid blend, or as two distinct interwoven strands, or as binaries with something else held in tension between them'.[16] I suggest that, more than a 'hybrid blend' or set of 'interwoven' binary 'strands', the text of *Rügen* is a continuous 'fabric' of expatriate identity performance. At no point is there a resolution (blend) between English and German perspectives because there cannot be. Nor can one side be teased out from the other because one side immediately gives way to the other and vice versa in this delightful novel.[17]

Prior even to the title page, the flickering back-and-forth of English and German perception begins in the fold-out map at the front (see Figure 7.1). The lie of the land, the route, the place names, the names of the sea and lakes on the map are all German, as in a map for Germans. But the title above the map and printer named below it are in English, this last including a British place name. The map legend visualises simultaneously English and German scales of measure (miles and kilometres), while 'Route' is both an English and a German word – a bilingual pun of the sort that von Arnim will use in her concluding chapter. Readers are left to imagine for themselves how 'Route' is pronounced; 'Elizabeth' can speak it both ways.

Yet the narrative itself, to state an obvious but consequential point, is in English (if peppered by German words), and the citation of Marianne North's *Recollections of a Happy Life* on page 2 additionally seems to foretell an English lens. The majority of North's text describes her adventurous travels to North America, the Caribbean, South America, and Asia; but her first chapter, 'Early Days and Home Life', details her family trips to Europe including their two-month stay in Rügen at Putbus in late summer 1848. The colourful floating jellyfish that North vividly describes make 'Elizabeth' determined to float in the sea beside them herself. North's Englishness absorbs other German elements besides the isle itself, including its prince in residence at Putbus, since 'The name of that place had become known to English people chiefly through its prince having been the representative of Prussia at the coronation of our Queen.'[18] Englishness also defines the one book 'Elizabeth' takes and opens frequently on her tour, a well-worn copy of Wordsworth's *Prelude*. Excepting a very brief mention of Wagner's *Tristan und Isolde*, all stars in the literary

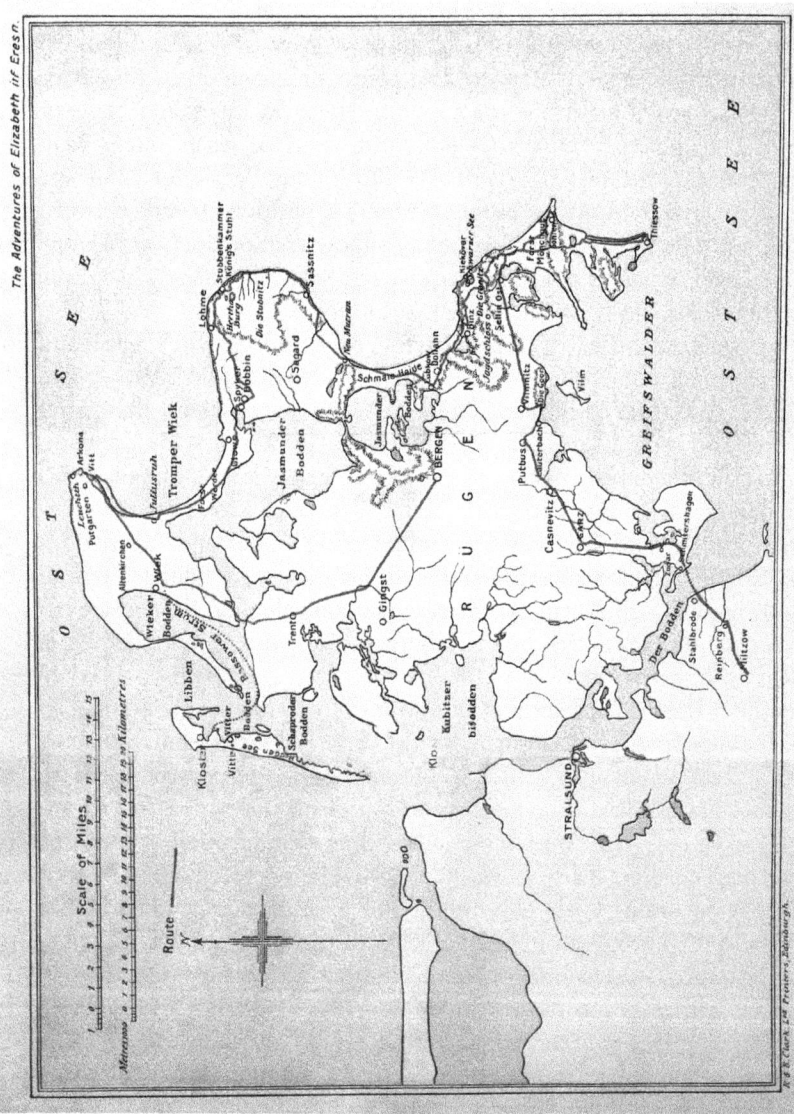

Figure 7.1. Fold-out map of Rügen affixed to the boards of *The Adventures of Elizabeth in Rügen*. Courtesy Mary Couts Burnett Library, Special Collections, TCU

firmament of 'Elizabeth' are English. As Stabler aptly notes, 'For exiled readers in particular, the voices of authors offer a constant form of companionship, and a link with the homeland left behind.'[19] A distinctly English outlook also marks the comic caricature of the impossibly sexist Professor Nieberlein, who absent-mindedly forgets his new wife on their wedding day when he becomes lost in deep philosophical thought and goes off on a walking tour – though he is ever alert to the soft, rounded bodies of attractive younger women who are so pleasurable to kiss, embrace, or merely chuck under the chin. He is especially made fun of when he cannot grasp the English hyphenated names of the Harvey-Brownes whom he meets, and a kind of 'who's on first' routine ensues when he tries to connect them to his prior acquaintances of one name or the other.[20]

Still, if English is the point of entrée linguistically and literarily, the character 'Elizabeth' materially and culturally enters a strictly German geographic zone within which she is a German-speaking citizen and wife with German relatives. Even Keats cannot prevail against this materiality when she attempts to recite his 'Ode on Melancholy' to curb her ecstasy over the beauties of nature she enjoys in the woods near Göhren:

> but the wood and the morning sun and the bread and butter were more than a match for it. No incantation of verse could make me believe that Joy's hand was for ever at his lips bidding adieu. Joy seemed to be sitting contentedly beside me sharing my bread and butter; and when I drove away towards Thiessow he got into the carriage with me, and whispered that I was going to be very happy there. (87)

Most characteristically, the expatriate narrator's restless, mobile consciousness whizzes from Englishness to Germanness and back again, as in her first encounter with the earnest intellectual youth Ambrose Harvey-Browne ('Brosy') when he is momentarily unaccompanied by his mother, the wife of an Anglican bishop who defines her identity through her husband's high English status. When Brosy attempts to take a Kodak snapshot on the small island of Vilm he inadvertently includes 'Elizabeth' in the viewer and immediately comes forward to apologise, pleasing her when he addresses her not as 'gnädige Frau' but as 'Fräulein' because of her youthful appearance. When 'Elizabeth' heads in another direction so that he can take his photos, she walks into another of them. As an expatriate, 'Elizabeth' knows immediately how to place Brosy given his English collar and way of speaking German: 'Again . . . did he call me *gnädiges Fräulein*, and again was I touched by so much innocence. And his German, too, was touching; it was so conscientiously grammatical, so laboriously put together, so like pieces of

Goethe learned by heart' (60–1). Despite his fine education Brosy cannot so easily negotiate German culture or place his German-speaking interlocutor. A devoted student of Professor Nieberlein, whom he has travelled to Germany in hopes of meeting, Brosy begins discussing his passion for the Absolute, and 'Elizabeth' responds as an adept in two cultures:

> I can't think what I have done that I should be talked to for twenty minutes by a nice young man who mistook me for a Fräulein about the Absolute. He evidently thought – the innocence of him! – that being German I must, whatever my sex and the shape of my head, be interested. I don't know how it began. It was certainly not my fault, for till that day I had had no definite attitude in regard to it. Of course I did not tell him that. Age has at least made me artful. A real Fräulein would have looked as vacant as she felt, and have said, 'What is the Absolute?' Being a matron and artful, I simply looked thoughtful – quite an easy thing to do – and said, 'How do *you* define it?' (62)

Because Brosy knows so little about German culture from within, she cannot think how to explain her German social rank when he asks whether she might know the professor: 'How impossible to explain to this scion of an unprejudiced race the limitless objection of the class called *Junker* – I am a female *Junker* – to mix on equal terms with the class that wears white satin ties in the evening' (63).[21] When Brosy then begins 'mansplaining' to the woman he addresses what German women are like, a comic moment blossoms as the utterly knowing expatriate narrator cuts him down to size without his having an inkling she is doing it:

> By the time we had reached the chestnut grove in front of the inn I had said so little that my companion was sure I was one of the most intelligent women he had ever met. I know he thought so, for he turned suddenly to me as we were walking past the Frau Förster's wash-house and rose-garden up to the chestnuts, and said, 'How is it that German women are so infinitely more intellectual than English women?'
> Intellectual! How nice. And all the result of keeping quiet in the right places.
> 'I did not know they were,' I said modestly; which was true.
> 'Oh but they are,' he assured me with great positiveness; and added, 'Perhaps you have noticed that I am English?'
> Noticed that he was English? From the moment I first saw his collar I suspected it; from the moment he opened his mouth and spoke I knew it; and so did everybody else ... who heard him speaking as he passed. But why not please this artless young man? So I looked at him with the raised eyebrows of intense surprise and said 'Oh, are you English?'
> 'I have been a good deal in Germany,' he said, looking happy. (64–5)

As 'Elizabeth' adds, 'The young man's belief in my intelligence was now unshakeable.' But she is not yet done with him. He assumes she will return to the mainland by the tourists' launch, but she has hired her own fishing smack. When he expresses surprise and remarks, '"How delightfully independent"', she rejoins, '"Have you not observed that the German Fräulein is as independent as she is intellectual?"' (65–6). As her smack rows away she recommends the 'compote' awaiting him at his lodging: '"It is lovely compote. It is what you would call in England glorified gooseberry jam."' With this she brings him up short:

> 'Glorified gooseberry jam?' echoed the young man, apparently much struck by these three English words. 'Why,' he added, speaking louder, for the golden strip [of water between them] had grown very wide, 'you said that without the ghost of a foreign accent!'
> 'Did I?' (68)

Even the word 'Fräulein' serves von Arnim's expatriate performance. When Brosy uses the term in his stiff German, it is italicised *as* foreign speech. When 'Elizabeth' uses it in her narration it is in roman type because it is no longer foreign. Brosy sincerely desires cultural exchange and later moves closer to that goal. In this encounter, however, he shows the worst of British provincialism and elite male education, and 'Elizabeth', all unbeknownst to him, puts him in his place.

Von Arnim's authorial performance of expatriate identity is even clearer when Charlotte, the German cousin of 'Elizabeth', enters the scene. Charlotte is in some ways an obverse image of 'Elizabeth'. While attending Oxford University as an international student, Charlotte met Professor Nieberlein as a great philosopher and married this much older widower with grown children. But after bearing six successive infants all named after her husband and dead within weeks, she left home and resurfaced in England giving lectures on women's rights and publishing bilingual German–English feminist pamphlets that assailed conventional domesticity and urged women to forge their true identities.

Von Arnim's expatriate narrative thus includes a German character who has journeyed in an opposite direction, from Germany – where Charlotte learned to admire British intellectual culture and elite academic institutions where women could study – to England, the language of which she knew well enough to enter as a participant. Von Arnim's bi-directional exploration of Anglo–German exchange marks a new development in her expatriate writing, and in *Rügen* its comic results are also turned against 'Elizabeth' and her English predilections. The day after her Vilm adventure

'Elizabeth' arrives at Thiessow and goes for a bathe. She had hoped, in her usual quest for solitude, to have the water all to herself and is disappointed when she spots the prior arrival of a woman whose voice 'Elizabeth' heard in the next room at her lodging. Her Englishness now manifests itself in as stereotypical an account of German women as Brosy's:

> German female tourists are apt to be extraordinarily cordial in the water. On land, laced into suppressive whalebone, dressed, and with their hair dry and curled, they cannot but keep within the limits set by convention; but the more clothes they take off the more do they seem to consider the last barrier between human creature and human creature broken down, and they will behave toward you, meeting you on this common ground of wateriness, as though they had known you and extravagantly esteemed you for years. Their cordiality, too, becomes more pronounced in proportion to the coldness and roughness of the water ... (95)

The German woman shrieks a full minute on plunging into the water from the cold, and when the scantily clad 'Elizabeth' emerges from the bath house to hear the bather shout '*prachtvoll*' (magnificent), she thinks perhaps the exclamation refers to her physique and is so thrown off that she falls in. Now she must shriek and clutch the German bather, since 'Elizabeth' has no rope to cling to. Once she gets her own rope she looks again at the woman in the India rubber swim cap and thinks she looks familiar, deciding that, after all her attempts to escape her routine life back home, she has been bathing with her dressmaker. But when the two women emerge in their street clothes from the bathing cells,

> With one accord we stopped dead and our mouths fell open. 'What,' she cried, it is *you*?'
> 'What,' I cried, 'it is *you*?'
> It was my cousin Charlotte whom I had not seen for ten years. (98)

Lightning quick, Englishness subsides and Germanness surfaces: Charlotte is not 'my German cousin' but simply 'my cousin', as a German would say. But 'Elizabeth' does not spare Charlotte or her limited grasp of English culture, either. Later, in contrast to the lyric impulses that Wordsworth inspires in 'Elizabeth' as she looks at the island's natural beauty, Charlotte borrows *The Prelude* and after reading it says, '"This is great rubbish"' (197). Some things do not translate, evidently.

On the English side Brosy's mother is a snob and self-satisfied English traveller; like Minora she thinks she speaks good German, but no Germans understand her either. She finds Charlotte fascinating only because she is the wife of the great professor and dismisses 'Elizabeth' as a nobody until, when 'Elizabeth' steps away, Charlotte explains her cousin's noble title. Mrs Harvey-Browne is all politesse when 'Elizabeth' returns while huffily dismissing the German man who asks if he can share her table since no others are available. Naturally, in this comic novel, she has snubbed the very professor her son diligently seeks.

The professor is seeking his wife; and in an uncharacteristic conformist moment, 'Elizabeth' affirms the legacies of both German and English traditions that wives belong with husbands whose rule wives should accept. 'Elizabeth' thus determines to try saving the marriage of Charlotte and the professor by chasing after the fleeing Charlotte herself.[22] When Charlotte takes refuge on a narrow island west of Wiek accessible only by boat, 'Elizabeth' hires a boat to Hiddensee with the professor aboard, then races back to the boat alone once they spot Charlotte, leaving the husband to embrace his wife. Certain that she has at last regained the solitude she craves, 'Elizabeth' exults: 'I laughed aloud for joy at the success of my plan ... I had certainly reunited them – reunited them and freed myself ... And never did well-doer glow with a warmer consciousness of having done well than I glowed as I lay on the deck' (293).

A further turn of the screw ends the novel. Summing up the best of Rügen for travellers on the last page, 'Elizabeth' pronounces Hiddensee the most beautiful, then adds a hasty narrative postscript:

> what became of the Nieberleins[?] I am sorry to say that I had letters from them both of a nature that positively prohibits publication; and a mutual acquaintance told me that Charlotte had applied for a judicial separation.
> When I heard it I was thunderstruck.
>
> The End (299)

An expatriate's Anglo–German pun had already provided a clue to this outcome in the setting at Hiddensee. In German, 'Hiddensee' is a place name designating the 'Island of Hedin' named after a legendary Norwegian king. But if read as two English words pushed together, it consists of an adjective implying something secret and an imperative command to view it – hide and seek, as it were. The pun encapsulates von Arnim's comedic expatriate technique throughout, in which now one national orientation, now another peeps out ready for detection (sometimes both showing at once). If the novel is a window on the dynamics of expatriate identity and consciousness, von Arnim's performance of it is a gleeful game, one turned on 'Elizabeth' herself in the novel's final sentence that leaves no stable ground but only more play and restlessness.

Escapist Expatriate Identity: *The Princess Priscilla's Fortnight* (1905)

When it is discussed at all, *The Princess Priscilla's Fortnight* (hereafter *Priscilla*) is usually seen as a misfire in von Arnim's developing writing career, the lightest of light *jeux d'esprit* that showed what could go wrong when von Arnim wandered from what she knew on her pulses. Römhild, for example, pronounces it 'weaker than her other novels'.[23] Its most oft-cited passage is on women who run away from home, like Charlotte in *Rügen*. The German princess, who has been taught by her idealist professor to loathe the artifice of court and the vulgarity of public appearances, wants to do the same:

> Priscilla wanted to run away. This, I believe, is considered an awful thing to do even if you are only a housemaid or somebody's wife. If it were not considered awful, placed by the world high up on its list of Utter Unforgivablenesses, there is, I suppose, not a woman who would not at some time or other have run ... [A]nd a wife who runs is pursued by social ruin, it being taken for granted that she did not run alone. I know at least two wives who did run alone. Far from wanting yet another burden added to them by adding to their lives yet another man, they were anxiously endeavouring to get as far as might be from the man they had got already. The world, foul hag with the downcast eyes and lascivious lips, could not believe it possible, and was quick to draw its dark mantle of disgrace over their shrinking heads. One of them, unable to bear this, asked her husband's pardon. She was a weak spirit, and now lives prostrate days, crushed beneath the unchanging horror of a husband's free forgiveness. The other took a cottage and laughed at the world. Was she not happy at last, and happy in the right way? I go to see her sometimes, and we eat the cabbages she has grown herself. Strange how the disillusioned find their peace in cabbages.[24]

This bites, especially in the superior delights of a cabbage head to a husband's.

The principal energy of the book, however, again lies in von Arnim's sustained comedic performance of expatriate identity. But this time she represents expatriate experience from a distance through an omniscient narrator who tells of an idealistic, stunningly beautiful princess and her crotchety, beloved bachelor tutor, the court archivist, who decamp at Priscilla's insistence once she gets a serious proposal of marriage that her father endorses. They travel incognito to England, where she hopes to live a simple life in a rural cottage just as her reading of Wordsworth has inspired her to do. After placing an Englishwoman in Germany in her 'Elizabeth' novels, then, von Arnim now imagines German central characters who perform (very imperfectly) the roles of niece and uncle abroad in a small rural English village.

Here, too, command of two languages is crucial to the narrative. Fritzing, the *Hofbibliothekar* (court librarian) elevated by the grand duke to the title of *Geheimarchivrath* (privy councillor archivist) (6), lived twenty years in England prior to arriving in Lothen-Kunitz, a fictional duchy in Germany near its southern border. An erudite scholar of English literature, he not only speaks English fluently but also knows a good deal about English culture and landscapes. Yet von Arnim takes care to mark his language, as she does Brosy's German, as formidably correct, hence not idiomatic or 'native', for he speaks 'quite as well as most Englishmen, if in a statelier, Johnsonian manner' (7–8). Priscilla, the daughter of an English mother, is a cultural hybrid from the outset; and unlike her sisters in this Catholic region of Germany, she has been raised Protestant. She has also inherited her mother's dangerous originality and disposition to think – unsettling, the courtiers deem, in a woman and disturbing in a grand duchess (1–2). Even so, Priscilla's English has a slight German trace discernible in her 'r's, which enables the vicar's son Robin to detect her foreign origins when he encounters her in the parish churchyard (80).

Von Arnim quickens the comedy when the two most eligible young men in the village are immediately attracted to the young woman who masquerades as the niece of a retired German teacher, though she holds a rank higher than either Englishman could ever imagine. The vicar's son gets his ears boxed when, thinking to vamp a lower-middle-class beauty from his socially superior status as a Cambridge student, he kisses her hair, while Tussie (Augustus), the sickly son of the local squire who aspires to poetry, falls in love and becomes seriously ill after exerting himself on her behalf in all weathers, actually proposing to her from his sickbed. (He recovers after she has left; as the narrator observes, 'he got over it. People do' [326].) A fortnight is not long enough for Priscilla to be an expatriate; she remains a visitor rather than resident. And her cultural mobility is limited because the one border she cannot cross is that of class. She cannot even imagine deferring to a vicar's wife, much less a self-righteous one like Mrs Morrison, and when she is bored and tired with the initial visit from Mrs Morrison and Lady Shuttleworth she dismisses them both, causing the former English lady-in-waiting to an English princess to suspect Priscilla's real identity (132, 326). As she has all her life, Priscilla goes about her business with no thought of consequences to others below the rank of her royal equals and presumes that the supply of money is endless.

The character most representative of expatriate experience is instead Fritzing in his comically fraught attempt to perform as a cultural insider and outsider at once. German allegiance to the princess, who commands that they decamp, brings him to England. He also owes allegiance as *Geheimarchivrath* to the grand duke and knows he has done wrong in spiriting away a royal princess without the duke's permission and keeping their location secret. His command of English village culture, moreover, is imperfect. Though he has lived in England two decades, he cannot grasp how ridiculous it is that he should walk into the land agent's office for Lady Shuttleworth and propose to buy two cottages on her land because Priscilla requires them to be happy. Nor can he imagine the suspicion awakened by the deference a supposedly retired German teacher pays to his young 'niece', who mysteriously appears to have the funds to buy not one but two cottages and build new cottages for the shoemaker and elderly widow they displace. German–English exchange is for Fritzi an angst-ridden burden as he attempts to live with one foot in England and the other at Lothen-Kunitz.

The farcical possibilities were endless, and after *Priscilla*'s popular success as a novel von Arnim was encouraged to adapt it for the London stage, where *Priscilla Runs Away* was a hit that ran for several months in 1910.[25] In both the novel and the play the dilemmas of Priscilla and Fritzing are resolved more or less fairy-tale-like. The prince who wants to marry Priscilla at the outset – grander and wealthier than her father the grand duke – speaks impeccable colloquial English, tracks her to her village, has the wisdom not to laugh at or pressure Priscilla (by now wearing threadbare clothing after the money is gone), and whisks her away. But not to any 'happily-ever-after'. Yet again von Arnim punctures the ending to which she has slowly built in the novel's last two sentences:

> Let it not however be imagined that a person who has been truthful so long as myself is going to lapse into easy lies at the last, and pretend that she was uninterruptedly satisfied and happy for the rest of her days. She was not; but then who is?
>
> THE END (329)

The ultimate expatriate in this fiction is the author who can slip in and out of satiric portraits of English provincialism, pettiness, and arrogance on one hand and German masculinity, idealism, and artificial German court life on the other. Though it may seem absurd to apply the deeply philosophical reflections of Said to this cream puff of a novel, his comment on an exile's binocular cultural vision nonetheless illuminates von Arnim's expatriate mode here:

> Seeing 'the entire world as a foreign land' makes possible originality of vision. Most people are principally aware of one culture, one setting, one home; exiles are aware of at least two, and this plurality of vision gives rise to an awareness of simultaneous dimensions, an awareness that – to borrow a phrase from music – is *contrapuntal.*
>
> For an exile, ... both the new and the old environments are vivid, actual, occurring together contrapuntally. There is a unique pleasure in this sort of apprehension, especially if the exile is conscious of other contrapuntal juxtapositions that diminish orthodox judgment and elevate appreciative sympathy. There is also a particular sense of achievement in acting as if one were at home wherever one happens to be.[26]

Moving swiftly from *Rügen* to *Priscilla*, von Arnim moved contrapuntally from showing the English abroad in Germany to Germans abroad in England. The two works were also linked by the metafictional, contrapuntal play of their paratexts. Above I noted the bilingual, bicultural map of *Rügen* and bilingual pun on 'Hiddensee'. On the title page of *Priscilla* is a German epigraph composed by von Arnim and accessible only to those who knew some German; even for those who did, it became fully decipherable only at the novel's close. For this apparent entrée to the novel is in fact a German postscript that continues von Arnim's English narrative:

> 'Oft habe ich die Welt durchwandert, und habe immer gesehen, wie das Grosse am Kleinlichen scheitert, und das Edle von dem ätzenden Gift des Alltäglichen zerfressen wird.'
>
> Fritzing, 'Erlebtes und Erlittenes.'
> Kunitz, 1904. Verlag von Biedermann und Meyer.[27]

As a retrospect, the epigraph enables readers to see that Fritzing wrote a book about his experiences and sufferings ('Erlebtes' and 'Erlittenes') after his return to court, publishing it in Kunitz before he left to become *Hofbibliothekar* to Priscilla's father-in-law. Von Arnim aims a final comic dart at Fritzing in his publisher's name. 'Biedermann' in German is 'an honest man', apt for an honourable publisher; but it can also be used pejoratively to designate philistines. Perhaps, von Arnim suggests, only philistine publishers would issue such rubbish as Fritzi's.

Few scholars see any relevance in *Priscilla* to von Arnim's life, the usual source of her best fiction.[28] But in 1905 she was writing a novel not just as an Englishwoman married to a German *Junker* and mother of several babies, as in *Elizabeth and Her German Garden*. She was now a mother of growing daughters who, like Priscilla and von Arnim's next protagonist Rose-Marie, were half-English, half-German, and who would have to work out their own relationship to Englishness. Imagining Germans responding to England and the English over three hundred pages additionally prepared von Arnim to write *Fräulein Schmidt and Mr Anstruther: Being the Letters of an Independent Woman* (1907), her first major novel. As well, *Priscilla* inspired von Arnim's next mode of authorial research. To gather background for *Fräulein Schmidt* she advertised herself as an English governess seeking improvement in German who could teach in exchange for lessons from the resident professor in Jena. By this means she could observe Jena and its surroundings and glimpse the life of a daughter charged with domestic duties ranging from cooking to mending. The reality was worse than expected, involving a cold attic room and extensive scrubbing. And it became dangerous when the young man of the house fell in love with her and proposed.[29] But von Arnim 'ran away' with the knowledge of her husband, who rescued her as the prince did Priscilla from her attempted disguise and a life devoid of aristocratic privilege. For von Arnim, then, *Priscilla* was not just a popular success that pitched expatriate experience in a comic register but also an important stepping stone to her most significant novel in the German phase of her life and career.

Innovating Expatriate Imagination in *Fräulein Schmidt and Mr Anstruther: Being the Letters of an Independent Woman* (1907)

In the 379 pages of *Fräulein Schmidt*, von Arnim reverts to first-person narrative but assumes the subjectivity of a lower-middle-class German woman of twenty-five to whom the English Mr Anstruther proposes after residing with the Schmidts while he studies German with Rose-Marie's father. He then drops her for a better prospect in marriage when he returns to England. When his new marital prospect fades, he expects to return to the former hero-worship and self-subordination of the German girl and proposes again near the novel's end. But Rose-Marie is no longer a naïve girl. She has learned to be independent and shuts him out. Part of von Arnim's achievement in this novel is delineating Rose-Marie's growth and change in the eighty-one English-language letters she writes to Anstruther over some fourteen months (6 November–25 January); his side of the correspondence is never given. The novel in this sense is an extended monologue that probes psychological process running beneath the external events Rose-Marie's letters report. The novel also represents von Arnim's fullest embrace of German identity and subjectivity in her career, though – like von Arnim's daughters and Princess Priscilla – Rose-Marie is also half-English.

In turning her back on modes that first won her a reputation and wide audience, von Arnim was taking risks. 'Elizabeth' had become a brand, and because reviewers looked for more of the same, they generally missed, in Usborne's words, that '[t]here is much in *Fräulein Schmidt and Mr. Anstruther* that reaches far beyond anything Elizabeth had attempted in her previous novels' or 'that Elizabeth had attained a deeply felt and serious pitch in her writing'.[30] One reviewer, Virginia Woolf, was even less receptive to the novel than her colleagues. Exercising rather than willingly suspending disbelief in her review, Woolf believed neither in Rose-Marie's German identity ('why should she be called Fräulein Schmidt and supplied with the troublesome properties of her part when she is really Elizabeth in a German lodging-house, or Princess Priscilla, or any other cultivated woman with a taste for poetry and a fluent pen?') nor in Mr Anstruther ('he does not exist'). At most Woolf granted the writing occasional charm that diversified otherwise dull triviality worth no critic's time.[31]

Pace Woolf, von Arnim's command of craft in this novel is impressive. Even as she sustained performance of Anglo–German expatriate identity, von Arnim interwove multiple Anglo–German literary traditions. As an epistolary novel, it derived from long eighteenth-century English *and* German literary precedents, from *Clarissa* to Johann von Goethe's *The Sorrows of Young Werther* [*Die Leiden des jungen Werthers*]). Von Arnim additionally channelled female-authored German Romanticism in *Fräulein Schmidt*, since a principal inspiration for its form came from the precursor who was also von Arnim's distant kin by marriage: Bettina von Arnim (1785–1859). In *Goethe's Correspondence with a Child* (*Goethes Briefwechsel mit einem Kinde*, 1835), Bettina pioneered a narrative evidently grounded in life writing but actually a novel, the form of von Arnim's own 'Elizabeth' books.[32] 'Bettina', the pseudonym of Elisabeth Catharina Ludovica Magdalena von Arnim, translated her novel into English in 1839, demonstrating *her* fluid cultural and linguistic mobility from German to English and back. In setting her own novel in Jena, not far from Weimar where the historical Bettina visited Johann von Goethe, the later von Arnim gestured towards her German female precursor.[33]

Von Arnim also adapted another Anglo–German literary form common to Johann von Goethe's *Wilhelm Meister's Apprenticeship* (*Wilhelm Meisters Lehrjahre*, 1795–6), Charlotte Brontë's *Jane Eyre* (1847), Charles Dickens's *David Copperfield* (1849–50), and Elizabeth Barrett Browning's verse novel *Aurora Leigh* (1856): the *Bildungsroman*.[34] And like the Victorian bildungsromans *David Copperfield* and W. M. Thackeray's *Pendennis* (1848–50), von Arnim's *Fräulein Schmidt* began as a serial novel, in ten instalments in *Cornhill Magazine* (September 1906–June 1907). By then serialisation was out of fashion, but this mode suited the slow unfolding of a psyche and the nuanced tonal shifts that helped register changes in mood or purpose in Rose-Marie's letters to Roger Anstruther. *Fräulein Schmidt*, however, reversed the Victorian serial convention of courtships concluding in happy marriage. Von Arnim's novel begins with Rose-Marie's ecstatic happiness over Anstruther's proposal and her conviction that she is loved. The rest of the novel represents her development towards the woman of the subtitle: not merely a single but an *independent* woman who embraces autonomy and the delights she finds in the aesthetic richness of solitary walks in nature, renewed companionship with her idiosyncratic, bluntly honest father, and the written word itself. By the novel's close Rose-Marie has rewritten her father's rambling German account of life in Jena in her own voice and had her book accepted for publication in England. Thus *Fräulein Schmidt* is also a künstlerroman, or novel of artistic development. If she begins by writing letters to Anstruther because she wants and needs to, she gradually begins to write for her own pleasure, taking joy in going where her thoughts lead her.

First, though, she must endure Anstruther's egocentric attempts to use her according to his selfish needs, starting with his proposal of marriage and a secret engagement on the very day he leaves for England, which guarantees both a fallback bride and a safety hatch for exit should he find better marriage prospects. Rose-Marie is transported by the proposal, which opens a potentially rich future emotional life in material comfort rather than the drudgery of her petty-bourgeois life with her uneducated, narrow-minded stepmother and her erudite father.

Inevitably Anstruther is attracted to 'Nancy', the daughter of wealthy family friends, and breaks his engagement to Rose-Marie to become the privileged Englishwoman's fiancé. Immediately adopting formal address ('Mr. Anstruther') in writing to 'Roger', Rose-Marie refuses self-abasement:

> I make you a present of everything; of the love and happy thoughts, of the pleasant dreams and plans, of the little prayers sent up, and the blessings called down – there were a great many every day – of the kisses, and all the dear sweetness. Take it all. I want nothing from you in return ... But do you suppose that, having given you all this, I am going to give you my soul as well? ... You are not worth it. (77)

Such palpable anger is never permitted to Victorian protagonists – though, like the jilted Cousin Phillis of Gaskell's eponymous novella (also serialised in *Cornhill Magazine* 1863–4), Rose-Marie falls seriously ill and three months pass before she writes again (in response to Anstruther's birthday greetings). Hereafter, von Arnim represents Rose-Marie's slow, uneven struggle towards self-respect, dignity, and self-reliance as she seeks to become something of a female Thoreau.[35]

When 'Nancy' jilts Anstruther for a duke, he returns to Germany and pursues Rose-Marie again just when she is socially and materially most disadvantaged. Her only friends have moved away, and she and her father are even poorer after the death of the stepmother (who had an annuity). In every material respect Anstruther is an eminently suitable husband: he is cultured and well-educated, has a higher social status than Rose-Marie, and enjoys an ample income with prospects of greater wealth to come. But she has learned to resist masculine power and privilege: 'Don't torment me with wild letters. I do not love you. I will not marry you. I cared for you sincerely as a friend ... I cannot look up to you ... Leave me alone' (371). The text devolves into five one-line letters scattered across facing pages (see Figure 7.2), visual and verbal fragments into which the prior narrative (and any connection with her former lover) fissures. The final fragment (4 February) says only, 'I shall not write again'; and where the balancing sixth fragment might appear, 'THE END' fills the space instead.

Von Arnim's anatomisation of Anstruther's egocentrism, selfishness, and entitlement bespeaks a more overt feminist critique and complex analysis. More strikingly, von Arnim innovates a proto-Modernist technique that I call 'subliminal narrative', narrative below the threshold of immediate visibility to readers, and sometimes to Rose-Marie herself. This is not yet James Joyce's or Woolf's stream of consciousness.[36] In subliminal narrative, psychic and emotional processes are ongoing beneath conscious rhetoric and at times rise momentarily to the surface only to subside again. In these instances, Rose-Marie's very act of writing a letter is not so much self-expression as a cover over complex psychological and emotional processing going on out of sight. Artful allusion as well as juxtapositions are the key techniques von Arnim adapts to signal this subliminal narrative, since what Rose-Marie thinks to quote in a given letter and her sudden turns of thought are clues to what motivates her.

An early instance occurs nearly a month after Rose-Marie resumes correspondence with Anstruther and agrees to be Anstruther's friend. By 9 April, she has received his self-centred letter about his trials with 'Nancy', his dislike of his father, and the pressure he feels regarding his engagement.

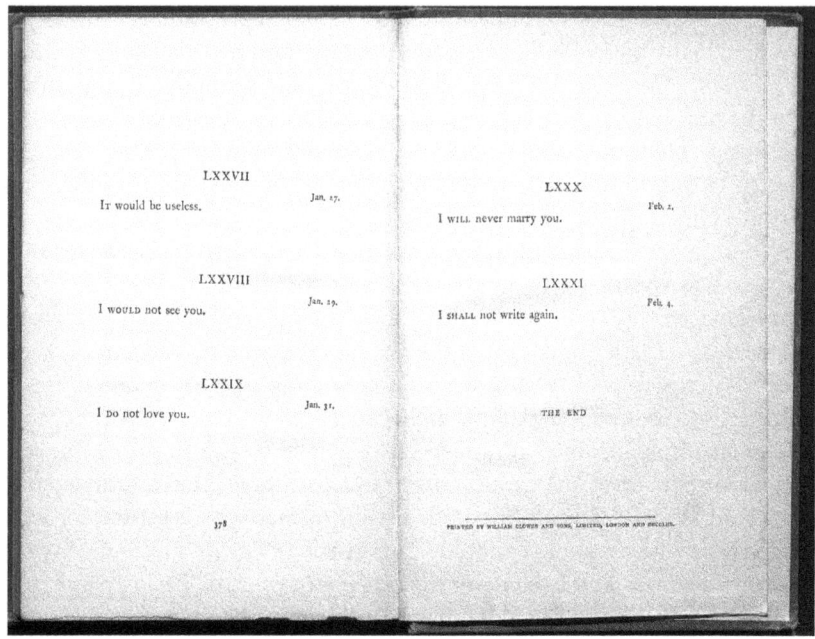

Figure 7.2. Concluding pages, *Fräulein Schmidt and Mr Anstruther* (378–9). Courtesy Mary Couts Burnett Library, Special Collections, TCU

He now looks back fondly to Jena. This Rose-Marie ignores, chatting instead about finding sustenance in her tasks and in nature, especially in the newly blossoming violets whose fragrance resurrects her sensibility and capacity for wonder and joy. That day even her peevish stepmother drops her haranguing to look out the window at 'how "proud-pied April, dressed in all his trim, / Hath put a spirit of youth in everything"' (84). Rather than an act of literary display, Rose-Marie's allusion to Shakespeare's Sonnet 98 sheds light on her underlying orientation towards Anstruther and their broken engagement as she writes of other things:

> From you have I been absent in the spring,
> When proud-pied April, dressed in all his trim,
> Hath put a spirit of youth in everything,
> That heavy Saturn laughed and leaped with him.
> Yet nor the lays of birds, nor the sweet smell
> Of different flowers in odor and in hue,
> Could make me any summer's story tell,
> Or from their proud lap pluck them where they grew.

Nor did I wonder at the lily's white,
Nor praise the deep vermilion in the rose.
They were but sweet, but figures of delight,
Drawn after you, you pattern of all those.
Yet seemed it winter still and, you away,
As with your shadow I with these did play.[37]

Rose-Marie's allusion, fully traced out, fissures her surface 'shadow play' of delight in nature and spring's rebirth to suggest her underlying continued desolation ('it seemed winter still'), the ongoing centrality of the absent, newly engaged Anstruther ('figures of delight, / Drawn after you, you pattern of all those'), and her inability as yet to tell a 'summer's story'. Beneath mere epistolary chat, von Arnim hints, lies persisting emotional anguish.

In her 28 July letter Rose-Marie acknowledges that her words express her feelings only partially: 'you mustn't suppose that my letters have always exactly represented my state of mind, and that my soul has made no pilgrimages during this half year' (146–7). But at least she can claim that her soul *has* come back to her, and she chides Anstruther for wanting to use her as 'medicine' for his own soul: 'I wholly repudiate the idea of being somebody's physic' (151–2). Yet when she turns to three lines from Ernest Dowson to assert her independence from him ('Now will I take me to a place of peace, / Forget mine heart's desire – / In solitude and prayer, work out my soul's release' [147]), her allusion telegraphs a counter-narrative. For the lines come from a book Anstruther had given her the year before as a birthday present. Mentioning the book unavoidably conjures memories of her jilting, and the title and concluding stanza of Dowson's lyric hint at the empty bravado of her letter's comic account of turning vegetarian and her pretence of strength:

Vain Resolves
I said: 'There is an end of my desire:
  Now have I sown, and I have harvested,
And these are ashes of an ancient fire,
  Which, verily, shall not be quickened.
Now will I take me to a place of peace,
    Forget mine heart's desire;
In solitude and prayer, work out my soul's release.

'I shall forget her eyes, how cold they were;
  Forget her voice, how soft it was and low,
With all my singing that she did not hear,
  And all my service that she did not know.

> I shall not hold the merest memory
>   Of any days that were,
> Within those solitudes where I will fasten me.'
>
> And once she passed, and once she raised her eyes,
>   And smiled for courtesy, and nothing said:
>   And suddenly the old flame did uprise,
>   And all my dead desire was quickened.
> Yea! as it hath been, it shall ever be,
>   Most passionless, pure eyes!
> Which never shall grow soft, nor change, nor pity me.[38]

In addition to allusions such as these, von Arnim extends her subliminal narrative by juxtaposing two September letters penned on successive days (204–28). The first recounts Rose-Marie's interactions with Vicky, the daughter of a poor aristocratic family who have rented the house below the Schmidt perch on Galgenberg (the hill above Jena) for the summer; the daughter is presumably named after Queen Victoria's daughter, called Vicky in childhood, who became Empress of Prussia. Vicky, Rose-Marie learns, has also been jilted, even more traumatically since her engagement had been made public and the wedding date was near. Sympathetic to her new friend, Rose-Marie discourses to Anstruther on the folly and futility of courtships and proposals alike; as she asks, 'what is there but pain in the end?' (216).

In her next letter to Anstruther, Rose-Marie explains that she had been side-tracked by Vicky's story the day before from writing about a book on English poets she has just read. The book infuriates her for giving the unsavoury biographical details of poets like Wordsworth and Shelley, whom she had long worshipped for their poetry and rated above the German poets Goethe, Schiller, and Heine. Then apparently apropos of nothing she alludes to Edward Fitzgerald and recalls the exact date – September 11 – when Anstruther and she drifted on a river and read *Omar Khayyam* together. This is a delayed reaction not to the poetry book but to Vicki's tale of jilting and the memories it jogged. Her hatred of the book's disillusioning details (she later burns it) also suggests her unacknowledged pain over disillusionment with love.

Rose-Marie's capping allusion in the letter is to two lines by 'that merry rhymer' Matthew Prior apropos of the repugnant critic's book: ''Tis long ago / Since gods came down incognito' (227). But Prior's poem 'The Ladle' is also very much about marriage. It tells how Jove and Mercury on a whim descend to earth to call on a long-married couple and grant them three wishes:

> The honest farmer and his wife,
> To years declined from prime of life,

> Had struggled with the marriage noose,
> As almost every couple does;
> Sometimes, my plague! sometimes, my darling!
> Kissing to-day, to-morrow snarling;
> Jointly submitting to endure
> That evil, which admits no cure.

Granted three wishes, the farmer's wife, thinking short-term, asks only for a ladle, which brings on the very funny and bawdy disaster:

> Thank ye, great gods, the woman says,
> Oh! may your altars ever blaze;
> A ladle for our silver dish
> Is what I want, is what I wish. –
> A ladle! cries the man, a ladle!
> 'Odzooks, Corisca, you have prayed ill;
> What should be great, you turn to farce;
> I wish the ladle in your a – .
>
> With equal grief and shame my Muse
> The sequel of the tale pursues;
> The ladle fell into the room,
> And stuck in old Corisca's bum.
> Our couple weep two wishes past,
> And kindly join to form the last;
> To ease the woman's awkward pain,
> And get the ladle out again.[39]

The arc of the two-letter sequence, from the transcendent power of poetry and love to a whiff of faeces in Prior's scatological satire, suggests subliminally Rose-Marie's own journey from initial ecstasy to disillusionment and abject misery.

In Rose-Marie's last substantive letter to Anstruther following his second proposal, she herself understands what has been ongoing beneath her letters' surface as she explains why she began writing in the first place, and thus brings the formerly subliminal narrative to the surface and to an end:

> It was because I thought I was making amends that way for having, though unconsciously, led you to fancy you cared for me last year. I wanted to be of some use to you ... By gradual degrees, as we both grew wiser, I meant my letters to be a help to you who have no sister, no mother, and a father you don't speak to ... [A]t first there was my own struggling to get out of the deep waters where I was drowning, and afterwards it seemed to be nothing but a staving off, a writing about other things, a determined telling of little anecdotes, of talk about our neighbours, ... about anything rather than your soul and my soul. (375)

Her soul's sufferings and growth now visible, Rose-Marie saves herself and dismisses Anstruther for good.

The 'little anecdotes' mentioned by Rose-Marie formed the 'charming' element that Woolf conceded to the novel: 'The experiences that admit of this treatment best are homely ones; vegetarianism, for example, and servants, and the pettiness of life in a small German town. There the humour is exhilarating and sufficient.'[40] Von Arnim has fun, for example, with Joey, a stolidly incurious English youth sent by his wealthy ironmonger father to study German with Professor Schmidt who falls in love with Vicky. He is baffled when her impoverished parents immediately return the expensive necklace he presents to their daughter. Rose-Marie recognises the defiant gesture of the aristocratic but poor mother proud to have been born a Dammerlitz. But Joey, befuddled as ever by German names, thinks he hears something very different[41] when Rose-Marie tries to explain:

> 'Ah – Dammerlitz,' I muttered, nodding with a complete comprehension.
> 'What?' exclaimed Joey, starting and looking greatly astonished.
> 'Go on,' said I.
> 'But I say,' said Joey, in tones of shocked protest.
> 'What do you say?' I asked.
> 'Why, how you must hate her,' said Joey, quite awestruck, and staring at me as though he saw me for the first time.
> 'Hate her?' I asked, surprised. 'Why do you think I hate her?'
> He whistled, still staring at me.
> 'Why do you think I hate her?' I asked again, patient as I always try to be with him.
> He murmured something about as soon expecting it of a bishop. (340)

Von Arnim had clearly retained her touch for cross-cultural comedy. By now a citizen and sixteen-years' resident of Germany, yet steeped in Englishness and Anglophone literature, von Arnim had more significantly mastered the performance of expatriate identity in both a comic and serious register. *Fräulein Schmidt* was the last of her 'German' novels written and published before she left Germany for good in the spring of 1909. Viewed retrospectively, *Fräulein Schmidt* was von Arnim's fond farewell to her bicultural experience. By then von Arnim had made her mark as a writer, with one foot in the nineteenth century, one in the twentieth broaching Modernism's radical innovations – just as she had one foot in Germany, one in England, spoofing and honouring them both like the expatriate she was.

CHAPTER 8

Queer Borders
Vernon Lee's Haunted Expatriate Writings

> I fancy an expatriated people, perhaps all really very independent ones are apt to pay this price ... I am too much of an alien, a cosmopolitan, an exception ...
> Vernon Lee to Mona Taylor, 12 August 1900[1]

> But of all the countries, the first to be good to me was Germany, coming, in the shape of my nurses and of my dear Bernese governess, fairy-like to my christening or thereabouts.
> *The Sentimental Traveller*, 1908[2]

Von Arnim became an expatriate after first growing up in England. Lee was an expatriate from birth. She carried an English passport yet knew England only as a destination for extended visits lasting a month or two.[3] As Vineta Colby remarks, Vernon Lee was in fact European. Born in France, until age seventeen she moved about with her parents and brother from one six months' residence to another in France, Germany, Switzerland, and Italy until the family settled in Florence – she for good.[4] More specifically, Lee was Pan-European, seeing all Europe and especially Western Europe as a single entity with people who shared common aims despite their differences in local languages, customs, and allegiances. She contained within her sole self, after all, the languages of English, French, German, and Italian.

Her repudiation of national boundaries as well as her sexuality give this chapter its title.[5] 'Queer' designates many aspects of Vernon Lee, beginning with her liminal sexuality – decidedly lesbian in inclination yet evidently celibate or asexual – and her appropriation of male and female traits with no care to police borders between them. She similarly ignored boundaries between past and present, actuality and imagination. For Lee, occupying any given position, whether in gender, geography, opinion, or emotion, meant being haunted by other possibilities that could and often did break through at any moment.[6]

Lee was also a pacifist who allied herself to British pacifists in the years leading up to World War I, a conviction directly related to her Pan-Europeanism.[7] Much earlier, a parallel pacifist movement had formed in Austria based on a philosophical outlook that illuminates Lee's own. In 1891 Alfred Fried (1864–1921), a Viennese Jew, joined the Austrian Peace Society and founded the German Peace Society the next year, returning to Austria after rampant German nationalism increased.[8] Fried was a pacifist, agnostic, and staunch supporter of democratic institutions, all traits shared by Lee; and both experienced marginality, Fried as a Jew, Lee as a woman. No evidence indicates that Lee read any of Fried's seventy-five books, manifold articles, or the journal he edited (*Die Friedens-Warte*, literally *Peace Perspective*), though her fluent German would have enabled her to. Nonetheless a central concept in his philosophy sheds light on Lee's Pan-Europeanism and her specific orientation towards Germanic lands and culture. It was Fried's conviction, according to historian Katherine Sorrels, that a society's bonds should be based on shared ideas and ideals rather than 'blood and soil' rights; expressed as *Deutschtum*, a Germanness that extended across national borders, this conception of German identity was predicated on shared participation in education, intellectual exchange, and achievement that in turn supported socialisation into a larger polity or union.[9]

Lee's participation in this orientation is evident in the second epigraph of this chapter, in which Lee makes no distinction between 'Germany' and the 'Bernese governess' who hailed from a German-speaking Swiss region. For her the border of Switzerland was an irrelevant datum to her mobile exploration of transnational German culture, just as she assumed that she could freely move across national borders. Lee has come to be identified so closely with Italy and its landscapes, art, and music that the Italianate Lee generally overrides other formative influences on her life and art. In this chapter I emphasise the important role of an encompassing '*Deutschtum*' or Germanic cultural legacy in waking Lee in childhood to the realms of wonder and imagination, large ideas, and profound affection. This legacy was directly connected to the hauntings that characterise her writing.

Opening the Door to Imagination

German elements appear in Lee's writing throughout her career, whether as German-language phrases, epigraphs, allusions, excerpts, or settings. Lee scholars have long recognised the importance of German aesthetic theory for Lee.[10] But German references also appear in her writing about Italy, as if a substrate of her subjectivity prior to her Italian awakening was an underlying constant. In 'Contemporary Italian Poets' in the 1877 *Quarterly Review*, for example, Lee asserted, 'Paganism, learnt from the Germans, and adopted with great readiness by the Latin race, has, indeed, a considerable hold among modern Italian poets, who regard themselves as the cousins of the Greeks, and the sons of the Renaissance; but it is a poetical and pure-minded paganism, like that of Goethe and of Schiller.' She closed by arguing that Johann von Goethe was the 'master' of contemporary Italian poet Alessandro Arnaboldi (1827–96).[11]

In *Belcaro* (1881), the character Baldwin endorses Goethe's description of genuine art, which he gives in untranslated German:

> My reason for restricting art to artistic aims is simply my principle that if things are to be fully useful they must be restricted to their real use, according to the idea of Goethe's Duke of Ferrara: –
> 'Nicht alles dienet uns auf gleicher Weise:
>
> > Wer viel gebrauchen will, gebrauche jedes
> > Nach seiner Art: so ist er wohl bedient.'[12]

As late as 1909, Lee took a sentence from Schiller for her epigraph to *Laurus Nobilis*, which began, 'Die Realität der Dinge ist der Dinge Werk'.[13] In these instances, Lee's Italian writing is, so to speak, 'haunted' by a coexistent Germanness.

'Faustus and Helena' (1880), in which Lee presents her theory of the supernatural in fiction, is a key text for her later supernatural tales and a clue to her emotional, intellectual, and erotic development. Lee articulates her theory by way of a crude medieval German legend telling how Faustus raised the ghost of Helena to be his 'paramour', a legend adapted by Christopher Marlowe for a brief scene in *Doctor Faustus* (1588) and by Johann von Goethe for the entire Act III, Part II, of *Faust* (1827; rpt. 1832).[14] Both adaptations, Lee contended, failed – Marlowe's because he presented the legend in a realistic episode peopled by contemporary Renaissance figures, Goethe's because he sought to realise the supernatural too concretely rather than activating the reader's mind and imagination through vague suggestion and outlines. The ghostly was most effective, she asserted, when 'the ghost is heard but not seen' or triggered by a rumoured site of haunting rather than a visible emanation, as in the medieval legend with which her essay begins: 'It does not give the complete and limited satisfaction of a work of art; it has the charm of the fantastic and fitful shapes formed by the flickering firelight or the wreathing mists; it haunts like some vague strain of music, drowsily heard in half-sleep.'[15]

Uncharacteristically, Lee indicates no historical source for the legend. A plausible reason is that Lee learned of it not through reading but through hearing it told, a frequent childhood experience for her when she was under the care of her beloved Bernese governess Marie Schülpach. Childhood listening in fact plays an important role in Lee's travel essays, which Colby rightly calls her most autobiographical work. Again and again, when Lee writes about revisiting Germany, memories of German scenes, oral tale telling, and a child's entrancement surface and fuse.[16] I propose that one reason they do is that they point to the formation of the adult writer's imagination from her experience of wonder in a liminally erotic context as a child.

Lee first mentions the impact of her governesses in *Hortus Vitae* (1903), a book published after her permanent break-up with longtime companion Kit Anstruther-Thomson, in which Lee explores how best we can cultivate and nurture our lives. Lee's dedication announces as the volume's theme that '*life must be begun many times anew*' (xiv). And the first chapter following the introduction ('The Garden of Life') is 'In Praise of Governesses', which contends, 'it is to our German governesses that we owe the power of understanding Germany, more than to German literature' – that is, to orality and affection more than reading.[17] Put another way, in Lee's childhood her governesses *were* her 'literature'. Italy, she contends, can enlarge sensibilities through its 'mere visible aspect and her history', while France 'explains itself to us through her books'. But 'the genius of Germany is, like her landscape, homely and sentimental, with the funny goodness and dearness of a good child; and we must learn to know it while we ourselves are children. And therefore it is from our governesses that we learn.'[18]

It is suggestive that Lee yokes two forms of orality, hearing and being fed, in a key childhood scene: 'It was long ago that I was, so to speak, a small German infant, fed on Teutonic romance and sentiment (and also funny Teutonic prosaicalness, bless it!) by a dim procession of Germania's daughters.' The 'best of all, dearest, far above all the others' was 'Marie S.', Marie Schülpach, 'charming enthusiastic young schoolmistress in that little town of pepper-pot towers and covered bridges'. More especially Lee recalls 'those hours which you and I, a girl of twenty and a child of eleven, spent in the little room above the rushing Alpine river, eating apples and drinking *café au lait*; hours in which a whole world of legend and poetry, and scientific fact and theory more wonderful still, passed from your ardent young mind into the little eager puzzled one of your loving pupil'.[19] If the inseparability of listening and feeding the body in the presence of a beloved woman can be read psychoanalytically in relation to Lee's emerging lesbian sexuality, the scene is also a tableau of total nurture: the child's mind, imagination, body, and affections are all being fed at once, enriched and enlarged by this German governess.

Karel Čapek, in theorising the fairy tale, begins and ends with the 'oldest theory', Plato's: 'fairy tales are tales told by nurses'.[20] For Čapek, the fairy tale originates as an oral, not written, tale told to a listener, born 'of the need to tell a story and of the delight of listening'. The longer the fairy tale told, the more magical the tale is for the child, for it sustains the pleasure of hearing' – and, I would add for Lee, the experience of being nurtured by a loved narrator.[21] Occupying a position between stand-in mother, salaried teacher, and companion, Schülpach could create a woman-loving environment even as she sought to expand through instruction and delight her charge's mind, imagination, and senses.

Ernst Bloch associates fairy tales with 'utopian longing' and 'creativity', a resonant pairing for the future writer Venon Lee.[22] Lee returns to a utopian scene of German orality in 'Säckingen and the Trumpeter' in *The Sentimental Traveller* (1908), which creatively recalls and re-enacts the magical effects of multiple childhood 'listenings' in Schülpach's presence. Before seeing Schülpach again in Switzerland for the first time in twenty-nine years, Lee detours to Säckingen near southern Germany's border with Switzerland. Her reason slyly foreshadows what is to come. Säckingen, she confides, is 'one of the realms of my childish fancy: Säckingen, the town of Scheffel's "Trompeter"', the epic poem of 1854 about successful cross-class love by Joseph Victor von Scheffel (1826–86). Lee buys a copy of the poem in the German town, then asks, 'Shall I ever read it?' (240). Her answer immediately resuscitates how she came to know it:

> I had not [read the tale] since my childhood. Or, speaking more correctly, I had never read it even then. It was doled out to me, quotations and *précis*, where it grew long-winded, in the little Swiss schoolroom twenty-nine years ago, over the copybooks and inkstands and the cups of coffee, by that dear, long-lost friend; the very one I was about to seek, plunging rather rashly into that gulf of Time. She used to bring the volume – just such a binding, only its gold and crimson embossings a little the worse for wear – to my daily lesson; and, if my sums and grammar and my *thème* were not too utterly disgraceful, she would reward me, and also her dear self, with the tale of how the roving musician (Germans have a way of roving for no visible reason, and it is so dear of them) fell in love with the daughter of the Baron of Säckingen, and how he made songs, and was counselled and consoled by the magic tomcat Hiddigeigei; and every one lived happy ever after …

> O dear German childhood in that schoolroom panelled with a porcelain stove where we baked apples! Dear German things never seen since: books heavily embossed or girt with orange labels – Konversations-Lexicons, bound years of *Gartenlaube*, stray volumes of Schiller and Goethe with their inspired curly heads in relief on the cover, and golden lyres and laurels ... best of all, the things unwritten – scraps of poetry, legends, tales of mystery, stored away behind the wide, candid brows, the kind young earnest eyes of my dear teacher: all summed up, symbolized for me in Scheffel's 'Trompeter,' and this little town of Säckingen.[23]

Place dematerialises: Säckingen is not a town but a utopian site of childhood mental, emotional, and physical repletion that resurfaces in adulthood as a haunted zone of memory and love to which orality is essential.

The chapter culminates in Lee's creative re-staging of this childhood experience after another apparent narrative detour. On arriving at Schülpach's home, Lee's hope of re-establishing connection to her former governess is baffled again and again, even on the last day, when Schülpach's daughters tactfully leave the two to themselves and they take an excursion into the country; '[we] never, in fact, found each other or ourselves'. But as they wait for a train back to town along the Aar River, the past suddenly reawakens and blossoms in the present:

> 'Do you remember,' I asked shyly, 'the story you used to tell me about some wonderful ladies – sisters – who lived, I don't quite know when, down by the river at Bern? It was very mysterious and strange, and it was called "The Light in the Corridor." Do you remember?'
>
> 'Yes,' she answered gravely. 'But you are mixing up two different stories. The "Light in the Corridor" was about a wicked stepmother – don't you recollect? – but it had nothing to do with the Aar. The one you are thinking of was the story of the five mysterious English sisters who lived at Bern.'
>
> 'Of course! And there was one who was called ... could it have been Zenobia?'
>
> 'Palmyra,' she corrected. 'There was Apollonia, Polydora, Palmyra!' She pronounced the *y* German fashion, as a diphthong *u*; and that name thus pronounced was the *Open, sesame* of my childhood.
>
> I recognized her earnest, dramatic voice, and recognized my own breathless listening. We sat there for an hour, waiting for the train, on the bench beneath the big trees, with the green, rushing river and the fantastic, sentimental old Swiss town in front of us, she telling stories and I listening.
>
> 'And when did it all happen?' I asked, at the conclusion of one of those well-known tales; and I remembered that I had always ended with that question.
>
> 'I suppose about a hundred years ago,' she answered.
>
> 'Surely,' I demurred, 'not anything as long ago? I thought only ... well, sixty or seventy?'

My friend turned round with her good, grave smile.
'Yes – *then*; but it is thirty years since last I told it you.'
Then she drew out her watch.
'The train is almost due; we must go,' she said, grasping her umbrella.
We rose and walked silently to the station. Our afternoon together was over. But we had found each other, ourselves, again.
So ended my excursion into my childhood, into the realms of the 'Trompeter von Säckingen.'[24]

The '*Open, sesame*' back to childhood closeness and wonder is a voiced German *y* diphthong, a *sound*, not a memory (which is faulty) or a specific narrative. In an artful flourish, Lee drops omniscient narration for dialogue and refrains from writing down the tale that she only hears, preserving the vagueness and suggestiveness of a voice, key elements of Lee's theory of supernatural fiction as well. Readers can only imagine Lee's auditory delight. 'Säckingen and the Trumpeter' thus replays an intricate collocation of thought, memories, feelings, and subtle eroticism from childhood to suggest one means by which her young self was awakened to wonder, imagination, and queer sexuality to become the adult writer Vernon Lee.

Lee's Supernatural Tales: *Hauntings* (1890) and 'Prince Alberic and the Snake Lady' (1896)

By the time Lee wrote her best supernatural tales she was a long-time resident of Florence and, in addition to *Studies of the Eighteenth Century in Italy* (1880), author of other writings on Italian art, music, and places. She had retained the legacy of her magical childhood experiences, to which Lee added the fruits of more than twenty years' intensive reading across multiple languages. The textual tutors of her supernatural writing, according to Colby and Christa Zorn, included the fairy tales of E. T. A. Hoffmann, Adelbert Chamisso, and folklore and ballads.[25] The written German tales did not conclude optimistically, Jack Zipes observes: 'Very few of the German romantic tales end on a happy note. The protagonists either go insane or die. The evil forces assume a social hue, for the witches and villains are no longer allegorical representations of evil in the Christian tradition but are symbolically associated with philistine society or the decadent aristocracy.' German romantic tales, then, strive less to enchant than 'to engage the reader in a serious discourse about art, philosophy, education, and love' – the preoccupations of three of Lee's most memorable supernatural stories.[26] All unfold in Italian, not German settings, yet all three have German connections.

The first two, 'Amour Dure' and 'Dionea', involve a German-sponsored scholar and German sculptor who (like the historical Johann von Goethe) make a transit from the Germanic north to the Italian south. This repeated scenario mirrored Lee's own transit from her early years in the north to the transformative effects of moving to Italy, a move as well from childhood to adulthood as she grew in intellect, aesthetic sensibility, and imagination. 'Amour Dure' introduces an 1885 journey from Germany to Urbania by the Polish protagonist Spiridion Trepka, author of a German book of scholarship who hates the scientism of contemporary German scholars as he hates (like Lee) the imperialist modern 'Vandal Germans' who have invaded his homeland as ancient Vandals invaded Rome. Trepka longs to repeat Goethe's own revelatory encounter with Italy, but he is thwarted at every turn: 'When I came to Italy first, I looked out for romance; I sighed, like Goethe in Rome, for a window to open and a wondrous creature to appear.'[27] Trepka ends up doing something quite German nonetheless. Out of the traces of the historical Medea da Carpi he finds in the Urbania archive, he creates a Gothic fairy tale, a Märchen of his own reimagining into which he then enters, finding his death in the process. Whether his death is due to supernatural agency of the Medea whose history he reassembles or a delusion, the story never clarifies: it invokes but never materialises the ghostly.[28]

Obsession and a haunting past destroy Lee's protagonist in 'Dionea' as well, which imagines an avatar of Venus returning in the nineteenth century to a Genoese village on the Gulf of La Spezia. Catherine Maxwell and Stefano Evangelista point to the precedents of both Walter Pater, whose 'Denys L'Auxerrois' and 'Apollo in Picardy' figure the return of Dionysus and Apollo to rural France, and Heinrich Heine's *The Gods in Exile*.[29] In 'Dionea' another German travels to Italy, a middle-aged sculptor with his self-effacing German wife, who requests that for once he sculpt a female figure, which unleashes through the beautiful, mysterious immigrant Dionea both violent desire and the deaths of the Germans. 'Dionea' can be read 'supernaturally' as a tale of the irresistible power of Venus, of whom Dionea is an avatar, 'naturally' as a tale of beauty's power, or psychologically as a story of male obsession. Both 'Dionea' and 'Amour Dure' are nightmare inversions of Goethe's Italian journey that kindled his mature creative powers (and amours); for Lee's Germans, apparent female supernatural powers overwhelm the puny efforts of masculine scholarship and art.

The most significant as well as most powerful of Lee's supernatural tales for this study, however, is 'Prince Alberic and the Snake Lady', first published in London's *Yellow Book* in July 1896. It has no German character travelling south and takes place in the fictional Italian Duchy of Luna.[30] Yet it breathes the very atmosphere of German romantic fairy tales and shares the traits identified by Zipes: 'The protagonists either go insane or die. The evil forces assume a social hue, for the witches and villains are no longer allegorical representations of evil in the Christian tradition but are symbolically associated with philistine society or the decadent aristocracy'; and the tales 'engage the reader in a serious discourse about art, philosophy, education, and love'.[31] The evil principle in 'Prince Alberic' is the debauched, vain, oppressive Duke Balthasar, grandfather to the innocent young prince, who is so neglected by his relation that the youth's only comfort is gazing upon a faded tapestry in the shabby rooms to which the prince is consigned. It depicts a knight and lady, 'Alberic the Blond and the Snake Lady Oriana', and is the youth's sole art and instruction, for the Gothic-style tapestry stirs his imagination and gives the prince knowledge of plants and animals, which he learns to name with his nurse's help.[32] Most of all he loves the tapestry's lady. When one day the furniture blocking his view is moved, he discovers that the woman's figure ends in a green and gold serpent's tail, and he then wonders, dreams, and imagines the more.

On impulse the duke deigns to look at his grandson's chamber one day, not to visit his heir but to consider the decorative possibilities of the space. He is repulsed by the faded tapestry and, since he is terrified of snakes, has it forthwith removed, replacing it with a sensual Susannah and the Elders tapestry that suits his tastes and lusts. The prince, furious at the removal of his beloved companion the tapestry, cuts this new tapestry to shreds with a sword and is forthwith sent away to the original home of the duchy, the Castle of Sparkling Waters, now largely a ruin. It becomes not the prison his grandfather intends as punishment but the prince's gateway to a paradise of nature, love, and nurturance, as if he had entered the very world depicted in the tapestry. This paradise is embodied above all in the green snake that comes to him near the deep well in the old garden, rising and swaying from the trough formed by an old sarcophagus, rubbing against his hand and becoming his daytime companion. At night his mysterious lovely godmother in green comes to him. She instructs him from the castle's richly stocked library and has him trained in swordsmanship and equestrian skills with the two horses he now acquires. Trained by her in probity and purity as well as strength of mind and body, he is incorruptible when the scheming, ambitious ministers to the duke visit and try to buy his affections and allegiance since he is destined to be duke himself one day.

This fairy tale clearly critiques the materialism, philistinism, and corruption of the Duke and his ministers. It also slips free of traditional Christianity and its symbolic codes, since the snake in paradise is not a Satan but a saviour, rescuing the child from the destructive forces and oppressions of court. Though the godmother, the magical snake woman Oriana, can be aligned with a phallic woman on the grounds of shape, both snake and woman are notably feminine in their affection, nurturance, and gentleness with the prince, as well as in their alignment with nature and its beauties. The prince learns the full story of Alberic the Blond and Oriana the Snake Lady from an itinerant tale teller, a quest romance that ends unhappily. Only when a knight summons the courage and fortitude to kiss the snake three times can Oriana assume her human form; and she can retain it only so long as the man is faithful to her. The first Alberic abandons Oriana to marry for wealth and power, fairy tale equivalents for capital-driven bourgeois marriage, while a second Alberic leaves Oriana for Christian salvation of his soul, a tacit critique of dogmatic Philistine religion.

Lee's tale ends unhappily as well. Now that the youth is princely and accomplished, the duke summons him to court to display him as heir to his people. The duke's ruinous decorative expenditures have bankrupted him, and he needs the prince to marry a wealthy bride to replenish the court coffers. The prince, however, refuses ever to marry. When the duke and his ministers visit the prince imprisoned in his chamber to coerce him, the duke sees the green snake in its corner and panics; he and his henchmen then crush the snake's head and slice it with swords. The prince dies not long after, as does the duke. When the prison room of the prince is cleared, 'the persons employed found in the corner, not the dead grass snake ... but the body of a woman, naked, and miserably disfigured with blows and sabre cuts' (343).

Lee's setting may be Italian, but her Gothic atmosphere, magical events, and dark ending bespeak German romantic fairy tales. 'Prince Alberic' is specifically indebted to E. T. A. Hoffmann's *Der goldene Topf* (the golden pot) (1814), as both Colby and Zorn affirm.[33] Hoffmann's title is unpromising, but even in translation it is an enchanting magical story, and unlike Hoffmann's more famous *Der Sandmann* (the Sandman) or Lee's 'Prince Alberic', which end violently, *Der goldene Topf* ends happily: a student's fidelity to his supernatural beloved enables him to achieve his quest and wed the beautiful snake woman Serpentina, who most often appears as a green and gold snake with magnetic large blue eyes expressing love.

Hoffmann's story, told in twelve parts, is intricate, with stories inside stories, but overall it pits the realm of Phosphorus, prince of Spirits, a site of overarching harmony with nature, within which humans of imagination can hear and understand nature's language, against a dark realm held in check only because Phosphorus keeps the black dragon who rules it enchained. It is very like a genesis story with paradisal harmony, beauty, and fulfillment pitted against dark greed, violence, and malevolence. Hoffmann's snakes are decided emblems of good to those with sufficient perception to see their beauty. A golden pot is given into the keeping of each of three snake daughters, whose father, the human Archivist Lindhorst, is suffering the penalty of human life for earlier disobeying a ban against marriage by Phosphorus. Lindhorst had disobeyed not from greed or rapaciousness but from overwhelming love for the fragile being enclosed within a golden lily who, when the lover embraced her, turned to ash. The pot's radiance reflects nature's harmony, and student Anselmus is promised that if he completes his quest, a golden lily will grow up from it replete with the fragrance dispersing harmony in an ongoing paradisal life.

That Lee's serpent lady is likewise a conduit of expansive love, beauty, goodness, and imagination rather than sin, as well as the sheer beauty of Hoffmann's and Lee's snakes, comprise the most forcible link between these tales; and the intertextuality confirms Lee's own deep-seated Anglo–German exchange that extended the arc of work by her Victorian precursors. Lee's dark turn at the end may have derived from the social factors identified by Stetz and others or the literary precedent of other German romantic fairy tales like Hoffmann's *Der Sandmann*.[34] No matter the underlying impulse, what lingers in the mind after reading 'Prince Alberic' is less the horror of that naked mutilated female body at the end than the utopian worlds of the tapestry and the Castle of Sparkling Waters. They represent realms of enchanted nature and radiant beauty – the enchanted world of childhood. And this world Lee knew not only from her Anglo–German exchange with German literary sources but also from her room over the river where she sat drinking coffee, eating apples, and experiencing the wonder of tales she drank in from her governess's lips.

Inventing an Alternative Ottilie

Germany's continuing importance to Lee beyond her childhood informed her choice of setting and characters for her first longer fiction, the novella *Ottilie* (1883), the story of a brother and sister in Questenberg, Franconia, during the nascent *Sturm und Drang* movement and rise of German romanticism in the late eighteenth century.³⁵ In some ways this work was a one-off production that led to nothing else, since it was neither an ambitious contemporary novel like *Miss Brown* (1884) nor one of Lee's supernatural tales. Lee later disparaged *Ottilie*, calling it 'the mere pretty fan painting of a child of eighteen', but she did so when she was smarting over what she deemed the critical failure of *Miss Brown*.³⁶ In contrast, *Ottilie* drew appreciative comments in 1883–4, and Fisher Unwin issued a second edition for his Pseudonym Library in 1893.³⁷ After writer Julia Wedgwood reviewed *Ottilie* in the *Contemporary Review*, Lee told Percy Bunting, editor of that journal, that she 'had been most pleased by her criticism'.³⁸ Wedgwood (1833–1913), the niece of Charles Darwin, had some reservations but nonetheless also offered praise:

> It is a sketch, delicately and lightly touched, of German provincial life in the Sturm und Drang period that produced Werther, and has all the interest and charm of a painting that records an actual excursion into an accessible past. It is too slight and purposeless, however, to attain fully the kind of interest at which it aims, and the reader is left with a sense of collapse and disappointment, though also with a great sense of power ... Vernon Lee is certainly to be one of our writers of the future; she has already acquired a style that is full of grace, and flavoured by a delicate humour, while it is also marked by that sure and rare sign of literary power – self-restraint. Moreover, she is original, in the sense that hardly any other young writer is original.³⁹

Alice Werner (1859–1935) likewise praised the finish of Lee's artistry but also singled out the author's intimate knowledge of Germany:

> her acquaintance with Germany, and the life and literature of the German people, would seem to be as complete as her other works show that her knowledge of Italy is. We do not mean to imply by this that any ponderous amount of learning is dragged into *Ottilie*. The book is just what it pretends to be – an idyl; a graceful little picture, too slight almost for criticism or detailed analysis, but charming all through ... We have applied the word slight to it, but it is the slightness, not of a sketch, but of a carefully finished miniature.⁴⁰

Scholars of the twentieth and twenty-first century offer mild praise, but *Ottilie* remains perhaps the least studied of Lee's works.⁴¹ It looks ahead to her travel writing on Germany yet is in some ways a sequel to Lee's *Studies of the Eighteenth Century in Italy*. Having demonstrated in-depth knowledge of Italy, *Ottilie* was her chance to do the same with late-eighteenth-century German culture.⁴²

Colby notes the work's biographical significance, its reflection of Lee's own situation in the 1870s. Just when publishing opportunities were beginning to open for her, the health and career of her half brother Eugene Lee-Hamilton collapsed. In this context Colby underscores

> the similarity of the melancholy, irresolute half brother Christoph and Eugene. Both leave university without taking degrees, both fail at careers and, still young, return home to live in passivity and dependency, writing undistinguished poetry. Ottilie, the older half sister, sacrifices her own promising future at court and later refuses offers of marriage ... Underlying her fictional heroine's lifetime of self-sacrifice and her brother's demands is a current of morbid and only partly repressed fear that Eugene was a threat both to her own dependence on her mother and to her independence as a woman.[43]

Lee endorsed a biographical approach when she told her beloved A. Mary F. Robinson that her 'fan painting' was that 'of a child of eighteen who has just read "*Aus Meinem Leben*"', that is, Johann von Goethe's *Aus meinem Leben: Dichtung und Wahrheit*, his autobiographical account of his life from childhood to his departure at age twenty-six for Weimar.[44]

Peter Gunn focuses almost exclusivly on Christoph in discussing the novella, since Gunn takes as a given that Ottilie, stuck in the provinces, would have had little awareness of the 'intellectual and spiritual ferment of the Sturm-und-Drang period'.[45] But Lee's artful framing of her story suggests the deliberateness of her title, which calls attention to the sister instead. Ottilie is distanced from readers by Lee's positioning of the narrative as an English-language translation of an old German manuscript left by Christoph ('"My Confession"'), who is known only as 'The Poet' in the village based on slight lyrics published in his youth. Readers first see the brother and sister in old age in an unidentified village (W –) through the eyes of the story's detached impersonal narrator. In summers the siblings walk daily to a bench by the river, he looking older and more worn than his older sister, who is still slender and upright where he is bent, and who seems to impart strength and encouragement to her fragile companion. The difference is partly accounted for by their being half-brother and half-sister. Never are they seen apart from each other until one day they are absent and after a space the brother comes alone, in black. One day he too ceases to appear and a second grave is dug in the village cemetery. The beginning of *Ottilie*, then, is the denouement of their life stories, the culmination of what they have amounted to. The title character is triply screened from view by the unnamed narrator, Christoph's manuscript, and temporal distance.

The prologue hints nonetheless at what lies at the tale's centre when the narrator reports village hearsay about the siblings:

> He had enjoyed some literary reputation at the end of the last century and the beginning of this one. His works, with the exception of a little volume of verse and some collections of popular legends which he had taken down from the mouth of the peasantry, were mostly tales of the fantastic, humorous, and pathetic style, slightly monotonous, and to our mind childish, which had been so popular in the time of Jean Paul and Hoffmann, and which are now wellnigh forgotten. People at W – maintained that in all these productions the sister had done at least half the work; and indeed the general opinion seems to have been that she was the master mind of the two.[46]

Since Eugene Lee-Hamilton had collaborated with his sister in collecting peasant folk narratives for *Tuscan Fairy Tales* (1880), issued by Lee's publisher of *Studies in the Eighteenth Century in Italy*, this back story again resonates strongly with Lee's youthful history.[47] But the village hearsay also points to an implied subterranean narrative that never rises to the surface, unfolding between – and haunting – the lines of Christoph's manuscript found in a 'mottled paper box' (24–5). Ottilie *is* the novella's main character, but her story is trapped, almost extinguished, by overlying male narratives just as this highly intelligent, gifted woman is trapped into constricted possibilities by the men in her life.

Lee shows this at every turn, and the result is a proto-feminist work that anticipates to a degree Virginia Woolf's *A Room of One's Own* (1929) and the life Woolf imagines for Judith Shakespeare. Alice Werner, the Anglo-German female critic, saw this clearly:

> It has often been remarked that there is no love and patience equal to the love and patience of a sister. It is to the sisters that the scapegrace of the family betakes himself when the father is inexorable and the mother indignant, and the brothers ... have finally determined 'to wash their hands of the fellow.' How many a sister has toiled patiently for years, giving up without a murmur all the brightness life might hold for herself, to give 'the boys' a fair start; and how many a one has worn out the rest of her days in the hopeless struggle to hide from friends and the world the worthlessness of one who ought to have been the pride and comfort of her life, to shield him from the consequences of his own folly and wrong-doing. And coupled with this is the fact that there is no ingratitude like that shown by brothers to sisters. Every brother, more or less, takes his sisters' services, great or small, as a matter of course.[48]

Lee's protagonist is not only systematically subordinated to her brother but is also, like Maggie Tulliver in Eliot's *The Mill on the Floss* (1860), the more intelligent sibling with greater potential. What follows is a feminist reading of the novella, surfacing the veiled narrative at its centre, and then an alternative *Ottilie* that fittingly concludes this study.

Ottilie's time at court before she surrenders possible advancement to come home and mother Christoph after their father's death means that she is fluent in the court language of French. But she is also a talented musician who plays harpsicord and has scouted out – a sure sign of endorsement by her creator – 'Italian canzonets', which she also sings (36). She becomes her half-brother's teacher and, in keeping with the advanced theories of education to which her court experiences have exposed her, opts first to inspire a 'love of literature' (38) by telling (like Lee's Bernese governess) her brother stories before teaching him to read. Ottilie's creative imagination, moreover, transforms through reinvention the traditional tales she recounts:

> [She would] begin telling me one of the many stories she was constantly collecting for my benefit. They were for the most part our popular fairy tales; but when, many years later, I chanced to hear or to read them in their original form, I was astonished to find how greatly they differed from my sister's version. It would seem as if her imagination refined and beautified all that passed through it: her knights were more gallant and courteous, her ladies more lovely and graceful, her fairies more ethereal and charming than the original ones, and the palaces and castles of our *Märchen* looked like so many hovels compared with the resplendent structures of her fancy. (39)

As Christoph matures the two begin to read English together, an avant garde turn away from French-dominated courts that follows the precedent of Johann von Goethe and others. Ottilie's keen intellectual interests expand still further when Dr Willibad is hired to tutor Christoph in classical languages, which Ottilie learns far more readily, supplementing Willibad's efforts with her own coaching of Christoph at night. The old-fashioned Willibad prefers French literature, but Ottilie's favourite poet is Friedrich Gottlieb Klopstock, whose experimental meters and innovative language in his adaptations of Milton for *Der Messias* (1749–55) inspired *Sturm und Drang* writers beginning in the 1760s.[49]

Christoph has learned well by this point the lesson noted by Alice Werner – his right to expect sisterly devotion as a matter of course. Indeed, he expects Ottilie's entire life to be built around him and intervenes whenever that privilege is threatened. Before Dr Willibad arrives Christoph has already ruined one chance for Ottilie to marry, breaking his promise to assist the suit of kindly Kasper, son of the local minister, whom Christoph considers too low on the social scale to marry into the family.

Lee makes clear that Ottilie's two other suitors are unworthy in the way that Christoph is: they want to fashion her for their own selfish needs. Willibad's marriage proposal is motivated as much by the delicious cinnamon cakes Ottilie bakes for him as by her intelligence and musical talents that provide the accompaniment to his viol de gamba in duets.

A far more promising candidate soon arrives, Councillor Moritz. Lee in this case referenced an actual historical figure, Karl Philipp Moritz (1756–93), as Colby notes.[50] In *Ottilie* Moritz is introduced as an advanced intellectual, published author, and rising star. For he, like Johann von Goethe, has made the transit south and discovered Italy and classical art as well as Johann Winckelmann's books on art.[51] Moritz possesses some of the young Goethe's glamour and is quite handsome to boot. Recognising this, Christoph insists on meeting Moritz, forms an acquaintance, and is introduced by him to classical art, the writings of Winckelmann, and Gotthold Lessing's *Laocoön* (1767). Moritz expects to be bored when Christoph invites Moritz to meet his sister, for he disdains the usual 'female inhabitant of a provincial town' (99). Instead he meets in Ottilie an intelligent, cultivated, and highly attractive young woman. Moritz and Ottilie first find intellectual and personal companionship in each other and in the new Italian opera music he brings her, and soon they fall in love (104). Though Ottilie never decreases her attentions, care, or concern for Christoph, nine years her junior, the jealous Christoph refuses to be dislodged however minutely from being 'my sister's sole thought, her life, her tyrant' (106). His tantrums and tears puzzle Ottilie, who seeks advice from Moritz, who flatly declares '"He has been spoilt"' and advises sending Christoph away to school (108).

Possible happiness for Ottilie ends when Moritz proposes marriage but dictates that '"Christoph . . . can be only one of two things to me – my son, or a stranger. As my son I shall insist on his being sent abroad and cured of this ridiculous morbidness, that he go into the world and there harden his absurd over-sensitive character; in this case I shall be acting for his own good"' (109–10). Christoph, more furious still, responds with his own ultimatum: '"Let her choose between us"' (111). The distraught Ottilie, who loves both, ultimately feels bound by duty to choose Christoph.

If Christoph's selfish infantilism is most glaringly visible, he is merely party to an overarching system of male dominance in which Moritz also participates, for his demand mirrors Christoph's:

> he was determined to make Ottilie his wife, but, as he declared before me, after one of my fits of jealous rage, his wife must be his and solely his . . . 'If you [Ottilie] refuse to let me deal with him as a son, I can regard him only

as an intruder, and his sentimental folly as a nuisance, and I shall be forced to keep him at a distance. I will permit of no middle course, I will endure no division of authority in my house.' (109, 110)

Unwilling to wait for Ottilie until Christoph finds his own way in life, Moritz simply leaves, doubling the betrayals of the men Ottilie loves most.

A succession of further betrayals by Christoph follows. He takes money she has saved by self-denial to go to university, joins the *Sturm und Drang* movement, publishes some minor lyrics, then leaves without a degree. He decides to marry Wilhelmine, the uneducated but pretty blonde cousin of Kasper, the parson's son, and ignores Ottilie's warning that their disparate intellects will be incompatible. He also pressures Otillie to humble herself and write a begging letter to her former royal patron the princess to get him a librarian's position in a small court, and fails there too – as he does in his marriage: after a five-year absence during which he has given no thought to his sister, Christoph returns home alone a final time:

> When my sister and I had met and embraced, we stood for a moment looking silently at each other. Six years ago I had left Questenburg scarcely more than a lad, now I returned older by twenty years. Ottilie was still slender and erect, but deep lines had formed round her mouth and eyes, and her serenity was that of a mind which has been victorious after long struggles. I felt that there now no longer existed any disparity of age between us; I had suffered as she had; but alas! while she had suffered from a generous sacrifice, I had suffered from my own selfish wilfulness. (187–8)

Despite his seeming confession, Christoph remains oblivious to Ottilie's separate self to the very end:

> She placed both her hands on my shoulders and looked into my face as she had done when I had first told her of my love for Wilhelmine. We were standing near a mirror; she noticed that I was looking at the white hairs among her brown ones. She smiled, but without any sadness.
> 'I have grown old,' she said.
> 'So have I,' I answered; 'but we should not complain of Time and his doings, since he has taught us that we were made only for each other.'
> And I kissed those few white hairs. (189–90)

He never hears what she is saying in announcing her arrival at old age. Behind this simple declaration lie the chance at marital happiness and family life squandered by Christoph and Moritz, the fact that she will now attract no other suitor, that years have passed without so much as a letter from the sibling to whom she had devoted her life's energies. In the novella's penultimate sentence he performs a culminating act of male privilege in appropriating her entire life and all that lies beneath her surface serenity to his needs and uses.

Seen through a feminist lens, the novel represents Ottilie's entrapment in a system of male dominance and entitlement, just as her story is trapped within Christoph's egocentric narrative. Lee enables readers to glimpse Ottilie's fuller story, but only at an angle. In the end Christoph's kiss is a kiss of death – not in stopping the breath but in delivering permanent stasis to his sister's existence. Ottilie's story continuously haunts the one that Christoph pens in 'My Confession' and belies its surface narrative.

This form of haunting points to another that emerges in Lee's preface to the novella, which involves her theory of fiction's relation to history. Lee turned to fiction rather than collected essays on eighteenth-century Germany, she explains, because of the frustrating limits imposed on the essayist, who may be able to imagine the contexts and characters of past events but can pen only what has been verified by documentary evidence:

> the Essayist has peculiarities which exclude him from the pleasant places of fiction, which render it proper that he should run along on the beaten roads of history, and be tied up in the narrow little stable of fact.
> Those who have not experienced it cannot guess how narrow, how very narrow, that stable of fact is; how straight and arid are often those roads of history. (10–11)

Because history writing cannot relay all that the historian intuits or imagines of certain scenes, every history is necessarily incomplete and contingent, so that the past itself becomes a haunted site:

> In studying any historical epoch ... there rise up before the unlucky Essayist vague forms of men and women whose names he does not know, whose parentage is obscure; in short, who have never existed, and who yet present him with a more complete notion of the reality of the men and women of those times than any real, contradictory, imperfectly seen creatures for whose existence history will vouch. (13)

Lee then applies the plenitude of imagined history versus the austerity of documentable history to her own case:

> I have been haunted ever since – it is now quite dreadfully long ago – the 18th century began to beckon to me, by certain persons living imaginary lives in a quiet imaginary German town – phantoms to whom I have often said 'avaunt,' performing over them all those spells with which the historically minded are wont to dispel the unreal creatures who thus torment them. But in vain; they have disappeared, but only to reappear again in a shape different, perhaps, but yet always familiar; till at last, after much

hesitation and much terror lest a person who, like myself, has dealt only with sober reality should be laughed at for seeing silly visions, I have determined to call in other folk, and ask them whether these are empty spectres, or such realities as the happy novelist creates out of nothing. (14–5)

Yet again haunting is a reference point for Lee the writer, and the preface suggests the aptness of half burying Ottilie's narrative in Christoph's, from whence the sister haunts the main narrative.

Karl Hillebrand, to whom *Ottilie* is dedicated, further illuminates Lee's narrative mode in *Ottilie*. His 16 July 1883 letter, while pointing out chronological inconsistencies, offered this praise:

> The chief merit ... of your novel is that characters are not psychologically analyzed or anatomically described, as is the fashion now a day's and that no moralizing intention is visible. Your persons show what they are by their acts and a few words, which is the only really artistic procédé. Ottilie and the Councillor are in this respect real models.[52]

By singling out Ottilie and Moritz as exemplary models in contrast to Christoph, with whom Lee approaches nearer to psychologising, Hillebrand pinpoints Lee's technique of impressionism that merely hints at psychologies and life processes. Impressionist technique is also what Lee advocates for effective supernatural writing. For like the 'vague forms of men and women' that present themselves to the historian, 'whose names he does not know, whose parentage is obscure', the supernatural is that

> which is beyond and outside the limits of the possible, the rational, the explicable – that supernatural which is due not to the logical faculties, argument from wrong premisses, but to the imagination wrought upon by certain kinds of physical surroundings ... But it is much more: it is the effect on the imagination of certain external impressions, it is those impressions brought to a focus, personified, but personified vaguely, in a fluctuating, ever-changing manner; the personification being continually altered, reinforced, blurred out, enlarged, restricted by new series of impressions from without, even as the shape which we puzzle out of congregated cloud-masses fluctuates with their every movement ...[53]

If one were to substitute for 'supernatural' the phrase 'perceived but undocumentable history', the passage would equally suit Lee's 1883 preface, which positions the historian as a spellmaker who attempts in vain to exorcise and put to rest the haunting figures that are generated by historical evidence but impossible to bring into clear focus or palpability. With such a self-conscious preface, the fiction that follows is both a story and a metafiction that reflects on how history is written and the contingent, incomplete result. The whole of *Ottilie* is in this context an allegory of history and history writing and a metafictional enactment of the contingency, flux, and liminality with which the historian grapples.

I conclude by taking a page from Lee's 1883 preface for myself to resituate *Ottilie* as an alternative, imagined history of the German woman who did so much to set in motion the fascination, beckoning freedoms, and literary opportunities of Germany for Victorian women writers: Ottilie von Goethe. Few scholars mention Lee's choice of the title character's name for her novella. That Lee intended a reference to the woman adored by Anna Jameson and Adele Schopenhauer is unlikely. Lee had many opportunities to allude to this female Goethe and undoubtedly knew of her, since in 'Goethe at Weimar' (1908) Lee registers detailed knowledge of the later life of Walther von Goethe, Ottilie von Goethe's elder son. In her travel essay Lee refers to the last Goethe only as a grandson, never a son. Even when Lee mentions the dusty Frauenplan residence and sees on display the pictured 'Lottes and Lilis and Maximilianes and Christianes, Suleikas, Gretchens and Ottilies, on whose love and love for him (as on the succulent roast ox-thighs of Homeric days) the god Wolfgang nourished and increased his own divinity', she is probably not referring with that last name to the 'Man-God's' *Schwiegertochter*, his daughter-in-law.[54] Most likely her novella's title was inspired by Johann von Goethe's 1809 novel, *Die Wahlverwandtschaften*, usually translated as *Elective Affinities*, in which Goethe explores the degree to which shifting erotic desires may, as with scientific laws governing chemistry or optics (about which he also wrote), involve similar regulatory laws that govern desires' realignments when new elements, new attractors, are introduced. In *Studies in the History of the Renaissance*, a book that influenced Lee profoundly, Walter Pater extolled Goethe's novel near the end of his chapter on Winckelmann.[55] Pater's endorsement and Lee's own immersion in the work of Goethe dating from her governesses' tutelage make it probable that she knew Goethe's novel, and it may well have come to mind when she envisioned Christoph's character, since Eduard, one of Goethe's four protagonists, insists on always fulfilling his immediate desires as a result of having been spoiled as a child. In the end Eduard's character trait leads to the death of his infant son and indirectly that of the younger woman with whom Eduard falls desperately in love: Ottilie, the niece and ward of Eduard's wife. Goethe's fictional Ottilie is meditative and philosophical, as seen in her diary excerpts in Part II. She loves Eduard deeply in return but is never permitted more than a few kisses despite German laws permitting divorce and remarriage. For like Lee's Ottilie,

Goethe's gives up her own desires and passions when she perceives that marriage to Eduard would inflict pain on others, here her aunt Charlotte, whom Eduard sleeps with again one night and impregnates.

Each time I read Lee's *Ottilie*, however, a narrative that Lee did not write or likely intend rises up ghostlike in the shadows of Lee's story: the life story of Ottilie von Goethe, another woman of creative literary talent, vitality, and passion who by Lee's day had virtually been erased from history and who in her own lifetime failed ever to find lasting fulfilment of her desires. Despite her fascinating conversation, sociability, charm, creativity, and esprit, her life story, too, was rapidly overlain and overshadowed by the men in her life to whom she subordinated herself.

At least this Ottilie's history is documentable, thanks to German feminist scholars and the documentary biography of Karsten Hein, which reprints many of Ottilie von Goethe's lyrics, sometimes playful but also at times confessional or meditative, written throughout her life. Hein also excerpts and sometimes prints in full this historical Ottilie's fictionalised letters or ripostes to other contributors in *Das Chaos*, the multilingual journal that she edited and circulated privately in Johann von Goethe's final years. Frederic Soret, who assisted her on the journal, described her as an original, full of imagination, sensitive, unpredictable, cleverer than most of her countrywomen, a lover of balls and parties but even more of literature, and, though as yet unpublished, a woman whose poetry and prose suggested that she would come to establish a literary reputation – an ironic guess in retrospect.[56] In most nineteenth- and twentieth-century accounts she figures merely as a daughter-in-law, reluctant wife, and frivolous romantic in love with one unattainable man after another. This ghostly Ottilie haunting Lee's *Ottilie* for me is a salutary reminder of all in Goethe's complicated social, sexual, emotional, psychological, and intellectual life, by turns vibrant and painful, that was once unquestionably present but eludes documentable history today.

Yet Ottilie von Goethe did have an impact on history – her own, her family's, and, far away in Britain, Englishwomen's lives. British women like Florence Nightingale would still have found their way to Germany had Ottilie von Goethe never met author Anna Jameson. But that meeting kindled not only Jameson's feelings for Goethe but also Jameson's love for a country and a culture where a woman's life could harmoniously combine sociability and intellectuality as a living reality, not an imagined dream. Women writers visited Germany for a complex range of motives, but the transit from Britain to a country notable for its challenging language especially beckoned a series of progressive women who were willing – and eager – to push at the borders of convention and female decorum. It seems appropriate, then, to glance back to the beginning of this study and bring it full circle, from the historical Ottilie to Lee's fictional Ottilie and back again. My alternative way of reading Lee's *Ottilie* may not square with documentable evidence. But as Lee claimed for her own version, in its own way it is true.

Nachwort/Afterword

This study closes after 1908 with good reason. 'The other Germany' beloved by Vernon Lee was destroyed by World War I. In preceding decades Germany was a brave new woman's world for Jameson in the 1830s, a strategic career and economic opportunity for the Howitts, a welcoming place to recuperate after her daughter's broken engagement for Gaskell, a refuge and source of increasing cosmopolitan sophistication for Eliot, a world of music and unconventional freedoms for Fothergill, an aesthetic archive for Michael Field, the home of Heine and his language for Levy, a catalyst for the expatriate identity and writing career for von Arnim, and a nurturing feminine zone for Lee and her imagination. After World War I and into the twentieth century, Germany became for most British writers, to invert Lee's words, precisely the country that sought to colonise and would eventually 'frighten the rest of the world in various ways'. Of course Germany's language and literary legacy remained, but the culture quickly became associated with military aggression and hostility rather than with a welcoming land for Britons. And with the dreadful slaughter of trench warfare and the Treaty of Versailles (1919), which demanded such stringent war reparations that it fuelled Germany's march to World War II, the very borders of Europe changed.

By the time World War I broke out in early August 1914, most of the writers of this study were dead or, in the case of Katharine Bradley, on her deathbed with less than two months to live. Only the expatriate writers survived to be confronted by what that war meant for them. Elizabeth von Arnim was literally caught by the war when it broke out. Her money was tied up in a Berlin bank, and she was barely able to arrange a transfer in francs before the Deutsche Bank closed. Von Arnim was then in Switzerland, where she had built a chalet after leaving Germany, but it was dangerous for her and her daughters – all German citizens – to stay put. Two of her daughters returned to Germany; her son, born in Britain, was already in England. She and her remaining two daughters needed to get to England quickly. To do so, she, Evi (her oldest), and Liebet had to borrow a friend's passport: their 'von Arnim' surnames and German citizenship would have denied them entry. To von Arnim's relief, the ruse worked, and her naturalisation papers as a British citizen arrived on 24 September 1914.[1]

Von Arnim did not renounce her authorial signature so closely tied to Germany but her feelings about Germany underwent a radical change. She had already portrayed the perspective of a Prussian military man in *The Caravaners* (1909), narrated by an oppressive Prussian husband in England. The novel is humorous, but the tensions between the Prussian narrator and the Englishmen in their holiday caravan anticipated conflict in national allegiances to come, and the narrative has been read as an anti-invasion and anti-German novel.[2] In June 1916 von Arnim received a telegram with the devastating news that her daughter Felicitas had died back in Germany, not from violence wrought by war but from pneumonia. Von Arnim's culminating novel on Germany, *Christine* (1917), was so bitter that she published it under a pseudonym to protect herself and Trixie, the daughter who remained in Germany. Von Arnim blamed Germany for her daughter's death – which forced her separation from her daughter if nothing else – and she utterly repudiated its claims on English artists through the character Christine, a gifted violist whose life is snuffed out by Germany's military machine.[3]

Vernon Lee never underwent such a *volte-face*, but she knew that her relation to Germany had been changed forever with the war; in effect the German part of her self was exiled. In the dedication to Mona Taylor in *The Golden Keys and other Essays on the Genius Loci* (1925), published well after the Armistice in 1918, Lee remarked that when the war broke out she immediately recognised it – presciently, as it turned out – 'as a war to bring about more wars'.[4] And in that volume's concluding essay, 'In Time of War', written in 1917, she testified to what the war destroyed:

> But as to them, dear clean, old-fashioned German towns, from Treves and Münster to innermost Franconia and the Harz, in which we two English friends were wont to take, year after year, our happiest holidays; *them* I shall, most likely, never again set foot in ... For though they stand intact in the material world and quite unchanged, no doubt, since we were there together, the thought of them has been sacked, burnt, defiled ten thousand times over by millions of indignant wills and by imaginations thirsty for reprisals.[5]

The war, in short, had not only destroyed lives on a horrific scale and changed the landscape, but it had also obliterated the past and with it the Germany that had been important to each of the writers in this study.

Worse was to come, both for Germany and for the rest of the world, when the fascism of Adolf Hitler began to take hold and erupted into the dreadful events of World War II. For decades after that conflict ended, to mention Germany was to call up associations with the Holocaust, a horror so terrible that it remains difficult to realise fully what it meant. Given the Marshall Plan in post-war Germany and defence of West Germany against the encroachments of the Soviets and East Germans, some support for the country always remained. Yet I will never forget that the first time I mentioned this book project and the name 'Germany' to a scholar I deeply respect and like, the immediate reaction was a grimace followed by an abrupt change of subject. It was understandable; I was talking to a British citizen who was born after 1945 but would have grown up with all the stories of the Blitzkrieg and struggles that Britons faced due to German aggression, just as the war has remained an active part of my own cultural memory since my father Andrew Michael Stauth, a German descendant, flew as flight engineer in 1943–4 on fifty bombing missions over Romania, Germany, and northern Italy in a B-24 before coming home and making my life possible. Between the threatening associations of twentieth-century Germany and the stereotype of ponderous German literature, philosophy, and prose style in nineteenth-century German culture, I wondered at times if anyone would want to read about what Victorian women writers discovered in Germany.

Since German reunification and the advent of Angela Merkel's leadership (which ended in December 2021), global citizens have had a chance through travel, economic markets, and diplomatic relations to develop far more receptive attitudes towards Germany. Though cultural stereotypes abide, mention of 'Germany' is as likely today to trigger positive as negative associations. All the world learned from Germany the dangers of military aggression wed to racist nationalism, and these dangers persist into our own time. But the delights and opportunities afforded by Germany for Victorian women writers can give us reasons to look back on nineteenth-century Germany with interest, a sense of discovery, and fresh appreciation.

Notes

Preface

1 John R. Davis's *The Victorians and Germany* (Oxford: Peter Lang, 2007) provides useful details but does not consider what German-speaking countries might have offered specifically to women, whose experiences were unlikely to replicate those of men.
2 Isabella Beeton was among the many who attended boarding school in Heidelberg; see Marianne von Remoortel, 'Women Editors' Transnational Networks in the *Englishwomen's Domestic Journal* and *Myra's Journal*', in *Women, Periodicals, and Print Culture in Britain, 1830s–1900s: The Victorian Period*, ed. Alexis Easley, Clare Gill, and Beth Rodgers (Edinburgh University Press, 2019), 48. Barbara Leigh Smith, later Bodichon, and Bessie Raynor Parkes travelled as unchaperoned tourists in Belgium, Germany, Austria, and Switzerland in 1850, a trip reflected in Anna Mary Howitt's novel *Sisters in Art*, serialised in eight parts in *The Illustrated Exhibitor and Magazine of Art*, July–December 1852. Elizabeth Rigby, the future Lady Eastlake, resided with her sister and mother for two years in Heidelberg to recover fully from typhoid fever – though she loathed German culture itself; see Davis, *The Victorians and Germany*, 100. Florence Nightingale famously received her nurse's training in Kaiserswerth, Germany, an experience that would figure in Anna Jameson's *Sisters of Charity Catholic and Protestant, Abroad and at Home* (London: Longman, Brown, Green, & Longmans, 1855).
3 This literary-historical inference is consistent with social psychologists' studies of the current effects of living abroad, for however short or long a period, on the creativity of those engaged in international business. As William Maddux and Adam Galinsky observe, openness to difference, adaptation to and voluntary immersion in the host culture promote 'lasting creative benefits from living abroad'; see Maddux and Galinsky, 'Multicultural Experiences: Making the World Creative, Innovative ... and Flat!', *INSEAD Knowledge*, open access online journal. This is a popular sequel to 'Cultural Borders and Mental Barriers: The Relationship Between Living Abroad and Creativity', *Journal of Personality and Social Psychology* 96.5 (2009), 1,047–61.

Introduction

1 Mercio P Gomes, 'Every Man Is an Island, Every Culture Is a Continent, and the Historical Process is Hyperdialectical', in *The Art of Cultural Exchange: Translation and Transformation between the UK and Brazil (2012–2016)*, ed. Paul Heritage and Ilana Strozenberg (Wilmington: Vernon Press, 2019), 51.
2 See Rosemary Ashton, *The German Idea: Four English Writers and the Reception of German Thought 1800–1860* (Cambridge: Cambridge University Press, 1980); Gerlinde Röder-Bolton, *George Eliot in Germany, 1854–55* (Aldershot: Ashgate, 2006); John Rignall, *George Eliot, European Novelist* (Farnham: Ashgate, 2011); Lesa Scholl, *Translation, Authorship and the Victorian Professional Woman: Charlotte Brontë, Harriet Martineau and George Eliot* (Farnham: Ashgate, 2011); Jennifer Raterman, 'Translation and the Transfer of Impressions in George Eliot', *Nineteenth-Century Literature* 68.1 (2013): 33–63, and Cristina Richieri Griffin, 'George Eliot's Feuerbach: Senses, Sympathy, Omniscience, and Secularism', *ELH* 84.2 (2017), 475–502.
3 Jameson had recently met Noel in England through Behnes Burlowe, a sculptor and Jameson's good friend; see Gerardine Macpherson, *Memoirs of the Life of Anna Jameson* (Boston: Roberts Brothers, 1878), 65. Noel knew Ottilie von Goethe from having lived in Germany for some time (G. H. Needler, ed., *Letters from Anna Jameson to Ottilie von Goethe* [Oxford University Press, 1939], 1, n.1).
4 Jameson too built upon precursors' experiences, including Madame de Staël and those eighteenth-century figures examined by Alessa Johns in *Bluestocking Feminism and British–German Cultural Transfer, 1750–1837* (Ann Arbor: University of Michigan Press, 2014).
5 In this study, 'Goethe' always refers to Ottilie von Goethe, consistent with my decision to call women writers by their last names – standard usage for male writers – rather than implying that women writers can inherently be approached more informally and intimately. I use full names for all others bearing that name, including the world-famous writer Johann von Goethe.
6 Judith Johnston, *Anna Jameson: Victorian, Feminist, Woman of Letters* (Aldershot: Ashgate, 1997), 7.
7 Karsten Hein, *Ottilie von Goethe (1796–1872): Biographie und literarische Beziehungen der Schwiegertochter Goethes* (Frankfurt am Main: Peter Lang, 2001), 419.
8 'For Anna – on Rahel, Bettine, and Charlotte.' Needler reprints the German text in his edition of *Letters*, 235–6. Carol Diethe translates an excerpt into English in *Towards Emancipation: German Women Writers of the Nineteenth Century* (New York: Berghahn Books, 1998), 65.
9 In northern Germany Prussia stretched westward to the Rhine, eastward to Königsberg (now Kaliningrad).
10 Germaine de Staël, *Germany; Translated from the French*, 3 vols. (London: John Murray, 1813), 1:39–40.
11 Ibid., 1:41–2.

12 Florence Nightingale, *Florence Nightingale's European Travels. Collected Works of Florence Nightingale*, vol. 7, ed. Lynn Mcdonald (Waterloo: Wilfrid Laurier University Press, 2004), 461–2.
13 Anna Jameson, *Visits and Sketches at Home and Abroad*, 4 vols. (London: Saunders & Otley, 1834).
14 Clara Thomas, *Love and Work Enough: The Life of Anna Jameson* (Toronto: University of Toronto Press, 1967), 45–6, 83.
15 Mary Howitt, *An Autobiography*, ed. Margaret Howitt, 2 vols. (London: William Isbister, 1889), 1:217; and Amice Lee, *Laurels and Rosemary: The Life of William and Mary Howitt* (London: Geoffrey Cumberlege, Oxford University Press, 1955), 119.
16 Vernon Lee, *The Sentimental Traveller: Notes on Places* (London: John Lane, The Bodley Head, 1908), x.
17 Elizabeth Gaskell had the most tenuous command of German (explored further in Chapter 3). Still, as William W. Maddux and Adam D. Galinsky report, there is a 'robust' correlation between living abroad and creativity. In addition to their study subjects, they posit Ernest Hemingway as an historical example, and I posit Gaskell as another. See 'Cultural Borders and Mental Barriers: The Relationship between Living Abroad and Creativity', *Journal of Personality and Social Psychology*, 96, no. 5 (May 2009), 1047–62, especially 1047–9, 1053, 1057.
18 Steven Vertovec and Robin Cohen, Introduction, *Conceiving Cosmopolitanism: Theory, Context, and Practice*, ed. S. Vertovec and R. Cohen (Oxford University Press, 2002), 1–10; see also Pauline Kleingeld, 'Six Varieties of Cosmopolitanism in Late Eighteenth-Century Germany', *Journal of the History of Ideas* 60.3 (1999), 505–6.
19 Kwame Anthony Appiah, *Cosmopolitanism: Ethics in a World of Strangers* (New York: W. W. Norton & Company, 2006), xv, xix, 165.
20 Vertovec and Cohen, Introduction, 1.
21 Immanuel Kant, 'Toward Perpetual Peace: A Philosophical Sketch', *Toward Perpetual Peace: and Other Writings on Politics, Peace, and History*, ed. Pauline Kleingeld, tr. David L. Colclasure et al. (New Haven: Yale University Press, 2006), 67–109.
22 See, e.g., Judith Walkowitz, 'Cosmopolitanism, Feminism, and the Moving Body', which extends the parameters of cosmopolitanism to include urban spaces such as music halls that were 'foreign' to middle-class women (*Victorian Literature and Culture* 38 [2010], 427–49).
23 Anna Jameson, *Characteristics of Women, Moral, Poetical, and Historical*, 2 vols. (London: Saunders & Otley, 1832).
24 Ludovico Ariosto, *Orlando Furioso*, tr. William S. Rose (London: John Murray, 1827), Canto XXVIII, St. XCVIII.
25 Jameson, *Visits and Sketches*, 1:7–8.
26 Ibid., 1:8.
27 For Lee's aesthetic theory and its German sources, see Vineta Colby, *Vernon Lee: A Literary Biography* (Charlottesville: University Press of Virginia, 2003), 154–5.

28 Vernon Lee, *Hortus Vitae: Essays on the Gardening of Life*, 2nd ed. (London: John Lane The Bodley Head, 1904), 18–19.
29 For a discussion of Lee, Appiah, and cosmopolitanism related to Italy, see Francesca Billiani and Stefano Evangelista, 'Carlo Placci and Vernon Lee: The Aesthetics and Ethics of Cosmopolitanism in *Fin-de-Siècle* Florence', *Comparative Critical Studies* 10, no. 2 (2013), 141–61.
30 James Buzard, *The Beaten Track: European Tourism, Literature, and the Ways to 'Culture' 1800–1918* (Oxford: Clarendon Press, 1993), 149–52.

Chapter 1

1 Gerardine Macpherson, *Memoirs of the Life of Anna Jameson*, 78. See also Mrs Steuart (Beatrice) Erskine, *Anna Jameson: Letters and Friendships (1812–1860)* (London: T. Fisher Unwin, 1915), 98; and Thomas, *Love and Work Enough*, 75.
2 Johnston, *Anna Jameson* (1997) and *Victorian Women and the Economies of Travel, Translation and Culture, 1830–1870* (Farnham: Ashgate, 2013).
3 Kimberly VanEsveld Adams, *Our Lady of Victorian Feminism: The Madonna in the Work of Anna Jameson, Margaret Fuller, and George Eliot* (Athens: Ohio University Press, 2001), 50–71; John Paul M. Kanwit, *Victorian Art Criticism and the Woman Writer* (Columbus: Ohio State University Press, 2013), 94, 101–3; Hilary Fraser, *Women Writing Art History in the Nineteenth Century: Looking Like a Woman* (Cambridge University Press, 2014), 10, 12, 17–22, 30–2, 107–10; and Caroline Palmer, '"A fountain of the richest poetry": Anna Jameson, Elizabeth Eastlake and the Rediscovery of Early Christian Art', *Visual Resources* 33.1–2 (2017), 54–66. Palmer makes the additional point that one reason for Jameson's (as well as Eastlake's) ability to appreciate early Christian art resulted directly from their fluent German and familiarity with current German art and art criticism. Adams argues that Jameson's analysis of the Madonna in *Legends of the Madonna, as Represented in the Fine Arts* (London: Longman, Brown, Green, and Longmans, 1852) influenced George Eliot's *Romola* (1862–3).
4 Though at times she showed more sympathy with English than with Irish opinion, she was proud of her Irish descent and often championed the Irish in conversation and commentaries.
5 Thomas, *Love and Work Enough*, 3–4, 11. That Jameson was raised Anglican rather than Catholic would have further enhanced her social mobility in England and in Protestant northern Germany.
6 Erskine, *Anna Jameson*, 48.
7 Jameson, *Diary of an Ennuyée* (London: Henry Colburn, 1826).
8 Erskine, *Anna Jameson*, 97–8; Thomas, *Love and Work Enough*, 75; Hein, *Ottilie von Goethe*, 364.
9 Jameson, *Visits and Sketches*, 1:15–16. During the 1829 visit Jameson had an extended conversation, in French, with sculptor Johann Heinrich von Danneker

in Stuttgart on his artistic career, which Jameson recounts in Part II of *Visits and Sketches*.
10 Erskine, *Anna Jameson*, 98.
11 Alessa John's *Bluestocking Feminism* instead emphasises the Personal Union of England and Germany (1714–1837), when Hanoverians assumed the British throne (1–3ff.), as the key factor enabling 'cultural transfer' for Jameson. As a Prussian residing in the grand ducal principality of Weimar, Goethe was removed from Hanoverian politics and relations, nor did Jameson have any political connection to Germany.
12 Erskine, *Anna Jameson*, 99.
13 Ibid., 98.
14 Sylke Kaufmann, *Henriette von Pogwisch und ihre Französische Lesegesellschaft* (Marburg: Tectum Verlag, 1994), 18, 24–6; and Hein, *Ottilie von Goethe*, 67.
15 In 1820 Henriette von Pogwisch initiated an uncontested divorce; see Ruth Rahmeyer, *Ottilie von Goethe: Eine Biographie* (Frankfurt am Main, Insel Verlag, 2002), 17–18, 29.
16 Johanna was also the mother of philosopher Arthur Schopenhauer (1788–1860), eleven years Adele's senior. Arthur moved to Weimar but never lived with the family, and when mutual hostilities between his mother and him peaked in 1814, Arthur had nothing more to do with her the rest of his life. See Angela Steidele, *Geschichte einer Liebe: Adele Schopenhauer und Sibylle Mertens* (Berlin: Insel Verlag, 2011), 50.
17 Hein, *Ottilie von Goethe*, 70.
18 Ibid., 64–6.
19 Ibid., 78. Johann von Goethe himself promoted the study of English language and literature rather than privileging all things French, as in most German courts; see Rahmeyer, *Ottilie von Goethe*, 47, and John Oxenford, tr., *Conversations of Goethe with Eckermann and Soret*, 2 vols. (London: Smith, Elder, 1850), 1:184.
20 Hein, *Ottilie von Goethe*, 67. Hein suggests that Johann von Goethe's recognition of Byron owed much to Henriette von Pogwisch (67–70). For the impact of Goethe and Byron on each other, see Fred Parker, '"Much in the mode of Goethe's Mephistopheles": *Faust* and Byron', *International Faust Studies: Adaptation, Reception, Translation*, ed. Lorna Fitzsimmons (London: Continuum, 2008), 107; Andrew Rutherford, ed., *Lord Byron: The Critical Heritage* (1970; rpt. London: Routledge, 2010), 119–20; and Frank Eirk Pointner and Achim Geisenhanslüke, 'The Reception of Byron in the German-Speaking Lands', *The Reception of Byron in Europe*, ed. Richard A. Cardwell, 2 vols. (London: Continuum, 2004), 2:254–6.
21 Hein, *Ottilie von Goethe*, 68. For Byron's poem, see Clara Tuite, *Lord Byron and Scandalous Celebrity* (Cambridge: Cambridge University Press, 2015), 65.
22 Goethe, 'Byron. Ein Traum', in *Das Chaos*, the journal Goethe edited 1829–32, which circulated privately among its contributors (Bern: Verlag Herbert Lang, 1936), 22. Goethe inserted her 1822 poem in the sixth number of *Das Chaos* (Hein, *Ottilie von Goethe*, 68). After Johann von Goethe's death

in 1832, she penned another prose fantasy, 'Drei Sterne' (Three Stars) about Schiller, Byron, and Goethe, which drew upon *Faust*, Part II. In it Byron, associated with a comet, fuses with the figure of Johann von Goethe's Euphorion, and altogether the celestial images materialise the three great writers' ideas and ideals (Hein, 342–3).

23 Thomas Moore, *Letters and Journals of Lord Byron: With Notices of His Life*, 3 vols., 3rd ed. (London: John Murray, 1833), 3:434.
24 Rahmeyer, *Ottilie von Goethe*, 127.
25 Steidele, *Geschichte einer Liebe*, 118. Steidele comments, 'Es war Liebe auf den ersten Blick – für Anna' (It was love at first sight – for Anna) (Steidele, 115).
26 Anna Jameson to Ottilie von Goethe, 23 July 1833, Goethe-Schiller Archiv 40/VIII, 4. Needler, the editor of Jameson's and Goethe's correspondence, omits this passage in the second letter of his edition. Many of the most telling passages in Jameson's letters were omitted by Needler, and consulting the originals at the Goethe- und Schiller-Archiv (GSA) in Weimar is vital to understanding Jameson's response and the women's evolving relationship over time. Captain Story's first name has never been discovered despite the efforts of scholars in Germany and North America.
27 Clara Thomas, *Love and Work Enough*, 78–9; Steidele, *Geschichte einer Liebe*, 113.
28 Erskine, *Anna Jameson*, 102. By October 1836 Jameson had mastered written German, as her letters to Mertens-Schaaffhausen attest. See Theo Clasen and Walther Ottendorff-Simrock, eds., *Briefe an Sibylle Mertens-Schaaffhausen* (Bonn: Ludwig Röhrscheid Verlag, 1974), 58–71.
29 My account is largely drawn from Steidele's sympathetic portrayal in which same-sex love plays a central role. For a somewhat less sympathetic English-language account that minimises lesbian desire but offers detailed analysis of Schopenhauer's fiction, see Diethe, *Towards Emancipation*, 55–61.
30 Steidele, *Geschichte einer Liebe*, 83, 171.
31 My translation of letters from Schopenhauer to Goethe, 1814, 7 May 1815, 19 July 1815, 19 October 1816, in Steidele, *Geschichte einer Liebe*, 44–5 ('mit jeder Kraft meines Daseyns liebe ich Dich, mit jedem Gefühle das in mir ist ... und glaube daß ich nicht leben kan [sic], wenn Du nicht glücklich bist, denn Du allein weißt alle meine Gedanken und empfindest ganz so wie ich ... Du bist ja nun mein Alles ... So wie Du gestern mein letzter Gedanke warst, bist Du, liebe Ottilie, auch Heut' mein 1ster ... jetzt weiß ich bestimmt: wir müßen immer vereint bleiben, denn wir sind zu fest verbunden ... Gottes Wille uns zusammenstelle, um vereint durch ein wunderlich verschlungenes Leben zu gehen'). For a fuller picture of nineteenth-century same-sex unions, see Martha Vicinus, *Intimate Friends: Women Who Loved Women, 1778–1928* (Chicago: University of Chicago Press, 2004).
32 Steidele, *Geschichte einer Liebe*, 44, 68–9.
33 Ibid., 18–23.
34 Ibid., 26–9.
35 Ibid., 54–7.

36 My translation of Schopenhauer to Goethe, 19 May 1828, in Steidele, *Geschichte einer Liebe*, 78, 79 ('*nicht so geliebt worden*'; '*ich liebe sie ... wie ich sie liebe werde ich wohl nie wieder jemanden lieben*').
37 Steidele, *Geschichte einer Liebe*, 82–3, 113; Diethe, *Towards Emancipation*, 55.
38 Monika Shafi, 'Annette Freiin von Droste-Hülshoff', *Nineteenth-Century German Writers to 1840*, ed. James N. Hardin and Siegfried Mews, *Dictionary of Literary Biography 133* (Detroit: Gale, 1993), 50; and Steidele, *Geschichte einer Liebe*, 57–8.
39 Steidele, *Geschichte einer Liebe*, 122–3.
40 Ibid., 129–32.
41 Ibid., 195, 283.
42 Joey [Ritta Jo] Horsley, rev. of *Geschichte einer Liebe*, by Angele Steidele, *Fembio* website for biographical research on women, 16 July 2010, n.p.
43 Steidele records only a fatal disease of the abdomen; Diethe's assumption that Schopenhauer's fatal illness was uterine cancer is persuasive (Diethe, *Towards Emancipation*, 61).
44 Steidele, *Geschichte einer Liebe*, 242.
45 Ibid., 226–8.
46 I translate from Steidele, *Geschichte einer Liebe*, 225 ('*die exentrischen Freundshaften der Mutter wurden vom Kind wie vom Vater wie Unrecht, Wahnwitz, Tollheit erfasst*). Steidele quotes from an unpublished biography of Mertens-Schaaffhausen by Schopenhauer.
47 Compare the impact and significance of a fictional parallel in George Eliot's *Romola*, when the classical collection so lovingly amassed by Romola's father during his lifetime is dispersed by Tito, Romola's husband, for profit.
48 Schlegel provided copy for *Visits and Sketches* as well as extending Jameson's German social network. See Hein, *Ottilie von Goethe*, 366; Erskine, *Anna Jameson*, 103–5; and Needler, *Letters*, 2–3.
49 Needler, *Letters*, 1–3; Erskine, *Anna Jameson*, 102–5; Steidele, *Geschichte einer Liebe*, 115–17.
50 My translation of Steidele, *Geschichte einer Liebe*, 116 ('*Anna liebt dich sehr, mehr noch seit dem sie mich kennt, und durch mich ohne daß ichs wußte, manche Erklärung über dich erhielt*'). Writing to Goethe almost four years later, Schopenhauer explicitly placed Jameson in the position that Schopenhauer once had held in Goethe's life, urging Goethe not to treat Jameson as poorly as she had her earlier (Steidele, *Geschichte einer Liebe*, 164–5). As Schopenhauer concluded, 'you are the poetry of her existence ... [and] can in the long run make her miserable' ('*Du bist die Poesie ihres Daseyns ... [und] köntest sie auf die Länge sehr elend machen*' [Steidele, *Geschichte einer Liebe*, 165]).
51 Erskine, *Anna Jameson*, 105.
52 My translation, Hein, *Ottilie von Goethe*, 370 ('*seit sie hier ist, habe ich zwar oft eine sehr wohlthuende Empfindung gefühlt, mich so geliebt zu sehen ...*').
53 Hein, *Ottilie von Goethe*, 370–1.

54 Needler, *Letters*, 5–6. Hein adduces Captain Story as the referent of the threat Jameson cites; see Jameson's 23 July 1833 letter mentioning Story above (Hein, *Ottilie von Goethe*, 369–70).
55 Letter of 16 October 1833; Needler, *Letters*, 15.
56 Sarah Austin, *Characteristics of Goethe. From the German of Falk, Von Müller, &c., with notes, original and translated, illustrative of German literature*, 3 vols. (London: E. Wilson, 1833).
57 I translate from the letter reproduced in Hein, *Ottilie von Goethe*, 13–14:

> Ich bin ungeheuer faul und indolent, wo es sich auf mich bezieht, aber ich habe eine eiserne Beharrlichkeit, wo etwas in Verbindung mit meinem Freunden steht, und verfolge dann durch alle Windungen des Lebens und jahrelang dieselben Zwecke, denn ein Aufgeben kenne ich eigentlich nicht, und dünkt mich unnatürlich, wodurch auch wol entstehen mag, daß ich gar keine Resignation habe. Ich habe eine unerschöpfliche Begeisterung für gewisse Ideen und bin nicht nur auf manche Punkte ein Gefühls-Don Quixote, sondern zeige es auch, und bin immer zum Lanzenbrechen bereit, weil ich die Furcht vor dem Ridicule, … der Gesellschaft jenen höheren Aufschwung untergräbt und ich für Zaghafte und Wankelmüthige an die Kraft des Wortes und des Beispieles glaube. (…) Mit einem wilden, angeborenen Freiheits-, ja Rebellensinn, war ich doch immer eine vollkommene Sklavin, wo ich liebte, und das Doppelurtheil, was von mir in der Welt herrscht, erklärt sich dadurch. So wenig es auf vielen Punkten den Anschein hat, so sehr ich eine gewisse Emancipation für die Frauen verlange, so war vielleicht Niemand, der wie ich sogar vollkommen glücklich in der Beschränkung eines Harems hätte sein können, wenn man dadurch die vollkommene Befriedigung verstand, alle Gedanken, Talente, Empfindungen nur als um und für Einen Menschen bezüglich zu fühlen, aber freilich mußte ich in meinem Harem mit ihm allein sein und mir keine Herzenstheilung zugemuthet werden.

Note Goethe's use of German to Austin, who was fluent in German, in contrast to her Anglophone letters to Jameson.
58 Erskine, *Anna Jameson*, 106.
59 Anna Jameson, ed., *Fantasien: Fancies; a series of subjects in outline, now first published from the original plates, by Moritz Retzsch* (London Saunders and Otley, 1834).
60 Hein, *Ottilie von Goethe*, 374; Needler, *Letters*, 11; Erskine, *Anna Jameson*, 107–8.
61 Macpherson, *Memoirs*, 83–4; Needler, *Letters*, 12.
62 Steidele asserts that Jameson was '*vorbehaltlos angetan*' (unreservedly taken with) Mertens-Schaaffhausen; Steidele, *Geschichte einer Liebe*, 116.
63 Jameson, *Visits and Sketches*, 1:51.
64 Steidele, *Geschichte einer Liebe*, 116. Both the 'Romantic Rhine' drawing and a decidedly erotic portrait of Mertens-Schaaffhausen noted below are reproduced in Steidele, *Geschichte einer Liebe*, opposite 99.
65 I translate from Thomas, *Love and Work Enough*, 79 ('*so lieb sie mir ist, so unendlich ich sie beklage, frappirt mich doch sehr, wie sie zu mir und zur Mertens stand denn jede glaubte mit ihr intimer zu sein … Sybille hat sich gewaltig exaltirt und mich sogar unfreundlich behandelt aus lauter Liebe zur Jameson, welche Sybillen wie eine Todkranke behandelt*'). For Jameson's troubled response to the two women's outpourings, see Needler, *Letters*, 18.

66 I translate from Thomas, *Love and Work Enough*, 79 ('*diese Art ist zwischen Frauen nicht natürlich*').
67 Needler, *Letters*, 17.
68 Schopenhauer reminded Goethe that with the death of her husband in 1830, her sole duty was to guard Germany's treasure and the 'Vater' who had long meant so much to her personally; Hein, *Ottilie von Goethe*, 306.
69 Rahmeyer, *Ottilie von Goethe*, 165–6.
70 Hein, *Ottilie von Goethe*, 351, 366.
71 Macpherson confirms the date of Jameson's arrival; see *Memoirs*, 97.
72 Hein, *Ottilie von Goethe*, 386; Erskine, *Anna Jameson*, 113–14.
73 See Erskine, *Anna Jameson*, 115, and Hein, *Ottilie von Goethe*, 389–90; Hein remarks that Goethe kept her pregnancy secret even from Schopenhauer, her earliest friend in life.
74 Both Jameson and Mertens-Schaaffhausen helped bear the costs of Goethe's sojourn in Vienna, the medical expenses of birth, and childcare. In recognition of them, Goethe named the baby Anna Sibylle Poiwisch and appointed both friends as godmothers. See Hein, *Ottilie von Goethe*, 396–7, 421.
75 Hein, *Ottilie von Goethe*, 396, 394.
76 See also Thomas, *Love and Work Enough*, 93–6.
77 Softest.
78 Dr Romeo Seligmann (1808–92), the personal physician called in to attend the birth. A scholar and intellectual as well as future professor of medicine, he became the friend (and romantic interest) of Goethe when she resided in Vienna from 1842 until late in the 1860s.
79 A miracle of beauty and spirit.
80 Like an embodiment of something divine.
81 GSA 40/VIII, 4, Letter 261a.
82 GSA 40/VIII, 4, Letter 258a. Later in the letter, Jameson details her visit to the baby: 'I will now tell you that I went this morning in a carriage to see Baby & found her quite well – she seized me by the hair with both her little hands & laughed at me – every thing was clean & nice & I saw her fed & put to sleep – the milk agrees with her perfectly ...'
83 Erskine, *Anna Jameson*, 123–7; Hein, *Ottilie von Goethe*, 397n.296, 399; Macpherson, *Memoirs*, 103. Jameson stayed in Weimar four months after falling ill, when she was largely nursed by Ulrike von Pogwisch, Goethe's younger sister (Hein, 406).
84 Jameson to Goethe, 16 August 1835, GSA 40/VIII, 4, Letter 266; Thomas, *Love and Work Enough*, 99–101.
85 Hein, *Ottilie von Goethe*, 394–5; Erskine, *Anna Jameson*, 117–18, 124.
86 Hein, *Ottilie von Goethe*, 479–80, 482–3; see also Thomas, *Love and Work Enough*, 147–8. Jameson, too, assisted by sharing her knowledge of Irish history and sending books from London. Kühne's novel was serialised in his weekly paper prior to the 1840 first edition.
87 For other indications of Jameson's collaborative writings with Goethe, see my 'Trace Collaboration and the Problem of Evidence: Anna Jameson and Ottilie

von Goethe', in *Studies in Victorian and Modern Literature: A Tribute to John Sutherland*, ed. William Baker (Madison: Fairleigh Dickinson University Press, 2015), 39–49.
88 Anna Sibylle Poiwisch died of consumption on 4 July 1836; after Goethe moved to Vienna she regularly visited her infant's grave (Hein, *Ottilie von Goethe*, 421, 482). For Jameson's own grief at the infant's death, which framed the older daughter's death in that city for both friends, see my '"Given in outline and no more": The Shared Life Writing of Anna Jameson and Ottilie von Goethe', *Forum for Modern Language Studies* 52.2 (2016), 166–9.
89 Macpherson, *Memoirs*, 211–13.
90 Hein, *Ottilie von Goethe*, 560–4.
91 Ibid., 595–6, 622; Thomas, *Love and Work Enough*, 215.
92 GSA 40/VIII, 4 Letter 9. Needler omitted this statement in his edition of *Letters* (35).
93 GSA 40/VIII, 4, Letter 42.
94 GSA 40/VIII, 6, Letter 76.
95 Jameson to Goethe, 2 June 1849, GSA 40/VIII, 6, Letter 118. Jameson's anxiety stemmed from the Continental revolutions of 1848–9. Jameson's 'book' was *Sacred and Legendary Art* (1848).
96 Rahmeyer, *Ottilie von Goethe*, 317–18.
97 GSA 40/VIII, 9, 1, Letter 321.

Chapter 2

1 Christopher M. Keirstead, *Victorian Poetry, Europe, and the Challenge of Cosmopolitanism* (Columbus: Ohio State University Press, 2011), 66.
2 Davis, *The Victorians and Germany*, 207–10. Other travelogues included Frances Trollope's *Belgium and Western Germany* in 1833 (Davis, 207). Macpherson first declared Jameson's significance in opening little-known German art museums to the British public, remarking that Carlyle's prior writing on Goethe and German letters contributed to Jameson's favourable reception. Jameson rather than Carlyle, however, was the first to outline the Niebelungen saga for the public (Macpherson, *Memoirs*, 86–9). In 1837 the book was also published in Germany under the title *Sketches of Germany. Art – Literature – Character* (listed in the British Library catalogue). By 1839 the London-issued *Visits and Sketches* reached a third edition.
3 *Athenaeum*, 28 June 1834, 489.
4 *Edinburgh Review* 60 (October 1834), 180–1.
5 See, e.g., Jameson's *Handbook to the Public Galleries of Art in and Near London* (1842), *Companion to the Private Galleries of Art in London* (1844), and *A Handbook to the Courts of Modern Sculpture* included in the *Official Handbooks of the Crystal Palace* (1854).
6 Jameson, *Characteristics of Women*, 1:xlix.

7 Jameson, *Visits and Sketches*, 1:7–8, 3–5. See the introduction for discussion of Jameson's affective female cosmopolitanism.
8 Jameson, *Visits and Sketches*, 1:6.
9 Jameson would also contrast German criticism's openness to cultural exchange with the English critical impulse towards narrow exclusivity in *Social Life in Germany* (1840):

> There existed, there still exists, in some degree, one strong distinction between the spirit of German and the spirit of English criticism: the Germans have deep sympathy, honest appreciation for what is most opposite to their own national nature and habits of life, united with a singular degree of nationality and individuality of character. Their very independence, in this sense, is the cause of their indulgence and universal spirit. The English critics, on the contrary, were long infected with the exclusive spirit ... Whatever was foreign to our own mode of existence was misunderstood ...

See Jameson, *Social Life in Germany*, 2 vols. (London: Saunders & Otley, 1840), 1:xiii. She happily conceded, however, that this orientation had lately begun to change.
10 Jameson, *Visits and Sketches*, 1:39–40.
11 Ibid., 1:52.
12 Ibid., 1:136. Jameson references Sarah Austin's translation, *Characteristics of Goethe from the German of Falk, von Müller* (London: Effingham Wilson, 1833).
13 Jameson, *Visits and Sketches*, 1:136.
14 Ibid., 1:138–40.
15 Ibid., 1:140. Jameson's accolades have seemed excessive to many. Another Englishman, however, confirms the German woman's mesmerising effect on men and women alike. In his novel *The Fergusons; or, Woman's Love and the World's Favour* (1839; rpt. Memphis: General Books, 2012), published only five years after *Visits and Sketches*, Edmund Phipps offers a portrait of Goethe, with whom he conversed at length during a visit to Weimar, with the thinnest of disguises, merely transporting her and her late father-in-law to an Italian rather than German setting. In the novel three Englishwomen discuss the Italian woman in these terms: 'I hear she is courted and respected by ladies as well as gentlemen; and, as for English, they say that not one of them can help falling in love with her. I know, for my part, I am already in love with her myself' (74).
16 Jameson, *Visits and Sketches*, 1:143.
17 Ibid., 1:144; A[braham] Hayward, tr., *Faust: A Dramatic Poem, by Goethe*, 2nd ed. (London: Edward Moxon, 1834), 305–6.
18 Hayward more explicitly references 'Madame de Goethe' in his *Faust* translation, vi, lxxii.
19 Hayward, *Faust*, 268. Hayward then appended a list of Jameson's books published up to 1834.
20 Jameson, *Visits and Sketches*, 1:150–6. In the second volume of *Visits* Jameson pointed out that the principal newspaper in Nuremburg was also entirely run by women (2:82).

21 Hayward, *Faust*, 350.
22 Jameson, *Visits and Sketches*, 2:19, 24–6, 122–4, 145. Fraser also notes Jameson's discussion of women painters in *Visits*, though Fraser places more emphasis on Italian painters (*Women Writing Art History*, 109–10).
23 Jameson, *Visits and Sketches*, 1:246–7.
24 Ibid., 1:249.
25 Cf. *Visits and Sketches*, 1:7–8.
26 Jameson, *Visits and Sketches*, 1:300.
27 Debra N. Mancoff, *The Arthurian Revival in Victorian Art* (New York: Garland, 1990), 65–100, 112–35. See also C. Palmer, '"A fountain of the richest poetry"', 61–2.
28 Jameson, *Visits and Sketches*, 2:51–2.
29 Ibid., 2:23.
30 Ibid., 2:35.
31 Ibid., 2:35–6. Jameson quotes John Gay, *The Shepherd's Week: In Six Pastorals* (1714). E. C. Stedman republishes another of Jameson's poems, 'Take Me, Mother Earth', in *A Victorian Anthology 1837–1895* (Boston: Houston, Mifflin and Company, 1895), 58.
32 Jameson, *Visits and Sketches*, 2:85. As Johns comments, travel writing, not just translations, circulated new ideas and 'discourses' on 'transnational political and social issues' (*Bluestocking*, 124–5). See also Scholl, *Translation, Authorship and the Victorian Professional Woman*, 129.
33 *Winter Studies and Summer Rambles in Canada*, 3 vols. (London: Saunders and Otley, 1838). Fittingly, the authoritative biography of Jameson was written by Canadian Clara Thomas, the York University professor who pioneered Canadian literary studies. Nora Shanahan, 'Obituary of Clara Thomas', *The Globe and Mail* (Toronto) 28 November 2013, web.
34 Johnston, *Victorian Women*, 102. For the German reception of *WSSR* as well as its connection to Jameson's German experiences, see Johns, *Bluestocking*, 126, 145–8.
35 For *WSSR*'s emphasis on women, see Johnston, *Victorian Women*, 96; Johns, *Bluestocking*, 152.
36 Jameson, *WSSR*, 1:v. Jameson also drew upon her Canadian letters to Mertens-Schaaffhausen, another tacit presence for Jameson in Canada. Jameson's 25 June 1837 letter to Mertens-Schaaffhaausen from Niagara Falls commented that Jameson always wore a ring that Mertens-Schaaffhausen gave her and had brought her friend's picture with her to Niagara Falls; see Theo Clasen and Walther Ottendorff-Simrock, eds., *Briefe an Sibylle Mertens-Schaaffhausen* (Bonn: Ludwig Röhrscheid Verlag, 1974), 66.
37 Jameson, *WSSR*, 1:39, 121; Charles Des Voeux, tr., *Torquato Tasso, a Dramatic Poem from the German of Goethe: with Other German Poetry* (London: Longman Rees, Orme, Brown, and Green, 1827). Goethe oversaw the issue of a second, corrected edition published in Weimar in 1833 and may have played a larger role in translating her father-in-law's work and the appended selection of additional German poems. See Hughes, 'Trace Collaboration', 40–1.

38 Oxenford, *Conversations of Goethe*, 1:289. A Jameson footnote more directly references Goethe as 'a near and dear relation of [Johann von] Goethe, who had lived for very many years in the closest communion with him'; see *WSSR*, 1:178–79n. Jameson later reveals that her own copy of Eckermann was a gift from Goethe; see 1:174.

39 Jameson, *WSSR*, 2:334–6.

40 See also Johnston, *Victorian Women*, 99; Bina Freiwald, 'Femininely Speaking: Anna Jameson's *Winter Studies and Summer Rambles in Canada*', in *A Mazing Space: Writing Canadian Women Writing*, ed. Shirley Neuman and Smaro Kamboureli (Edmonton: Longspoon & NeWest Presses, 1986), 67–8; Thomas M. F. Gerry, '"I am Translated": Anna Jameson's Sketches and *Winter Studies and Summer Rambles in Canada*', *Journal of Canadian Studies* 25.4 (1990–1), 43; and Christa Zeller Thomas, '"I shall take to translating": Transformation, Translation and Transgression in Anna Jameson's *Winter Studies and Summer Rambles in Canada*', in *Translators, Interpreters, Mediators: Women Writers 1700–1900*, ed. Gillian E. Dow (Oxford: Peter Lang, 2007), 183.

41 Jameson, *WSSR*, 1:230. *Specimens of the Table Talk of the Late Samuel Taylor Coleridge* edited by his son-in-law Henry Nelson Coleridge had appeared in two volumes in 1835 (London: John Murray) – i.e. shortly before Jameson herself began writing what became *Winter Studies*. If Jameson's 'talk' was self-recorded, so was William Hazlitt's in his *Table-Talk*, 1821–2.

42 Needler, *Letters*, 73.

43 Doris Starr Guilloton, 'Rahel Varnhagen von Ense', *Dictionary of Literary Biography 90: German Writers in the Age of Goethe, 1789–1832*, ed. James Hardin and Christoph E. Schweitzer (Detroit: Gale, 1989), 340. For Rahel's legacy, see Heidi Thomann Tewarson, *Rahel Levin Varnhagen: The Life and Work of a German Jewish Intellectual* (Lincoln: University of Nebraska Press, 1998).

44 Jameson, *WSSR*, 2:26n. Thomas identifies late November as the book's release date (*Love and Work Enough*, 126).

45 [Thomas Carlyle,] 'Varnhagen von Ense's Memoirs', *London and Westminster Review* 32 (December 1838), 78, 75.

46 Translated by Diethe, *Towards Emancipation*, 65. Rahel's full acknowledgment as a writer by German scholars and her canonical status today are verified by the ten-volume scholarly edition of Rahel's complete writings (*Gesammelte Werke*); see Tewarson, *Rahel Levin Varnhagen*, 5–6.

47 Diethe, *Towards Emancipation*, 65.

48 Needler, *Letters*, 57; see also 88.

49 Jameson, *WSSR*, 3:315.

50 Ibid., 2:33. The online *Dictionary of Canadian Biography*, vol. 12, transliterates MacMurray's Ojibwa name as Oge-Buno-Quay (web).

51 Jameson, *WSSR*, 2:33–4. Jameson's 1 June 1837 letter verifies that she had Goethe in mind: '[Mrs. MacMurray] is an Indian Squaw by birth, and charming, she speaks English like you with the same kind of accent'

(Needler, *Letters*, 90). Jameson's racist term 'squaw' indicates her limited cross-cultural understanding.
52 Jameson, *Visits and Sketches*, 1:7.
53 See, for example, Jameson, *WSSR*, 3:57.
54 For Jameson's privileged status as white visitor, see Mary Louise Pratt, *Imperial Eyes: Travel Writing and Transculturation* 2nd ed. (New York: Routledge, 2008), 201.
55 Jameson, *WSSR*, 3:36–7.
56 Kate Flint, *The Transatlantic Indian, 1776–1930* (Princeton: Princeton University Press, 2009), 5ff.; Jameson, *WSSR*, 3:69–70.
57 Jameson, *WSSR*, 3:184–5.
58 Ibid., 3:185.
59 Ibid., 3:186; see also 188.
60 See, for example, Thomas M. F. Gerry, who comments of the sketches Jameson made of the Ojibwa, some of which he publishes for the first time, 'The sketches bespeak her great power of sympathy – of being able to translate herself into the positions of other, very different, people'; '"I am Translated"', 45.
61 Jameson, *WSSR*, 3:194–5.
62 Ibid., 3:199–200. Susan Birkwood casts doubt on the authenticity of Jameson's narrative based on Henry Schoolcraft's counter-narrative in his memoirs that he attributes to June Schoolcraft; see Birkwood, 'True or False: Anna Jameson on the Position of Women in European and in Anishinaube Society', *Nineteenth-Century Feminisms* 2 (2000), 39. According to Schoolcraft, Jameson initiated the adoption, and he implies her difficulties as a cultural outsider. See Henry Rowe Schoolcraft, *Personal Memoirs of a Residence of Thirty Years with the Indian Tribes on the American Frontiers* (Philadelphia: Lippincott, Grambo, & Co., 1851), 563. June Schoolcraft had died in 1842, several years before Henry Schoolcraft's 1851 memoir appeared; he then married the American daughter of a South Carolina enslaver. Caution regarding both narratives seems advisable.
63 See Thomas, *Love and Work Enough*, 126–7; Johnston, *Victorian Women*, 121; and Friewald, '"Femininely Speaking"', 66.
64 Jameson, *WSSR*, 3:305. See Birkwood, 'True or False', who compellingly traces Jameson's challenge to enlightenment history and its four stages of development in citing Ojibwa women to underscore European women's lack of progress.
65 Needler, *Letters*, 75–6. The customary spelling of the princess's name is Amalia.
66 Ibid., 105.
67 Ibid., 106.
68 For *Society in America* and *How to Observe. Morals and Manners* (1838) as founding documents in the discipline of sociology, see Susan Hoecker-Drysdale, *Harriet Martineau: First Woman Sociologist* (Oxford: Berg, 1992).
69 Needler, *Letters*, 51.

70 Johnston, *Anna Jameson*, 143. Johnston does not reference Martineau.
71 Advert for *Social Life in Germany*, *Examiner*, 9 February 1840, 96.
72 Jameson, *Social Life in Germany*, 2 vol. (London: Saunders & Otley, 1840), 2:151.
73 Ibid., 2:155. See also the conclusion to von Arnim's *Princess Priscilla's Fortnight* in chapter 7.
74 Rev. of *Social Life in Germany*, *Athenaeum*, 15 February 1840, 125–6. The *Monthly Review* similarly remarked of the work, 'In England, we trust a recent alliance will present no parallel to this picture. Hitherto, indeed, there has been no resemblance; see *Monthly Review* 1 (March 1840), 419.
75 Rev. of *Social Life*, *Athenaeum*, 125.
76 Jameson, *Social Life in Germany*, 1:xxix. A similar 'statement of... principles' in Jameson's hand is housed at Weimar but includes six points. In this statement unpublished in her lifetime, Jameson affirms the holiness of marriage but only insofar as its obligations are equally binding upon men *and* women. And she redefines 'maternity' not as 'the actual state of motherhood – which is not necessary nor universal – but the maternal organisation, common to all women'; see Needler, *Letters*, 233–4. Jameson's private and published credo demonstrate again the intimate link of Jameson's thought and writing at this time to Germany.
77 [Marian Evans], 'Three Months in Weimar', *Fraser's Magazine* 51 (June 1855), 699–706.
78 Jameson, *Social Life*, 1:24n., 132.
79 Ibid., 2:5–7.
80 Ibid., 1:149, 131.
81 Ibid., 1:131.
82 Thomas J. Williams, 'The Beginnings of Anglican Sisterhoods', *Historical Magazine of the Protestant Episcopal Church* 16.4 (December 1947), 350–1.
83 Rahmeyer, *Ottilie von Goethe*, 29; Hein, *Ottilie von Goethe*, 110.
84 Jameson, *Social Life in Germany*, 2:158–9.
85 Ibid., 2:160.
86 Needler, *Letters*, 121.
87 Ibid., 124. See also Hughes, 'Trace Collaboration', 43.
88 Johnston, *Anna Jameson*, 221.
89 See Janice Schroeder, 'Speaking Volumes: Victorian Feminism and the Appeal of Public Discussion', *Nineteenth-Century Contexts* 25.2 (2003), 98, 101–7.
90 Thomas, *Love and Work Enough*, 209–10.
91 Ibid. See also Martha Vicinus, *Independent Women: Work and Community for Single Women, 1850–1920* (Chicago: University of Chicago Press, 1985), 15, 24, 46.
92 Johnston, *Anna Jameson*, 219, 227.
93 Jameson, *Sisters of Charity Catholic and Protestant, Abroad and at Home* (London: Longman, Brown, Green, and Longmans, 1855), vi, 52. Hookham was not the publisher but the bookshop on Bond Street at which the pamphlet was available. The title page lists the publisher as 'Inmates of the

Ragged Colonial Training School' – perhaps a source that Jameson veiled because she wanted to emphasise middle-class gentility and femininity (Jameson, *Sisters of Charity*, 52).
94 Lynn Mcdonald, ed., *Florence Nightingale's European Travels. Collected Works of Florence Nightingale*, vol. 7 (Waterloo: Wilfrid Laurier University Press, 2006), 492.
95 Jameson, *Sisters of Charity*, 27, 30, 60, 75, 78.
96 Ibid., 25–6.
97 Letter to Goethe, 8 March 1856, GSA 40/VIII, 8.
98 Letters to Goethe, 9 May 1856, GSA 40/VIII, 8; 28 November 1857, in Needler, *Letters*, 220. In the end no appendix on *Stifte* appeared in the enlarged edition.
99 Hein, *Ottilie von Goethe*, 617; Jameson to Goethe, with appended list of questions, 28 November 1857, GSA 40/VIII, 8.
100 A. J[ameson]., 'The Damen-Stifter in Germany', *Athenaeum*, 1 January 1859, 18.
101 Ibid. This reference glances back at the context provided for *Social Life in Germany* by the marriage of Queen Victoria herself in 1840.
102 S. A., 'Damen-Stifter', *Athenaeum*, 8 January 1859, 50. S. A. may have been right in all the writer asserted, but the desire to publish seems connected to ongoing feminist debates in England. One reason to suspect Austin's hand is that by this point in her life, according to Joseph Hamburger, she had become more conservative: 'While asserting the intellectual equality of women and condemning their subordination such as she had observed in Germany, [Austin] refused to support the feminist movement in Britain and upheld traditional, family-centred roles for women'; Joseph Hamburger, 'Austin, Sarah (1793–1867)', *Oxford Dictionary of National Biography* (Oxford: Oxford University Press, 2004; 2008, online edition).

Chapter 3

1 Subsequently I refer to Mary Howitt as 'Howitt', her daughter as 'Anna Mary', and her husband as 'William Howitt'.
2 Joanne Shattock, 'Researching Periodical Networks: William and Mary Howitt', in *Researching the Nineteenth-Century Periodical Press: Case Studies*, ed. Alexis Easley, Andrew King, and John Morton (London: Routledge, 2018), 62, 66.
3 A. Lee, *Laurels and Rosemary*, 122–50; Linda H. Peterson, *Becoming a Woman of Letters: Myths of Authorship and Facts of the Victorian Market* (Princeton: Princeton University Press, 2009), 118–19. By 1845 Anna Mary published her first professional work, [Anna Mary Howitt, tr.], *The Betrothed Lovers: A Milanese Story of the Seventeenth Century*, 3 vols. (London: Longman, Green, Brown, and Longmans, 1845), a translation of Alessandro Manzoni's *I promessi sposi* (1827). An 1843 letter from Howitt to her sister confirms that

William Howitt was first invited to translate the novel but due to other commitments delegated the task to Anna Mary (University of Nottingham Manuscripts and Special Collections, Ht/1/1/137/1).
4 Jenny Uglow, *Elizabeth Gaskell: A Habit of Stories* (New York: Farrar Strauss Giroux, 1993), 101, 117–18, 121. William Howitt was in London when the Gaskells arrived to arrange publication of *The Student-Life of Germany* (London: Longman, Brown, Green, and Longmans, 1841). See Howitt, *Autobiography*, 1:302.
5 Uglow, *Habit of Stories*, 182–3.
6 Howitt, *Autobiography*, 1:310; 2:57; 66, 77, 84; Anna Mary Howitt, *An Art-Student in Munich*, 2 vols. (London: Longman, Brown, Green, and Longmans), 1853.
7 Uglow, *A Habit of Stories*, 416, 446–8, 450–3, 490–1.
8 Jameson, *Visits and Sketches*, 1:68; Howitt, *Autobiography*, 1:294. Jameson also provided the Howitts with a letter of introduction to Wolfgang von Goethe, son of Ottilie von Goethe (*Autobiography*, 1:294), though they formed no close relationship with him or his family.
9 Howitt, *Sketches of Natural History* (London: Effingham Wilson, 1834), 123–8. In 2002 the ballad was illustrated by Tony DiTerlizzi and awarded a Caldecott Medal in the US, then reissued in a tenth anniversary edition in 2012.
10 Howitt, *Autobiography*, 1:217.
11 Mary Howitt to Anna Harrison, 30 September 1829, University of Nottingham Manuscripts and Special Collections, Ht/1/1/54.
12 A. Lee, *Laurels and Rosemary*, 122, 136. The existence of the nanny is effaced in Howitt's *Autobiography*, which quotes a letter only to the effect that 'My young Friend in the nursery, Eliza, is a real jewel. It is quite affecting to me to see her nice methods, and to visit her and the children at the nursery-breakfast' (*Autobiography*, 1:291). In the autobiographical series published in *Good Words* in the mid-1880s, Howitt is much clearer: 'As a considerable portion of my time was now given to literature, I had engaged an excellent young woman Friend, Eliza F., to superintend the care of these little ones. She lived with us for about five-and-twenty years'; Howitt, 'Some Reminiscences of My Life. Chapter V', *Good Words* 26 (December 1885), 666.
13 Howitt, *Autobiography* 2:22, 1:298–9; A. Lee, *Laurels and Rosemary*, 132.
14 Howitt, 'Preface', *Fisher's Drawing-Room Scrapbook* (London: Fisher, Son, & Co., 1842), ii.
15 Howitt, 'Heidelberg, on the Neckar', *Fisher's Drawing-Room Scrapbook* (1842), 33.
16 Howitt, 'Boaz and Ruth. / A Harvest Scene', *Fisher's Drawing-Room Scrapbook* (1842), 58–60. Cf. William Howitt in the same year about Heidelberg environs: 'You ... feel a lively sympathy with those who make so large a proportion of the people of the land, especially as you compare their form of life and comforts with those of the same class in your own country'; William Howitt, *The Rural and Domestic Life of Germany: with Characteristic Sketches of its Cities and Scenery* (London: Longman, Brown, Green, and Longmans, 1842), 17.

17 Howitt also published translations of Heine in the January and July 1841 issues of *Bentley's Miscellany* and in her volume *Ballads and Other Poems* (1847); her translation of 'Des Knaben Tod' by Johann Ludwig Uhland, whom the Howitts met on their tour of Germany, appeared as 'The Youth's Death' in the July 1842 *Bentley's Miscellany*.
18 Carl R. Woodring, *Victorian Samplers: William and Mary Howitt* (Lawrence: University of Kansas Press, 1952), 85; William Stupp, 'The German Experience of William and Mary Howitt', in *Anglo-German and American-German Crosscurrents*, vol. 4, ed. Arthur O. Lewis, W. LaMarr Kopp, and Edward J. Danis (Lanham: University Press of America, 1990), 87. Howitt provides an account of their travels in *Autobiography* (1:304–20), which covered an immense deal of ground, from the Rhine and Munich to Bavaria, Vienna, Prague, Dresden, Berlin, and Leipzig before they returned to Heidelberg in mid-October.
19 See, e.g., William Howitt, *German Experiences: Addressed to the English; Both Stayers at Home, and Goers Abroad* (London: Longman, Brown, Green, and Longmans, 1844), 4, 18–20, 24–5.
20 Howitt, *Autobiography*, 1:321, 323.
21 For detailed accounts of the journal and its relation to liberalism as well as social reform, see Brian Maidment, 'Magazines of Popular Progress and the Artisans', *Victorian Periodicals Review* 17 (Fall 1984): 83–94; Peterson, *Becoming a Woman of Letters*, 96, 114–8; and Clare Pettitt, *Serial Forms: The Unfinished Project of Modernity, 1815–1848* (Oxford: Oxford University Press, 2020), 251–86. For Howitt's role as the journal's poetry editor, see Hughes, 'Mary Howitt and the Business of Poetry', *Victorian Periodicals Review* 50.2 (Summer 2017), 273–94.
22 William Howitt, 'The Month in Prospect – January', *Howitt's Journal* 1 (2 January 1847), 9.
23 Howitt, 'The Lover. From the German of Heinrich Voss', *Howitt's Journal* 1 (20 February 1847): 100.
24 A. Lee, *Laurels and Rosemary*, 114.
25 Howitt, *Which Is the Wiser: Or, People Abroad. A Tale for Youth*, 2nd ed. (London: Thomas Tegg, 1842), 36. Subsequent page references are given in the text.
26 Cf. the similar figure of Blanche Ingram in *Jane Eyre*.
27 Howitt appears to have drawn inspiration for Von Rosenberg from the career (if not the Jewish heritage) of Felix Mendelssohn, who became a sensation upon his first visit to England in 1829.
28 A. Lee, *Laurels and Rosemary*, 131.
29 Howitt's young adult tale sold well enough to go into a second edition despite a disapproving *Athenaeum* review that ridiculed her integration of German words into a 'child's book' and its more favourable treatment of German peasant life compared to the poor back home:

> this book of Mary Howitt's is no laughing matter. There is malice prepense in it. The under-current purpose is to contrast the state of society and of morals in

Germany and in England; so far well; but the malice prepense is shown in this, that all the Herrs and Vons and Geheimraths, all the German *dramatis personae*, down to serving maids and paupers, are pure, intellectual, high-minded, or good; while the English, with one solitary exception, a girl in love with German life and German students, are proud, insolent, or in some way offensive or contemptible. Fortunately, the book is in other respects so objectionable, that it cannot become popular.

The care Howitt takes to show initial prejudice in both Mrs Hoffman and Mrs Palmer might have tempered such a judgement. See Rev. of *Which Is the Wiser?*, *Athenaeum*, 22 January 1842, 87.

30 Stupp, 'The German Experience of William and Mary Howitt', 101; David Blamires, *Telling Tales: The Impact of Germany on English Children's Books 1780–1918* (Cambridge: Open Book Publishers, 2009), 4, 321.
31 Howitt, *Child's Picture and Verse Book: Commonly Called Otto Speckter's Fables. With the Original German and With French. Translated into English* (London: Longman, Brown, Green, and Longmans, 1844), v.
32 Blamires, *Telling Tales*, 322.
33 Stupp, 'The German Experience of William and Mary Howitt', 101.
34 Howitt, *Child's Picture and Verse Book*, 16–17.
35 The French translations appear to be Howitt's, but I cannot verify this.
36 Blamires, *Telling Tales*, 142.
37 Rev. of *Child's Picture and Verse Book*, *Tait's Edinburgh Magazine* 11 (February 1844), 136; *Eclectic Review* 15 (March 1844), 368–70.
38 Letter from Mary Howitt to Anna Harrison, 28 October 1839, University of Nottingham Manuscripts and Special Collections, Ht/1/1/125.
39 Howitt, *Autobiography*, 2:89. Howitt's book received a short notice on 19 March 1853; *Art-Student* was advertised on 30 April as 'Nearly ready' and due out the following Monday (2 May). See Rev. of *Stories of English and Foreign Life*, *Athenaeum*, 19 March 1853, 351; Advert for *An Art-Student in Germany*, *Athenaeum*, 30 April 1853, 518.
40 Howitt, *Margaret von Ehrenberg, The Artist-Wife*, in *Stories of English and Foreign Life* (London: Henry G. Bohn, 1853), 53. Subsequent page numbers are given in the text.
41 Anna Mary Howitt, *Art-Student*, 2:181–2.
42 Ibid., 2:189.
43 Margaret's aspirations are proto-feminist. As Babette Bohn and Alexandra K. Wettlaufer point out, from the Renaissance forwards history painting enjoyed the highest prestige but was presumed to be 'masculine', in contrast to 'feminine' portraiture. See Bohn, *Women Artists, Their Patrons, and Their Publics in Early Modern Bologna* (Philadelphia: Pennsylvania State University Press, 2021), 5; and Wettlaufer, *Portraits of the Artist as a Young Woman: Painting and the Novel in France and Britain, 1800–1860* (Columbus: Ohio State University Press, 2011), 195–6.
44 Cf. Jane Eyre's symbolic paintings in Charlotte Brontë's 1847 novel.
45 Throughout the novella Margaret's hybrid identity as an Anglo–German woman is marked by her appearing 'neither English' nor like a German

baroness, but 'very like "the Artist"' (10), though her adherence to English tea-drinking is mentioned repeatedly (26). A. Lee mentions the 'Germans' antipathy to *tea* observed by the Howitts during their Heidelberg residence (*Laurels and Rosemary*, 143).

46 This rare representation of bankruptcy shadows Howitt's experience in 1848, when she and William faced public humiliation and were forced to sell off prized possessions, move to smaller quarters, and write unrelentingly to pay off their debts and maintain the family. See Howitt, *Autobiography*, 2:45–56; A. Lee, *Laurels and Rosemary*, 177–98.

47 We approach the novella's depiction of English and German women quite differently, however. Losano ties Margaret's emancipatory freedoms to her being a foreigner and hence free from German women's gossip and prejudice. Yet the censorious views of Margaret's aunt are equally narrow and hostile to careers for women. See Losano, *The Woman Painter in Victorian Literature* (Columbus: Ohio State University Press, 2008), 87–8.

48 Wettlaufer, *Portraits of the Artist*, 196. Gillies' friendship with Howitt is confirmed by several mentions in Howitt's *Autobiography*, including an 1847 tribute to Gillies' 'warm heart' and an 1877 outing the friends made in Rome; Howitt, *Autobiography* 2:30–1, 262–3.

49 Bateman, who himself left for Australia in 1853, left his mark in that country as a garden designer. See Daniel Thomas, 'Bateman, Edward La Trobe (1815–1897)', *Australian Dictionary of Biography*, vol. 3 (1969; rpt. online, National Centre of Biography, Australian National University).

50 Lenore Ann Beaky, 'The Letters of Anna Mary Howitt to Barbara Leigh Smith Bodichon', Ph.D. dissertation, Columbia University, 1974, 147–8.

51 Beaky, 'Letters of Anna Mary Howitt', 157; A. Lee, *Laurels and Rosemary*, 185–6, 207.

52 Wettlaufer, *Portraits of the Artist*, 101–6. Their shared feminist network is also indicated in Bessie Rayner Parkes's letters at Girton College, which include several from Howitt (which mention Anna Mary several times) and from Jameson. Howitt and Anna Mary both rallied around Barbara Bodichon's petition for a Married Women's Property Act. As Anna Mary's letter of 13 March 1856 stated, 'The petition about married women's property has already been announced in Parliament. It is spoken of as the petition of Elizabeth Barrett Browning, Anna Jameson, Mary Howitt, Mrs. Gaskell, &c.' (Howitt, *Autobiography*, 2:116).

53 Richard Scully, *British Images of Germany: Admiration, Antagonism & Ambivalence, 1860–1914* (Houndmills: Palgrave Macmillan, 2012), 73. Interest in the 1880 performance was also indicated in the *Jewish Chronicle*, which, as I note in Chapter 6, sent a reporter to cover the event amidst the backdrop of rising anti-Semitic activism in Germany.

54 Howitt, *Autobiography*, 2:57–9.

55 A[nna]. M[ary]. H[owitt]., 'The Miracle-Play in the Ammergau. In Two Letters', *Ladies Companion* 2 (17 August, 24 August 1850), 113–15, 129–31.

56 Howitt, *Autobiography*, 2:66. Chorley, according to Howitt, also encouraged Anna Mary to make a book of her short periodical descriptions; see Howitt, 'Reminiscences of My Later Life. Second Paper', *Good Words* 27 (1886), 173.
57 A. M. H., 'Miracle-Play', 115.
58 Anna Mary Howitt, 'Consecration of the Basilica', *Athenaeum*, 7 December 1850, 1,285–6; Howitt, *Autobiography*, 2:64.
59 Howitt, *Autobiography*, 2:65–6.
60 A. M. H., 'Miracle-Play', 114.
61 Howitt's own contributions of Swedish verse translations and original ballads to *Household Words* began in the 18 May 1850 issue. In 1850 she also published a sixty-six-page German translation of Berthold Auerbach ('The Professor's Wife') and prepared *Mary Howitt's Story Book* for publication. This included reprints of some of her earlier translations and stories first published in *Howitt's Journal*.
62 Beaky, 'Letters of Anna Mary Howitt', 155–6.
63 All told, Anna Mary's periodical publications represented twelve of *Art-Student*'s forty-four chapters.
64 A decade later, in 1860, a woman art student was finally admitted. See Amy Bluett, '"Striving after excellence": Victorian women and the fight for arts training', International Women's Day series, Royal Academy online blog, 4 March 2015.
65 Anna Mary Howitt, *Art-Student*, 1:67, 70, 90. Justina also finds zest in being freed from upper-class convention, 'the life of first-class travelling, of couriers, of the grandest hotels, of English solemnity, and aristocratic propriety' (1:90).
66 See Wettlaufer, *Portraits of the Artist*, 69–74, for *Art-Student* as a feminist narrative of professional vocation; Peterson, *Becoming a Woman of Letters*, 118–21, for it as family collaboration, especially since Anna Mary frequently references subjects that figured in her parents' German writings; and Julie F. Codell, *The Victorian Artist: Artists' Lifewritings in Britain, ca. 1870–1910* (Cambridge University Press, 2003), 143–6, for it as an artist's life writing.
67 Anna Mary Howitt, *Art-Student*, 1:10.
68 [Anna Mary Howitt], 'Bits of Life in Munich: The Holy Week', *Household Words*, 7 June 1851, 261; *Art-Student*, 2:10–11.
69 [Anna Mary Howitt], 'The Holy Week, 262–3; *Art-Student*, 14–15.
70 Anna Mary Howitt, *Art-Student*, 2:21–2.
71 William A. Cohen, *Embodied: Victorian Literature and the Senses* (Minneapolis: University of Minnesota Press, 2008), 6.
72 Anna Mary Howitt, *Art-Student*, 2:140.
73 Ibid., 2:141–2.
74 Howitt, *Autobiography*, 2:90–1.
75 Anna Mary Howitt, *Art-Student*, 2:142.
76 Ibid., 2:143. 'Isabel' is the pseudonym of Anna Mary's cousin Mary Harrison, who joined Anna Mary in November 1851 as a companion; see Beaky, 'Letters to Anna Mary Howitt', 32.

77 Anna Mary Howitt, *Art-Student*, 2:149.
78 Ibid., 2:143.
79 Ibid., 2:147–8.
80 Codell, *Victorian Artist*, 145.
81 Anna Mary Howitt, *Art-Student*, 2:181,183–4.
82 Ibid., *Art-Student*, 2:191. 'Day's work, Evening's guests! / Sour weeks: happy festivals!' (my literal translation). The toast is likewise rendered in simple German: 'Long live the city of Munich and Munich art and artists!" (my translation).
83 Uglow, *A Habit of Stories*, 416–7, 437.
84 Ibid., 445–6.
85 For the relation of 'The Grey Woman' to sensation fiction, see my introduction and headnote to the tale in *The Works of Elizabeth Gaskell, Volume 4. Novellas and Shorter Fiction: Cousin Phillis and other Tales from* All the Year Round *and the* Cornhill Magazine *1859–64* (London: Pickering & Chatto, 2006), x, xiii–xiv, 125–7; and Julia McCord Chavez, 'Gaskell's Other Wives and Daughters: Reimagining the Gothic and Anticipating the Sensational in "Lois the Witch" and "The Grey Woman"', *Gaskell Society Journal* 29 (2015), 61, 67–70.
86 Anna Unsworth, 'Elizabeth Gaskell and German Romanticism', *Gaskell Society Journal* 8 (1994), 7; for Gaskell's own very limited German, see her letter of early August 1860, when she confided to daughter Marianne, 'I think I am cowardly in shrinking from the journey to Cologne[,] with my no-knowledge of German'; *The Letters of Mrs Gaskell*, ed. J. A. V. Chapple and Arthur Pollard (1966; rpt. Manchester: Mandolin/Manchester University Press, 1997), 625.
87 Unsworth, 'Elizabeth Gaskell', 8.
88 Gaskell, *Letters*, 539; Uglow, *A Habit of Stories*, 450–1.
89 Peter Skrine, 'Elizabeth Gaskell and Germany', *Gaskell Society Journal* 7 (1993), 39–40, 47; Skrine, 'Elizabeth Gaskell and Her German Stories', *Gaskell Society Journal* 12 (1998), 11–12; '; J. A. V. Chapple, 'Elizabeth Gaskell's "Six Weeks at Heppenheim": Art and Life', *Revista di studi vittoriani* 2.3 (1997), 8–9.
90 Gaskell, 'The Grey Woman', *All the Year Round*, 5 January 1861, 300, 303.
91 Ibid., 5 January, 301.
92 Ibid., 19 January, 352, 353.
93 Ibid., 19 January, 354.
94 Gaskell, 'Six Weeks at Heppenheim', *Cornhill Magazine* 5 (May 1862), 560–87; Chapple, 'Elizabeth Gaskell's', 9. Subsequent page references to the story, which appeared in a single instalment, are given in the text.
95 Gaskell references *A Simple Story*, the 1791 novel by Elizabeth Inchbald.
96 See also Chapple, 'Elizabeth Gaskell's', 10–11.
97 Gaskell, 'The Grey Woman', 12 January, 321.
98 Skrine, 'Elizabeth Gaskell and her German Stories', 10.
99 Jameson, *Characteristics of Women*, 1:94, 99–100, 102.

Chapter 4

1 Her long insistence that she was 'Mrs Lewes' indicates that she believed in committed partnerships but was not dismayed when a state-approved legalisation of the bond was impossible. After Lewes's death she married John W. Cross, who became her first biographer after her death in 1880.
2 As Rosemary Ashton points out, Lewes kept Karl Varnhagen von Ense, widower of Rahel and Lewes's earliest friend in Berlin, 'regularly informed about Agnes and their family' starting in 1841; Ashton, *G. H. Lewes: A Life* (Oxford: Clarendon Press, 1991), 32.
3 *The Letters of George Henry Lewes*, 3 vols., ed. William Baker (Victoria: University of Victoria, 1995–9), 1:266–7.
4 Gerlinde Röder-Bolton, *George Eliot in Germany, 1854–55* (Aldershot: Ashgate, 2006). More recently, Kathleen McCormack has analysed Eliot's and Lewes's visits to German spa towns and the salons they hosted there; see McCormack, *George Eliot in Society: Travels Abroad and Sundays at the Priory* (Columbus: Ohio State University Press, 2013), 14–16, 21, 37–56, 111–31, 137–53.
5 Röder-Bolton, *George Eliot*, 12, 23–35; [Evans, tr.], *The Life of Jesus Critically Examined*, by David Friedrich Strauss, 3 vols. (London: Chapman, Brothers, 1846).
6 *The George Eliot Letters*, 9 vols., ed. Gordon S. Haight (New Haven: Yale University Press, 1954–78), 2:184n.5, 193.
7 *George Eliot Letters*, 2:449, 468n.7; *The Journals of George Eliot*, ed. Margaret Harris and Judith Johnston (Cambridge: Cambridge University Press, 1998), 303, 306, 311. By 1858 Evans had adopted the publishing signature of George Eliot. To avoid confusion, however, I refer to her as Evans here.
8 Evans to Sarah Hennell, 28 July 1858, *George Eliot Letters*, 2:471. In *Visits and Sketches*, Jameson called the Sistine Madonna the 'divinest image that ever shaped itself in palpable hues and forms to the living eye' (*Visits and Sketches*, 2:103). Evans elaborated on Raphael's impact in her journal: [I experienced] 'a sort of awe, as if I were suddenly in the living presence of some glorious being', which 'made my heart swell too much for me to remain comfortably, and we hurried out of the room'; *Journals of George Eliot*, 325.
9 Nancy Henry, *The Life of George Eliot: A Critical Biography* (Malden: Wiley-Blackwell, 2012), 263; *Journals of George Eliot*, 207–8.
10 McCormack, *George Eliot in Society*, 146.
11 *Letters of George Eliot*, 7:308.
12 George Eliot, *Daniel Deronda* (1976; rpt. Oxford: Oxford University Press, 1984), 3.
13 Ashton, *G. H. Lewes*, 4, 25; Ashton, *The German Idea. Four English Writers and the Reception of German Thought 1800–1860* (Cambridge: Cambridge University Press, 1980), 105.
14 Ashton, *The German Idea*, 105.
15 Röder-Bolton, *George Eliot*, 57, 69–70n.1.

16 Gordon S. Haight, *George Eliot: A Biography* (Oxford: Oxford University Press, 1968), 130; Julia Kuehn, 'Realism's Connections: George Eliot's and Fanny Lewald's Poetics', *George Eliot–George Henry Lewes Studies* 68.2 (2016), 94.
17 Röder-Bolton, *George Eliot*, 3, 10.
18 Ibid., 2, 12, 48, 85.
19 *Letters of George Eliot*, 8:124.
20 Haight, *George Eliot*, 124.
21 *Letters of George Eliot*, 8:129–30.
22 Needler, *Letters*, 209.
23 *Letters of George Eliot*, 2:70, 105.
24 Ibid., 2:171; Röder-Bolton, *George Eliot*, 7.
25 Röder-Bolton, *George Eliot*, 159.
26 When Stahr finally won a divorce from his wife in 1855, he and Lewald quickly married – on the very day, 6 February 1855, that Lewes and Evans tried to call on them. See *Journals of George Eliot*, 45; Margaret E. Ward, *Fanny Lewald: Between Rebellion and Renunciation* (New York: Peter Lang, 2006), 145.
27 *Journals of George Eliot*, 22, 25. See also McCormack, *George Eliot in Society*, 40.
28 Röder-Bolton, *George Eliot*, 95, 101–2, 104n.50; *Journals of George Eliot*, 26–8.
29 *Journals of George Eliot*, 25–9. The couple were more routinely accepted in Berlin and visited several homes there; see Röder-Bolton, *George Eliot*, 159–60.
30 *Letters of George Eliot*, 8:120–1.
31 Needler, *Letters*, 35.
32 Hein, *Ottilie von Goethe*, 585.
33 *Letters of George Henry Lewes*, 1:232.
34 Hein, *Ottilie von Goethe*, 586.
35 Evans's journal noted only that on the morning of 11 August Lewes called on 'Frau von Goethe'; *Journals of George Eliot*, 22.
36 [Marian Evans], 'Three Months in Weimar', *Fraser's Magazine* 51 (June 1855), 705.
37 Jameson, *Visits and Sketches*, 1:136.
38 [Evans], 'Three Months in Weimar', 704.
39 George Henry Lewes, *The Life and Works of Goethe*, 2 vols. (London: David Nutt, 1855), 2:404, 450.
40 Lewes, *Life and Works of Goethe*, 2:423; Heinz Bluhm, 'Die Neue Goetheana in der Newberry Library', in *Ottilie von Goethe: Tagebücher und Briefe von und an Ottilie von Goethe 1839–1841*, vol. 1, ed. Heinz Bluhm (Vienna: Bergland Verlag, 1962), xx.
41 Ottilie von Goethe to Anna Jameson, 21 August 1854, GSA 40, XXI, 6.
42 *Journals of George Eliot*, 246.
43 See, e.g., *Journals of George Eliot*, 9.

44 Röder-Bolton, *George Eliot*, 4, 10, 85, 87; *Journals of George Eliot*, 22. On Eliot's limited response to class difference, see also Cheri Larsen Hoeckley, 'Reframing Difference in George Eliot's Early *Fraser's Magazine* Articles after Kimberlé Crenshaw's Intersectionality', *Encountering Difference: New Perspectives on Genre, Travel and Gender*, ed. Gigi Adair and Lenka Filipova (Wilmington: Vernon Press, 2020), 100.
45 Hoeckley, 'Reframing Difference', 98; [Evans], 'Liszt, Wagner, and Weimar', *Fraser's Magazine* 52 (July 1855), 48–62 .
46 Eliot, 'Lizst, Wagner, and Weimar', 59. Evans's comments on German female freedoms are confined to a short paragraph.
47 Fionnuala Dillane, *Before George Eliot: Marian Evans and the Periodical Press* (Cambridge: Cambridge University Press, 2013), 200–1; [Evans], rev. of *Life and Works of Goethe*, by G. H. Lewes, *Leader*, 3 November 1855, 1058–61.
48 [Evans], 'Belles Lettres', *Westminster Review* 64 (July 1855), 307; 'Memoirs of the Court of Austria', *Westminster Review* 63 (April 1855), 330. In *Visits and Sketches*, Jameson's seven-page survey of women writers observed that Pichler was well-known in England (1:153).
49 Letter of 9 January 1855, *Letters of George Eliot*, 2:190.
50 [Evans], 'German Wit: Heinrich Heine', *Westminster Review* 65 (January 1856), 12.
51 Ibid., 33.
52 [Evans], 'Recollections of Heine', *Leader*, 23 August 1856: 811–12.
53 Ibid., 811.
54 For the role of 'house style' in Evans's anonymous reviews, see Dillane, *Before George Eliot*, 80–2.
55 *Journals of George Eliot*, 25.
56 Deborah Hertz, *How Jews Became Germans: the History of Conversion and Assimilation in Berlin* (New Haven: Yale University Press, 2007), 170–1.
57 *Journals of George Eliot*, 34, 29, 245. Note Solmar's fluent French and command of English, which underlay Evans's ready exchanges with her.
58 *Journals of George Eliot*, 392. Ahlefeldt's lover was Carl Leberecht Immermann (1796–1840).
59 *Journals of George Eliot*, 35; Stilling (1740–1817) was best known for his autobiography.
60 *Letters of George Eliot*, 2:454.
61 Ward, *Fanny Lewald*, 138–9, 143. When Lewald resisted Stahr's erotic overtures despite their mutual attraction, Goethe proved a warm friend indeed. On 5 February 1846 she invited Lewald and Stahr to her house, and when Goethe left the room, Stahr immediately embraced the woman he loved. The next day, during a ride in Mertens-Schaaffhausen's carriage with the owner, the couple declared their love for each other and spent the rest of the day at Mertens-Schaaffhausen's mansion alternately listening to the Trevi fountain and embracing (Ward, 146). When at last Stahr was free to marry, they deliberately chose to wed on 6 February 1855 in memory of their first mutual declaration of love – the day when Lewes and Evans called on them but found them absent.

62 Gisela Argyle, 'The Horror and the Pleasure of Un-English Fiction: Ida von Hahn-Hahn and Fanny Lewald in England', *Comparative Literature Studies* 44.1–2 (2007), 159; Ward, *Fanny Lewald*, 158, 185–6.
63 Kuehn, 'Realism's Connections', 94.
64 Irene Stocksieker Di Maio, 'Fanny Lewald', *Dictionary of Literary Biography 129: Nineteenth-Century German Writers, 1841–1900*, ed. James Hardin (Detroit: Gale, 1993), 210.
65 *Journals of George Eliot*, 35–6. See also Evans's entry for 29 December, which records her lively conversation with Stahr about Johann von Goethe's novel *Elective Affinities* (*Die Wahlverwandschaften*) (*Journals*, 41). Lewald herself, in contrast, noted in her journal the conversation she had with Evans when they first met, while Varnhagen von Ense wrote that the two women 'had much to say to one another' at his coffee on 4 December (Kuehn, 'Realism's Connections', 95).
66 *Journals of George Eliot*, 247.
67 See Alan T. Levenson, 'Writing the Philosemitic Novel: *Daniel Deronda* Revisited', *Prooftexts* 28.2 (2008), 129–56.
68 Röder-Bolton, *George Eliot*, 28.
69 *Journals of George Eliot*, 39.
70 Ibid., 324.
71 [Evans], 'Heine's Poems', *Leader* 1 September 1855, 843; *Journals of George Eliot*, 246.
72 John Rignall, *George Eliot, European Novelist* (Farnham: Ashgate, 2011), 19. The second edition of Charles Des Voeux's translation of Johann von Goethe's *Torquato Tasso*, on which Ottilie von Goethe collaborated, included a translation of Heine's 'The Solitary Tear' ('Was will die einsame Träne?'). Among British reviewers, Heine received a favourable if brief notice of his *Reisebilder* (2nd ed., 1830) in the *Edinburgh Review* in 1832 and a full-length *Quarterly Review* essay on his *Zur Geschichte der Neueren Schönen Literatur in Deutschland* ('On the History of New Belles-Lettres in Germany', 1833), in which Heine attacked the German Romantic School of poetry and credited Goethe with killing it off; see 'Recent German Lyrical Poetry', *Edinburgh Review* 56 (October 1832), 37–51, and [Abraham Hayward], 'Recent German Belles-Lettres', *Quarterly Review* 53 (February 1835), 215–19. Hayward called Heine a 'new star' in German letters who had succeeded Jean Paul Richter as the representative of German wit, albeit an 'outlaw' in Germany for his attacks on all sides (215–16). For fuller details of the British reception of Heine before 1856, see Armin Arnold, *Heine in England and America* (London: Linden Press, 1959), 17–31, 41–57.
73 This was one reason Carlyle, the great advocate of German literature in the 1820s and 1830s, refused anything to do with Heine. In 1835 he mentioned 'Heine's new Sacrilege of a Book' in a letter to his brother; the next year he tersely commented to Ralph Waldo Emerson, 'Blackguard Heine is worth very little.' See *The Collected Letters of Thomas and Jane Welsh Carlyle*, ed. Charles Richard Sanders et al., 48 vols. (Durham: Duke University Press, 1970–), 8:149, 9:85.
74 [Hayward], 'Recent German Belles-Lettres', 229.

238 Notes to pages 99–107

75 'Heine, His Works and Times', *Tait's Edinburgh Magazine* 18 (October–November 1851), 618, 622.
76 [Evans], 'Heine's Poems', 843. 'Morale' here indicated 'The morals or morality of a person or group' (*OED*).
77 [Evans], 'German Wit', 1–4; Matthew Arnold, 'The Functions [sic] of Criticism at the Present Time', *National Review* 1 (November 1864), 232–3, 240.
78 [Evans], 'German Wit', 7–9, 15–16, 18, 22–3.
79 Ibid., 6.
80 Ibid., 10.
81 'Heine, His Works and Times', 619.
82 Jeffrey Sammons, *Heinrich Heine: A Modern Biography* (1980; rpt. Princeton: Princeton University Press, 2014), 15, 17.
83 Heinrich Heine, *Reisebilder* (1827), 2:166–7; digitised in facsimile and in transliterated modern German, at *Deutsches Textarchiv. Grundlage für ein Referenzkorpus der neuhochdeutschen Sprache. Herausgegeben von der Berlin-Brandenburgischen Akademie der Wissenschaften, Berlin 2020* (web).
84 [Evans], 'German Wit', 10.
85 Ibid., 12.
86 Ibid., 22–3.
87 Ibid., 31, 19–20.
88 *Journals of George Eliot*, 33.
89 Heinrich Heine, *Buch der Lieder* (1827; rpt. Heidelberg: Verlag Lambert Schneider, 1956), 171, 173.
90 *Letters of George Eliot*, 2:205.
91 [Evans], 'German Wit', 12.
92 *Journals of George Eliot*, 58, 63.
93 [Evans], 'Recollections of Heine', *Leader*, 30 August 1856, 811.
94 Charles Lee Lewes, Preface, *Essays and Leaves from a Notebook*, by George Eliot (Edinburgh: William Blackwood and Sons, 1884), v–vi.
95 *Essays of George Eliot*, ed. Thomas Pinney (New York: Columbia University Press, 1963), 254n.28.
96 Matthew Arnold, 'Heinrich Heine', *Cornhill Magazine* 8 (August 1863), 233, 236.
97 *Letters of George Eliot*, 4:130.
98 Ward, *Fanny Lewald*, 262.

Chapter 5

1 Headnote to *The First Violin* excerpt, in *The International Library of Famous Literature: Selections from the World's Great Writers, Ancient, Mediaeval, and Modern*, vol. 20., comp. Nathan Haskell Dole et al., introductory notes by Donald G. Mitchell [author Ik Marvel] and Andrew Lang (New York: Merrill and Baker, 1898), 9,739.

2 In recent scholarship only Phyllis Weliver and Anna Peak mention the novel in passing; Weliver also briefly compares it to *Daniel Deronda*, and Anna Peak remarks on the specificity of the composers Fothergill mentions and the novel's reprinting 'multiple times in England, the United States, and Australia and translated into various languages'. See Weliver, 'George Eliot and the Prima Donna's "Script"', *Yearbook of English Studies* 40.1–2 (2010), 103n.3, and Peak, 'Music and New Woman Aesthetics in Mona Caird's *The Daughters of Danaus*', *Victorian Review* 40.1 (Spring 2014), 141. A German translation of the novel by Emma von Sichart as *Der Konzertmeister* was published in 1903.
3 Heyse's mother, Julie Saaling, was Jewish and had been a member of Rahel Varnhagen von Ense's salon prior to marriage. Jewish novelist Rebecca Friedländer, a close friend of Rahel's, was Heyse's aunt. See Deborah Hertz, *Jewish High Society in Old Regime Berlin* (New Haven: Yale University Press, 1988), 177; and Charles H. Helmetag, 'Paul Heyse', *Dictionary of Literary Biography 330: Nobel Prize Laureates in Literature, Part 2: Kipling-Faulkner* (Detroit: Gale, 2007), 357. In his Nobel Prize biographical statement, Heyse identified himself as the second son of Karl Heyse, a royal university professor, and 'Julie, née Saaling, who came from a Jewish family' (reprinted in Helmetag, 'Paul Heyse', 366).
4 Fothergill subscribed to the National Manchester Society for Women's Suffrage in 1882 and published an article on the imperative of imbuing girls with a sense of responsibility. See 'National Manchester Society of Woman's Suffrage [List of subscribers]', *Women's Suffrage Journal* 13 (February 1882), 31, and Fothergill, 'Girls and the Sense of Responsibility', *Women's Suffrage Journal* 13 (February 1882), 13–14. As Wendy Williams notes in *George Eliot, Poetess* (Farnham: Ashgate, 2014), Eliot was ambivalent about feminism and the Woman Question (72–8).
5 Helen C. Black, *Notable Women Authors of the Day* (Glasgow: David Bryce and Son, 1893), 190–1.
6 Review of *The First Violin*, *New York Times*, 17 November 1878, 10.
7 Hans Robert Jauss, *Toward an Aesthetic of Reception*, tr. Timothy Bahti (Minneapolis: University of Minnesota Press, 1982), 3–45.
8 George Eliot, *Daniel Deronda*, ed. Graham Handley (1984; rpt. Oxford: Oxford University Press, 2009), 39. Later Eliot's narrator comments that Klesmer has set poetry by Heine to music (208). Franz Liszt, a character on whom Klesmer is in part based, himself composed *Freudvoll und Leidvoll* (1848) set to the same Goethe lyric; see *Oxford Lieder*, an open-access online database. For the partial resemblance of Klesmer to both Liszt and Wagner, see David A. Reibel, 'Hidden Parallels in George Eliot's *Daniel Deronda*: Julius Klesmer, Richard Wagner, Franz Liszt', *George Eliot–George Henry Lewes Studies* 64/65 (October 2013), 16–52. Haight and Delia de Sousa Correa instead point to Anton Rubenstein as Klesmer's model; see Haight, *George Eliot*, 489–90, and Correa, *George Eliot, Music and Victorian Culture* (Houndmills: Palgrave Macmillan, 2003), 133. Subsequent page references to Eliot's novel are given in the text.

9 See chapters 34, 39, 42, and 62.
10 Henry James, 'Daniel Deronda: A Conversation', *Partial Portraits* (1888; rpt. London: Macmillan, 1894), 73.
11 Haight, *George Eliot*, 257; Mathilde Blind, *George Eliot* (London: W. H. Allen and Co., 1883), 69.
12 Blind, *George Eliot*, 67. Blind does not consider that Lewes may have influenced Eliot or that, as Susan McPherson suggests, their 1854–6 writings were collaborative; see McPherson, 'Companionship and Collaboration: Marian Evans, George Henry Lewes, and *The Life and Works of Goethe*', *The Victorian* 1.2 (November 2013), n.p.
13 Blind, *George Eliot*, 69.
14 The British Library holds a complete run of *Lippincott's Magazine* from 1868 to 1914 and the freestanding reprint of Heyse's story is dated 1870. *Lippincott's* was thus accessible to library members in London and presumably in bookshops.
15 *Letters of George Eliot*, 5:158.
16 'The Lonely Ones. From the German of Paul Heyse', anon. tr., *Lippincott's Magazine* 4 (October 1869), 396.
17 Heyse, 'The Lonely Ones', 401–2.
18 Ibid., 402–3.
19 See Chapters 1–2 of this study.
20 Fothergill read *Kinder der Welt* in the original language, since the English translation *Children of the World* did not appear until 1882, after *First Violin* had been published.
21 Heyse, *Kinder der Welt: Roman in sechs Büchern*, 3 vols. (Berlin: Verlag von Wilhelm Hertz, 1873). Heyse's publication history was cited in the English review of the novel; see 'Germany', *Illustrated Review*, 29 May 1873, 581. Since the novel was ably translated in 1882, I quote from that version.
22 To enhance accessibility for its diverse readership, *Temple Bar* provided translations in notes to Fothergill's text during its serialisation; the three-volume novel occasionally does so as well.
23 Jessie Fothergill, *The First Violin: A Novel*, 3 vols. (London: Richard Bentley and Son, 1878), 1:15–16. Subsequent page references are given in the text.
24 'Elberthal' may be an Anglo–German pun on 'Albert Hall'; the Royal Albert Hall opened in 1871 and immediately began offering music performances. '*Thal*' or '*Tal*' is the German noun for valley.
25 Raff's Fifth Symphony, the 'Lenore', is a programmatic composition based on Gottfried Bürger's ballad 'Lenore'. The *Monthly Musical Record* published a two-part synopsis, including Raff's march in the third movement introduced by first violins and horns, which marks the lovers' separation when he leaves for the war. See C. A. Barry, 'Joachim Raff's Symphony, "Lenore"', *Monthly Musical Record* 5 (August, September 1875), 121. This, the first Raff symphony ever heard in London, was performed at the Crystal Palace on 14 November 1874. Ebenezer Prout, the *Academy* music critic, observed that 'Seldom, if ever, has a new symphony received such an ovation as that

bestowed on "Lenore"'; see 'Crystal Palace Concerts', *Academy*, 21 November 1874, 573. Fothergill adopts Raff's 'Lenore' as a musical leitmotif for her male protagonist after the manner of Wagner to signal Eugen's entrances, using a melody that London concertgoers would have recognised and might hum along with while reading. Eugen's leitmotif reinforces his position in the orchestra as concertmaster and 'first violin'.

26 'Eugen' is the German equivalent of the English 'Eugene' and often accented on the second syllable ('oi**gain**).

27 A next train is soon available; only much later is it clear that Courvoisier, taken with May's directness, naiveté, and beauty, is allowing himself a rare holiday from strict self-discipline and the chance to enjoy an afternoon and early evening with a charming companion.

28 With their meeting, the text shifts from the English 'Cologne' to the German Köln, so that the text itself registers May's enfolding into a German setting and culture.

29 See Weliver, 'George Eliot and the Prima Donna's "Script"', 103n.3, for the significance of Fothergill's choice of a Wagnerian opera.

30 For an account of the nineteenth-century tradition of middle-class dilettanti's participation in Düsseldorf's choral concerts and rehearsals, as well as the tenure of distinguished composer-conductors Felix Mendelssohn (1833–5) and Robert Schumann (1850–4) in the city, see Cecelia Hopkins Porter, 'The Reign of the "Dilettanti": Düsseldorf from Mendelssohn to Schumann', *Musical Quarterly* 73.4 (1989), 476–512. Helen Black comments on Fothergill's 'wonderful discovery of German music' in Düsseldorf (Black, *Notable Women Authors*, 190). There she could have attended rehearsals as well as concerts, or joined the chorus as an amateur singer. Either option would have enabled the close observation of musical practices on which much of *First Violin* seems based.

31 Fothergill also intervenes in conventional Victorian gender norms in a subplot that both echoes and diverges from Eliot's story of Gwendolen. Like Gwendolen, May's sister Adelaide is tall, 'beautiful, proud, clever' (1:18), and like Gwendolen with Grandcourt, Adelaide weds Sir Peter convinced that she can control the wealthy older man. Instead Sir Peter sadistically controls her every step. When the couple visit May in Elberthal, May moves her voice lessons from her narrow room to Adelaide's luxurious quarters, and in the process von Francius and Adelaide fall deeply in love. As noted earlier, Adelaide ultimately dares what Gwendolen does not, first separating from Sir Peter and then, when her husband's cruel provocations continue, elopes like Marian Evans to a town in Germany. Sir Peter divorces Adelaide, leaving her ashamed at the mess she has made of her life through an inept first choice of mate. In Germany she at least does not face the radical ostracisation of divorcées in England, and Adelaide and von Francius marry once she is free. Later, after she nurses soldiers during the Franco-Prussian war, she becomes a beloved figure in her adopted country for her wartime service. Unlike Gwendolen, then, Adelaide acts to claim agency and end her husband's abusive power over her – though the novel tempers her eventual happiness in marriage in giving von Francius an early death.

32 Fothergill's carnival ball closely resembles Anna Mary Howitt's description of the artists' ball in *Art Student*, discussed in Chapter 3.

33 I use 'queer' in the sense articulated by Noreen Giffney: 'Queer is more often embraced to point to fluidity in identity, recognising identity as a historically-contingent and socially-constructed fiction that prescribes and proscribes against certain feelings and actions. It signifies the messiness of identity, the fact that desire and thus desiring subjects cannot be placed into discrete identity categories, which remain static for the duration of people's lives.' See Giffney, 'Introduction: The "q" Word', in *Queer Interventions: The Ashgate Research Companion to Queer Theory*, ed. Noreen Giffney and Michael O'Rourke (Farnham: Ashgate, 2009), 2.

34 The German noun *Friede* signifies peace, *Helm* a helmet, and the verb *helfen* 'to help' or 'assist'.

35 The chapter represents professional musicianship in detail, including the orchestra's internal politics, the nuts and bolts of choral rehearsal as the conductor stops to correct and sharply criticise individual performers (many of them amateurs), and May's approach to professional performance as she ceases to be nervous about her solo and begins to feel part of the orchestra under von Francius's leadership.

36 Friedhelm's reading includes Schopenhauer and Eduard von Hartmann, whose three-volume *Die Philosophie des Unbewussten* (1870) was translated as *The Philosophy of the Unconscious* in 1884. Schopenhauer, the brother of Adele Schopenhauer (see Chapter 1) had become well known before he died in 1860.

37 Heyse, *Children of the World: A Novel. Translated from the German of Paul Heyse*, 3 vols. (London: Chapman & Hall, 1882), 3:250–9.

38 Fothergill mistakes her chronology; Courvoisier could not buy *Kinder der Welt* until 1873, but the Franco-Prussian war began in 1870.

39 The Victorian meteorologist Robert H. Scott verified that strong cyclones causing severe flooding along the Rhine were on record for Germany; see Scott's *Elementary Meteorology*, 5th ed., International Science Series 46 (London: Kegan Paul, Trench, Trübner & Co., 1890), 378, 382.

40 As if not entirely satisfied with this resolution, Fothergill gave May's singing career a momentary reprise in *The Wellfields* (1880), when the English woman painter Sara Ford attends a soiree at which 'A certain young Englishwoman, married to one Count Eugen of Rothenfels, was the first to sing. The fair soprano was filling the room with a flood of melody . . .'; see *The Wellfields*, 3 vols. (London: Richard Bentley and Son, 1880), 1:63. May then disappears from the story.

Chapter 6

1 Virginia H. Blain, 'Bradley, Katharine Harris [*pseud*. Michael Field] (1846–1914)', *Oxford Dictionary of National Biography* (Oxford: Oxford University Press, 2004, 2021), n.p.; and Linda Hunt Beckman, *Amy Levy: Her Life and Letters* (Athens: Ohio University Press, 2000), 37, 55.

2 The Fields did, however, travel to Germany for family reasons in 1897, as discussed below.
3 These modern transportation networks also brought hordes of middle-class Anglophone tourists on guided tours as well as working-class groups on sponsored excursions, so that British or American visitors became far more familiar to Germans. Michelle M. Strong comments on the unwarranted neglect of 'specific nineteenth-century modes of foreign study that presage today's university language programmes, vocational work/study classes, and holiday learning tours abroad'; see Strong, *Education, Travel, and the 'Civilisation' of the Victorian Working Classes* (Houndmills: Palgrave Macmillan, 2014), 4.
4 As a small child Bradley additionally had a German nurse, just as Vernon Lee had German-speaking Swiss governesses in her adolescence. See Emma Donoghue, *We Are Michael Field* (Bath: Absolute Press, 1998), 7. As Lesa Scholl observes, reading in a foreign culture exposed women to alternatives beyond dominant voices at home, and if women additionally entered into another culture through travel, they intensified their encounter with foreignness and foreign ideas; Scholl, *Translation, Authorship and the Victorian Professional Woman: Charlotte Brontë, Harriet Martineau and George Eliot* (Farnham: Ashgate, 2011), 3, 6–8. See also Johnston, *Economies of Travel*, 48–9; and Susan David Bernstein, *Roomscape: Women Writers in the British Museum from George Eliot to Virginia Woolf* (Edinburgh: Edinburgh University Press, 2013), 36.
5 Scholl, *Translation, Authorship and the Victorian Professional Woman*, 6; Annemarie Drury, *Translation as Transformation in Victorian Poetry* (Cambridge: Cambridge University Press, 2015), 1–56.
6 See Lori Chamberlain, 'Gender and the Metaphorics of Translation', *Signs* 13.3 (1988), 455; Oana-Helene Andone, 'Gender Issues in Translation', *Perspectives: Studies in Translatology* 10.2 (2002), 142, 147, 149; Sherry Simon, *Gender in Translation. Cultural Identity and the Politics of Transmission* (London: Routledge, 1996); and Luise von Flotow, *Translation and Gender: Translating in the 'Era of Feminism'* (Manchester and Ottawa: St Jerome Publishing and University of Ottawa Press, 1997), 35–6.
7 'Arran Leigh' [Katharine Bradley], *The New Minnesinger and Other Poems* (London: Longmans, Green and Co., 1875), 2–3.
8 Rev. of *The New Minnesinger*, *Academy*, 3 July 1875, 9.
9 [Bradley], *The New Minnesinger*, 86.
10 Ibid., 103–4.
11 Ibid., 108–9; Roger Paulin, 'Some Remarks on the Occasion of the New Edition of the Works of Wilhelm Müller', *Modern Language Review* 92.2 (April 1997), 366.
12 Michael Field, *Works and Days*, entry for 31 May 1889, British Library Additional MS 46777, 74. Hereafter I give only the date of each entry and the ms reference and folio.
13 [Bradley], *The New Minnesinger*, 97.
14 Arnold, *Heine in England and America*, 12.

15 Entry for 7 August 1891, British Library Additional MS 46779, 67r.
16 Entry for 2 August 1891, British Library Additional MS 46779, 61v. As Alex Murray notes, the Fields perforce relied on the 'infrastructure' of tourist travel but loathed the 'vulgar[ity]' of tourism and its travellers; they instead sought to transform their journeys into 'Bacchic and spiritual travel'. See '"Profane Travelers": Michael Field, Cornwall, and Modern Tourism', in *Michael Field: Decadent Moderns*, ed. Sarah Parker and Ana Parejo Vadillo (Athens: Ohio University Press, 2019), 167.
17 Entry for 7 August 1891, British Library Additional MS 46779, 64r-v. For an alternative reading of this scene, see Fraser, *Women Writing Art History*, 94.
18 Michael Field, *Stephania: A Trialogue* (London: Elkin Mathews & John Lane, 1892), 77, 83.
19 Cooper notes Bryce's role in the entry of c. 20 September 1890, British Library Additional MS 46778, 115r. See James Bryce, *The Holy Roman Empire*, revised ed. (London: Macmillan, 1866), 159–60.
20 T. Sturge Moore and D. C. Sturge Moore, eds., *Works and Days* (London: John Murray, 1933), 59. The Fields had great hopes for their drama, but it was one of their least-reviewed and least favourably received, as a journal entry dated 26 January 1893 indicates; see Marion Thain and Ana Parejo Vadillo, eds., *Michael Field, The Poet: Published and Manuscript Materials* (Peterborough: Broadview Press, 2009), 258. There was no reason to follow up with later German-related work.
21 Norns, or Scandinavian goddesses of fate, are the Fields's sobriquet for the two elderly German women.
22 Entry for 7 August 1891, British Library Additional MS 46779, 64v–66r.
23 It was while in hospital that Cooper added the scene of Otho's 'delirium' in the final act; see the 4 September 1891 entry, British Library Additional MS 46779, 101.
24 Cooper records their brief German conversation with each other in the entry for 15 September 1891, British Library Additional MS 46779, 103–4.
25 Undated entry [Friday], British Library Additional MS 46779, 110.
26 Undated entry [Thursday], British Library Additional MS 46779, 105. 'Amy' is Cooper's sister, Bradley's niece.
27 Moore and Moore, eds., *Works and Days*, 62–5; 'Saturday' entry, British Library Additional MS 46779, 111v.
28 Christiane's letter stated, '*Wenn Ihnen stet[?] ist so wollen wir heute dichten – Sie die rote Rose, und ich die letze Rose*'; undated entry, British Library Additional MS 46779, 119. My translation of Cooper's poem (on the same page of the journal) is as follows: 'Summer brings the first rose, though she is [actually] summer's creation; dear youth sings of love, which gives him power. In May the rose has a glow that you miss in the hot sun, and first love has a rage that misses life's ultimate joy.' Clearly Cooper had advanced in German language skills due to her extended Dresden residence.
29 Marion Thain, '*Michael Field': Poetry, Aestheticism and the Fin de Siècle* (Cambridge: Cambridge University Press, 2007), 16.

30 Michael Field, *Sight and Song* (London: Elkin Mathews and John Lane, 1892), v.
31 See in particular Fraser, *Women Writing Art History*, 83–4, 93. I briefly survey prior readings and discuss the modes of aesthetic perception the Fields brought to each painting, especially their turn towards visual formalism rather than narrative content, in Hughes, 'Michael Field: *Sight and Song* and Significant Form', *The Oxford Handbook of Victorian Poetry*, ed. Matthew Bevis (Oxford: Oxford University Press, 2013), 563–78.
32 Michael Field, *Sight and Song*, 1–15.
33 Ibid., 27–46.
34 See Alison Byerly, *Are We There Yet? Virtual Travel and Victorian Realism* (Ann Arbor: University of Michigan Press, 2013), 1–14. Yeats in fact compared *Sight and Song* to a guidebook in his review in the *Bookman* 2 (1892), 117. It was not a compliment. Fraser suggests that the volume functioned as a *musée imaginaire* rather than travel guide (*Women Writing Art History*, 84).
35 Michael Field, *Sight and Song*, 98–105, 81.
36 Bradley had read Jameson's work on sacred art, which she mentions in a 9 September 1880 letter to Cooper; see Sharon Bickle, ed., *The Fowl and the Pussycat: Love Letters of Michael Field, 1876–1909* (Charlottesville: University of Virginia Press, 2008), 28, 30n.5.
37 Michael Field, *Sight and Song*, 98–9. The phrase 'grace, and purity' comes from Jameson's *Visits and Sketches*, 2:103.
38 Michael Field, *Sight and Song*, 39–41; Jameson, *Memoirs of the Early Italian Painters*, 2 vols. (London: Charles Knight & Co., 1845), 2:258; Jameson, *Visits and Sketches*, 2:112.
39 John Slatter, 'Jaakoff Prelooker and *The Anglo-Russian*', *Immigrants and Minorities* 2.3 (1983), 52–3.
40 British Library Additional MS 46779, 143r–v. Cooper's 24 December entry registers suspicion that he wanted to flirt with her, perhaps another factor in her lack of interest. References to Prelooker in the journal cease thereafter.
41 Entries labeled 'Tiefen Kastell' and 3 August 1896, British Library Additional MS 46785, 101v, 106v. Cooper evidently misheard the name of Tiefenkasten. For most British tourists, Switzerland rather than Dresden or Bayreuth remained the most popular destination; see Scully, *British Images of Germany*, 64.
42 Undated entry, British Library Additional MS 46785, 109.
43 Entry for 9 August 1896, British Library Additional MS 46785, 113r–113v. Redhill, Surrey, is a commuter town near Reigate.
44 This and the preceding quotation come from an undated entry ('Sunday'), British Library Additional MS 46785, 114v.
45 Undated entry, British Library Additional MS 46785, 121v, 125v.
46 Undated entry ('Thursday'), British Library Additional MS 46785, 131.
47 Undated entries, British Library Additional MS 46786, 83, 84. The telegram announcing that James Cooper was missing arrived on 25 June 1897; these entries were presumably written in July.

48 Undated entry, British Library Additional MS 46786, 86. Franz, their guide, had accompanied them through parts of Switzerland in 1896. Marion Thain suggests that 'Franz' was Franz Andenmatten (personal communication, 11 June 2016).
49 Undated entry ('Friday'), British Library Additional MS 46786, 92v.
50 Undated entry, British Library Additional MS 46786, 137v.
51 Jill Ehnenn reproduces part of their 31 July 1898 journal entry recounting their ceremony in '"Drag(ging) at memory's fetter": Michael Field's Personal Elegies, Victorian Mourning, and the Problem of Whym Chow', *The Michaelian* (online) 1 (June 2009), n.p.
52 Ehnenn, '"Drag(ging) at memory's fetter"', n.p.
53 Beckman, *Amy Levy*, 12–14, 29, 277.
54 Levy, 'In Holiday Humour', *London Society* 46 (August 1884): 177–84. For the magazine's holiday travel themes, see Beth Palmer, '*London Society* (1862–1898)', in *Dictionary of Nineteenth-Century Journalism in Great Britain and Ireland*, ed. Laurel Brake and Marysa Demoor (Ghent and London: Academia Press and the British Library, 2009), 377.
55 Levy, 'In Holiday Humour', 178–9.
56 Ibid., 183–4; Shakespeare, *As You Like It*, IV.i.68–9.
57 Levy, 'In Retreat: A Long Vacation Experience', *London Society* 46 (September 1884), 332–5. Following the defeat of France in the Franco-Prussian War (1870–1), Prussia annexed Alsace-Lorraine.
58 The narrator adds in a postscript that if her reader is interested in learning more about St Odile, 'read Katherine Lee's book, *In the Alsatian Mountains*' ('In Retreat', 335). A travel guide complete with a table of expenses, *In the Alsatian Mountains* (London: Richard Bentley, 1883) is dedicated by author Katherine Lee Jenner to her young daughter Ysolt in a poem that mentions leaving her child behind while she and her husband rambled among the Vosges Mountains to discover how Alsatians regarded Prussian rule (Lee, vii), a New Woman record of untraditional marriage. Lee's eleventh chapter focuses on St Odile, where Lee and her husband conversed with nuns and visitors in French; in Gaskell's narrative set in the Vosges Mountains in 'The Grey Woman', French is likewise spoken. Levy's use of German in her story is thus quite deliberate.
59 Levy, 'In Retreat', 333–4.
60 Ibid., 335.
61 Ibid., 332. 'Camford' could also allude to both Cambridge and Oxford, which could intensify the fictionality of the story. For Levy's contributions to *Cambridge Review*, see Hughes, 'Reading Amy Levy Through Victorian Newspapers', *Women, Periodicals and Print Culture in Britain, 1830s–1900s: The Victorian Period*, ed. Alexis Easley, Clare Gill, and Beth Rodgers (Edinburgh University Press, 2019), 457–63.
62 Since Ida weds the prince in the end, it is not deemed progressive today. But in the late 1840s it was welcomed by Elizabeth Cady Stanton among others; see Hughes, '*The Princess* and the Generosity of Tennyson's Imagination', *Tennyson Research Bulletin* 11.2 (2018), 119–20.

63 'In the Black Forest', *London Society* 46 (October 1884), 392–4.
64 Ibid., 393–4.
65 Ibid., 392–3.
66 Ibid., 394.
67 Levy's 'Princess' series continued into two more tales, but these are set in England: 'Easter-Tide at Tunbridge Wells', *London Society* 47 (May 1885), 481–3, and 'Out of the World', *London Society* 49 (January 1886), 53–6, set in Cornwall.
68 See 'Jewish Women and "Women's Rights"' from the 7 and 28 February 1879 *Jewish Chronicle* in *Reuben Sachs*, ed. Susan David Bernstein (Peterloo, Ontario: Broadview Press, 2006), 171–5.
69 Untitled paragraph, *Jewish Chronicle*, 6 February 1880, 11. The paper was edited by Asher I. Myers.
70 'The "Judenhetze" in Germany', 'Notes of the Week', *Jewish Chronicle*, 27 February 1880, 4; 'Notes from Germany', *Jewish Chronicle*, 9 January 1880, 11.
71 'The Jews of Frankfurt', *Jewish Chronicle*, 25 June 1880, 13.
72 Beckman, *Amy Levy*, 232–7.
73 Ibid., 233. Beckman also comments on Levy's repulsion when she visited a Dresden synagogue and commented on the plausibility of German anti-Semitism towards such folk; Beckman reads this reaction as Jewish self-hatred generated by British racist attitudes towards Anglo-Jewry (7–11, 236).
74 Beckman, *Amy Levy*, 233–4.
75 Christine Pullen, *The Woman Who Dared: A Biography of Amy Levy* (Kingston upon Thames: Kingston University Press, 2010), 57–8. Pullen describes the Hotel Sonnenberg where the women stayed and provides photographs of the building and scenery visible from the hotel (52–3, 103).
76 Levy, 'In Holiday Humour', 182; Beckman, *Amy Levy*, 241. Olivia's last name of 'Longcroft' in the story echoes the name of Levy's travel companion Ellen Crofts.
77 Pullen, *The Woman Who Dared*, 60. Levy's travels to the Black Forest and Switzerland also inspired poems, including 'In Switzerland', *London Society* 46 (July 1884), 120, never reprinted; and 'To E.', *London Society* 49 (May 1886), 447. Levy placed 'To E.', another reference to her travelling companion Ellen Crofts, at the end of the posthumously published *A London Plane-Tree and Other Verse* (London: T. Fisher Unwin, 1889), 92–4. Levy's volume thus ends, 'The cloud descends', in contrast to the dedicatory poem to Clementina Black that ends in hope. See also Beckman on 'To E.', *Amy Levy*, 95.
78 Beckman, *Amy Levy*, 77; Pullen, *The Woman Who Dared*, 57.
79 As Pullen reports, a diary entry by Levy's London friend Dollie Radford confirms Levy's and Smith's stop in the Vosges Mountains; *The Woman Who Dared*, 80. David Goslee observes that Tennyson's fictional professor Lady Blanche, mother of Melissa, is 'the voice of orthodox feminism'; see 'Character and Structure in Tennyson's *The Princess*', *SEL: Studies in English Literature* 14.4 (Autumn 1974), 568. For details of Blanche Smith, see Beckman, *Amy Levy*, 244–5, and Gillian Sutherland, *In Search of the New*

Woman: Middle-Class Women and Work in Britain 1870–1914 (Cambridge: Cambridge University Press, 2015), 63.
80 Beckman, *Amy Levy*, 246. For details of this English crowd, including Harry Bond, future Master of Trinity Hall, Cambridge, and Karl Pearson, a leading radical of the fin de siècle, both of whom Levy had known in a Cambridge discussion circle, see Beckman, *Amy Levy*, 245, 248 and Pullen, *The Woman Who Dared*, 35–6, 68.
81 I have silently corrected Beckman's 'Gottieil' and restored the umlaut omitted by Beckman in *Amy Levy*, 250, based on my examination of the letter in the Amy Levy Archive owned by Camellia PLC. Walter Gottheil was a playwright who would go on to publish *Berliner Märchen* (Berlin fairy tales) in 1902.
82 I adopt Pullen's reproduction of the letter (*The Woman Who Dared*, 84–5) since it includes German translations but substitute 'at his house' for 'by him' to translate 'bei ihm' and silently correct other mistranscriptions. Pullen notes that Miss Corfe, born in 1856, attended Newnham from 1874–9 (Pullen, 218n.199).
83 Beckman, *Amy Levy*, 76. A 2012 study found that women studying abroad face five times the risk of rape during a study abroad semester in a non-English speaking country than on home campuses, a consequence less of predatory foreign 'others' than of women's unfamiliarity with local terrain and relevant social codes even if they have considerable proficiency in the local language. See Elizabeth Redden, 'Sexual Assault and Study Abroad', *Inside Higher Ed* [online], 19 December 2012, n.p.
84 Her association of priests with villainy would be consistent with Heine's anti-clericalism in his essay 'The Romantic School'; see *The Complete Works of Heinrich Heine, Volume 5*, tr. Charles Leland (London: William Heinemann, 1892), 274–6, 283–4.
85 'Notes from Germany', *Jewish Chronicle*, 21 May 1880, 10, and 28 May 1880, 11.
86 Beckman, *Amy Levy*, 16.
87 As Beckman notes, Levy also wrote a letter to the *Jewish Chronicle* about Heyse in 1883 (*Amy Levy*, 166).
88 Drury, *Translation as Transformation in Victorian Poetry*, 14, 20.
89 Levy, 'The Shepherd', *Cambridge Review*, 9 June 1880, 158; Johann von Goethe, 'Der Schäfer', *Goethes Sämtliche Werke* [Goethe's Collected Works], *Erster Band: Gedichte Erster Teil* [vol.1: *Poems*, Part I] (Stuttgart: Verlag der I. G. Cotta'schen Buchhandlung, 1893), 33.
90 For Victorian prosodists' association of iambic pentameter with Englishness, see Yopie Prins, 'Victorian Meters', *The Cambridge Companion to Victorian Poetry*, ed. Joseph Bristow (Cambridge: Cambridge University Press, 2000), 90–4, and Meredith Martin, *The Rise and Fall of Meter: Poetry and English National Culture, 1860–1930* (Princeton: Princeton University Press, 2012), 101–2. Prins notes George Saintsbury's assertion in his 1908 study of English prosody that the '"German or Germanised ear"' could not properly hear the '"elasticity combined with form"' in English prosody (Prins, 94).
91 Beckman, *Amy Levy*, 236.

92 Jameson, *Winter Studies and Summer Rambles*, 1:286–7.
93 Rev. of *Xantippe and Other Verse*, *Cambridge Review*, 8 June 1881, 382–3; Levy, 'From Grillparzer's Sappho', *Cambridge Review*, 1 February 1882, 141.
94 Beckman, *Amy Levy*, 77, 239. T. D. Olverson more overtly suggests the debt of Levy's 'Medea' to Grillparzer's *Medea*, analysing Levy's fragment in the context of Levy's articulation of Anglo-Jewish identity; see '"Such Are Not Woman's Thoughts": Amy Levy's "Xantippe" and "Medea"', in *Amy Levy: Critical Essays*, ed. Naomi Hetherington and Nadia Valman (Athens: Ohio University Press, 2010), 122–8. Olverson also notes Levy's translation from Grillparzer's *Sappho* but only in passing (125).
95 As F. J. Lamport points out, German dramatists began to adopt Elizabethan drama's blank verse as a preferred mode after Gotthold Lessing's *Nathan der Weise* (1779), becoming standard for serious German dramas from Goethe and Schiller onward. See Lamport, *German Classical Drama: Theatre, Humanity and Nation, 1750–1870* (Cambridge: Cambridge University Press, 1990), 83.
96 Levy, 'Translated from Geibel', *Xantippe, and Other Verse* (Cambridge: E. Johnson, 1881), 23–4; this translation was added to the posthumous reprinting of Levy's *A Minor Poet* in 1891.
97 'From Heine' (270) in the 26 April 1882 *Cambridge Review* follows Heine's form (six trimeter quatrains and a rhyme scheme of abcb defe etc.) as well as his characteristic ironic twist at the end.
98 'A Farewell / (After Heine)', *A Minor Poet and Other Verse* (London: T. Fisher Unwin, 1884), 92–3; reprinted and slightly revised from 'Imitation of Heine', *Cambridge Review*, 7 December 1881, 127.
99 William Rose, Introduction, in Arnold, *Heine in England and America*, 8.
100 Heine, *Buch der Lieder*, 133.
101 For additional discussion of Levy's university depictions in prose, see Lisa C. Robertson, 'Time and Memory in Amy Levy's Collegiate Writing: "My Present Mind"', *ELT: English Literature in Transition* 61.2 (2018), 211–31, as well as Levy's story 'Cohen of Trinity' (1889). Increasing deafness and her lesbian sexuality would have further distanced Levy from many Newnham students.
102 The term 'assimilative creativity' is Naomi Levine's; see Levine, 'Tirra-Lirrical Ballads: Source Hunting with the Lady of Shalott', *Victorian Poetry* 54.4 (Winter 2016), 444.
103 Heine, *Buch der Lieder*, 96; Levy, *Xantippe, and Other Verse*, iii. My thanks to Jenny Hodge, Special Collections Assistant at the UC-Davis-Shields Library, University of California-Davis, for sharing an image of the epigraph from Levy's first volume.
104 Heine, *Buch der Lieder*, 127. In his *Heinrich Heine: Selected Verse* (London: Penguin Books, 1968), 44, Peter Branscombe provides this literal prose translation of the lyric:

> The night is still, the streets are at rest, my darling dwelt in this house, she left the town long ago, but the house still stands in the same place.
> A man stands there too and stares up, and wrings his hands in the violence of his pain; I shudder when I see his face – the moon shows me my own form.
> You double-ganger! pale fellow! Why do you imitate the pain of love which tormented me in this very place so many nights in times gone by?

105 Levy, *A London Plane-Tree*, 57.
106 Alex Goody, 'Passing in the City: The Liminal Spaces of Amy Levy's Late Work', in *Amy Levy: Critical Essays*, ed. Naomi Hetherington and Nadia Valman (Athens: Ohio University Press, 2010), 170. Goody further asserts that both Levy's older and younger selves function as ghosts, one of the past, one of the future.
107 See Beckman's description of the ms letter in *Amy Levy*, 257–8n.8.
108 Beckman, *Amy Levy*, 116, 120–1.
109 Levy, *A London Plane-Tree*, 58.
110 'Neue Liebe, Neues Leben', Amy Levy Archive. My transcription of the poem differs slightly from that of Beckman (*Amy Levy*, 257–8).
111 Lee wrote of Levy to her mother in September 1888, 'I don't love her'. More galling still, Lee appropriated the German-language title of Levy's poem for an inscription on an envelope holding a white rose and letters to Kit Anstruther-Thomson that marked the beginning of their love affair (Beckman, *Amy Levy*, 208, 148). See also Sally Newman, 'The Archival Traces of Desire: Vernon Lee's Failed Sexuality and the Interpretation of Letters in Lesbian History', *Journal of the History of Sexuality* 14.1–2 (January–April 2005), 51–75.
112 Beckman, *Amy Levy*, 257n.8.
113 Levy, *A London Plane-Tree*, 74. The 1889 volume, from which I quote here, presents no significant variants from the paired poems. Fittingly, the blackthorn is identified with 'difficulty' in the facsimile Edwardian hand-painted dictionary of flowers in my possession.
114 Levy, *A London Plane-Tree*, 40.
115 The Heine echo in 'The Birch-Tree' was sufficiently clear that Levy's *Athenaeum* reviewer pointed it out, expressing dissatisfaction that 'The Birch-Tree' was 'too reminiscent of Heine'; the University of Ghent *Athenaeum* index identifies the reviewer as Mabel C. Birchenough. See [Birchenough], 'Recent Verse', *Athenaeum*, 14 December 1889, 818.
116 Heine, *Buch der Lieder*, 94–5. In *Dramatic Pictures: English Rispetti Sonnets and Other Verses* (London: Chatto and Windus, 1894), Alexander H. Japp translated this lyric as follows (137):

> A fir-tree stands all lonely
>   In the north, on a cold gray height;
> He slumbers, as round him ice and snow
>   Weave a mantle of spotless white.
>
> He dreams of a palm-tree towering
>   Afar in the Eastern land,
> Alone, and silently dreaming
>   'Mid rocks and burning sand.

For a finer, more recent translation, see Hal Draper's version in Peter Simon, ed., *The Norton Anthology of World Literature, Volume 2*, shorter 2nd ed. (New York: W. W. Norton, 2009), 454.

117 Philipp Veit, 'Fichtenbaum und Palme', *Germanic Review* 51 (1976), 17. For the birch's gendering, see Fred Hageneder, *The Meaning of Trees: Botany – History – Healing – Lore* (London: Chronicle Books, 2005), 42–3.
118 Qtd. by Beckman, *Amy Levy*, 82.
119 Levy, 'Jewish Humour', *Jewish Chronicle*, 20 August 1886, 9–10; rpt. in Melvyn New, ed., *The Complete Novels and Selected Writings of Amy Levy 1861–1889* (Gainesville: University Press of Florida, 1993), 522. New identifies Levy's Heine source in a note (562n.33).

Chapter 7

1 After her husband's death she resettled in Switzerland; with the outbreak of World War I she returned to Britain and was repatriated in 1914. See 'Nachwort/Afterword' for further details.
2 Jennifer Walker, *Elizabeth of the German Garden: A Literary Journey* (Sussex: Book Guild Publishing, 2013), 16–21. Unusual for women at the time, von Arnim studied and performed Bach's fugues for organ in academy student recitals (Walker, 20).
3 Hein, *Ottilie von Goethe*, 164, 421–2, 598–9. Ottilie von Goethe's grandmother left it to her two children, and after Goethe's mother died in 1851, the Goethes became part owners. Eventually the Goethes sold their portion to their uncle, Graf von Donnersmerck; Henning von Arnim-Schlagenthin's father bought it when the von Donnersmerck heirs sold it. See Karen Usborne, *'Elizabeth': The Author of Elizabeth and Her German Garden* (London: The Bodley Head, 1986), 56.
4 Henning von Arnim-Schlagenthin's declining health had rendered him unable to manage the estate by 1909, and in 1910 he died.
5 For von Arnim's knowledge of Johann von Goethe and Bettina, see Usborne, *'Elizabeth'*, 59. Usborne suggests that the publishing name of 'Elizabeth' was partly inspired by Bettina von Arnim since 'Bettina' is a diminutive of the German personal name 'Elisabeth' (*'Elizabeth'*, 67).
6 Amanda Klekowski von Koppenfels, *Migrants or Expatriates? Americans in Europe* (Houndmills: Palgrave Macmillan, 2014), 43, 48–50.
7 Edward Said, *Representations of the Intellectual: The 1993 Reith Lectures* (1994; rpt. New York: Vintage Books, 1996), 61–2.
8 Carmel S. Saad et al., 'Multiculturalism and Creativity: Effects of Cultural Context, Bicultural Identity, and Ideational Fluency', *Social Psychological and Personality Science* 4.3 (2013), 369–75.
9 Said, *Representations*, 60, 53.
10 I use 'Elizabeth' within quotes when I reference von Arnim's fictional stand-ins for herself in her 1898 and 1904 novels to avoid confusion between von Arnim the historical subject and her narrators.
11 See also Hughes, 'von Arnim, Elizabeth, the German Novels of', *The Palgrave Encyclopedia of Victorian Women's Writing*, ed. Lesa Scholl (Cham: Palgrave

Macmillan, 2020). For the von Arnim novel closest to representations of ethnoexocentrism by earlier Victorian women writers, see *The Benefactress* (1901), in which Anna Estcourt, daughter of a German mother and affluent English father, disdains the conventional expectations of 'advantageous' marriage for daughters of wealthy English families and, on unexpectedly inheriting a Pomeranian estate from her uncle, decides to settle there to escape family match-making and pursue a meaningful life. She naively founds a home for German gentlewomen of slender means to free them from obligatory marriage or economic dependence. She has much to learn about German culture and is assisted by the kindly bachelor owner of neighbouring farmland who mentors her through her cultural negotiations and land management. Ultimately these two fall in love and Anna will settle for good in her new home country.

12 As Talia Schaffer notes, 'Elizabeth' omits realist description of the garden, an indication that the novel is invested in its narrator's subjectivity more than in horticulture; see *The Forgotten Female Aesthetes: Literary Culture in Late-Victorian England* (Charlottesville: University Press of Virginia, 2000), 64–5.

13 [Elizabeth von Arnim], *Elizabeth and her German Garden* (London: Macmillan, 1898), 3, 9–10. I give subsequent page numbers in the text.

14 Juliane Römhild, *Femininity and Authorship in the Novels of Elizabeth von Arnim* (Madison: Fairleigh Dickinson University Press, 2014), 82–4.

15 Usborne, 'Elizabeth', 70, 89; Römhild, *Femininity and Authorship*, 75, 80.

16 Jane Stabler, *The Artistry of Exile: Romantic and Victorian Writers in Italy* (Oxford: Oxford University Press, 2013), 24.

17 To ensure clarity, however, I at times discuss the displays of Germanness and Englishness alternately.

18 Marianne North, *Recollections of a Happy Life, Being the Autobiography of Marianne North*, 2 vols., ed. Mrs John Addington Symonds (New York and London: Macmillan, 1894), 23.

19 Stabler, *The Artistry of Exile*, 227.

20 [von Arnim], *The Adventures of Elizabeth in Rügen* (New York and London: Macmillan, 1904), 221–2. Page numbers of subsequent citations are given in the text. 'Who's on first' refers to a famous American baseball sketch debuted by comedians Abbott and Costello in the 1930s.

21 *Junker*: 'A member of a class of aristocratic Prussian landholders, who dominated the Prussian military and later also the government of the German Empire' (*OED*). Junkers were notorious for their conservatism socially and politically.

22 'I have had much leisure for reflection, and my reflections have led me to the conclusion, erroneous perhaps, but fixed, that having got a husband, taken him of one's own free will, taken him sometimes even in the face of opposition, the least one can do is to stick to him' (*Rügen*, 114).

23 Römhild, *Femininity and Authorship*, 102.

24 [von Arnim], *The Princess Priscilla's Fortnight* (London: Smith, Elder, 1905), 11–12. Subsequent page numbers are given in the text.

25 Walker, *Elizabeth*, 116.

26 Said, *Reflections on Exile and Other Essays* (Cambridge: Harvard University Press, 2000), 186.
27 'Often have I wandered through the world, seeing always how greatness is undone by pettiness, and how what is noble becomes corroded by the caustic poison of everyday life' (my translation).
28 See, for example, Usborne, *'Elizabeth'*, 115.
29 Leslie De Charms [pseud. of Liebet von Arnim], *Elizabeth of the German Garden: A Biography* (London: Heinemann, 1958), 122–3; Usborne, *'Elizabeth'*, 116; Walker, *Elizabeth*, 87–8.
30 Usborne, *'Elizabeth'*, 118. Similarly, De Charms posits a 'profound gulf' between the 'naïve adventures of *Priscilla*' and *Fräulein Schmidt*, which rises 'to the deeply-felt and serious plane of Elizabeth's future *Vera* and final *Mr. Skeffington*' (*Elizabeth*, 121).
31 [Virgina Woolf], 'Fräulein Schmidt and Mr Anstruther', *Times Literary Supplement*, 10 May 1907: 149. Isobel Maddison notes this review in surveying the novel's reception; see *Elizabeth von Arnim: Beyond the German Garden* (Farnham: Ashgate. 2013), 17, 29–30. Woolf had published only reviews to this point, though she had begun *The Voyage Out* (1915). The spectacle of von Arnim publishing her sixth novel since her first in 1898 would have done little to cheer Woolf. It was a dark time for Woolf altogether, since her brother Thoby had died of typhoid fever in November 1906 and Vanessa Bell, much to Woolf's disappointment, had married Clive Bell in February 1907. Rose-Marie's early, florid letters to Anstruther would hardly have struck a responsive chord in Woolf.
32 Usborne, *'Elizabeth'*, 44–5, 65, 67.
33 As noted in Chapter 2, Bettina's successful example also inspired other German women, including Ottilie von Goethe, who asserted that 'appreciation of female genius' descended from Rahel and Bettina. See Diethe, *Towards Emancipation*, 65.
34 Laura M. Green, 'Bildungsroman', *The Encyclopedia of Victorian Literature*, 4 vols., ed. Dino Felluga; assoc. eds. Pamela Gilbert and Linda K. Hughes (Chichester: Wiley Blackwell, 2015), 1:126–32. Rose-Marie alludes to *Aurora Leigh* at one point; see *Fräulein Schmidt and Mr Anstruther* (London: Smith, Elder, 1907), 101. Subsequent page references are given in the text.
35 Von Arnim greatly admired Thoreau and references him in *Fräulein Schmidt* (92–3). See also De Charms, *Elizabeth*, 67; Usborne, *'Elizabeth'*, 117; and Römhild, *Femininity and Authorship*, 15. As De Charms observes, von Arnim was reading Thoreau again while writing *Princess Priscilla's Fortnight* (110).
36 The closest literary precursors of von Arnim's subliminal narrative are the experimental monologues of Tennyson's *Maud* (1855) and Browning's juxtaposed Guido monologues in *The Ring and the Book* (1868–9) as well as Arthur Hugh Clough's epistolary *Amours de Voyage* (1855). In these, too, readers are invited to discern ongoing psychic processes that are never explicitly narrated.
37 Shakespeare, *Shakespeare: Complete Works*, ed. G. B. Harrison (New York: Harcourt, Brace & World, 1952), 1613.

38 Ernest Dowson, *The Poems of Ernest Dowson* (London: John Lane, The Bodley Head, 1905), 41–2.
39 Matthew Prior, 'The Ladle', in *The Poetical Works of Matthew Prior. With Memoir and Critical Dissertation* by Rev. George Gilfillan (Edinburgh: James Nichol, 1858), 98–100, lines 79–86, 133–48.
40 Woolf, 'Fräulein Schmidt and Mr. Anstruther', 149.
41 'Damn her lips', presumably.

Chapter 8

1 Mandy Gagel, 'Selected Letters of Vernon Lee (1856–1935)', Ph.D. dissertation, Boston University, 2008, 618, 620.
2 Vernon Lee, *The Sentimental Traveller* (London: John Lane The Bodley Head, 1908), x.
3 Lee and von Arnim became acquainted after von Arnim moved to Switzerland; Lee mentions *Fräulein Schmidt and Mr Anstruther* in a chapter on Jena in *The Tower of the Mirrors* (London: John Lane The Bodley Head, 1914), 108.
4 Colby, *Vernon Lee*, 251.
5 In some respects the impetus to creativity and contrapuntal perception that Said identifies with expatriate intellectuals parallels Dustin Friedman's analysis of nineteenth-century aesthetes' queer subjectivities founded upon Hegelian negativity, a process by which the subject encounters obstacles to self-development or destruction of assumptions, freeing the subject to discover or create alternative perspectives hitherto unseen. For queer aesthetes, according to Friedman, the obstacles are most often homophobia and social condemnation of non-normativity, while the avenue to new perceptions is the experience of beauty in art, until aesthetic experience leading to detachment from convention itself becomes freedom. See Friedman, *Before Queer Theory: Victorian Aestheticism and the Self* (Baltimore: Johns Hopkins University Press, 2019), 2–4, 10.
6 See Sudeep Dasgupta and Mireille Rosello, 'Introduction: Queer and Europe: an Encounter', in their essay collection *What's Queer about Europe? Productive Encounters and Re-Enchanting Paradigms* (New York: Fordham University Press, 2014), 1–23. As they explain, 'Queer discourses question the way in which queer objects are conceptualized and articulated. For, contrary to what readers who are not familiar with the field may think, Queer Theory has never been reducible to sexuality let alone to the sexual politics of gays and lesbians' (4). They add, 'Queering is a permanent process that undermines normativity at the same time that it wards off the paradoxical threat of reinstating non-normativity as a desired and stable program. To that extent, queering possesses the perpetual uncertainty of a negative dialectical habit of mind without hypostasizing and reifying litanies of in-betweenness or the interval' (9). For a foundational work that links lesbian queerness to ghosts and haunting, see Terry Castle, *The Apparitional Lesbian: Female Homosexuality and Modern Culture* (New York: Columbia University Press, 1993).

7 Lee allied herself with members of the British Union of Democratic Control in 1911 prior to its official founding in 1914. She was reviled, sometimes even by friends, for her pacificism during World War I (Colby, *Vernon Lee*, 290–1, 296–7). Her refusal to elevate one European nation over another was part of a deliberate strategy to oppose devastating wars.
8 Fried received the Nobel Peace Prize in 1911; see Katherine Sorrels, *Cosmopolitan Outsiders: Imperial Inclusion, National Exclusion, and the Pan-European Idea, 1900–1930* (New York: Palgrave Macmillan, 2016), 3, 23–7.
9 Sorrels, *Cosmopolitan Outsiders*, 37. Fried in turn influenced Count Richard Coudenhove-Kalergi (1894–1972), the half Bohemian, half Japanese author of *Paneuropa* (1923), today considered the '"grandfather of European unity"' (*Cosmopolitan Outsiders*, 2).
10 See, e.g., Christa Zorn, *Vernon Lee: Aesthetics, History, and the Victorian Female Intellectual* (Athens: Ohio University Press, 2003), 9; Stefano Evangelista, *British Aestheticism and Ancient Greece: Hellenism, Reception, Gods in Exile* (Houndmills: Palgrave Macmillan, 2009), 58.
11 Lee, 'Contemporary Italian Poets', *Quarterly Review* 144 (October 1877), 465, 474.
12 Lee, *Belcaro: Being Essays on Sundry Æsthetical Questions* (London: W. Satchell & Co., [1881]), 247. Baldwin's name is itself Franco-Germanic; see Patrick Hanks et al., *A Dictionary of First Names*, 2nd ed. (Oxford: Oxford University Press, 2006), online edition. Baldwin's quote comes from Goethe's *Torquato Tasso* V.i, which gives 'brauchen' rather than 'gebrauchen'. Charles Des Voeux rendered the lines as 'All does not similarly serve our turn; / Who much would use, must ev'ry thing employ / In its own manner, then is he well serv'd'; *Torquato Tasso: A Dramatic Poem from the German of Goethe: With Other German Poetry* (London: Longman, Rees, Orme, Brown, and Green, 1827), 179. As I note in 'Trace Collaboration', Des Voeux was assisted by Ottilie von Goethe, who wrote the preface to his posthumous second edition (40).
13 Lee, *Laurus Nobilis: Chapters on Art and Life* (London: John Lane The Bodley Head, 1909), vi. Reginald Snell translates the quotation from Letter 26 of Friedrich Schiller's work (1794) thus: 'The reality of things is the work of the things: the appearance of things is the work of Man, and a nature which delights in appearance no longer takes pleasure in what it receives, but in what it does'; see Snell, tr., *On the Aesthetic Education of Man, in a Series of Letters* (New Haven: Yale University Press, 1954), 125.
14 Lee, 'Faustus and Helena', *Cornhill Magazine* 42 (August 1880), 212. This essay was reprinted in *Belcaro*.
15 Lee, 'Faustus and Helena', 227, 223, 212. See also Friedman, *Before Queer Theory*, 119. Friedman emphasises Lee's 'queer historicism' rather than, as I do, the legend's relation to oral sources.
16 See Colby, *Vernon Lee*, 8, 261, 251.
17 Lee, *Hortus Vitae: Essays on the Gardening of Life*, 2nd ed. (London: John Lane The Bodley Head), 1904, 17–8.

18 Ibid., 18–9.
19 Ibid., 20–2. The 'little town' is Thun, Switzerland.
20 Karel Čapek, *In Praise of Newspapers and Other Essays on the Margin of Literature*, tr. M. and R. Weatherall (New York: Arts, Inc., 1951), 49, 72–3.
21 Ibid., 59–60, 68. See also Maria Tatar, *Enchanted Hunters: The Power of Stories in Childhood* (New York: W. W. Norton, 2009), 54–63.
22 Jack Zipes, *Grimm Legacies: The Magic Spell of the Grimms' Folk and Fairy Tales* (Princeton: Princeton University Press, 2015), 190.
23 Lee, *The Sentimental Traveller*, 240–2.
24 Ibid., 244–6.
25 Colby, *Vernon Lee*, 225; Zorn, 142–3. Zorn also connects Hoffmann to Lee's 'Faustus and Helena'.
26 Zipes, 'The Changing Function of the Fairy Tale', *The Lion and the Unicorn* 12.2 (December 1988), 18–19.
27 Vernon Lee, *Hauntings and Other Fantastic Tales*, ed. Catherine Maxwell and Patricia Pulham (Peterborough: Broadview Press, 2006), 54. Maxwell and Pulham's edition follows Lee's first.
28 Zorn persuasively argues that E. T. A. Hoffmann's tale *Der Sandmann* (the Sandman) influenced 'Amour Dure'; see *Vernon Lee*, 142, and E. T. A. Hoffmann, *The Golden Pot and Other Tales*, tr. Ritchie Robertson (Oxford: Oxford University Press, 1992), 85–118.
29 Catherine Maxwell, *Second Sight: The Visionary Imagination in Late Victorian Literature* (Manchester: Manchester University Press, 2008), 120–1; Evangelista, *British Aestheticism and Ancient Greece*, 81–8. Evangelista views these two tales' 'spectral classicism' as Lee's critique of male aesthetes' Hellenism. See also Patrick Bridgwater, *Anglo–German Interactions in the Literature of the 1890s* (European Humanities Research Centre, University of Oxford: Legenda, 1999), 10–43.
30 This well-known tale has been linked to Lee's lesbianism, her sympathetic response to Oscar Wilde's imprisonment, and her perspectives on aestheticism and decadence. See, e.g., Martha Vicinus, 'The Adolescent Boy: Fin de Siècle Femme Fatale?', *Journal of the History of Sexuality* 5.1 (July 1994), 90–114; Margaret Stetz, 'The Snake Lady and the Bruised Bodley Head: Vernon Lee and Oscar Wilde in the *Yellow Book*', in *Vernon Lee: Decadence, Ethics, Aesthetics*, ed. Catherine Maxwell and Patricia Pulham (Basingstoke: Palgrave Macmillan, 2006), 112–22; Sondeep Kandola, *Vernon Lee* (Tavistock: Northcote House, 2010), 33–7; and Friedman, *Before Queer Theory*, 142–6.
31 Zipes, 'The Changing Function of the Fairy Tale', 18–19.
32 Lee, 'Prince Alberic and the Snake Lady', *The Yellow Book* 10 (July 1896), 290–2. Subsequent page references are given in the text.
33 Colby, *Vernon Lee*, 230; Zorn, *Vernon Lee*, 190n.6; Hoffmann, *The Golden Pot*, 1–83.
34 The snake lady's name of 'Oriana' may further indicate lesbian significance if the name is an allusion to Tennyson's 'The Ballad of Oriana', in which the

knight aiming his arrow at a foe kills his betrothed Oriana instead: 'The damnèd arrow glanced aside / And pierced thy heart, my love, my bride' (lines 41–2), in *The Poems of Tennyson*, ed. Christopher Ricks (London: Longmans, 1969), 249. Relative to 'Prince Alberic', Tennyson's Oriana suggests heteronormative love's potential for destruction. As Friedman notes, the prince's love for Oriana opens a space for multiple forms of non-normative love (*Before Queer Theory*, 142–4).

35 Franconia encompasses parts of Saxony, Thuringia, and Bavaria. Lee wrote *Ottilie* some time before late June 1881, when she reported that Longman had refused the story since it was too long to appear in a single number of *Longman's Magazine*; letter of 29–30 June 1881 to her mother in Amanda Gagel, ed., *Selected Letters of Vernon Lee 1856–1935: Volume 1, 1865–1884* (London: Routledge, 2017), 302.
36 A. Gagel, *Selected Letters*, 612.
37 The *Contemporary Review*, *Academy*, *Saturday Review*, and *Westminster Review* all published notices of *Ottilie* upon its initial publication.
38 A. Gagel, *Selected Letters*, 616.
39 [Julia Wedgwood], rev. of *Ottilie*, by Vernon Lee in 'Contemporary Records', *Contemporary Review* 44 (November 1883), 784–5.
40 A[lice]. Werner, rev. of *Ottilie*, by Vernon Lee, *Academy*, 30 June 1883, 448. Werner (1859–1935), the daughter of a German professor and English mother, was born and partly raised in Germany before the family moved to England; later famous for her work with Bantu languages, she had attended Newnham and was contributing to other periodicals at the time *Ottilie* appeared.
41 See Colby, *Vernon Lee*, 83; and Peter Gunn, *Vernon Lee* (London: Oxford University Press, 1964), 83.
42 On this point see Werner, rev. of *Ottilie*, 448; Colby, *Vernon Lee*, 84–5; and Gunn, *Vernon Lee*, 82.
43 Colby, *Vernon Lee*, 84.
44 A. Gagel, *Selected Letters*, 612.
45 Gunn, *Vernon Lee*, 83–4.
46 Lee, *Ottilie: An Eighteenth Century Idyl* (London: T. Fisher Unwin, 1883), 21–2. Subsequent page references are given in the text.
47 See Colby, *Vernon Lee*, 46. Neither sibling's name appeared on the title page of the collected fairy tales, and in official bibliographical records today the work is listed only under Lee's name.
48 Werner, rev. of *Ottilie*, 448.
49 Klopstock's admirers included Johann von Goethe, who alludes to Klopstock in *Die Leiden des jungen Werthers*; see Beth Bjorklund. 'Friedrich Gottlieb Klopstock', *Dictionary of Literary Biography 97: German Writers from the Enlightenment to Sturm und Drang, 1720–1764*, ed. James N. Hardin and Christoph E. Schweitzer (Detroit: Gale, 1990), 154–5.
50 Colby, *Vernon Lee*, 86. Moritz, Colby explains, was 'a novelist and essayist who rose from humble circumstances to become privy councillor to Prince Karl August in Berlin'.

51 See Gunn, *Vernon Lee*, 83, for the historical liberties Lee takes with Moritz. Moritz indeed has a place in literary history, but he was never quite the leading light that he appears in Lee's story.
52 Karl Hillebrand, letter of 16 July 1883, in Perley M. Leighton, '"TO MY FRIEND, KARL HILLEBRAND": The Dedication in *Ottilie* and its Aftermath', *Colby Library Quarterly* ser. 3.12 (November 1953), 187–8. Leighton's article marked the first publication of Hillebrand's letter.
53 Lee, 'Faustus and Helena', 215.
54 Lee, *Sentimental Traveller*, 52.
55 For Pater's influence, see among the many others who might be cited Colby, *Vernon Lee*, 56–8. As Pater comments in the Winckelmann essay,

> necessity ... is a magic web woven through and through us, like that magnetic system of which modern science speaks, penetrating us with a network subtler than our subtlest nerves, yet bearing in it the central forces of the world. Can art represent men and women in these bewildering toils so as to give the spirit at least an equivalent for the sense of freedom? Goethe's *Wahlverwandtschaften* is a high instance of modern art dealing thus with modern life.

Pater, *Studies in the History of the Renaissance* (London: Macmillan, 1873), 205–6. See also Stefano Evangelista, '"Life in the Whole": Goethe and English Aestheticism'", *Publications of the English Goethe Society* 82.3 (2013), 184–5.
56 I have loosely and selectively translated Soret's words in Hein:

> [Ottilie ist] klein, braun, mit feurigen, geistblitzenden Augen, lebhaft, originell, empfindsam, kokett (in allen Ehren, versteht sich), voll Phantasie, ab und zu auch launenhaft; sie verdreht den Männern ein wenig die Köpfe, liebt Gesellschaft, Bälle, Toiletten und noch mehr geistreiche Leute und Literatur. (...) Sie dichtet und schriftstellert, und ihre Versuche sind keineswegs ohne Wert, wenn auch von allzu jugendlichem Sturm und Drang, aber das mag hingehen. Klüger als die Mehrzahl ihrer Landsmänninnen, hat sie, so viel ich weiß, bisher nichts veröffentlicht, aber im Lauf der Zeit wird sie zu literarischem Ansehen kommen (*Ottilie von Goethe*, 128).

Afterword

1 Walker, *Elizabeth*, 171–7.
2 See Maddison, *Elizabeth von Arnim*, 11; Walker, *Elizabeth*, 113.
3 Walker, *Elizabeth*, 194–5, 199, 201–3.
4 Lee, *The Golden Keys and other Essays on the Genius Loci* (London: John Lane: The Bodley Head, 1925), ix.
5 Ibid., 247–8.

Bibliography

Adams, Kimberly VanEsveld. *Our Lady of Victorian Feminism: The Madonna in the Work of Anna Jameson, Margaret Fuller, and George Eliot.* Athens: Ohio University Press, 2001.
Advert, 'An Art-Student in Munich'. *Athenaeum*, 30 April 1853, 518.
'Social Life in Germany'. *Examiner*, 9 February 1840, 96.
Andone, Oana-Helene. 'Gender Issues in Translation'. *Perspectives: Studies in Translatology* 10.2 (2002), 135–50.
Appiah, Kwame Anthony. *Cosmopolitanism: Ethics in a World of Strangers.* New York: W. W. Norton, 2006.
Argyle, Gisela. 'The Horror and the Pleasure of Un-English Fiction: Ida von Hahn-Hahn and Fanny Lewald in England'. *Comparative Literature Studies* 44.1–2 (2007), 144–65.
von Arnim, Elizabeth. *The Adventures of Elizabeth in Rügen.* New York and London, Macmillan, 1904.
— *Elizabeth and Her German Garden.* London: Macmillan, 1898.
— *Fräulein Schmidt and Mr Anstruther.* London: Smith, Elder, 1907.
— *The Princess Priscilla's Fortnight.* London: Smith, Elder, 1905.
Arnold, Armin. *Heine in England and America.* London: Linden Press, 1959.
Arnold, Matthew. *Culture and Anarchy.* Ed. Samuel Lipman. New Haven: Yale University Press, 1994.
— 'The Functions [sic] of Criticism at the Present Time'. *National Review* 1 (November 1864), 230–51.
— 'Heinrich Heine'. *Cornhill Magazine* 8 (August 1863), 233–49.
Advert, S. 'Damen-Stifter'. *Athenaeum*, 8 January 1859, 50.
Ashton, Rosemary. *The German Idea: Four English Writers and the Reception of German Thought 1800–1860.* Cambridge: Cambridge University Press, 1980.
— *G. H. Lewes: A Life.* Oxford: Clarendon Press, 1991.
Austin, Sarah, tr. *Characteristics of Goethe from the German of Falk, von Müller, &c.* 3 vols. London: Effingham Wilson, 1833.
Barry, C. A. 'Joachim Raff's Symphony "Lenore"'. *Monthly Musical Record* 5 (August, September 1875), 109–11, 121–3.
Beaky, Lenore Ann. 'The Letters of Anna Mary Howitt to Barbara Leigh Smith Bodichon'. PhD dissertation, Columbia University, 1974.

Beckman, Linda Hunt. *Amy Levy: Her Life and Letters*. Athens: Ohio University Press, 2000.
Bernstein, Susan. *Roomscape: Women Writers in the British Museum from George Eliot to Virginia Woolf*. Edinburgh: Edinburgh University Press, 2013.
Bickle, Sharon, ed. *The Fowl and the Pussycat: Love Letters of Michael Field, 1876–1909*. Charlottesville: University of Virginia Press, 2008.
Billiani, Francesca, and Stefano Evangelista. 'Carlo Placci and Vernon Lee: The Aesthetics and Ethics of Cosmopolitanism in *Fin-de-Siècle* Florence'. *Comparative Critical Studies* 10.2 (2013), 141–61.
[Birchenough, Mabel C.] 'Recent Verse'. *Athenaeum*, 14 December 1889, 817–18.
Birkwood, Susan. 'True or False: Anna Jameson on the Position of Women in European and in Anishinaubae Society'. *Nineteenth-Century Feminisms* 2 (2000), 32–47.
Bjorklund, Beth. 'Friedrich Gottlieb Klopstock'. *Dictionary of Literary Biography 97: German Writers from the Enlightenment to Sturm und Drang, 1720–1764*. Ed. James N. Hardin and Christoph E. Schweitzer. Detroit: Gale, 1990, 148–59.
Black, Helen C. *Notable Women Authors of the Day*. Glasgow: David Bryce and Son, 1893.
Blain, Virginia H. 'Bradley, Katharine Harris [*pseud*. Michael Field] (1846–1914)'. *Oxford Dictionary of National Biography*. Oxford: Oxford University Press, 2004; 2021. Online edition.
Blamires, David. *Telling Tales: The Impact of Germany on English Children's Books 1780–1918*. Cambridge: Open Book Publishers, 2009.
Blind, Mathilde. *George Eliot*. London: W. H. Allen & Co., 1883.
Bluett, Amy. 'Victorian Women and the Fight for Arts Training'. International Women's Day series. Royal Academy blog, 2 March 2021.
Bluhm, Heinz. 'Die Neue Goetheana in der Newberry Library'. *Ottilie von Goethe: Tagebücher und Briefe von und an Ottilie von Goethe 1839–1841*. Vol. 1. Ed. Heinz Bluhm. Wien: Bergland Verlag, 1962, v–xxiii.
Bohn, Babette. *Women Artists, Their Patrons, and Their Publics in Early Modern Bologna*. Philadelphia: Pennsylvania State University Press, 2021.
[Bradley, Katharine] 'Arran Leigh'. *The New Minnesinger and Other Poems*. London: Longmans, Green and Co., 1875.
Branscombe, Peter, ed., tr. *Heinrich Heine. Selected Verse*. London: Penguin Books, 1968.
Bridgwater, Patrick. *Anglo–German Interactions in the Literature of the 1890s*. European Humanities Research Centre, University of Oxford: Legenda, 1999.
Bryce, James. *The Holy Roman Empire*. Rev. ed. London: Macmillan, 1866.
Buzard, James. *The Beaten Track: European Tourism, Literature, and the Ways to 'Culture' 1800–1918*. Oxford: Clarendon Press, 1993.
Byerly, Alison. *Are We There Yet? Virtual Travel and Victorian Realism*. Ann Arbor: University of Michigan Press, 2013.

Čapek, Karel. *In Praise of Newspapers and Other Essays on the Margin of Literature.* Tr. M. and R. Weatherall. New York: Arts, Inc., 1951.
[Carlyle, Thomas.] 'Varnhagen von Ense's Memoirs'. *London and Westminster Review* 32 (December 1838), 60–84.
Carlyle, Thomas, and Jane Carlyle. *The Collected Letters of Thomas and Jane Welsh Carlyle.* Eds. Charles Richard Sanders et al. 48 vols. Durham: Duke University Press, 1970.
Castle, Terry. *The Apparitional Lesbian: Female Homosexuality and Modern Culture.* New York: Columbia University Press, 1993.
Chamberlain, Lori. 'Gender and the Metaphorics of Translation'. *Signs* 13.3 (1988), 454–72.
Chapple, J. A. V. 'Elizabeth Gaskell's "Six Weeks at Heppenheim": Art and Life'. *Revista di Studi Vittoriani* 2.3 (1997), 5–17.
Chavez, Julia McCord. 'Gaskell's Other Wives and Daughters: Reimagining the Gothic and Anticipating the Sensational in "Lois the Witch" and "The Grey Woman"'. *Gaskell Society Journal* 29 (2015), 59–78.
Clasen, Theo, and Walther Ottendorff-Simrock, eds. *Briefe an Sibylle Mertens-Schaaffhausen.* Bonn: Ludwig Röhrscheid Verlag, 1974.
Codell, Julie F. *The Victorian Artist: Artists' Lifewritings in Britain, ca. 1870–1910.* Cambridge: Cambridge University Press, 2003.
Cohen, William A. *Embodied: Victorian Literature and the Senses.* Minneapolis: University of Minnesota Press, 2008.
Colby, Vineta. *Vernon Lee: A Literary Biography.* Charlottesville: University of Virginia Press, 2003.
Correa, Delia de Sousa. *George Eliot, Music and Victorian Culture.* Houndmills: Palgrave Macmillan, 2003.
Dasgupta, Sudeep, and Mireille Rosello. 'Introduction: Queer and Europe: An Encounter'. *What's Queer about Europe?: Productive Encounters and Re-Enchanting Paradigms.* Ed. M. Rosello and S. Dasgupta. New York: Fordham University Press, 2014, 1–23.
Davis, John R. *The Victorians and Germany.* Oxford: Peter Lang, 2007.
De Charms, Leslie [Liebet von Armin]. *Elizabeth of the German Garden: A Biography.* London: Heinemann, 1958.
Des Voeux, Charles, tr. *Torquato Tasso: A Dramatic Poem from the German of Goethe: With Other German Poetry.* London: Longman, Rees, Orme, Brown, and Green, 1827.
Diethe, Carol. *Towards Emancipation: German Women Writers of the Nineteenth Century.* New York: Berghahn Books, 1998.
Dillane, Fionnuala. *Before George Eliot: Marian Evans and the Periodical Press.* Cambridge: Cambridge University Press, 2013.
Di Maio, Irene Stocksieker. 'Fanny Lewald'. *Dictionary of Literary Biography 129: Nineteenth-Century German Writers, 1841–1900.* Ed. James Hardin. Detroit: Gale, 1993, 202–13.
Donoghue, Emma. *We Are Michael Field.* Bath: Absolute Press, 1998.

Dowson, Ernest. *The Poems of Ernest Dowson*. London: John Lane, The Bodley Head, 1905.
Drury, Annemarie. *Translation as Transformation in Victorian Poetry*. Cambridge: Cambridge University Press, 2015.
Ehnenn, Jill. '"Drag(ging) at memory's fetter': Michael Field's Personal Elegies, Victorian Mourning, and the Problem of Whym Chow', *The Michaelian* 1 (June 2009), online.
Eliot, George. *Daniel Deronda*. 1976. Rpt. Oxford: Oxford University Press, 1984.
Essays and Leaves from a Note-book. Edinburgh: W. Blackwood and Sons, 1884.
Essays of George Eliot. Ed. Thomas Pinney. New York: Columbia University Press, 1963.
The George Eliot Letters. 9 vols. Ed. Gordon S. Haight. New Haven: Yale University Press, 1954–1978.
The Journals of George Eliot. Ed. Margaret Harris and Judith Johnston. Cambridge: Cambridge University Press, 1998.
Erskine, Mrs Steuart [Beatrice]. *Anna Jameson: Letters and Friendships (1812–1860)*. London: T. Fisher Unwin, 1915.
Evangelista, Stefano. *British Aestheticism and Ancient Greece: Hellenism, Reception, Gods in Exile*. Houndmills: Palgrave Macmillan, 2009.
'"Life in the Whole": Goethe and English Aestheticism'. *Publications of the English Goethe Society* 82.3 (2013), 180–92.
[Evans, Marian.] 'Belles Lettres'. *Westminster Review* 64 (July 1855), 288–307.
Evans, Marian. 'German Wit: Heinrich Heine'. *Westminster Review* 65 (January 1856), 1–33.
'Heine's Poems'. *Leader*, 1 September 1855, 843–4.
'Liszt, Wagner, and Weimar'. *Fraser's Magazine* 52 (July 1855), 48–62.
'Memoirs of the Court of Austria'. *Westminster Review* 63 (April 1855), 303–35.
'Recollections of Heine'. *Leader*, 30 August 1856, 811–12.
Rev. of *Life and Works of Goethe*, by G. H. Lewes. *Leader*, 3 November 1855, 1,058–61.
'Three Months in Weimar'. *Fraser's Magazine* 51 (June 1855), 699–706.
tr. *The Essence of Christianity*, by Ludwig Feuerbach. London: John Chapman,1854.
tr. *The Life of Jesus Critically Examined*, by David Friedrich Strauss. 3 vols. London: Chapman, Brothers, 1846.
Field, Michael. *Sight and Song*. London: Elkin Mathews & John Lane, 1892.
Stephania: A Trialogue. London: Elkin Mathews & John Lane, 1892.
Underneath the Bough. London: George Bell & Sons, 1893.
Wild Honey from Various Thyme. London: T. Fisher Unwin, 1908.
Works and Days. British Library, BL Additional MS 46777.
Flint, Kate. *The Transatlantic Indian, 1776–1930*. Princeton: Princeton University Press, 2009.

von Flotow, Luise. *Translation and Gender: Translating in the 'Era of Feminism'*. Manchester and Ottawa: St. Jerome Publishing and University of Ottawa Press, 1997.
Fothergill, Jessie. *The First Violin: A Novel*. 3 vols. London: Richard Bentley and Son, 1878.
—— *The First Violin*. Excerpt, in *The International Library of Famous Literature: Selections from the World's Great Writers, Ancient, Mediaeval, and Modern*, vol. 20. Comp. by Nathan Haskell Dole, et al., introductory notes by Donald G. Mitchell [Ik Marvel] and Andrew Lang. New York: Merrill and Baker, 1898, 9,739–52.
—— 'Girls and the Sense of Responsibility'. *Women's Suffrage Journal* 13 (February 1882), 13–4.
—— *The Wellfields*. 3 vols. London: Richard Bentley and Son, 1880; rpt. 3rd popular edition, 1881; rpt. London: British Library Historical Print Editions, n.d.
Fraser, Hilary. *Women Writing Art History in the Nineteenth Century: Looking Like a Woman*. Cambridge: Cambridge University Press, 2014.
Freiwald, Bina. 'Femininely Speaking: Anna Jameson's *Winter Studies and Summer Rambles in Canada*'. *A Mazing Space: Writing Canadian Women Writing*. Ed. Shirley Neuman and Smaro Kamboureli. Edmonton: Longspoon & NeWest Presses, 1987, 61–73.
Friedman, Dustin. *Before Queer Theory: Victorian Aestheticism and the Self*. Baltimore: Johns Hopkins University Press, 2019.
Gagel, Amanda, ed. *Selected Letters of Vernon Lee 1856–1935*. Vol. 1: 1865–1884. London: Routledge, 2017.
Gagel, Mandy. 'Selected Letters of Vernon Lee (1856–1935)'. Ph.D. dissertation, Boston University, 2008.
Gaskell, Elizabeth. 'The Grey Woman'. *All the Year Round*, 5–19 January 1861, 300–6, 321–8, 347–55.
—— *The Letters of Mrs Gaskell*. Ed. J. A. V. Chapple and Arthur Pollard. 1966. Rpt. Manchester: Mandolin/Manchester University Press, 1997.
—— 'Six Weeks at Heppenheim'. *Cornhill Magazine* 5 (May 1862), 560–87.
'Germany'. *Illustrated Review*, 29 May 1873, 581–2.
Gerry, Thomas M. F. '"I am Translated": Anna Jameson's Sketches and *Winter Studies and Summer Rambles in Canada*'. *Journal of Canadian Studies* 25.4 (1990–1), 34–49.
Giffney, Noreen. 'Introduction: The "q" Word'. *The Ashgate Research Companion to Queer Theory*. Ed. Noreen Giffney and Michael O'Rourke. Farnham: Ashgate, 2009, 1–17.
Goethe, Johann von Wolfgang. *Goethes Sämtliche Werke. Erster Band: Gedichte Erster Teil*. Stuttgart: Verlag der I. G. Cotta'schen Buchhandlung, 1893.
Goethe, Ottilie von. 'Für Anna — Über Rahel, Bettine und Charlotte'. *Letters from Anna Jameson to Ottilie von Goethe*. Ed. G. H. Needler, Oxford: Oxford University Press, 1939, 235–6.

ed. and tr. *Torquato Tasso: A Dramatic Poem from the German of Goethe: With Other German Poetry*, tr. Charles Des Voeux. 2nd ed. Weimar: privately printed, 1833.

Gomes, Mercio P. 'Every man is an island, every culture is a continent, and the historical process is hyperdialectical'. *The Art of Cultural Exchange: Translation and Transformation between the UK and Brazil (2012–2016)*. Ed. Paul Heritage and Ilana Strozenberg. Wilmington: Vernon Press, 2019, 46–61.

Goody, Alex. 'Passing in the City: The Liminal Spaces of Amy Levy's Late Work'. *Amy Levy: Critical Essays*. Ed. Naomi Hetherington and Nadia Valman. Athens: Ohio University Press, 2010, 157–79.

Goslee, David. 'Character and Structure in Tennyson's *The Princess*'. *SEL: Studies in English Literature* 14.4 (Autumn 1974), 563–73.

Green, Laura M. 'Bildungsroman'. *The Encyclopedia of Victorian Literature*. 4 vols. Ed. Dino Felluga; assoc. ed. Pamela Gilbert and Linda K. Hughes. Chichester: Wiley Blackwell, 2015, 126–32.

Griffin, Cristina Richieri. 'George Eliot's Feuerbach: Senses, Sympathy, Omniscience, and Secularism'. *ELH* 84.2 (2017), 475–502.

Guilloton, Doris Starr. 'Rahel Varnhagen von Ense'. *Dictionary of Literary Biography 90: German Writers in the Age of Goethe, 1789–1832*. Ed. James Hardin and Christoph E. Schweitzer. Detroit: Gale, 1989, 340–4.

Gunn, Peter. *Vernon Lee*. London: Oxford University Press, 1964.

Hageneder, Fred. *The Meaning of Trees: Botany – History – Healing – Lore*. London: Chronicle Books, 2005.

Haight, Gordon S. *George Eliot: A Biography*. Oxford: Oxford University Press, 1968.

Hamburger, Joseph. 'Austin, Sarah (1793–1867)'. *Oxford Dictionary of National Biography*. Oxford University Press, 2004; 2008. Online edition.

Hanks, Patrick, Kate Hardcastle, and Flavia Hodges. *A Dictionary of First Names*. 2nd ed. Oxford: Oxford University Press, 2006.

Harris, Margaret, and Judith Johnston, eds. *The Journals of George Eliot*. Cambridge: Cambridge University Press, 1998.

Hayward, A[braham], tr. *Faust: A Dramatic Poem, by Goethe*. 2nd ed. London: Edward Moxon, 1834.

[Hayward, Abraham.] 'Recent German Belles-Lettres'. *Quarterly Review* 53 (February 1835), 215–29.

Hein, Karsten. *Ottilie von Goethe (1796–1872): Biographie und literarische Beziehungen der Schwiegertochter Goethes*. Frankfurt am Main: Peter Lang, 2001.

'Heine, His Works and Times'. *Tait's Edinburgh Magazine* 18 (October–November 1851), 618–22, 679–83.

Heine, Heinrich. *Buch der Lieder*. Heidelberg: Verlag Lambert Schneider, 1956.

'The Romantic School'. *The Complete Works of Heinrich Heine, Volume 5*. Tr. Charles Leland. London: William Heinemann, 1892.

Helmetag, Charles H. 'Paul Heyse'. *Dictionary of Literary Biography 330: Nobel Prize Laureates in Literature, Part 2: Kipling–Faulkner*. Detroit: Gale, 2007, 351–67.

Henry, Nancy. *The Life of George Eliot: A Critical Biography*. Malden: Wiley-Blackwell, 2012.
Hertz, Deborah. *How Jews Became Germans: The History of Conversion and Assimilation in Berlin*. New Haven: Yale University Press, 2007.
Jewish High Society in Old Regime Berlin. New Haven: Yale University Press, 1988.
Heyse, Paul. *Children of the World: A Novel. Translated from the German of Paul Heyse*. 3 vols. London: Chapman & Hall, 1882.
Kinder der Welt: Roman in sechs Büchern. 3 vols. Berlin: Verlag von Wilhelm Hertz, 1873.
'The Lonely Ones. From the German of Paul Heyse'. *Lippincott's Magazine* 4 (October 1869): 389–403.
Hoecker-Drysdale, Susan. *Harriet Martineau: First Woman Sociologist*. Oxford: Berg, 1992.
Hoeckley, Cheri L. Larsen. 'Reframing Difference in George Eliot's Early *Fraser's Magazine* Articles after Kimberlé Crenshaw's Intersectionality'. *Encountering Difference: New Perspectives on Genre, Travel and Gender*. Ed. Gigi Adair and Lenka Filipova. Wilmington: Vernon Press, 2020, 93–107.
Hoffmann, E. T. A. *The Golden Pot and Other Tales*. Tr. Ritchie Robertson. Oxford: Oxford University Press, 1992.
Horsley, Joey [Ritta Jo]. Rev. of Geschichte einer Liebe, by Angele Steidele. *Fembio* website for biographical research on women, July 2010.
Howitt, Anna Mary. *An Art-Student in Munich*. 2 vols. London: Longman, Brown, Green, and Longmans, 1853.
'Bits of Life in Munich: The Holy Week'. *Household Words*, 7 June 1851, 261–4.
'Consecration of the Basilica'. *Athenaeum*, 5 December 1850, 1,285–6.
'The Miracle-Play in the Ammergau. In Two Letters'. *Ladies Companion*, 17 August, 24 August 1850, 113–15, 129–31.
Sisters in Art. The Illustrated Exhibitor and Magazine of Art 2 (July–December 1852): 214–26, 238–40, 262–3, 286–8, 317–19, 334–6, 347–9, 362–4.
[—, tr.]. *The Betrothed Lovers: A Milanese Story of the Seventeenth Century*. 3 vols. London: Longman, Brown, Green, and Longmans, 1845.
Howitt, Mary. *An Autobiography*. Ed. Margaret Howitt. 2 vols. London: William Isbister, 1889.
Ballads and Other Poems. London: Longman, Brown, Green, and Longmans, 1847.
'Boaz and Ruth. / A Harvest Scene'. *Fisher's Drawing-Room Scrapbook*. London: Fisher, Son, & Co., 1842, 58–60.
Child's Picture and Verse Book: Commonly Called Otto Speckter's Fables. With the Original German and With French. Translated into English. London: Longman, Brown, Green, and Longmans, 1844.
'Heidelberg, on the Neckar'. *Fisher's Drawing-Room Scrapbook*. London: Fisher, Son, & Co., 1842, 33–4.

'The Lover. From the German of Heinrich Voss'. *Howitt's Journal* 1 (1847), 100.
Popular Tales for Household Reading. New York: Derby & Jackson, 1857.
'Preface'. *Fisher's Drawing-Room Scrapbook*. London: Fisher, Son, & Co., 1842, ii.
'Reminiscences of My Later Life. Second Paper'. *Good Words* 27 (1886), 172–9.
Sketches of Natural History. London: Effingham Wilson, 1834.
'Some Reminiscences of My Life. Chapter V'. *Good Words* 26 (December 1885), 660–7.
Which Is the Wiser: Or, People Abroad. A Tale for Youth. 2nd ed. London: Thomas Tegg, 1842.
'The Youth's Death'. *Bentley's Miscellany* 12 (July 1842), 462.

Howitt, William. *German Experiences: Addressed to the English; Both Stayers at Home, and Goers Abroad*. London: Longman, Brown, Green, and Longmans, 1844.
'The Month in Prospect—January'. *Howitt's Journal* 1 (1847), 9–10.
The Rural and Domestic Life of Germany: With Characteristic Sketches of its Cities and Scenery, Collected in a General Tour, and during a Residence in the Country in the Years 1840, 41 and 42. London: Longman, Brown, Green, and Longmans, 1842.
The Student-Life of Germany. London: Longman, Brown, Green, and Longmans, 1841.

Howitt, William, and Mary Howitt. *Stories of English and Foreign Life*. London: Henry G. Bohn, 1853.

Hughes, Linda K. '"Given in Outline and No More": The Shared Life Writing of Anna Jameson and Ottilie von Goethe'. Special issue, Co-Constructions of Self: Nineteenth-Century Collaborative Life-Writing, ed. Lynn M. Linder. *Forum for Modern Language Studies* 52.2 (2016), 160–71.
'Mary Howitt and the Business of Poetry'. *Victorian Periodicals Review* 50.2 (Summer 2017), 273–94.
'Michael Field: Sight and Song and Significant Form'. *The Oxford Handbook of Victorian Poetry*. Ed. Matthew Bevis. Oxford: Oxford University Press, 2013, 563–78.
'*The Princess* and the Generosity of Tennyson's Imagination'. *Tennyson Research Bulletin*, 11.2 (2018), 110–28.
'Reading Poet Amy Levy through Victorian Newspapers'. *Women, Periodicals and Print Culture in Britain, 1830s–1900s: The Victorian Period*. Ed. Alexis Easley, Clare Gill, and Beth Rodgers. Edinburgh: Edinburgh University Press, 2019, 456–69.
'Trace Collaboration and the Problem of Evidence: Anna Jameson and Ottilie von Goethe'. *Studies in Victorian and Modern Literature: A Tribute to John Sutherland*. Ed. William Baker. Madison: Fairleigh Dickinson University Press, 2015, 39–49.

'von Arnim, Elizabeth, the German Novels of'. *The Palgrave Encyclopedia of Victorian Women's Writing*. Ed. Lesa Scholl. Cham: Palgrave Macmillan, 2020.

Hughes, Linda K. ed. *The Works of Elizabeth Gaskell, Volume 4. Novellas and Shorter Fiction: Cousin Phillis and other Tales from* All the Year Round *and the* Cornhill Magazine *1859–64*. London: Pickering & Chatto, 2006.

James, Henry. *Partial Portraits*. 1888. Rpt. London: Macmillan, 1894.

J[ameson]., A[nna]. 'The Damen-Stifter in Germany'. *Athenaeum*, 1 January 1859, 18–19.

Jameson, Anna Brownell. *Characteristics of Women, Moral, Poetical, and Historical*. 2 vols. London: Saunders and Otley, 1832.

The Communion of Labour: A Second Lecture on the Social Employments of Women. London: Longman, Brown, Green, Longmans, & Roberts, 1856.

Diary of an Ennuyée. London: Henry Colburn, 1826.

Legends of the Madonna, as Represented in the Fine Arts. London: Longman, Brown, Green, and Longmans, 1852.

Sisters of Charity Catholic and Protestant, Abroad and at Home. London: Longman, Brown, Green, and Longmans, 1855.

Social Life in Germany. 2 vols. London: Saunders and Otley, 1840.

Visits and Sketches at Home and Abroad. 4 vols. London: Saunders and Otley, 1834.

Winter Studies and Summer Rambles in Canada. 3 vols. London: Saunders and Otley, 1838.

Japp, Alexander H. *Dramatic Pictures: English Rispetti Sonnets and Other Verses*. London: Chatto & Windus, 1894.

Jauss, Hans Robert. *Toward an Aesthetic of Reception*. Tr. Timothy Bahti. Minneapolis: University of Minnesota, 1982.

Johns, Alessa. 'Anna Jameson in Germany: "A. W." and Women's Translation'. *Translation and Literature* 19 (2010): 190–5.

Bluestocking Feminism and British-German Cultural Transfer, 1750–1837. Ann Arbor: University of Michigan Press, 2014.

Johnston, Judith. *Anna Jameson: Victorian, Feminist, Woman of Letters*. Aldershot: Ashgate, 1997.

Victorian Women and the Economies of Travel, Translation and Culture, 1830–1870. Farnham: Ashgate, 2013.

'The "Judenhetze" in Germany'. 'Notes of the Week'. *Jewish Chronicle*, 27 February 1880, 4.

Kandola, Sondeep. *Vernon Lee*. Tavistock: Northcote House, 2010.

Kant, Immanuel. 'Toward Perpetual Peace: A Philosophical Sketch'. *Toward Perpetual Peace and Other Writings on Politics, Peace, and History*. Ed. Pauline Kleingeld; tr. David L. Colclasure et al. New Haven: Yale University Press, 2006. 67–109.

Kanwit, John Paul M. *Victorian Art Criticism and the Woman Writer*. Columbus: Ohio State University Press, 2013.

Kaufmann, Sylke. *Henriette von Pogwisch und ihre Französische Lesegesellschaft*. Marburg: Tectum Verlag, 1994.
Keirstead, Christopher. *Victorian Poetry, Europe, and the Challenge of Cosmopolitanism*. Columbus: Ohio State University Press, 2011.
Kleingeld, Pauline. 'Six Varieties of Cosmopolitanism in Late Eighteenth-Century Germany'. *Journal of the History of Ideas* 60.3 (1999), 505–24.
von Koppenfels, Amanda Klekowski. *Migrants or Expatriates? Americans in Europe*. Basingstoke: Palgrave Macmillan, 2014.
Kuehn, Julia. 'Realism's Connections: George Eliot's and Fanny Lewald's Poetics'. *George Eliot–George Henry Lewes Studies* 68.2 (2016), 91–115.
Lamport, F. J. *German Classical Drama: Theatre, Humanity and Nation, 1750–1870*. Cambridge: Cambridge University Press, 1990.
Latour, Bruno. *Reassembling the Social: An Introduction to Actor-Network-Theory*. Oxford: Oxford University Press, 2005.
Lee, Amice. *Laurels and Rosemary: The Life of William and Mary Howitt*. London: Geoffrey Cumberlege, Oxford University Press, 1955.
Lee, Vernon. *Belcaro: Being Essays on Sundry Æsthetical Questions*. London: W. Satchell & Co., [1881].
— 'Contemporary Italian Poets'. *Quarterly Review* 144 (October 1877), 446–74.
— 'Faustus and Helena'. *Cornhill Magazine* 42 (August 1880), 212–28.
— *Genius Loci: Notes on Places*. London: Grant Richards, 1899.
— *The Golden Keys and Other Essays on the Genius Loci*. London: John Lane: The Bodley Head, 1925.
— *Hauntings and Other Fantastic Tales*. Ed. Catherine Maxwell and Patricia Pulham. Peterborough: Broadview Press, 2006.
— *Hortus Vitae: Essays on the Gardening of Life*. 2nd ed. London: John Lane The Bodley Head, 1904.
— *Laurus Nobilis: Chapters on Art and Life*. London: John Lane The Bodley Head, 1909.
— *Ottilie: An Eighteenth Century Idyl*. London: T. Fisher Unwin, 1883.
— 'Prince Alberic and the Snake Lady'. *The Yellow Book* 10 (July 1896), 289–344.
— *The Sentimental Traveller: Notes on Places*. London: John Lane The Bodley Head, 1908.
— *The Tower of the Mirrors*. London: John Lane The Bodley Head, 1914.
[—, with Eugene Lee-Hamilton]. *Tuscan Fairy Tales, Taken Down from the Mouths of the People*. London: W. Satchell, [1880].
Leighton, Perley M. '"TO MY FRIEND, KARL HILLEBRAND": The Dedication in *Ottilie* and Its Aftermath'. *Colby Library Quarterly* ser. 3.12 (November 1953), 185–9.
Levenson, Alan T. 'Writing the Philosemitic Novel: *Daniel Deronda* Revisited'. *Prooftexts* 28.2 (2008), 129–56.
Levine, Naomi. 'Tirra-Lirrical Ballads: Source Hunting with the Lady of Shalott'. *Victorian Poetry* 54.4 (Winter 2016): 439–54.
Levy, Amy. 'Easter-Tide at Tunbridge Wells'. *London Society* 47 (May 1885), 481–3.

'From Grillparzer's Sappho'. *Cambridge Review*, 1 February 1882, 141.
'From Heine'. *Cambridge Review*, 26 April 1882, 270.
'Imitation of Heine'. *Cambridge Review*, 7 December 1881, 127.
'In Holiday Humour'. *London Society* 46 (August 1884), 177–84.
'In Retreat: A Long Vacation Experience'. *London Society* 46 (September 1884), 332–5.
'In Switzerland'. *London Society* 46 (July 1884), 120.
'In the Black Forest'. *London Society* 46 (October 1884), 392–4.
'Jewish Humour'. *Jewish Chronicle*, 20 August 1886, 9–10. Rpt. Melvyn New, ed. *The Complete Novels and Selected Writings of Amy Levy 1861–1889*. Gainesville: University Press of Florida, 1993, 521–24.
'Lohengrin'. *Academy*, 20 March 1886, 201.
A London Plane-Tree and Other Verse. London: T. Fisher Unwin, 1889.
A Minor Poet and Other Verse. London: T. Fisher Unwin, 1884.
A Minor Poet and Other Verse. 2nd. ed. London: T. Fisher Unwin, 1891.
'Out of the World'. *London Society* 49 (January 1886), 53–6.
Reuben Sachs: A Sketch. Ed. Susan David Bernstein. Peterborough: Broadview Press, 2006.
'The Shepherd (From Goethe)'. *Cambridge Review*, 9 June 1880, 158.
'To E.' *London Society* 49 (May 1886), 447.
Lewes, Charles Lee. 'Preface'. *Essays and Leaves from a Notebook* by George Eliot. Ed. Charles Lee Lewes. Edinburgh: William Blackwood and Sons, 1884, v–vi.
Lewes, George Henry. *The Letters of George Henry Lewes*. 3 vols. Ed. William Baker. Victoria, B.C.: University of Victoria, English Literary Studies, 1, 995–9.
The Life and Works of Goethe. 2 vols. London: David Nutt, 1855.
Losano, Antonia. *The Woman Painter in Victorian Literature*. Columbus: Ohio State University Press, 2008.
Macpherson, Gerardine. *Memoirs of the Life of Anna Jameson*. Boston: Roberts Brothers, 1878.
Maddison, Isobel. *Elizabeth von Arnim: Beyond the German Garden*. Farnham: Ashgate, 2013.
Maddux, William W., and Adam D. Galinsky. 'Cultural Borders and Mental Barriers: The Relationship between Living Abroad and Creativity'. *Journal of Personality and Social Psychology* 96.5 (May 2009), 1,047–62.
Maidment, Brian. 'Magazines of Popular Progress and the Artisans'. *Victorian Periodicals Review* 17 (Fall 1984), 82–94.
Mancoff, Debra N. *The Arthurian Revival in Victorian Art*. New York: Garland, 1990.
Martin, Meredith. *The Rise and Fall of Meter: Poetry and English National Culture, 1860–1930*. Princeton: Princeton University Press, 2012.
Maxwell, Catherine. *Second Sight: The Visionary Imagination in Late Victorian Literature*. Manchester: Manchester University Press, 2008.
McCormack, Kathleen. *George Eliot in Society: Travels Abroad and Sundays at the Priory*. Columbus: Ohio State University Press, 2013.

McDonald, Lynn, ed. *Florence Nightingale's European Travels. Collected Works of Florence Nightingale*. Vol. 7. Waterloo: Wilfrid Laurier University Press, 2004.

McPherson, Susan. 'Companionship and Collaboration: Marian Evans, George Henry Lewes, and *The Life and Works of Goethe*'. *The Victorian* 1.2 (November 2013), online.

Moore, T. Sturge, and D. C. Sturge Moore, eds. *Works and Days*. London: John Murray, 1933.

Moore, Thomas. *Letters and Journals of Lord Byron: With Notices of His Life*. 3 vols. 3rd ed. London: John Murray, 1833.

Murray, Alex. '"Profane Travelers": Michael Field, Cornwall, and Modern Tourism'. *Michael Field: Decadent Moderns*. Ed. Sarah Parker and Ana Parejo Vadillo. Athens: Ohio University Press, 2019, 167–87.

'National Manchester Society of Woman's Suffrage'. *Women's Suffrage Journal* 13 (February 1882), 31.

Needler, G. H., ed. *Letters from Anna Jameson to Ottilie von Goethe*. Oxford: Oxford University Press, 1939.

Newman, Sally. 'The Archival Traces of Desire: Vernon Lee's Failed Sexuality and the Interpretation of Letters in Lesbian History'. *Journal of the History of Sexuality* 14.1–2 (January–April 2005), 51–75.

Nightingale, Florence. *Florence Nightingale's European Travels: Collected Works of Florence Nightingale*, vol. 7. Ed. Lynn McDonald. Waterloo: Wilfrid Laurier University Press, 2004.

North, Marianne. *Recollections of a Happy Life, Being the Autobiography of Marianne North*. 2 vols. Ed. Mrs. John Addington Symonds. New York and London: Macmillan and Co., 1894.

'Notes from Germany'. *Jewish Chronicle*, 9 January 1880, 11.

'Notes from Germany'. *Jewish Chronicle*, 21 May 1880, 10.

'Notes from Germany'. *Jewish Chronicle*, 28 May 1880, 11.

'Notes of the Week'. *Jewish Chronicle*, 3 February 1882, 4.

Olverson, T. C. '"Such Are Not Woman's Thoughts": Amy Levy's "Xantippe" and "Medea"'. *Amy Levy: Critical Essays*. Ed. Naomi Hetherington and Nadia Valman. Athens: Ohio University Press, 2010, 110–34.

Oxenford, John, tr. *Conversations of Goethe with Eckermann and Soret*. 2 vols. London: Smith, Elder, 1850.

Palmer, Beth. '*London Society* (1862–1898)'. *Dictionary of Nineteenth-Century Journalism in Great Britain and Ireland*. Ed. Laurel Brake and Marysa Demoor. Ghent and London: Academia Press and The British Library, 2009, 376–7.

Palmer, Caroline. '"A Fountain of the Richest Poetry": Anna Jameson, Elizabeth Eastlake and the Rediscovery of Early Christian Art'. *Visual Resources* 33.1–2 (2017), 48–73.

Parker, Fred. '"Much in the mode of Goethe's Mephistopheles": *Faust* and Byron'. *International Faust Studies: Adaptation, Reception, Translation*. Ed. Lorna Fitzsimmons. London: Continuum, 2008, 107–23.

Pater, Walter. *Studies in the History of the Renaissance*. London: Macmillan, 1873.
Paulin, Roger. 'Some Remarks on the Occasion of the New Edition of the Works of Wilhelm Müller'. *Modern Language Review* 92.2 (April 1997), 363–78.
Peak, Anna. 'Music and New Woman Aesthetics in Mona Caird's *The Daughters of Danaus*'. *Victorian Review* 40.1 (2014), 135–54.
Peterson, Linda H. *Becoming a Woman of Letters: Myths of Authorship and Facts of the Victorian Market*. Princeton: Princeton University Press, 2009.
Pettitt, Clare. *Serial Forms: The Unfinished Project of Modernity, 1815–1848*. Oxford: Oxford University Press, 2020.
Phipps, Edmund. *The Fergusons; or, Woman's Love and the World's Favour*, 1839. Rpt. Memphis: General Books, 2012.
Pointner, Frank Eirk, and Achim Geisenhanslüke. 'The Reception of Byron in the German-Speaking Lands'. *The Reception of Byron in Europe*. Ed. Richard A. Cardwell. 2 vols. London: Continuum, 2004, 2:235–68.
Pratt, Mary Louise. *Imperial Eyes: Travel Writing and Transculturation*. 2nd ed. New York: Routledge, 2008.
Prins, Yopie. 'Victorian Meters'. *The Cambridge Companion to Victorian Poetry*. Ed. Joseph Bristow. Cambridge: Cambridge University Press, 2000, 89–113.
Prior, Matthew. *The Poetical Works of Matthew Prior: With Memoir and Critical Dissertation* by Rev. George Gilfillan. Edinburgh: James Nichol, 1858.
Pullen, Christine. *The Woman Who Did: A Biography of Amy Levy*. Kingston upon Thames: Kingston University Press, 2010.
Rahmeyer, Ruth. *Ottilie von Goethe: Eine Biographie*. Frankfurt am Main und Leipzig: Insel Verlag, 2002.
Raterman, Jennifer. 'Translation and the Transfer of Impressions in George Eliot'. *Nineteenth-Century Literature* 68.1 (2013), 33–63.
'Recent German Lyrical Poetry'. *Edinburgh Review* 56 (October 1832), 37–51.
Redden, Elizabeth. 'Sexual Assault and Study Abroad'. *Inside Higher Ed*, 19 December 2012, online.
Reibel, David A. 'Hidden Parallels in George Eliot's *Daniel Deronda*: Julius Klesmer, Richard Wagner, Franz Liszt'. *George Eliot–George Henry Lewes Studies* 64/65 (October 2013), 16–52.
von Remoortel, Marianne. 'Women Editors' Transnational Networks in the *Englishwoman's Domestic Journal* and *Myra's Journal*'. *Women, Periodicals, and Print Culture in Britain, 1830s–1900s: The Victorian Period*. Ed. Alexis Easley, Clare Gill, and Beth Rodgers. Edinburgh University Press, 2019, 46–56.
Rev. of *Characteristics of Women* and *Visits and Sketches*. *Edinburgh Review* 60 (October 1834), 180–201.
Rev. of *The Child's Picture and Verse Book*. *Tait's Edinburgh Magazine* 11 (February 1844), 136.
Rev. of *The First Violin*. *New York Times*, 17 November 1878, 10.
Rev. of *The New Minnesinger*, *Academy*, 3 July 1875, 9.
Rev. of *Stories of English and German Life*. *Athenaeum*, 19 March 1853, 351.

Rev. of *Which Is the Wiser*, *Athenaeum*, 22 January 1842, 87.
Rev. of *Xantippe and Other Verse*. *Cambridge Review*, 8 June 1881, 382–3.
Rignall, John. *George Eliot, European Novelist*. Farnham: Ashgate, 2011.
Robertson, Lisa C. 'Time and Memory in Amy Levy's Collegiate Writing: "My Present Mind"'. *ELT: English Literature in Transition* 61.2 (2018), 211–31.
Röder-Bolton, Gerlinde. *George Eliot in Germany, 1854–55*. Aldershot: Ashgate, 2006.
Römhild, Juliane. *Femininity and Authorship in the Novels of Elizabeth von Arnim*. Madison: Fairleigh Dickinson University Press, 2014.
Rose, William. Introduction. *Heine in England and America*, by Arnim Arnold. London: Linden Press, 1959, 7–9.
Rutherford, Andrew, ed. *Lord Byron: The Critical Heritage*. 1970. Rpt. London: Routledge, 2010.
Saad, Carmel S. et al. 'Multiculturalism and Creativity: Effects of Cultural Context, Bicultural Identity, and Ideational Fluency'. *Social Psychological and Personality Science* 4.3 (2013), 369–75.
Said, Edward W. *Reflections on Exile and Other Essays*. Cambridge: Harvard University Press, 2000.
Representations of the Intellectual: The 1993 Reith Lectures. 1994; rpt. New York: Vintage Books, 1996.
Sammons, Jeffrey. *Heinrich Heine: A Modern Biography*. 1980; rpt. Princeton: Princeton University Press, 2014.
Schaffer, Talia. *The Forgotten Female Aesthetes: Literary Culture in Late-Victorian England*. Charlottesville: University Press of Virginia, 2000.
Schiller, Friedrich. *On the Aesthetic Education of Man, in a Series of Letters*. Tr. Reginald Snell. New Haven: Yale University Press, 1954.
Scholl, Lesa. *Translation, Authorship and the Victorian Professional Woman: Charlotte Brontë, Harriet Martineau and George Eliot*. Farnham: Ashgate, 2011.
Schoolcraft, Henry Rowe. *Personal Memoirs of a Residence of Thirty Years with the Indian Tribes on the American Frontiers*. Philadelphia: Lippincott, Grambo, & Co., 1851.
Schroeder, Janice. 'Speaking Volumes: Victorian Feminism and the Appeal of Public Discussion'. *Nineteenth-Century Contexts* 25.2 (2003), 97–117.
Scott, Robert H. *Elementary Meteorology*. 5th ed. International Science Series 46. London: Kegan Paul, Trench, Trübner & Co., 1890.
Scully, Richard. *British Images of Germany: Admiration, Antagonism & Ambivalence, 1860–1914*. Houndmills: Palgrave Macmillan, 2012.
Shafi, Monika. 'Annette Freiin von Droste-Hülshoff'. *Nineteenth-Century German Writers to 1840*. Ed. James N. Hardin and Siegfried Mews. *Dictionary of Literary Biography 133*. Detroit: Gale, 1993, 49–60.
Shakespeare, William. *Shakespeare: The Complete Works*. Ed. G. B. Harrison. New York: Harcourt, Brace & World, 1952.
Shanahan, Nora. Clara Thomas Obituary. *The Globe and Mail* (Toronto), 28 November 2013, online edition.

Shattock, Joanne. 'Researching Periodical Networks: William and Mary Howitt'. *Researching the Nineteenth-Century Periodical Press: Case Studies*. Ed. Alexis Easley, Andrew King, and John Morton. London: Routledge, 2018, 60–73.
Simon, Peter, ed. *The Norton Anthology of World Literature, Volume 2*. Shorter Second Edition. New York: W. W. Norton, 2009.
Simon, Sherry. *Gender in Translation. Cultural Identity and the Politics of Transmission*. London: Routledge, 1996.
Skrine, Peter. 'Elizabeth Gaskell and Germany'. *Gaskell Society Journal* 7 (1993), 37–49.
'Elizabeth Gaskell and Her German Stories'. *Gaskell Society Journal* 12 (1998), 1–13.
Slatter, John. 'Jaakoff Prelooker and *The Anglo-Russian*'. *Immigrants and Minorities* 2.3 (1983), 48–66.
Sorrels, Katherine. *Cosmopolitan Outsiders: Imperial Inclusion, National Exclusion, and the Pan-European Idea, 1900–1930*. New York: Palgrave Macmillan, 2016.
Stabler, Jane. *The Artistry of Exile: Romantic and Victorian Writers in Italy*. Oxford: Oxford University Press, 2013.
Staël, Germaine de. *Germany; Translated from the French*. 3 vols. London: John Murray, 1813.
Stedman, Edmund Clarence, ed. *A Victorian Anthology 1837–1895*. Boston: Houghton, Mifflin & Company, 1895.
Steidele, Angela. *Geschichte einer Liebe: Adele Schopenhauer und Sibylle Mertens*. Berlin: Insel Verlag, 2011.
Stetz, Margaret. 'The Snake Lady and the Bruised Bodley Head: Vernon Lee and Oscar Wilde in the *Yellow Book*'. *Vernon Lee: Decadence, Ethics, Aesthetics*. Ed. Catherine Maxwell and Patricia Pulham. Basingstoke: Palgrave Macmillan, 2006, 112–22.
Strong, Michelle M. *Education, Travel, and the 'Civilisation' of the Victorian Working Classes*. Houndmills: Palgrave Macmillan, 2014.
Stupp, William. 'The German Experience of William and Mary Howitt'. *Anglo–German and American–German Crosscurrents*. Vol. 4. Ed. Arthur O. Lewis, W. LaMarr Kopp, and Edward J. Danis. Lanham: University Press of America, 1990, 86–110.
Sutherland, Gillian. *In Search of the New Woman: Middle-Class Women and Work in Britain 1870–1914*. Cambridge: Cambridge University Press, 2015.
Tatar, Maria. *Enchanted Hunters: The Power of Stories in Childhood*. New York: W. W. Norton, 2009.
Tennyson, Alfred Lord. *The Poems of Tennyson*. Ed. Christopher Ricks. London: Longmans, 1969.
Tewarson, Heidi Thomann. *Rahel Levin Varnhagen: The Life and Work of a German Jewish Intellectual*. Lincoln: University of Nebraska Press, 1998.
Thain, Marion. *'Michael Field': Poetry, Aestheticism and the Fin de Siècle*. Cambridge: Cambridge University Press, 2007.

Thain, Marion, and Ana Parejo Vadillo, eds. *Michael Field, The Poet: Published and Manuscript Materials*. Peterborough: Broadview Press, 2009.

Thomas, Christa Zeller. '"I Shall Take to Translating": Transformation, Translation and Transgression in Anna Jameson's *Winter Studies and Summer Rambles in Canada*'. *Translators, Interpreters, Mediators: Women Writers 1700–1900*. Ed. Gillian E. Dow. Oxford: Peter Lang, 2007, 175–90.

Thomas, Clara. *Love and Work Enough: The Life of Anna Jameson*. Toronto: University of Toronto Press, 1967.

Thomas, Daniel. 'Bateman, Edward La Trobe (1815–1897)'. *Australian Dictionary of Biography*. Vol. 3, 1969; rpt. online, National Centre of Biography, Australian National University.

Tuite, Clara. *Lord Byron and Scandalous Celebrity*. Cambridge: Cambridge University Press, 2015.

Uglow, Jenny. *Elizabeth Gaskell: A Habit of Stories*. New York: Farrar Straus Giroux, 1993.

Unsworth, Anna. 'Elizabeth Gaskell and German Romanticism'. *Gaskell Society Journal* 8 (1994), 1–14.

Usborne, Karen. *'Elizabeth': The Author of Elizabeth and Her German Garden*. London: The Bodley Head, 1986.

Vertovec, Steven, and Robin Cohen. 'Introduction'. *Conceiving Cosmopolitanism: Theory, Context, and Practice*. Ed. Steven Vertovec and Robin Cohen. Oxford: Oxford University Press, 2002, 1–22.

Veit, Philipp F. 'Fichtenbaum und Palme'. *Germanic Review* 51 (1976), 13–27.

Vicinus, Martha. 'The Adolescent Boy: Fin de Siècle Femme Fatale?' *Journal of the History of Sexuality* 5.1 (July 1994), 90–114.

Independent Women: Work and Community for Single Women, 1850–1920. University of Chicago Press, 1985.

Walker, Jennifer. *Elizabeth of the German Garden: A Literary Journey*. Sussex: Book Guild Publishing, 2013.

Walkowitz, Judith R. 'Cosmopolitanism, Feminism, and the Moving Body'. *Victorian Literature and Culture* 38 (2010), 427–49.

Ward, Margaret E. *Fanny Lewald: Between Rebellion and Renunciation*. New York: Peter Lang, 2006.

[Wedgwood, Julia.] Rev. of *Ottilie*, by Vernon Lee. 'Contemporary Records'. *Contemporary Review* 44 (November 1883), 784–5.

Weliver, Phyllis. 'George Eliot and the Prima Donna's "Script"'. *Yearbook of English Studies* 40.1–2 (2010), 103–20.

Werner, A[lice]. Rev. of *Ottilie*, by Vernon Lee. *Academy*, 30 June 1883, 448–9.

Wettlaufer, Alexandra K. *Portraits of the Artist as a Young Woman: Painting and the Novel in France and Britain, 1800–1860*. Columbus: Ohio State University Press, 2011.

Williams, Thomas J. 'The Beginnings of Anglican Sisterhoods'. *Historical Magazine of the Protestant Episcopal Church* 16.4 (December 1847), 350–72.

Williams, Wendy S. *George Eliot, Poetess*. Farnham: Ashgate, 2014.

Woodring, Carl Ray. *Victorian Samplers: William and Mary Howitt*. Lawrence: University of Kansas Press, 1952.
[Woolf, Virginia]. 'Fräulein Schmidt and Mr Anstruther'. *Times Literary Supplement*, 10 May 1907, 149.
Yeats, W. B. Rev. of *Sight and Song*. *The Bookman* 2 (July 1892), 116–17.
Zipes, Jack. 'The Changing Function of the Fairy Tale'. *The Lion and the Unicorn* 12.2 (December 1988), 7–31.
   Grimm Legacies: The Magic Spell of the Grimms' Folk and Fairy Tales. Princeton: Princeton University Press, 2015.
Zorn, Christa. *Vernon Lee: Aesthetics, History, and the Victorian Female Intellectual*. Athens: Ohio University Press, 2003.

Index

Aachen, 134
Academy, 131
Accademia of Venice, 138
accidental immigrant, 163, See also Elizabeth von Arnim
aestheticism, 134
agnosticism, 87, 106–7, 114, 156
Ainsworth's Magazine, 94
Albert, Prince, 7, 37, 45, See Queen Victoria
All the Year Round, 79
Anstruther-Thomson, Kit, 190, See also Vernon Lee
anti-Semitism, 98, 103, 147, 151
Antwerp, 90
Appiah, Kwame Anthony, 9
Arnim, Bettina von, 5, 163, 179
  Goethe's Correspondence with a Child (Goethes Briefwechsel mit einem Kinde), 5, 179
Arnim, Elizabeth von, 3–4, 162–86, 209
  Adventures of Elizabeth in Rügen, The, 164, 166–74
  Caravaners, The, 210
  Christine, 210
  Elizabeth and Her German Garden, 164–6, 177
  Fräulein Schmidt and Mr. Anstruther Being the Letters of an Independent Woman, 178–86
  Princess Priscilla's Fortnight, The, 164, 174–8
Arnim-Schlagenthin, Count Henning von, 5, 162, See also Elizabeth von Arnim
Arnold, Matthew, 100, 105
  Culture and Anarchy, 105
Assing, Ludmilla, 96, 103
Athenaeum, 32, 46, 53, 55, 70–1, See also Anna Jameson
Austen, Jane, 115
Austin, Sarah, 23
  Characteristics of Goethe, 34

Bach, Johann Sebastian
  St. Matthew's Passion ('Matthäus Passion'), 118

Baden, 149
baptism, 102
Bavaria, 24, 67, 70–1, 73, 96, 135
Bayreuth, 140
Beauchamp, Mary, 162–3, See Elizabeth von Arnim
Benham, Jane, 71, 88
Berlin, 6–7, 26, 29, 33, 41, 62, 87, 89, 91–2, 94–8, 102–3, 114–15, 140, 162, 209
bicultural identity, 163, 167, 170, 188–9
Bildungsroman, 180
Black Forest, 145, 147
Black, Clementina, 156
Blackwood's Edinburgh Magazine, 55
Blind, Mathilde, 109, 112
Blitzkrieg, 211
boarding house, 107, 119, 124, 133, 148
Bodichon, Barbara, 51, 70, 72, 90, 94
Bonn, 15, 17–18, 20–2, 24–5, 29
Bradley, Katharine, 3, 129–30, 133–4, 136, 140–1, 143, 152, 209, See also Michael Field
  'New Minnesinger, The', 131
  New Minnesinger and Other Poems, The, 4, 130–3
  'Youth Time', 131
Braun, Emil, 21
Bray, Charles, 90
Brontë, Charlotte
  Jane Eyre, 179
Browning, Elizabeth Barrett
  Aurora Leigh, 180
Browning, Robert, 4, 75
  Christmas-Eve and Easter-Day, 75
Byron, Lord George Gordon, 16, 132

Cambridge Review, 145, 151–4
Canada, 28
canoe, 43
Carlyle, Jane, 97

Carlyle, Thomas, 41, 58, 89, 132
  'Varnhagen Von Ense's Memoirs', 41
  On Heroes, Hero-Worship, and the Heroic, 41
Catholicism, 71, 73–4, 76, 102, 145
Chapman, John, 90, 94, See *Westminster Review*
Chartism, 58
children's literature, 1, 56, 64
Chippewa. See Ojibwa
Chorley, H. F., 7
Christiane, Sister, 136–7
Christianity, 43, 97, 101–2, 195–6
citizenship, 9
class, 93, 112, 114–15, 180
  middle class, 14, 116–17, 120, 149
Cohen, Robin, 9
Colby, Vineta, 187, 190, 193, 196, 199, 202
Coleridge, Samuel Taylor, 85, 132
  Table Talk, 40
Collége de France, 129
Cologne (Köln), 18–20, 33, 87, 89, 116, 121, 233, 241
Combe, George, 90–1
Contemporary Review, 198
Cooper, Edith, 3, 129, 133, 136–7, 140–1, 143, See also Michael Field
Cooper, James, 141–2, See also Katharine Bradley and Edith Cooper
Cornhill Magazine, 81, 105, 180–1
cosmopolitanism, 1, 8–9, 11, 36, 42, 54, 68, 88, 94, 105, 107, 116, 222
Crimea, 51
Crofts, Ellen, 148, See also Newnham College, Cambridge
Cross, Eleanor, 149, See also George Eliot
Cross, John W., 88
Cross, Mrs., 88, See George Eliot
Cross, Willie, 88, See also John W. Cross
cultural difference, 1, 71, 94, 98, 106–7, 109, 114, 118–19, 121–2, 129, 145, 150, 163, See cultural exchange
cultural exchange, 54, 60, 74, 76, 79, 85, 88, 106, 120, 137, 143, 146, 151, 159–60, 176
cultural hybridity, 108, 163–4, 166–7, 175–6
cultural transfer, 59

Damenstift, 52, See lay-convent
Danneker, Johann von, 24
Darwin, Charles, 198
Darwin, Francis, 148
Das Chaos, 207
de Staël, Madame, 6
des Voeux, Charles
  Tasso, 39, See also translation
Deutschtum, 188, See also national identity

Dickens, Charles
  David Copperfield, 179
Die Friedens-Warte (Peace Perspective), 188, See Alfred Fried
divorce, 6, 48, 81, 114
double narrative, 114
Dowson, Ernest
  'Vain Resolves', 183–4
Dresden, 8, 13, 24, 28–9, 36, 67, 88, 93, 133, 135–6, 138–40, 147–8, 153, 159, 165, 244
Droste-Hülshoff, Annette von, 20
Dryden, John, 151
Düsseldorf, 8, 102, 107, 116

East Germany, 211
Edinburgh Review, 33, See also Anna Jameson
Eliot, George, 2, 87–107, 126, 138, 149, 209, See Marian Evans
  Adam Bede, 106
  Daniel Deronda, 89, 98, 107–12, 128–9
  Essays and Leaves from a Note-book, 99
  'German Wit', 94–105
  Middlemarch, 107
  Mill on the Floss, The, 127, 200
  'Recollections of Berlin', 95, 98
English Woman's Journal, 51, 53–4
ethnoexocentrism, 1, 44, 55, 60, 85, 93, 106, 116, 130, 134, 145
Evans, Marian, 47, 58, 71, 87–106, 129, 133–4, 240–1, See George Eliot
expatriate identity, 163–6, 169, 171, 173–4, 176, 179, 186–7

fairy tale, 191, 194, 196
family, 55
fascism, 211
Fatherland, 165
feminism, 51, 70, 73, 107, 116, 121, 123–4, 127, 130–1, 143, 145, 149, 162, 165, 181, 186, 200, 204
Field, Michael, 3–4, 8, 106, 129–30, 133–43, 148, 160, 162, 209, See Katharine Bradley and Edith Cooper
  'Halcyon, The', 142
  'Longer Allegiance, The', 142
  'Pen-Drawing of Leda, A / Sodoma / The Grand Duke's Palace at Weimar', 138
  'Rescue, The', 139
  Sight and Song, 8, 137–9, 148
  'Sleeping Venus, The / Giorgione / The Dresden Gallery', 138
  Stephania. A Trialogue, 130, 134–5
  'Turning Homeward', 142

Field, Michael (cont.)
 Wild Honey from Various Thyme, 142
 Works and Days, 137, See also journal
First Nations, 40, 42, 44, See also Native American
Fisher's Drawing-Room Scrapbook, 57–8
Florence, 21, 156, 158, 187, 193
Ford, Helen, 149
Ford, John Rowlinson, 149
Fothergill, Jessie, 3–4, 8, 106–7, 133, 160, 162, 209
 First Violin, The, 4, 107, 112–28
Frankfurt, 15, 17, 22, 26, 33, 80, 87, 108, 138, 147
Fraser's Magazine, 92
Fried, Alfred, 188

Gaskell, Elizabeth, 3, 55, 71, 78–89, 129, 151, 181, 209
 'Six Weeks at Heppenheim', 8, 56, 78, 81–5
 'The Grey Woman', 56, 78–81
 The Life of Charlotte Brontë, 78
Gaskell, Meta, 78, See also Elizabeth, Gaskell
Gaskell, William, 55, 78, 89
Geibel, Emanuel, 4
 'In der Ferne' (In the distance), 153
Geldern, Peira van, 101, See also Heinrich Heine
gender, 2, 94, 114, 118–19, 123, 129, 148, 155, 187–8
 gaze, 118, 122, 139
 gender roles, 115, 125–6, 128–9, 139, 146
 girlhood subjectivity, 131
 homosociality, 145
Genoa, 17, 110
Giorgione
 Sleeping Venus, The, 138, 141, See also *Sight and Song* (Michael Field)
Glyptothek, 36–7, 88
Goethe, Alma von, 29, See also Ottilie von Goethe
Goethe, Anna von. See Ottilie von Goethe
Goethe, Johann von, 4–5, 8, 14–15, 25–6, 34–5, 39–40, 87, 91–4, 99–100, 103, 108, 131–2, 147, 151–2, 163, 184, 189, 194, 201
 Aus meinem Leben Dichtung und Wahrheit, 199
 Conversations with Goethe, 40
 'Das Veilchen' (the violet), 131
 'Der Schäfer' (The Shepherd), 152
 Elective Affinities (Die Wahlverwandtschaften), 5, 206
 'Freudvoll, Leidvoll, Gedankenvoll' (joyful, sorrowful, thankful), 108
 Faust, 189, See also translation

Sorrows of Young Werther, The [*Die Leiden des jungen Werthers*], 179
Wilhelm Meister's Apprenticeship (Wilhelm Meisters Lehrjahre), 179
Goethe, Ottilie von, 2, 13, 16–17, 22–3, 25–31, 34–5, 44, 90–2, 97, 138, 206–8
 'Byron. Ein Traum. Den 27ten October 1822' (Byron: A Dream). See also Byron, George Gordon
 illegitimate daughter, 26, See Anna Sibylle von Poiwisch
 Tasso, 39, See also Charles des Voeux, translation
Gomes, Mercio Pereira, 1, 9
governess, 5, 8, 14–15, 62, 127, 143, 165, 178, 187–8, 190–2, 197, 201
Grillparzer, Franz, 29, 153
 Medea, 153
 Sappho, 153
Gruppe, Mrs., 98
Gruppe, Otto, 94, 98

Hahn-Hahn, Countess, 95, 105
Hayward, Abraham, 35
Heidelberg, 7, 51, 55–62, 65, 71, 78, 81, 88
Heidelberg University, 7
Hein, Karsten, 207
Heine, Heinrich, 4, 58, 94, 98–105, 108–9, 130–1, 133, 151, 153–5, 159, 184, 209
 Buch der Lieder (book of songs), 94, 133, 154–5
 'Die Lotosblume', 116
 'Donna Clara', 103
 'Ein Fichtenbaum steht einsam' (A fir-tree stands lonely), 159
 Gods in Exile, The, 194
 Heimkehr (homecoming), 94, 104, 154–5
 "Ich hab' dich geliebet und liebe dich noch" (I have loved you and love you still), 109
 'Lyrisches Intermezzo', 155
 Neue Gedichte (new poems), 133
 'Neuer Frühling XIII' ('Die blauen Frühlingsaugen') (new spring, no. 13 [the blue eyes of spring]). See also translation
 Reisebilder, 102
 'Still ist die Nacht', 155
 'Wer zum ersten Male liebt' (Whoever loves for the first time), 159
Hemans, Felicia, 7, 57
Hennell, Sara, 88, 96, 104
Heyse, Paul, 4, 107, 109, 112, 114–15, 126, 151
 'Das Mädchen von Treppi' (The Girl from Treppi), 110
 'Die Einsamen' (The Lonely Ones), 110–12
 Kinder der Welt (Children of the World), 114–15, 120, 126–7, 151

Hillebrand, Karl, 205
Hitler, Adolf, 211
Hoffmann, E.T.A., 5, 16, 193
   Der goldene Topf (the golden pot), 196
   Der Sandmann (the Sandman), 196–7
Hohenhausen, Elise von, 95
Holocaust, 211
Household Words, 55, 70–1, 73
Howitt, Anna Mary, 3, 51, 55, 65, 70–7, 87–8, 106, 121, 129, 209
   Art-Student in Munich, An, 7, 56, 66–7, 70, 88
   Sisters in Art, 70
Howitt, Mary, 3, 55–65, 71, 87–8, 94, 106, 108, 129–30, 133, 209
   Artist-Wife, The, 66–70, 79
   'Boaz and Ruth. / A Harvest Scene', 58
   Child's Picture and Verse Book, 64
   'The Spider and the Fly', 56
   Which Is the Wiser, 59–63, 108
Howitt, William, 55, 88
   German Experiences. Addressed to the English, Both Goers Abroad and Stayers at Home, 58
   Student Life in Germany, 63
Howitt's Journal, 7, 58, 65, 72

iambic pentameter, 38, 152–3
Illustrated Exhibitor, 70
imperialism, 130
Indian Rebellion, 1857, 78
Innsbruck, 140
intertextuality, 35, 108, 114

James, Henry, 108
   Partial Portraits, 108
Jameson, Anna, 2, 13–15, 17–18, 22–50, 56, 70, 87–8, 90–4, 97, 106, 116, 129, 138–9, 206–7, 209
   'Alone. In the Gallery of Sculpture at Munich', 37
   Characteristics of Women, 10, 14, 33, 85
   Communion of Labour, The, 51–2
   Diary of an Ennuyée, 14
   Sacred and Legendary Art, 32
   Sisters of Charity, 51–2
   Social Life in Germany, 6, 30, 32, 44–50
   Visits and Sketches at Home and Abroad, 6, 11, 14, 24, 26, 30, 32–8, 67, 73, 82
   Winter Studies and Summer Rambles, 29–30, 32, 38–44, 153, *See also* Canada
Jameson, Robert Sympson, 14, 28, 38, 49
Jewish Chronicle, 147, 151, 159
Jewishness, 97–103, 105, 107, 109, 112–14, 147, 151, 154, 188
   Anglo-Jewish, 147

Jewsbury, Geraldine, 97
journal, 8, 39, 91, 93, 95–7, 130, 133–6, 140, 142–3, 212, 216, 234, 244, 246
Judaism, 94, 98, 101–2, 147
Judenhetze, 151

Kaiserswerth, 6, 52
Karl Alexander, Grand Duke, 91
Kaulbach, Wilhelm, 7, 55, 59, 65, 73
Keats, John
   'Ode on Melancholy', 169
Klopstock, Friedrich Gottlieb
   Der Messias, 201
Kühne, Gustav, 29
   Die Rebellen von Irland, 29
   Zeitung für die elegante Welt, 29
künstlerroman, 180

Ladies' Companion, 55, 70–1
Landon, Letitia, 57
Langham Place group, 51
lay-convent, 49
Leader, 94–5, 98, 101, 105, *See also* George Henry Lewes
Lee, Vernon, 1–5, 9, 11, 130, 156–7, 159–60, 162, 187–209
   'Amour Dure', 194
   'Contemporary Italian Poets', 189
   'Dionea', 194
   'Faustus and Helena', 189–90
   'Goethe at Weimar', 206
   Golden Keys and other Essays on the Genius Loci, The, 210
   Hortus Vitae, 190
   Laurus Nobilis, 189
   Miss Brown, 198
   Ottilie, 197–207
   'Prince Alberic and the Snake Lady', 5, 194–7, *See also* paganism
   Sentimental Traveller, The, 191–3
   Studies of the Eighteenth Century in Italy, 193, 198, 200
   'In Time of War', 210
   Tuscan Fairy Tales, 200
Lee-Hamilton, Eugene, 199–200, *See also* Vernon Lee
Lenau, Nikolaus, 4
Lenzkirch, 149
Leubrunn, 108
Levy, Amy, 3–4, 8, 94, 106, 129–30, 133, 143–60, 162, 209
   'Birch-Tree at Loschwitz, The', 155, 157–9
   'In the Black Forest', 146–7, 155
   'Confessions Book', 151
   'From Grillparzer's Sappho', 152–3

Levy, Amy (cont.)
'In Holiday Humour', 143–5, 148
'Ida Grey', 143
'Imitation of Heine' ['A Farewell. / (After Heine.)'], 154–5
'Jewish Humour', 159
'Lohengrin', 155
London Plane-Tree and Other Verse, A, 155, 157–9
'Medea (A Fragment in Drama Form)', 153
A Minor Poet, 154
'Neue Liebe, Neues Leben', 156–7
'Old House, The', 155
'In Retreat, A Long Vacation Experience', 145–6
'Shepherd, The', 151–2, See also translation
'Sonnet' ['The Two Terrors'], 155
'Translated from Geibel', 153
'To Vernon Lee', 155, 157–9
Xantippe, and Other Verse, 153
Lewald, Fanny, 89, 91, 96–7, 106
Wandlungen (Changes), 97
Lewes, Charles Lee, 105, See also George Henry Lewes
Lewes, George Henry, 4, 8, 87–93, 96, 112, 134, See also George Eliot
'Realism in Art: Recent German Fiction', 109
Lippincott's Magazine, 110, 112
Liszt, Franz, 91
London Society, 143, 146–7
Loschwitz, 159
Louvre, 138
Lucerne, 143, 147–9
Lutheran Church, 102

MacMurray, Charlotte, 42
Mainz, 17
Maria Pavlovna, Grand Duchess, 91
marital immigrant, 164
Marlow, Christopher
Doctor Faustus, 189
marriage, 4, 7, 14–15, 18–19, 22, 46–7, 50, 54, 57, 62, 67–70, 78–9, 81–3, 85, 89, 93, 104, 106, 111, 114–16, 118, 121, 125–7, 144–5, 162, 173–4, 176, 178–81, 184, 196–7, 199, 201–2, 207, 226, 236, 239, 241, 246, 252
Martineau, Harriet, 45, 90
Society in America, 45
Marx, Eleanor, 159
masculinity, 84
Meissner, Alfred, 95
Recollections of Heine, 104
memoirs, 1

Merkel, Angela, 211
Mertens, Louis. See Sibylle Mertens-Schaaffhausen
Mertens-Schaaffhausen, Sibylle, 18–22, 24–5, 33, 97, See also queer sexuality
middle class, 3
Morgenstern, Lina, 140
Moritz, Karl Philipp, 202
Morris, William, 4
Müller, Wilhelm, 132
'Vineta', 132
multilingualism, 18
Munich (München), 7, 22–4, 36, 51, 65–7, 69–73, 76–7, 88, 109–10, 121, 140
Murphy, Denis Brownell. See Anna Jameson
music, 107–10, 113–18, 120–5, 127–8, 140–1, 201–2, 209
Muslims, 76

Naples, 110
Nassenheide, 163
National Association for the Promotion of Social Science, 51
National Gallery, London, 138
national identity, 107, 109, 113, 179
nationalism, 188, 211
Native American, 42
New Woman, 4, 73, 114, 119–22, 127–30, 138–9, 143–7, 151, 153, 160, 162, 165
Newnham College, Cambridge, 4, 129, 143, 149, 151
Nightingale, Florence, 6, 51, 94, 207
Noel, Robert, 2, 90, 92–3
North, Marianne
Recollections of a Happy Life, 166–7
Nuremberg, 29

Oberammergau, 70, 75, 77, 151
Ojibwa, 39, 42–4
orality, 191–2
Orientalism, 76

Paalzow, Henriette von, 94
Citizen of Prague, 94, See also Mary Howitt
Jacob van der Neess, 94
pacifism, 188
paganism, 138, 189, 196, See also Michael Field
Paget, Violet, 3, 162, See Vernon Lee
pan-Europeanism, 188
Parkes, Bessie, 70
Pater, Walter, 194
Studies in the History of the Renaissance, 206
Pereira-Arnstein, Henriette, 29
The Pelican, 143
philosemitism, 98

piano, 121
Pichler, Karoline, 29
pogroms, 147
Pogwisch, Baron Wilhelm Julius von, 15, *See* Henriette von Pogwisch
Pogwisch, Henriette von, 15, 49, 91
Poiwisch, Anna Sibylle von, 40
Prague, 98
Prelooker, Jaakoff, 139
Prior, Matthew
  'The Ladle', 184
property rights. *See* citizenship
Protestantism, 5, 72–4, 114, 147
proto-feminism, 47
proto-Modernism, 181
Prussia, 102

Quarterly Review, 189

race, 2, 42, 93, 100–1, 105, 114, 147, 189, 211
Raff, Joachim
  'Lenore', 124, 127
rape, 115
Raphael
  Sistine Madonna, 138
Rauch, Christian, 96
realism, 107, 109
religious conversion, 97, 102, 104, 115
remarriage, 114
Retzsch, Moritz, 24
Rome, 3, 21, 78, 97
Royal Academy of Music, 162
Rügen, 163, 166–7, 171, 173–4, 177, 211, 252

Säckingen, 191–3
Said, Edward, 163
salon, 20
Sauppe, Hedwig, 105
Scheffel, Joseph Victor von
  Der Trompeter von Säckingen, 191–3
Schiller, Friedrich, 4, 85, 131–2, 184, 189
  Death of Wallenstein, The, 85
Schlegel, August von, 20
Schlosser, Friedrich, 7, 56
Schöll, Adolf, 89, 93
Schoolcraft, Henry, 42
Schoolcraft, June Johnston, 42
Schopenhauer, Adele, 15, 18–21, 24–5, 34, 97, 206, *See also* queer sexuality
Schopenhauer, Johanna, 15, 21, 26, 35
Schreiner, Olive
  Story of an African Farm, 121
Schülpach, Marie, 5, 190–3, *See also* Vernon Lee, governess

Schumann, Robert
  Kinderszenen (childhood scenes), 123
  Lied. *See also* 'Die Lotosblume'
  Träumerei (reverie), 122
secular sisterhood, 49
secularism, 105
serialisation, 70, 94, 107–8, 114, 180–1
sexual predation, 118, 150
stalking, 137
sexualities, 2
  asexuality, 187
  celibacy, 187
  extra-legal marital unions, 95
  female eroticism, 141
  heteronormativity, 20
  intimate friendship, 18
  lesbianism, 129, 159, 187, 191
  mistress, 115
  queer family, 19, 125–6
  queer sexuality, 17–25, 123–4, 143–4, 193
  romantic male friendship, 113, 123–5, 128
Shakespeare, William, 98
  As You Like It, 144
  Sonnet 98, 182
  Twelfth Night, 144
Smith, Barbara Leigh. *See* Barbara Bodichon
Smith, Blanche, 4, 149
Solmar, Henriette, 95–7
Sophie, Grand Duchess, 91
Soret, Frederic, 207
Spener Zeitung, 114
Spinola, Laurina, 91
Städel'sche Institut, Frankfurt, 138
Stahr, Adolf, 89, 91, 94, 97
  Torso, 94
Sterling, Charles, 16–17, 25
Stöcker, Adolf, 147
Story, Captain, 26
Strauss, David Friedrich, 87
study abroad, 4, 150
Sturm und Drang movement, 198, 201, 203
subliminal narrative, 181, 185, *See also* Elizabeth von Arnim
suicide, 19, 115, 125–6, 130, 153
supernatural writing, 189, 193–4, 196, 198, 205

Tait's Edinburgh Magazine, 99, 101
Temple Bar, 107
Tennyson, Lord Alfred
  'Lady of Shalott, The', 139
  Princess, The, 145–6, 149
Thackeray, William Makepeace
  Pendennis, 180
Tieck, Ludwig, 24
Toronto, 40

translation, 1, 4, 35, 45, 50, 56, 59, 63–4, 85, 99, 102, 110, 130–1, 133, 138, 145, 151–5, 196, 199
transnational mobility, 3
transnationalism, 188
Traunsee, 28
travel writing, 1, 7, 15, 32, 42, 58, 167
  virtual travel, 138
Treaty of Versailles, 209
Treitschke, Heinrich von, 147

University College, Bristol, 129

Varnhagen von Ense, Karl, 89, 92, 104
  'Denkwurdigkeiten' (memoirs), 104
Varnhagen von Ense, Rahel, 41, 94–5, 103
Vayal, Marquis Ferrière de, 91
Vehse, Edward, 94
Vertovec, Steven, 9
Victoria, Queen, 7, 45
Vienna, 3, 26, 40, 89
voting rights. *See* citizenship

Wagner, Richard, 113, 140, 156
  Das Rheingold, 141
  Lohengrin, 119
  Ring cycle, 140

Tristan und Isolde, 167
Walküre, Die, 141
Wallraf, Ferdinand Franz, 19
Wedgwood, Julia, 198
Weimar, 5, 13, 15–19, 22, 24–6, 28–30, 34, 47, 53–4, 71, 87, 89–95, 105, 132, 138, 179, 199
Werner, Alice, 198, 200–1
West Germany, 211
Westminster Review, 41, 90, 99, 109
Wildbad, 88
Wittgenstein, Princess, 91, 94–5
women painters, 36
women's education, 33
women's suffrage, 149
Woolf, Virginia, 179, 186, *See also Fräulein Schmidt and Mr. Anstruther*
  Room of One's Own, A, 200
Wordsworth, William
  Prelude, The, 167, 172
World War I, 209–10
World War II, 209, 211

Yellow Book, The, 5, 195

Zermatt, 141–2
Zunz, Leopold, 108

CAMBRIDGE STUDIES IN NINETEENTH-CENTURY
LITERATURE AND CULTURE

General Editors
Kate Flint, *University of Southern California*
Clare Pettitt, *King's College London*

Titles published

1. *The Sickroom in Victorian Fiction: The Art of Being Ill*
   MIRIAM BAILIN, *Washington University*
2. *Muscular Christianity: Embodying the Victorian Age*
   edited by DONALD E. HALL, *California State University, Northridge*
3. *Victorian Masculinities: Manhood and Masculine Poetics in Early Victorian Literature and Art*
   HERBERT SUSSMAN, *Northeastern University, Boston*
4. *Byron and the Victorians*
   ANDREW ELFENBEIN, *University of Minnesota*
5. *Literature in the Marketplace: Nineteenth-Century British Publishing and the Circulation of Books*
   edited by JOHN O. JORDAN, *University of California, Santa Cruz* and ROBERT L. PATTEN, *Rice University, Houston*
6. *Victorian Photography, Painting and Poetry*
   LINDSAY SMITH, *University of Sussex*
7. *Charlotte Brontë and Victorian Psychology*
   SALLY SHUTTLEWORTH, *University of Sheffield*
8. *The Gothic Body: Sexuality, Materialism and Degeneration at the Fin de Siècle*
   KELLY HURLEY, *University of Colorado at Boulder*
9. *Rereading Walter Pater*
   WILLIAM F. SHUTER, *Eastern Michigan University*
10. *Remaking Queen Victoria*
    edited by MARGARET HOMANS, *Yale University* and ADRIENNE MUNICH, *State University of New York, Stony Brook*
11. *Disease, Desire, and the Body in Victorian Women's Popular Novels*
    PAMELA K. GILBERT, *University of Florida*
12. *Realism, Representation, and the Arts in Nineteenth-Century Literature*
    ALISON BYERLY, *Middlebury College, Vermont*
13. *Literary Culture and the Pacific*
    VANESSA SMITH, *University of Sydney*
14. *Professional Domesticity in the Victorian Novel: Women, Work and Home*
    MONICA F. COHEN
15. *Victorian Renovations of the Novel: Narrative Annexes and the Boundaries of Representation*
    SUZANNE KEEN, *Washington and Lee University, Virginia*

16. *Actresses on the Victorian Stage: Feminine Performance and the Galatea Myth*
    GAIL MARSHALL, *University of Leeds*
17. *Death and the Mother from Dickens to Freud: Victorian Fiction and the Anxiety of Origin*
    CAROLYN DEVER, *Vanderbilt University, Tennessee*
18. *Ancestry and Narrative in Nineteenth-Century British Literature: Blood Relations from Edgeworth to Hardy*
    SOPHIE GILMARTIN, *Royal Holloway, University of London*
19. *Dickens, Novel Reading, and the Victorian Popular Theatre*
    DEBORAH VLOCK
20. *After Dickens: Reading, Adaptation and Performance*
    JOHN GLAVIN, *Georgetown University, Washington D C*
21. *Victorian Women Writers and the Woman Question*
    edited by NICOLA DIANE THOMPSON, *Kingston University, London*
22. *Rhythm and Will in Victorian Poetry*
    MATTHEW CAMPBELL, *University of Sheffield*
23. *Gender, Race, and the Writing of Empire: Public Discourse and the Boer War*
    PAULA M. KREBS, *Wheaton College, Massachusetts*
24. *Ruskin's God*
    MICHAEL WHEELER, *University of Southampton*
25. *Dickens and the Daughter of the House*
    HILARY M. SCHOR, *University of Southern California*
26. *Detective Fiction and the Rise of Forensic Science*
    RONALD R. THOMAS, *Trinity College, Hartford, Connecticut*
27. *Testimony and Advocacy in Victorian Law, Literature, and Theology*
    JAN-MELISSA SCHRAMM, *Trinity Hall, Cambridge*
28. *Victorian Writing about Risk: Imagining a Safe England in a Dangerous World*
    ELAINE FREEDGOOD, *University of Pennsylvania*
29. *Physiognomy and the Meaning of Expression in Nineteenth-Century Culture*
    LUCY HARTLEY, *University of Southampton*
30. *The Victorian Parlour: A Cultural Study*
    THAD LOGAN, *Rice University, Houston*
31. *Aestheticism and Sexual Parody 1840–1940*
    DENNIS DENISOFF, *Ryerson University, Toronto*
32. *Literature, Technology and Magical Thinking, 1880–1920*
    PAMELA THURSCHWELL, *University College London*
33. *Fairies in Nineteenth-Century Art and Literature*
    NICOLA BOWN, *Birkbeck, University of London*
34. *George Eliot and the British Empire*
    NANCY HENRY *The State University of New York, Binghamton*
35. *Women's Poetry and Religion in Victorian England: Jewish Identity and Christian Culture*
    CYNTHIA SCHEINBERG, *Mills College, California*
36. *Victorian Literature and the Anorexic Body*
    ANNA KRUGOVOY SILVER, *Mercer University, Georgia*

37. *Eavesdropping in the Novel from Austen to Proust*
    ANN GAYLIN, *Yale University*
38. *Missionary Writing and Empire, 1800–1860*
    ANNA JOHNSTON, *University of Tasmania*
39. *London and the Culture of Homosexuality, 1885–1914*
    MATT COOK, *Keele University*
40. *Fiction, Famine, and the Rise of Economics in Victorian Britain and Ireland*
    GORDON BIGELOW, *Rhodes College, Tennessee*
41. *Gender and the Victorian Periodical*
    HILARY FRASER, *Birkbeck, University of London* JUDITH JOHNSTON and STEPHANIE GREEN, *University of Western Australia*
42. *The Victorian Supernatural* edited by NICOLA BOWN, *Birkbeck College, London* CAROLYN BURDETT, *London Metropolitan University* and PAMELA THURSCHWELL, *University College London*
43. *The Indian Mutiny and the British Imagination*
    GAUTAM CHAKRAVARTY, *University of Delhi*
44. *The Revolution in Popular Literature: Print, Politics and the People*
    IAN HAYWOOD, *Roehampton University of Surrey*
45. *Science in the Nineteenth-Century Periodical: Reading the Magazine of Nature*
    GEOFFREY CANTOR, *University of Leeds* GOWAN DAWSON, *University of Leicester* GRAEME GOODAY, *University of Leeds* RICHARD NOAKES, *University of Cambridge* SALLY SHUTTLEWORTH, *University of Sheffield* and JONATHAN R. TOPHAM, *University of Leeds*
46. *Literature and Medicine in Nineteenth-Century Britain from Mary Shelley to George Eliot*
    JANIS MCLARREN CALDWELL, *Wake Forest University*
47. *The Child Writer from Austen to Woolf*
    edited by CHRISTINE ALEXANDER, *University of New South Wales* and JULIET MCMASTER, *University of Alberta*
48. *From Dickens to Dracula: Gothic, Economics, and Victorian Fiction*
    GAIL TURLEY HOUSTON, University of New Mexico
49. *Voice and the Victorian Storyteller*
    IVAN KREILKAMP, *University of Indiana*
50. *Charles Darwin and Victorian Visual Culture*
    JONATHAN SMITH, *University of Michigan-Dearborn*
51. *Catholicism, Sexual Deviance, and Victorian Gothic Culture*
    PATRICK R. O'MALLEY, *Georgetown University*
52. *Epic and Empire in Nineteenth-Century Britain*
    SIMON DENTITH, *University of Gloucestershire*
53. *Victorian Honeymoons: Journeys to the Conjugal*
    HELENA MICHIE, *Rice University*
54. *The Jewess in Nineteenth-Century British Literary Culture*
    NADIA VALMAN, *University of Southampton*
55. *Ireland, India and Nationalism in Nineteenth-Century Literature*
    JULIA WRIGHT, *Dalhousie University*

56. *Dickens and the Popular Radical Imagination*
    SALLY LEDGER, *Birkbeck, University of London*
57. *Darwin, Literature and Victorian Respectability*
    GOWAN DAWSON, *University of Leicester*
58. *'Michael Field': Poetry, Aestheticism and the* Fin de Siècle
    MARION THAIN, *University of Birmingham*
59. *Colonies, Cults and Evolution: Literature, Science and Culture in Nineteenth-Century Writing*
    DAVID AMIGONI, *Keele University*
60. *Realism, Photography and Nineteenth-Century Fiction*
    DANIEL A. NOVAK, *Lousiana State University*
61. *Caribbean Culture and British Fiction in the Atlantic World, 1780–1870*
    TIM WATSON, *University of Miami*
62. *The Poetry of Chartism: Aesthetics, Politics, History*
    MICHAEL SANDERS, *University of Manchester*
63. *Literature and Dance in Nineteenth-Century Britain: Jane Austen to the New Woman*
    CHERYL WILSON, *Indiana University*
64. *Shakespeare and Victorian Women*
    GAIL MARSHALL, *Oxford Brookes University*
65. *The Tragi-Comedy of Victorian Fatherhood*
    VALERIE SANDERS, *University of Hull*
66. *Darwin and the Memory of the Human: Evolution, Savages, and South America*
    CANNON SCHMITT, *University of Toronto*
67. *From Sketch to Novel: The Development of Victorian Fiction*
    AMANPAL GARCHA, *Ohio State University*
68. *The Crimean War and the British Imagination*
    STEFANIE MARKOVITS, *Yale University*
69. *Shock, Memory and the Unconscious in Victorian Fiction*
    JILL L. MATUS, *University of Toronto*
70. *Sensation and Modernity in the 1860s*
    NICHOLAS DALY, *University College Dublin*
71. *Ghost-Seers, Detectives, and Spiritualists: Theories of Vision in Victorian Literature and Science*
    SRDJAN SMAJIĆ, *Furman University*
72. *Satire in an Age of Realism*
    AARON MATZ, *Scripps College, California*
73. *Thinking About Other People in Nineteenth-Century British Writing*
    ADELA PINCH, *University of Michigan*
74. *Tuberculosis and the Victorian Literary Imagination*
    KATHERINE BYRNE, *University of Ulster, Coleraine*
75. *Urban Realism and the Cosmopolitan Imagination in the Nineteenth Century: Visible City, Invisible World*
    TANYA AGATHOCLEOUS, *Hunter College, City University of New York*

76. *Women, Literature, and the Domesticated Landscape: England's Disciples of Flora, 1780–1870*
    JUDITH W. PAGE, *University of Florida* ELISE L. SMITH, *Millsaps College, Mississippi*
77. *Time and the Moment in Victorian Literature and Society*
    SUE ZEMKA, *University of Colorado*
78. *Popular Fiction and Brain Science in the Late Nineteenth Century*
    ANNE STILES, *Washington State University*
79. *Picturing Reform in Victorian Britain*
    JANICE CARLISLE, *Yale University*
80. *Atonement and Self-Sacrifice in Nineteenth-Century Narrative*
    JAN-MELISSA SCHRAMM, *University of Cambridge*
81. *The Silver Fork Novel: Fashionable Fiction in the Age of Reform*
    EDWARD COPELAND, *Pomona College, California*
82. *Oscar Wilde and Ancient Greece*
    IAIN ROSS, *Colchester Royal Grammar School*
83. *The Poetry of Victorian Scientists: Style, Science and Nonsense*
    DANIEL BROWN, *University of Southampton*
84. *Moral Authority, Men of Science, and the Victorian Novel*
    ANNE DEWITT, *Princeton Writing Program*
85. *China and the Victorian Imagination: Empires Entwined*
    ROSS G. FORMAN, *University of Warwick*
86. *Dickens's Style*
    edited by DANIEL TYLER, *University of Oxford*
87. *The Formation of the Victorian Literary Profession*
    RICHARD SALMON, *University of Leeds*
88. *Before George Eliot: Marian Evans and the Periodical Press*
    FIONNUALA DILLANE, *University College Dublin*
89. *The Victorian Novel and the Space of Art: Fictional Form on Display*
    DEHN GILMORE, *California Institute of Technology*
90. *George Eliot and Money: Economics, Ethics and Literature*
    DERMOT COLEMAN, *Independent Scholar*
91. *Masculinity and the New Imperialism: Rewriting Manhood in British Popular Literature, 1870–1914*
    BRADLEY DEANE, *University of Minnesota*
92. *Evolution and Victorian Culture*
    edited by BERNARD LIGHTMAN, *York University, Toronto* and BENNETT ZON, *University of Durham*
93. *Victorian Literature, Energy, and the Ecological Imagination*
    ALLEN MACDUFFIE, *University of Texas, Austin*
94. *Popular Literature, Authorship and the Occult in Late Victorian Britain*
    ANDREW MCCANN, *Dartmouth College, New Hampshire*
95. *Women Writing Art History in the Nineteenth Century: Looking Like a Woman*
    HILARY FRASER *Birkbeck, University of London*

96. *Relics of Death in Victorian Literature and Culture*
    DEBORAH LUTZ, *Long Island University, C. W. Post Campus*
97. *The Demographic Imagination and the Nineteenth-Century City: Paris, London, New York*
    NICHOLAS DALY, *University College Dublin*
98. *Dickens and the Business of Death*
    CLAIRE WOOD, *University of York*
99. *Translation as Transformation in Victorian Poetry*
    ANNMARIE DRURY, *Queens College, City University of New York*
100. *The Bigamy Plot: Sensation and Convention in the Victorian Novel*
    MAIA MCALEAVEY, *Boston College, Massachusetts*
101. *English Fiction and the Evolution of Language, 1850–1914*
    WILL ABBERLEY, *University of Oxford*
102. *The Racial Hand in the Victorian Imagination*
    AVIVA BRIEFEL, *Bowdoin College, Maine*
103. *Evolution and Imagination in Victorian Children's Literature*
    JESSICA STRALEY, *University of Utah*
104. *Writing Arctic Disaster: Authorship and Exploration*
    ADRIANA CRACIUN, *University of California, Riverside*
105. *Science, Fiction, and the* Fin-de-Siècle *Periodical Press*
    WILL TATTERSDILL, *University of Birmingham*
106. *Democratising Beauty in Nineteenth-Century Britain: Art and the Politics of Public Life*
    LUCY HARTLEY, *University of Michigan*
107. *Everyday Words and the Character of Prose in Nineteenth-Century Britain*
    JONATHAN FARINA, *Seton Hall University, New Jersey*
108. *Gerard Manley Hopkins and the Poetry of Religious Experience*
    MARTIN DUBOIS, *Newcastle University*
109. *Blindness and Writing: From Wordsworth to Gissing*
    HEATHER TILLEY, *Birkbeck College, University of London*
110. *An Underground History of Early Victorian Fiction: Chartism, Radical Print Culture, and the Social Problem Novel*
    GREGORY VARGO, *New York University*
111. *Automatism and Creative Acts in the Age of New Psychology*
    LINDA M. AUSTIN, *Oklahoma State University*
112. *Idleness and Aesthetic Consciousness, 1815–1900*
    RICHARD ADELMAN, *University of Sussex*
113. *Poetry, Media, and the Material Body: Autopoetics in Nineteenth-Century Britain*
    ASHLEY MILLER, *Albion College, Michigan*
114. *Malaria and Victorian Fictions of Empire*
    JESSICA HOWELL, *Texas A&M University*
115. *The Brontës and the Idea of the Human: Science, Ethics, and the Victorian Imagination*
    edited by ALEXANDRA LEWIS, *University of Aberdeen*

116. *The Political Lives of Victorian Animals: Liberal Creatures in Literature and Culture*
    ANNA FEUERSTEIN, *University of Hawai'i-Manoa*
117. *The Divine in the Commonplace: Recent Natural Histories and the Novel in Britain*
    AMY KING, *St John's University, New York*
118. *Plagiarizing the Victorian Novel: Imitation, Parody, Aftertext*
    ADAM ABRAHAM, *Virginia Commonwealth University*
119. *Literature, Print Culture, and Media Technologies, 1880–1900: Many Inventions*
    RICHARD MENKE, *University of Georgia*
120. *Aging, Duration, and the English Novel: Growing Old from Dickens to Woolf*
    JACOB JEWUSIAK, *Newcastle University*
121. *Autobiography, Sensation, and the Commodification of Identity in Victorian Narrative: Life Upon the Exchange*
    SEAN GRASS, *Rochester Institute of Technology*
122. *Settler Colonialism in Victorian Literature: Economics and Political Identity in the Networks of Empire*
    PHILLIP STEER, *Massey University, Auckland*
123. *Mimicry and Display in Victorian Literary Culture: Nature, Science and the Nineteenth-Century Imagination*
    WILL ABBERLEY, *University of Sussex*
124. *Victorian Women and Wayward Reading: Crises of Identification*
    MARISA PALACIOS KNOX, *University of Texas Rio Grande Valley*
125. *The Victorian Cult of Shakespeare: Bardology in the Nineteenth Century*
    CHARLES LAPORTE, *University of Washington*
126. *Children's Literature and the Rise of 'Mind Cure': Positive Thinking and Pseudo-Science at the Fin de Siècle*
    ANNE STILES, *Saint Louis University, Missouri*
127. *Virtual Play and the Victorian Novel: The Ethics and Aesthetics of Fictional Experience*
    TIMOTHY GAO, *Nanyang Technological University*
128. *Colonial Law in India and the Victorian Imagination*
    LEILA NETI, *Occidental College, Los Angeles*
129. *Convalescence in the Nineteenth-Century Novel: The Afterlife of Victorian Illness*
    HOSANNA KRIENKE, *University of Wyoming*
130. *Stylistic Virtue and Victorian Fiction: Form, Ethics and the Novel*
    MATTHEW SUSSMAN, *The University of Sydney*
131. *Scottish Women's Writing in the Long Nineteenth Century: The Romance of Everyday Life*
    JULIET SHIELDS, *University of Washington*
132. *Reimagining Dinosaurs in Late Victorian and Edwardian Literature: How the 'Terrible Lizard' Became a Transatlantic Cultural Icon*
    RICHARD FALLON, *The University of Birmingham*

133. *Decadent Ecology in British Literature and Art, 1860–1910: Decay, Desire, and the Pagan Revival*
    DENNIS DENISOFF, *University of Tulsa*
134. *Vagrancy in the Victorian Age: Representing the Wandering Poor in Nineteenth-Century Literature and Culture*
    ALISTAIR ROBINSON, *New College of the Humanities*
135. *Collaborative Writing in the Long Nineteenth Century: Sympathetic Partnerships and Artistic Creation*
    HEATHER BOZANT WITCHER, *Auburn University, Montgomery*
136. VISUAL CULTURE AND ARCTIC VOYAGES: PERSONAL AND PUBLIC ART AND LITERATURE OF THE FRANKLIN SEARCH EXPEDITIONS *Eavan O'Dochartaigh, Umeå Universitet, Sweden*
137. *Music and the Queer Body in English Literature at the* Fin de Siècle
    FRASER RIDDELL, *University of Durham*
138. *Victorian Women Writers and the Other Germany: Cross-Cultural Freedoms and Female Opportunity*
    LINDA K. HUGHES, *Texas Christian University*

For EU product safety concerns, contact us at Calle de José Abascal, 56–1°,
28003 Madrid, Spain or eugpsr@cambridge.org.

www.ingramcontent.com/pod-product-compliance
Ingram Content Group UK Ltd.
Pitfield, Milton Keynes, MK11 3LW, UK
UKHW020845180325
456407UK00008B/237